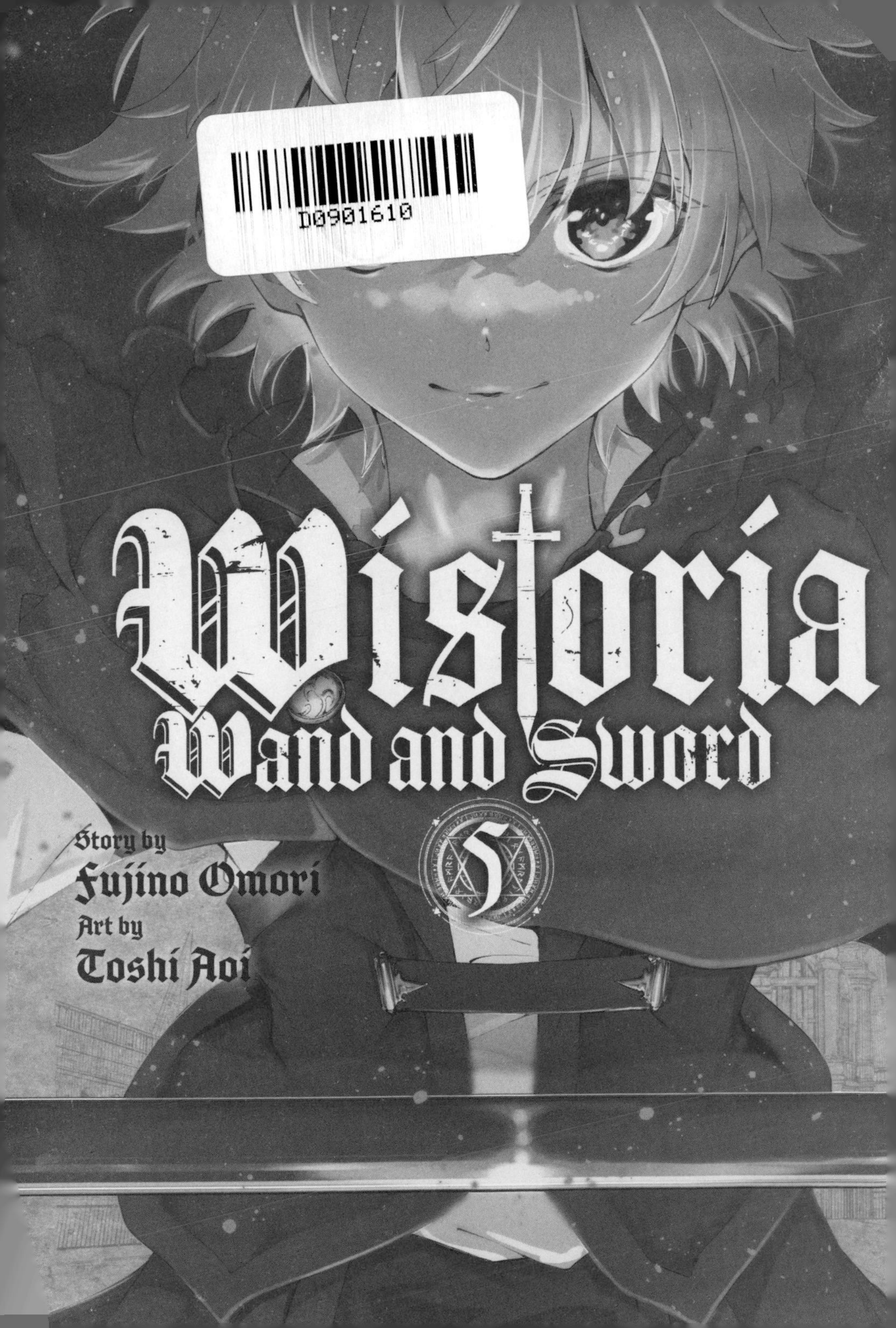
Wistoria
Wand and Sword
5
Story by
Fujino Omori
Art by
Toshi Aoi

Fujino Omori   Toshi Aoi

Wistoria
Wand and Sword
5

contents

Chapter 17: Rise Above Despair   003

Chapter 18: The True Shape
           of Cowardice   053

Chapter 19: Wand and Sword   099

Chapter 20: Final Exams   151

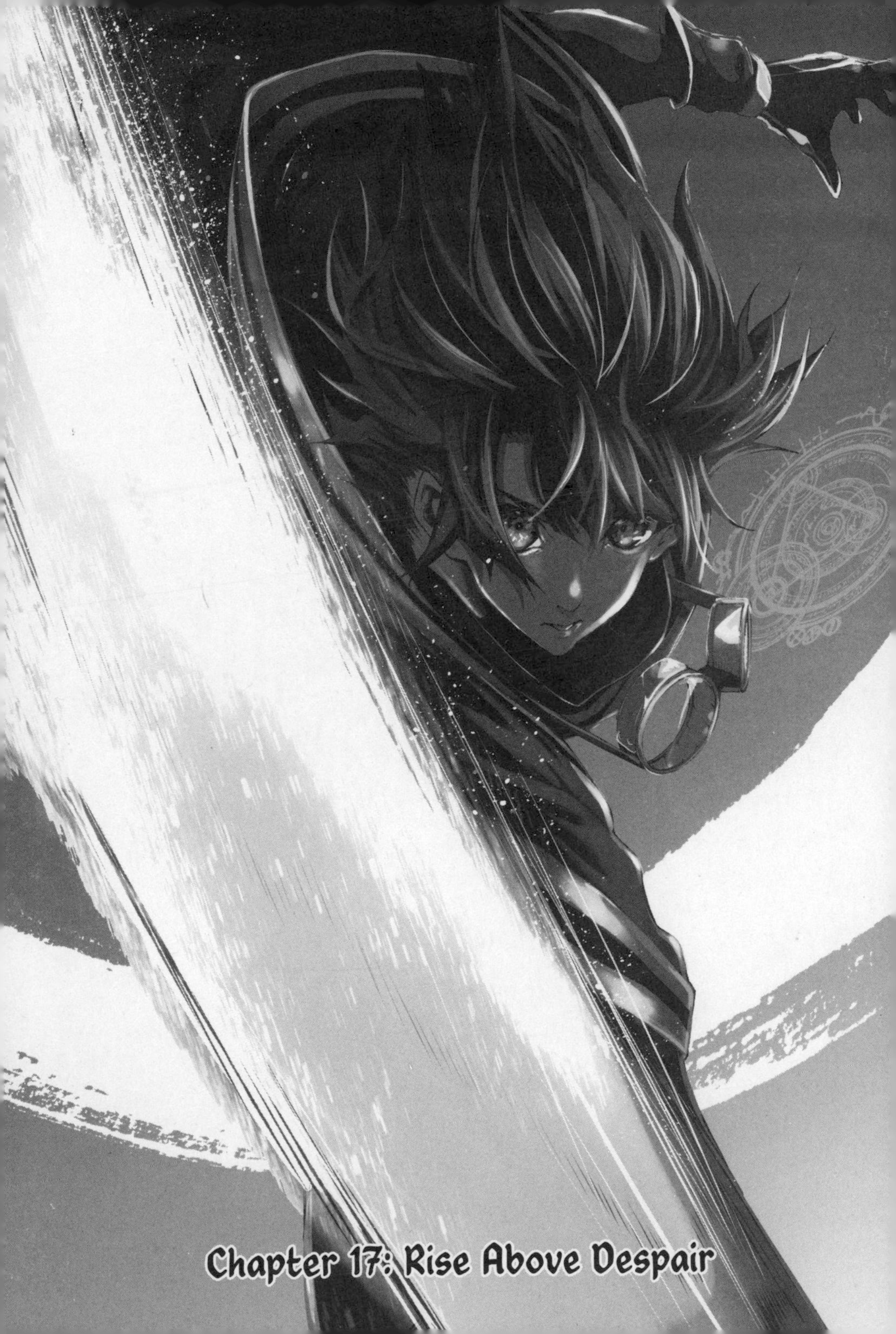

Chapter 17: Rise Above Despair

Wistoria
Wand and Sword

They call it the "1/1000 rule."

THE TOWER USES CREDITS AS A MEASURE OF A MAGE'S ABILITIES. WHEN CONVERTING THEM...
...EACH CREDIT ASSIGNED TO A MONSTER IS EQUAL TO 1,000 MAGE CREDITS.

...A 270-CREDIT MONSTER.

IN OTHER WORDS, IF YOU WERE TO CALCULATE THE TOTAL NUMBER OF CREDITS EARNED FROM A 270-CREDIT MONSTER, IT WOULD COME OUT TO...

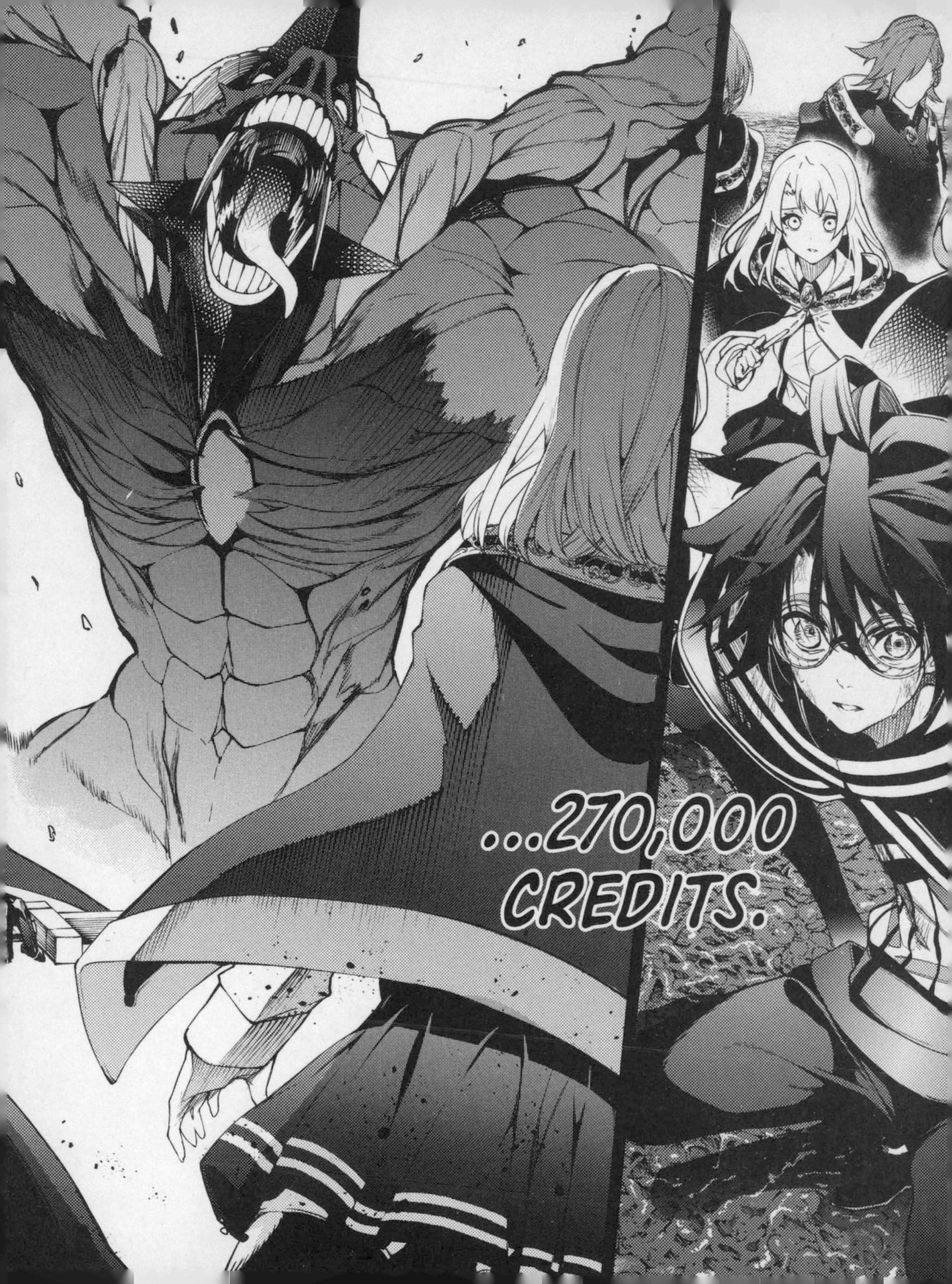
...270,000 CREDITS.

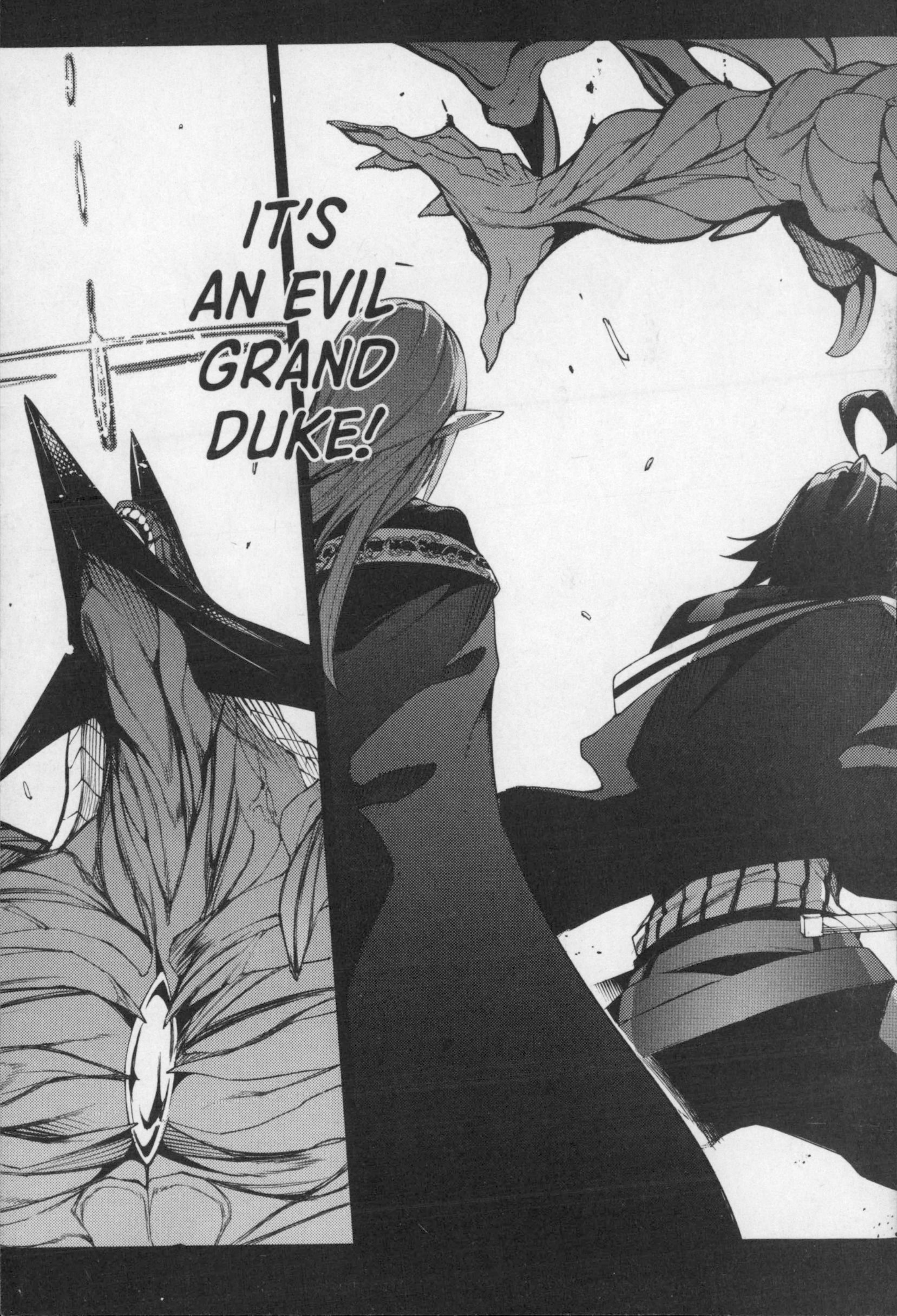
IT'S AN EVIL GRAND DUKE!

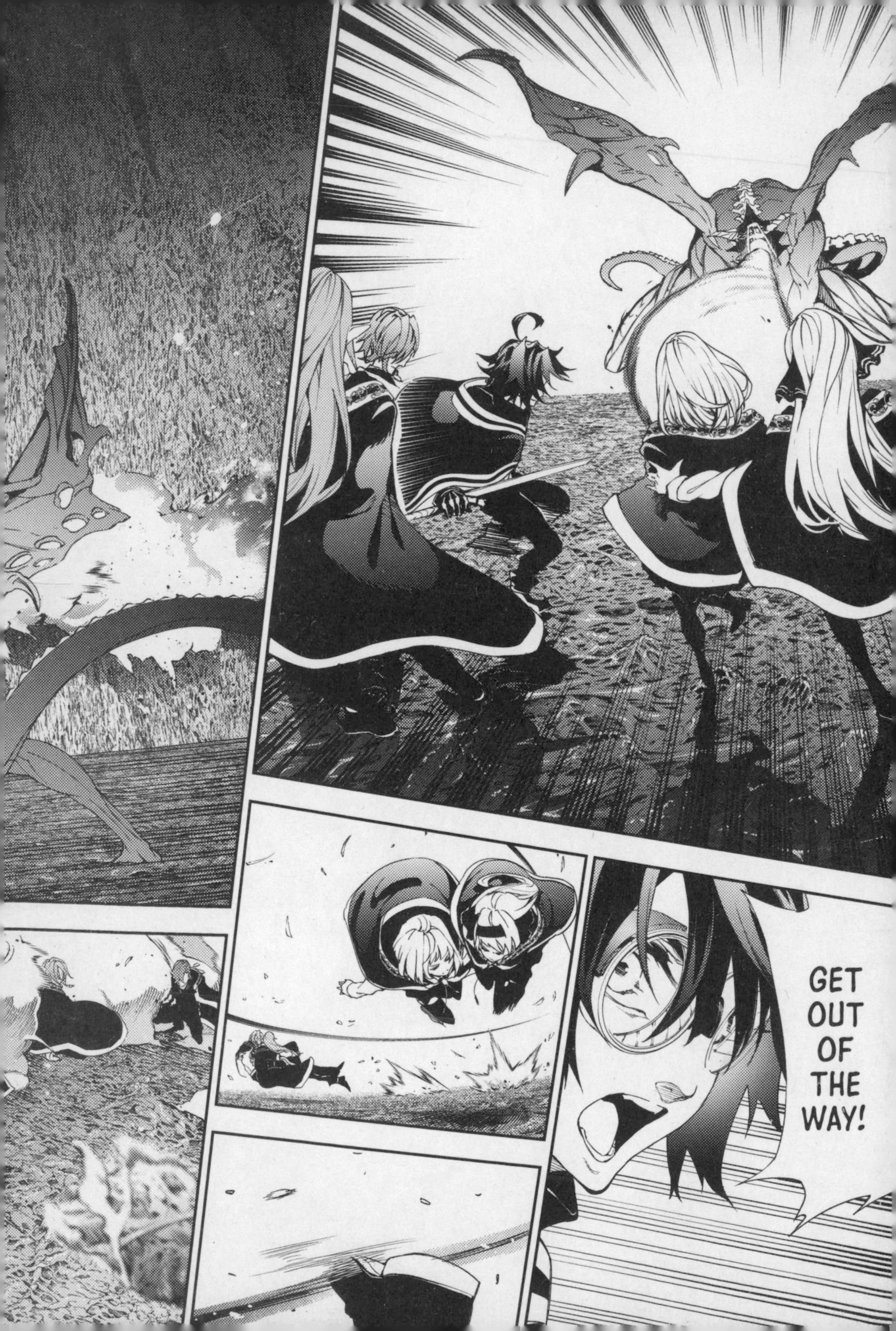
GET OUT OF THE WAY!

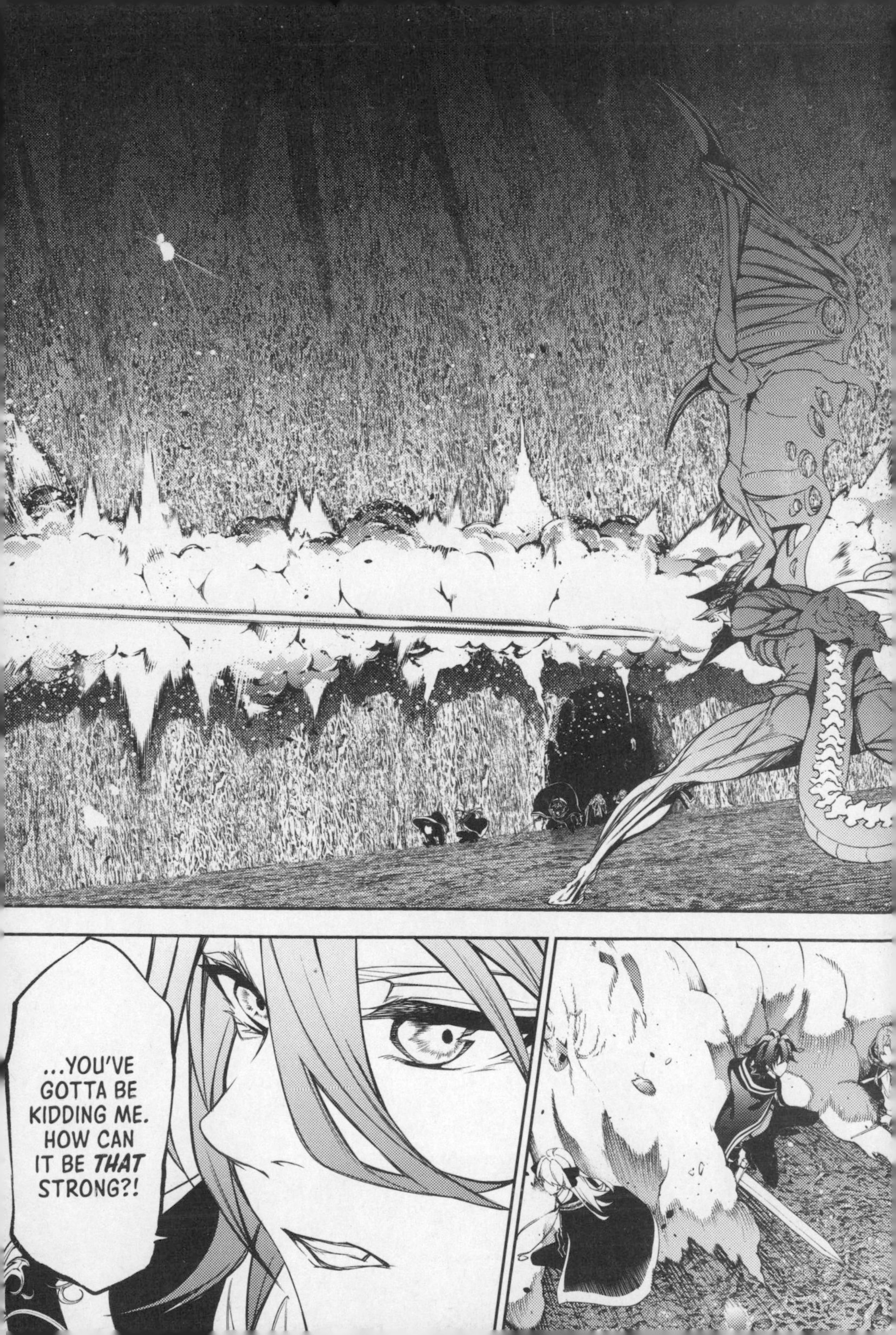
...YOU'VE GOTTA BE KIDDING ME. HOW CAN IT BE THAT STRONG?!

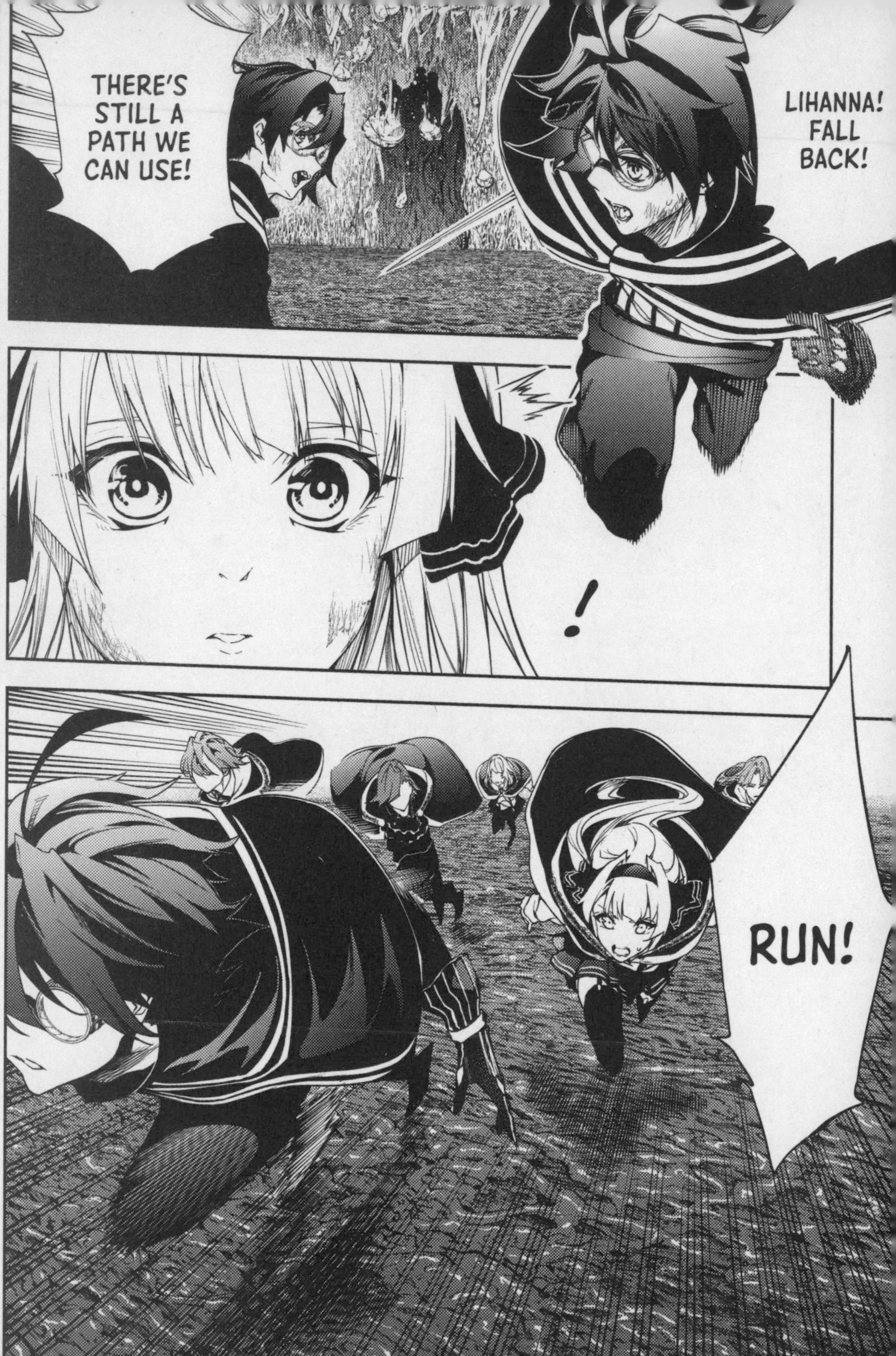
LIHANNA! FALL BACK!
THERE'S STILL A PATH WE CAN USE!
!
RUN!

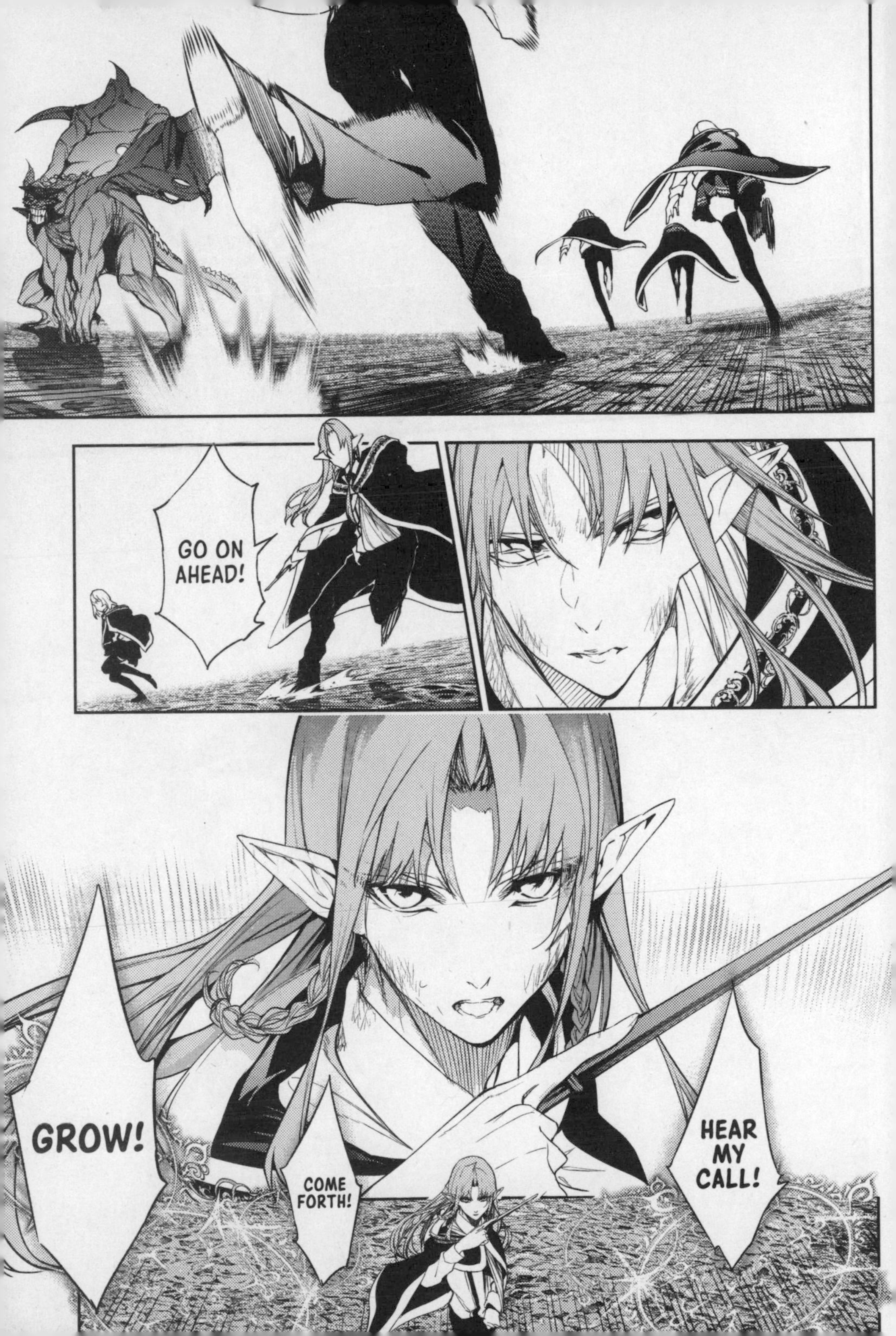
GO ON AHEAD!
HEAR MY CALL!
COME FORTH!
GROW!

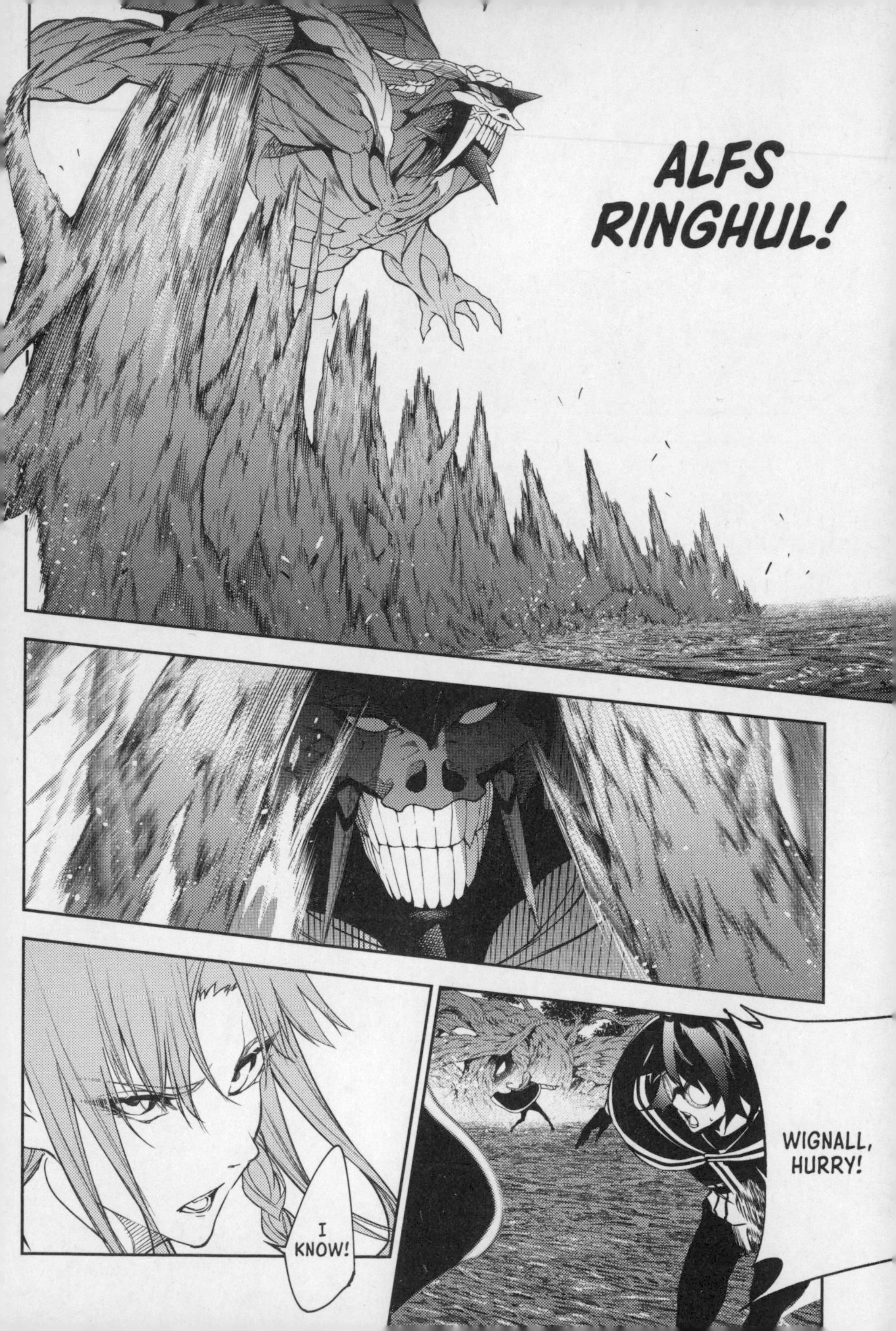
ALFS RINGHUL!
WIGNALL, HURRY!
I KNOW!

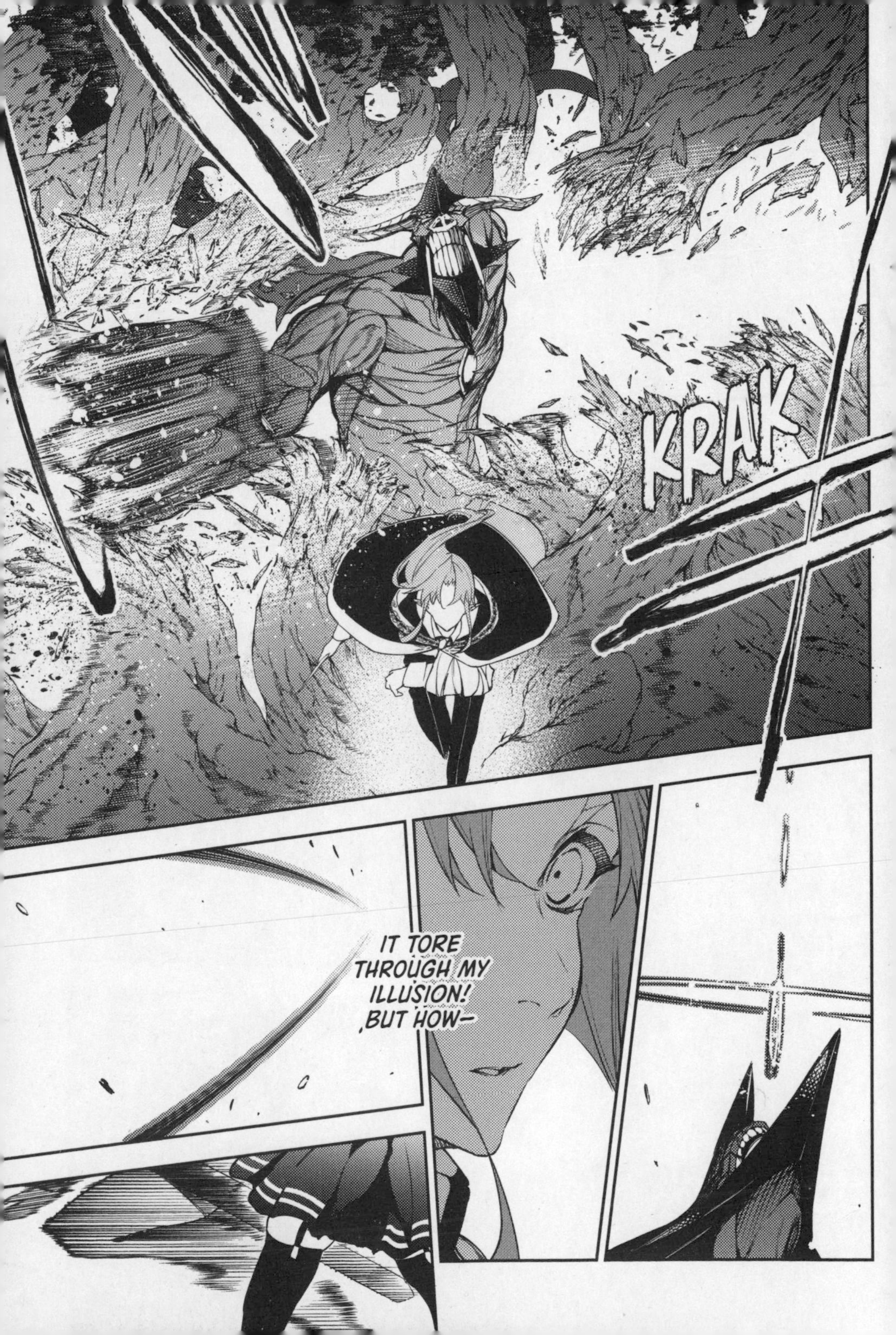
KRAK
IT TORE THROUGH MY ILLUSION! BUT HOW–

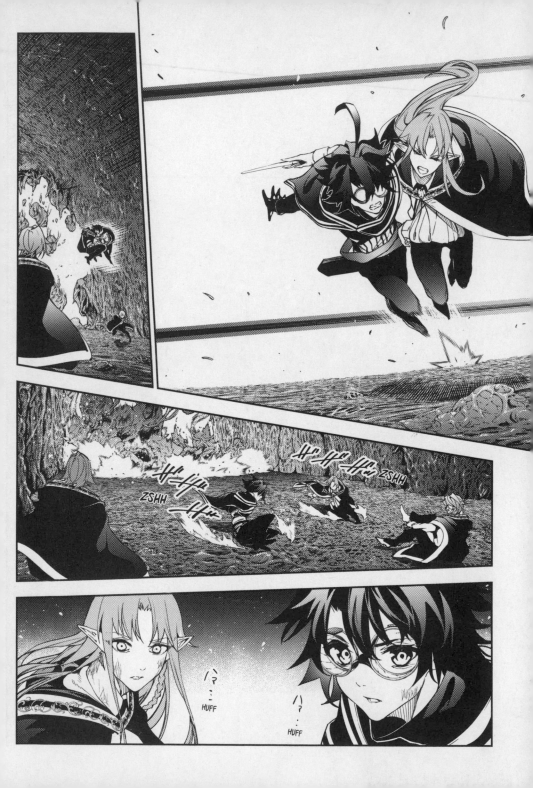

ZSHH

ZSHH

HUFF

HUFF

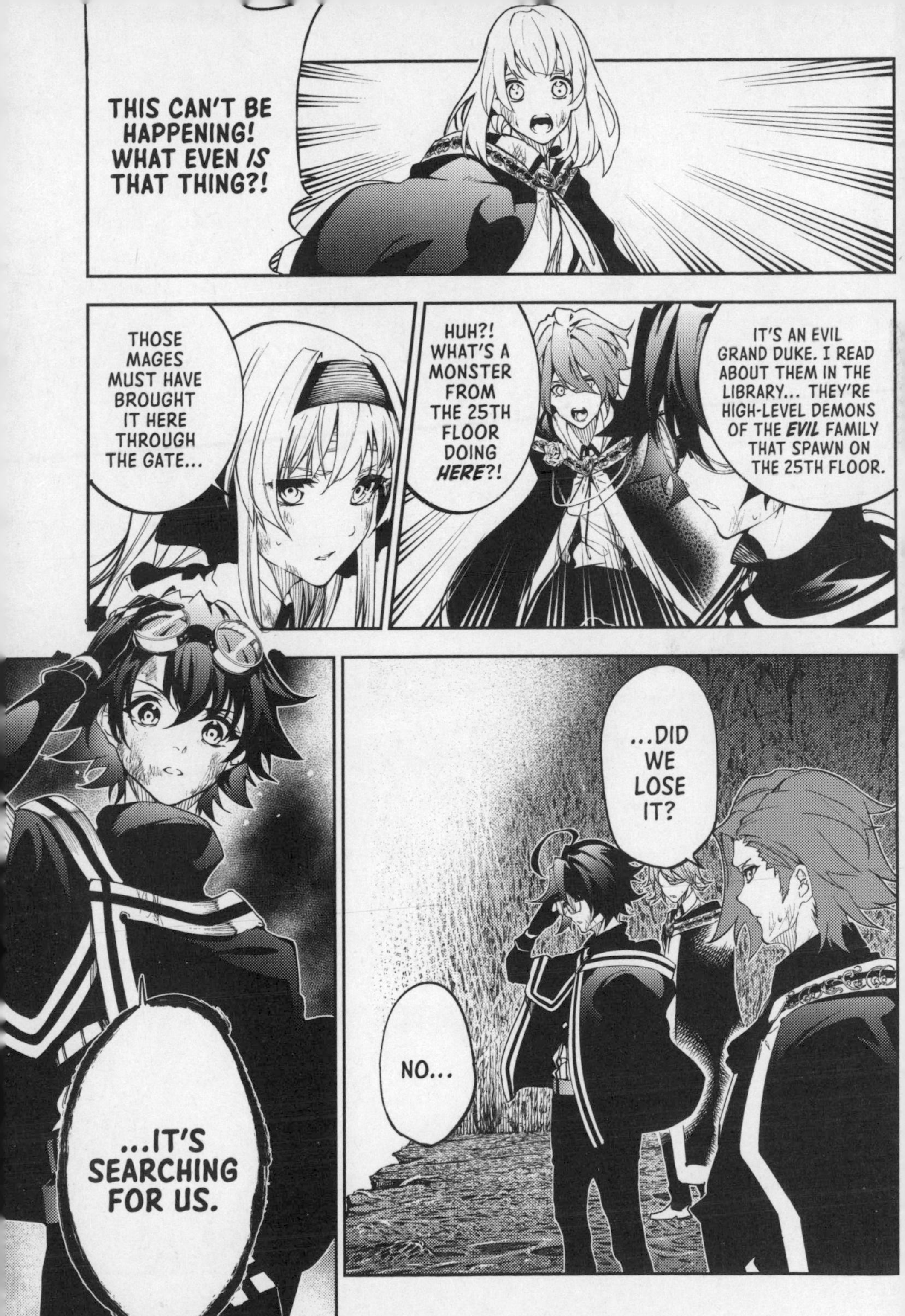
THIS CAN'T BE HAPPENING! WHAT EVEN *IS* THAT THING?!
IT'S AN EVIL GRAND DUKE. I READ ABOUT THEM IN THE LIBRARY... THEY'RE HIGH-LEVEL DEMONS OF THE *EVIL* FAMILY THAT SPAWN ON THE 25TH FLOOR.
HUH?! WHAT'S A MONSTER FROM THE 25TH FLOOR DOING *HERE*?!
THOSE MAGES MUST HAVE BROUGHT IT HERE THROUGH THE GATE...
...DID WE LOSE IT?
NO...
...IT'S SEARCHING FOR US.

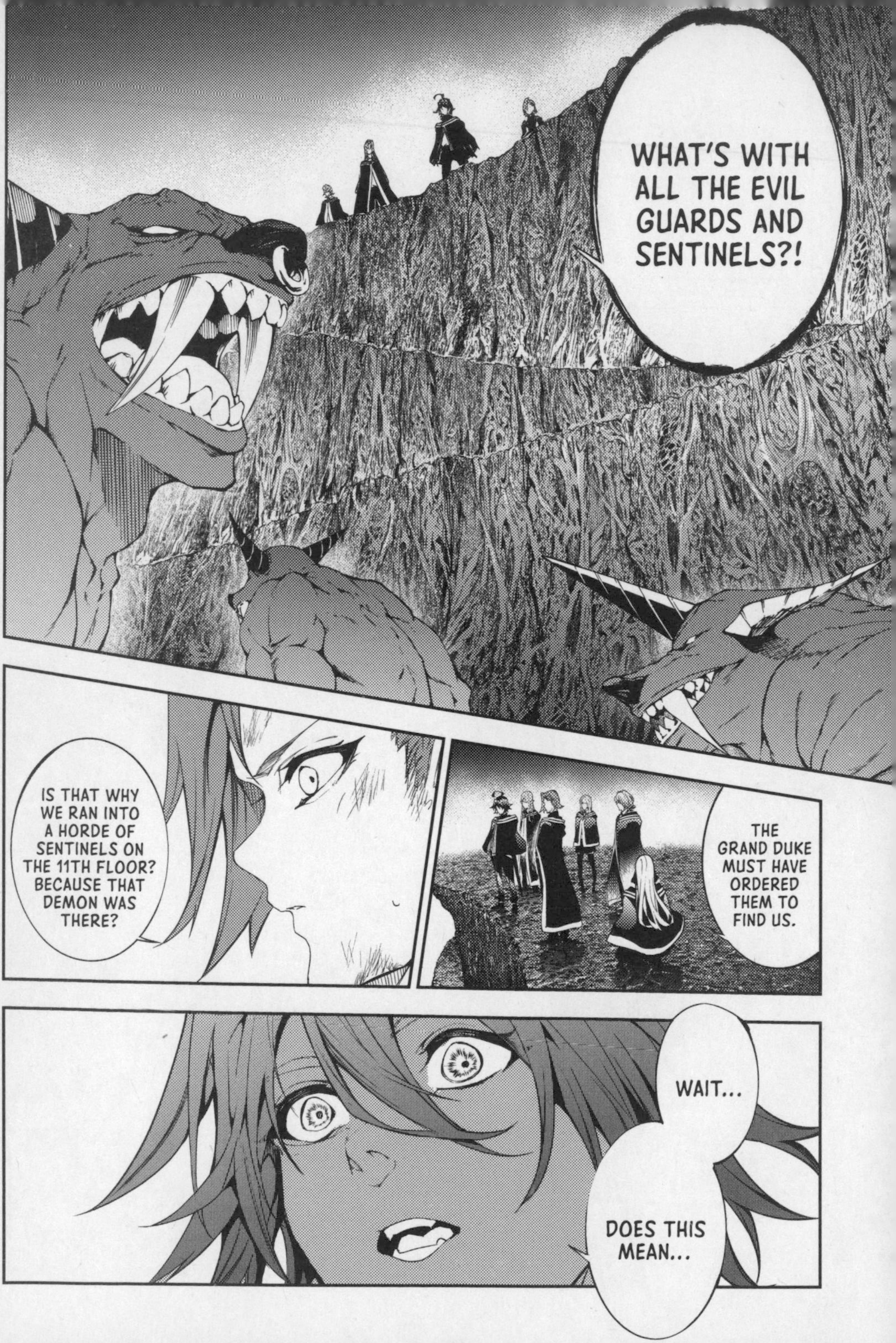
WHAT'S WITH ALL THE EVIL GUARDS AND SENTINELS?!
THE GRAND DUKE MUST HAVE ORDERED THEM TO FIND US.
IS THAT WHY WE RAN INTO A HORDE OF SENTINELS ON THE 11TH FLOOR? BECAUSE THAT DEMON WAS THERE?
WAIT...
DOES THIS MEAN...

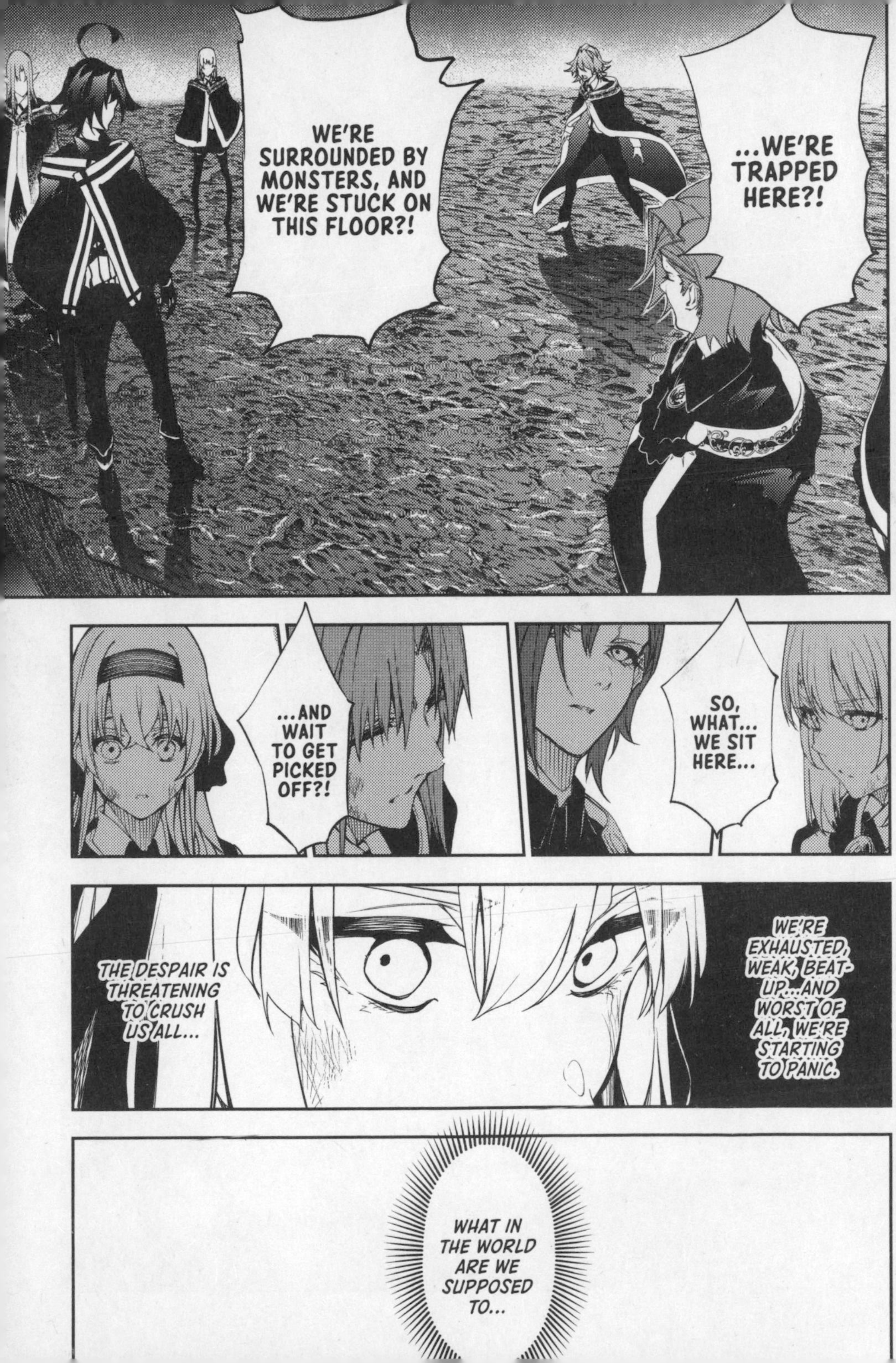
...WE'RE TRAPPED HERE?!
WE'RE SURROUNDED BY MONSTERS, AND WE'RE STUCK ON THIS FLOOR?!
SO, WHAT... WE SIT HERE...
...AND WAIT TO GET PICKED OFF?!
WE'RE EXHAUSTED, WEAK, BEAT-UP...AND WORST OF ALL, WE'RE STARTING TO PANIC.
THE DESPAIR IS THREATENING TO CRUSH US ALL...
WHAT IN THE WORLD ARE WE SUPPOSED TO...

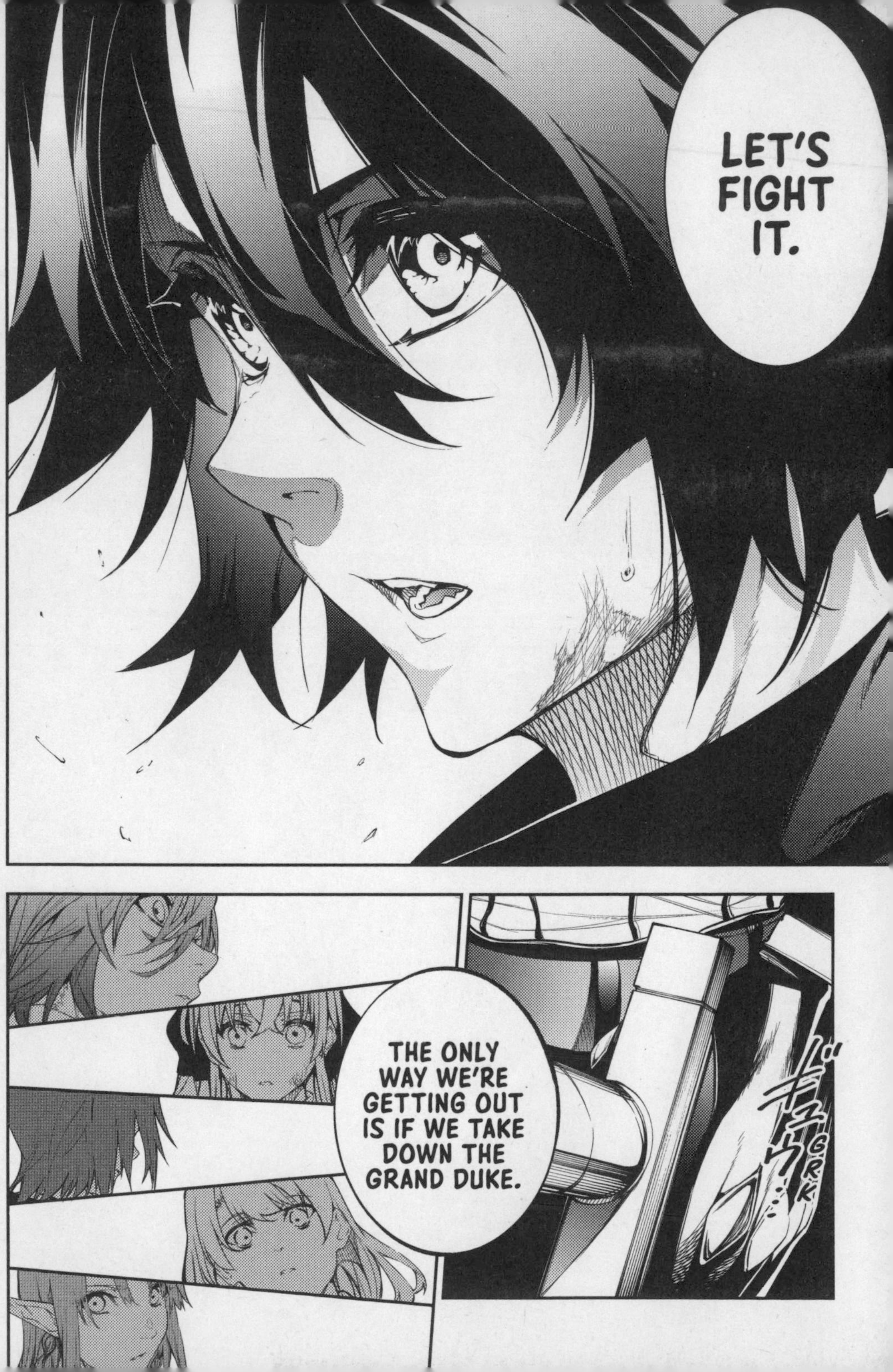
LET'S FIGHT IT.
GRK
THE ONLY WAY WE'RE GETTING OUT IS IF WE TAKE DOWN THE GRAND DUKE.

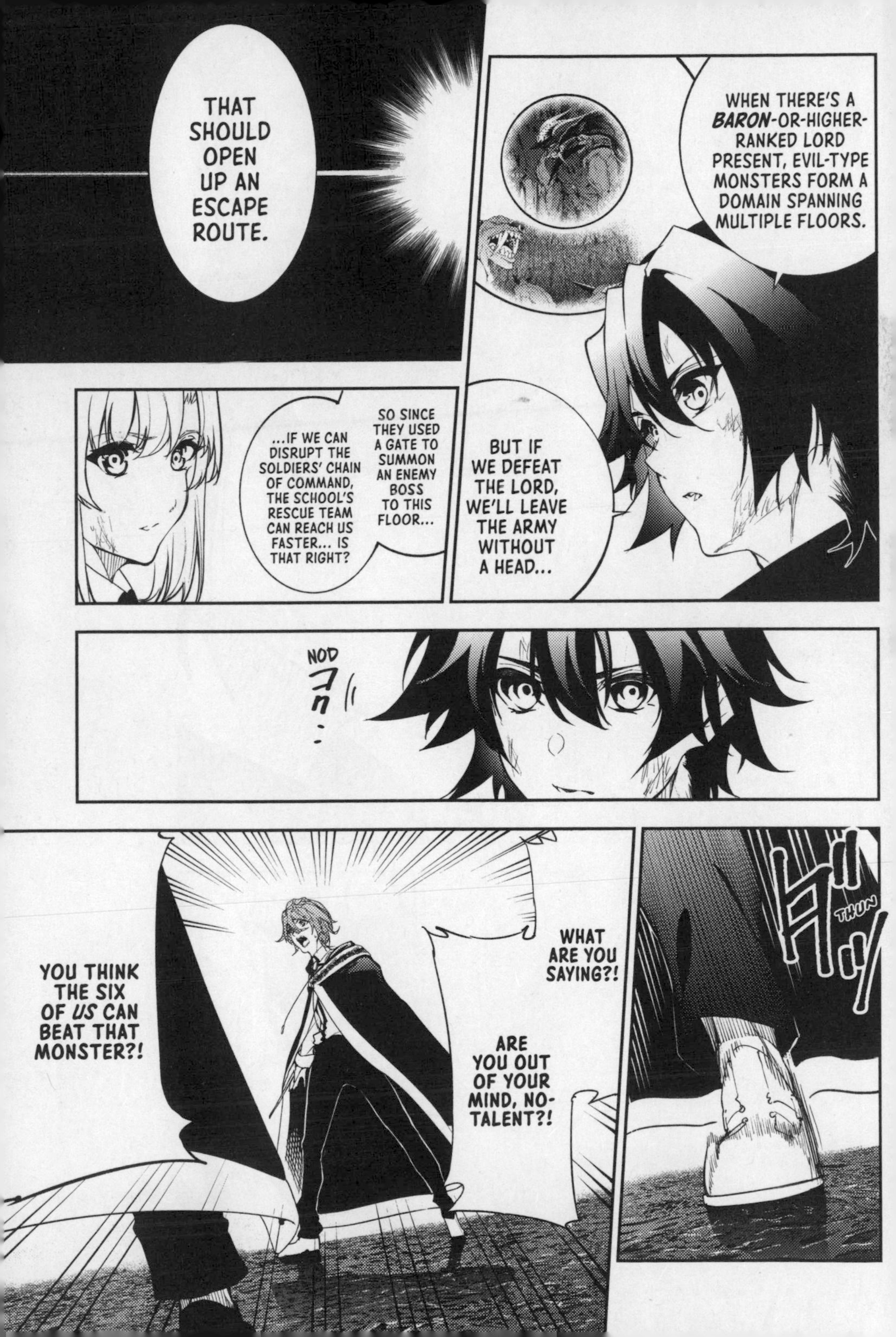
WHEN THERE'S A *BARON*-OR-HIGHER-RANKED LORD PRESENT, EVIL-TYPE MONSTERS FORM A DOMAIN SPANNING MULTIPLE FLOORS.
BUT IF WE DEFEAT THE LORD, WE'LL LEAVE THE ARMY WITHOUT A HEAD...
THAT SHOULD OPEN UP AN ESCAPE ROUTE.
SO SINCE THEY USED A GATE TO SUMMON AN ENEMY BOSS TO THIS FLOOR...
...IF WE CAN DISRUPT THE SOLDIERS' CHAIN OF COMMAND, THE SCHOOL'S RESCUE TEAM CAN REACH US FASTER... IS THAT RIGHT?
NOD
THUN
WHAT ARE YOU SAYING?!
ARE YOU OUT OF YOUR MIND, NO-TALENT?!
YOU THINK THE SIX OF *US* CAN BEAT THAT MONSTER?!

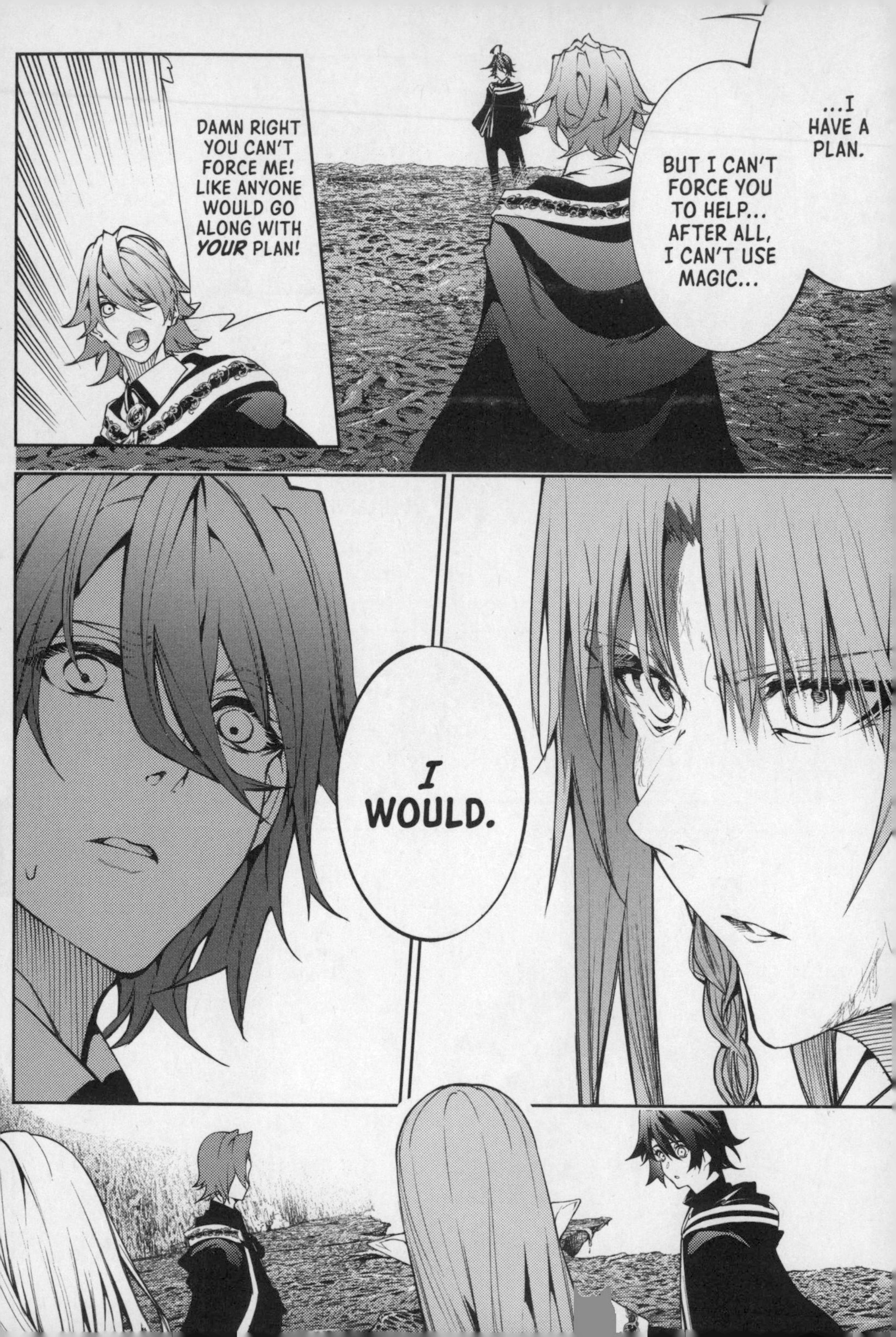
...I HAVE A PLAN.
BUT I CAN'T FORCE YOU TO HELP... AFTER ALL, I CAN'T USE MAGIC...
DAMN RIGHT YOU CAN'T FORCE ME! LIKE ANYONE WOULD GO ALONG WITH *YOUR* PLAN!
I WOULD.

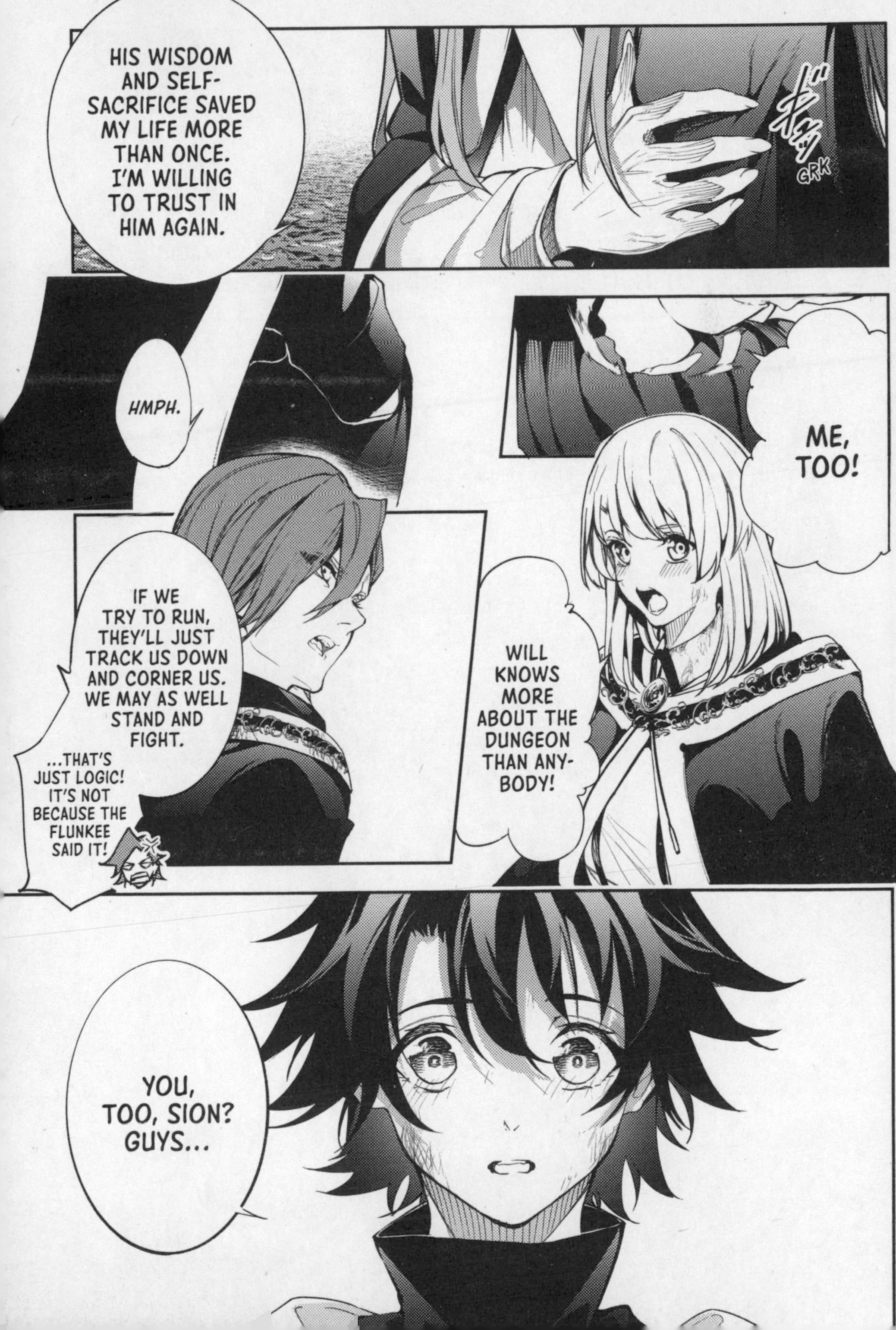
GRK
HIS WISDOM AND SELF-SACRIFICE SAVED MY LIFE MORE THAN ONCE. I'M WILLING TO TRUST IN HIM AGAIN.
ME, TOO!
WILL KNOWS MORE ABOUT THE DUNGEON THAN ANY-BODY!
HMPH.
IF WE TRY TO RUN, THEY'LL JUST TRACK US DOWN AND CORNER US. WE MAY AS WELL STAND AND FIGHT.
...THAT'S JUST LOGIC! IT'S NOT BECAUSE THE FLUNKEE SAID IT!
YOU, TOO, SION? GUYS...

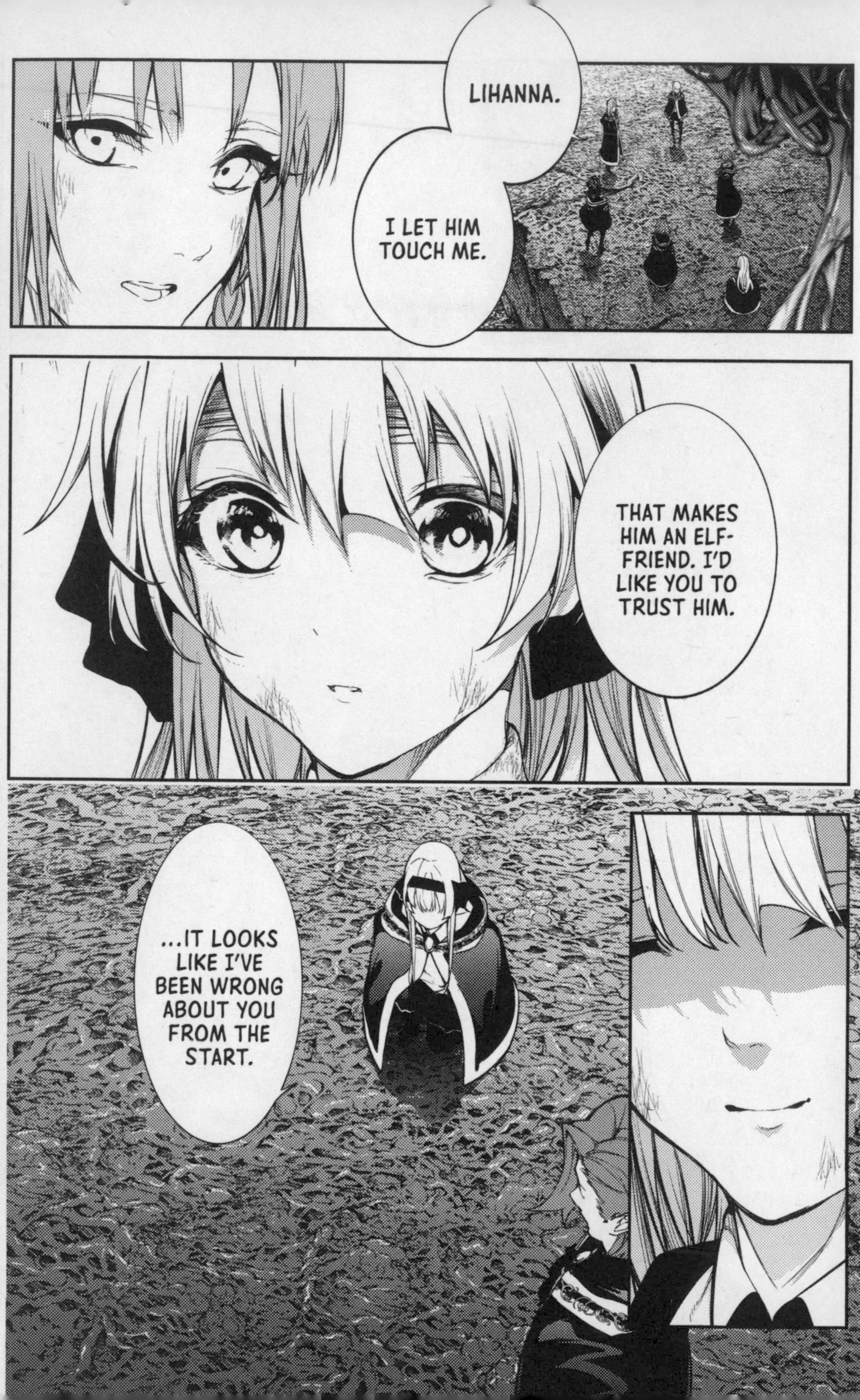
LIHANNA.
I LET HIM TOUCH ME.
THAT MAKES HIM AN ELF-FRIEND. I'D LIKE YOU TO TRUST HIM.
...IT LOOKS LIKE I'VE BEEN WRONG ABOUT YOU FROM THE START.

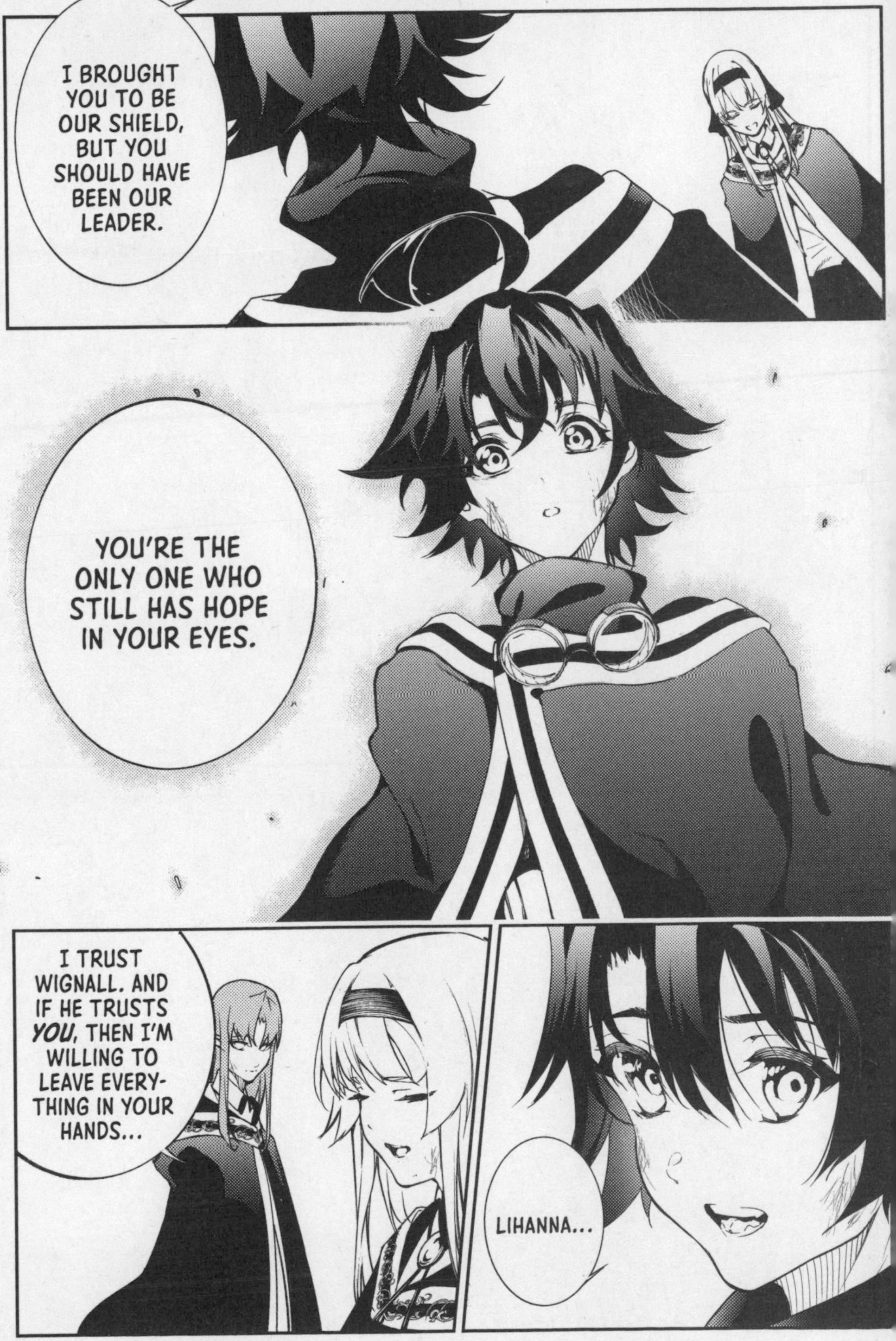
I BROUGHT YOU TO BE OUR SHIELD, BUT YOU SHOULD HAVE BEEN OUR LEADER.
YOU'RE THE ONLY ONE WHO STILL HAS HOPE IN YOUR EYES.
LIHANNA...
I TRUST WIGNALL. AND IF HE TRUSTS *YOU*, THEN I'M WILLING TO LEAVE EVERY-THING IN YOUR HANDS...

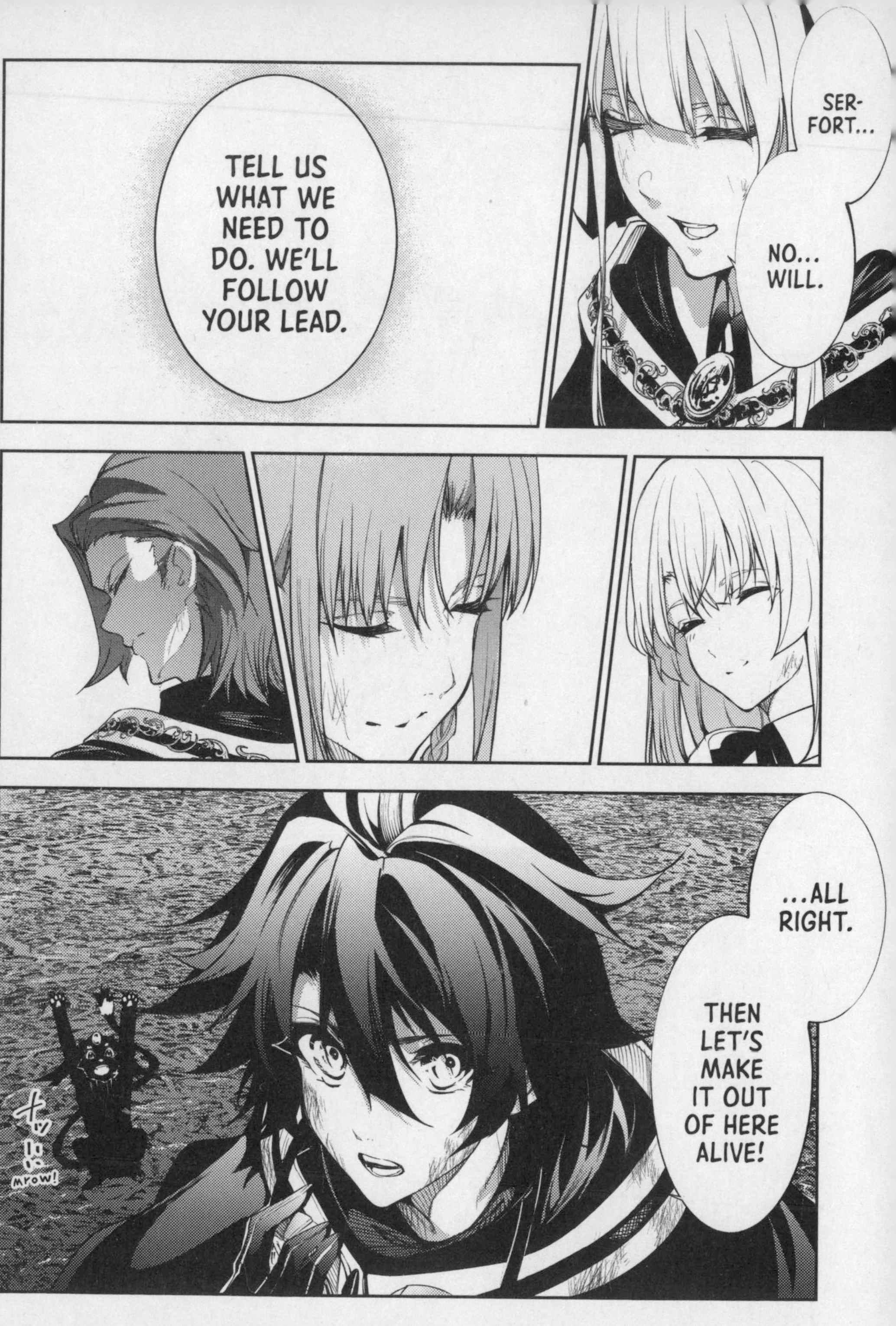
SER-FORT...
NO... WILL.
TELL US WHAT WE NEED TO DO. WE'LL FOLLOW YOUR LEAD.
...ALL RIGHT.
THEN LET'S MAKE IT OUT OF HERE ALIVE!
mrow!

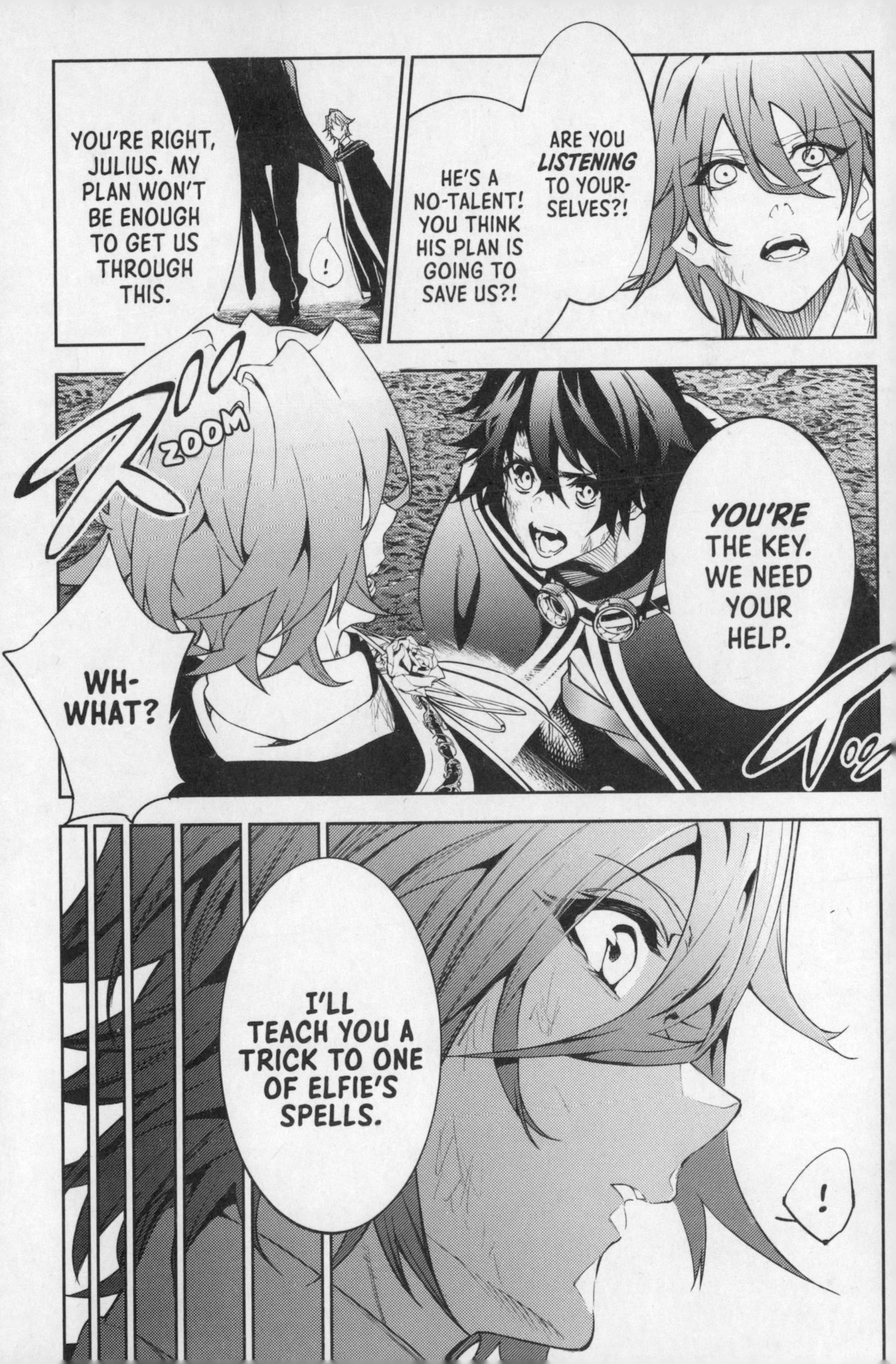
ARE YOU *LISTENING* TO YOURSELVES?!
HE'S A NO-TALENT! YOU THINK HIS PLAN IS GOING TO SAVE US?!
!
YOU'RE RIGHT, JULIUS. MY PLAN WON'T BE ENOUGH TO GET US THROUGH THIS.
YOU'RE THE KEY. WE NEED YOUR HELP.
ZOOM
WH-WHAT?
I'LL TEACH YOU A TRICK TO ONE OF ELFIE'S SPELLS.
!

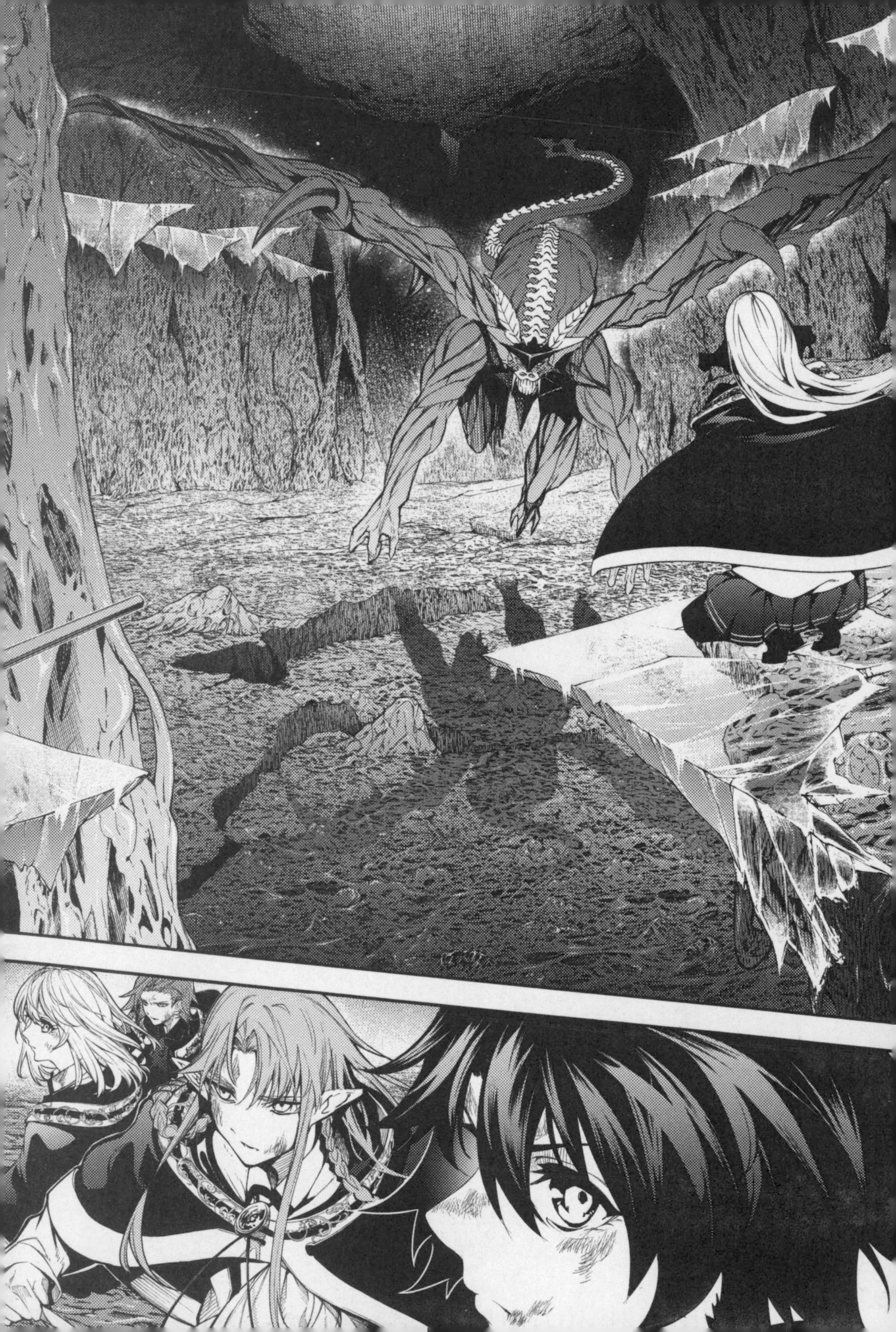

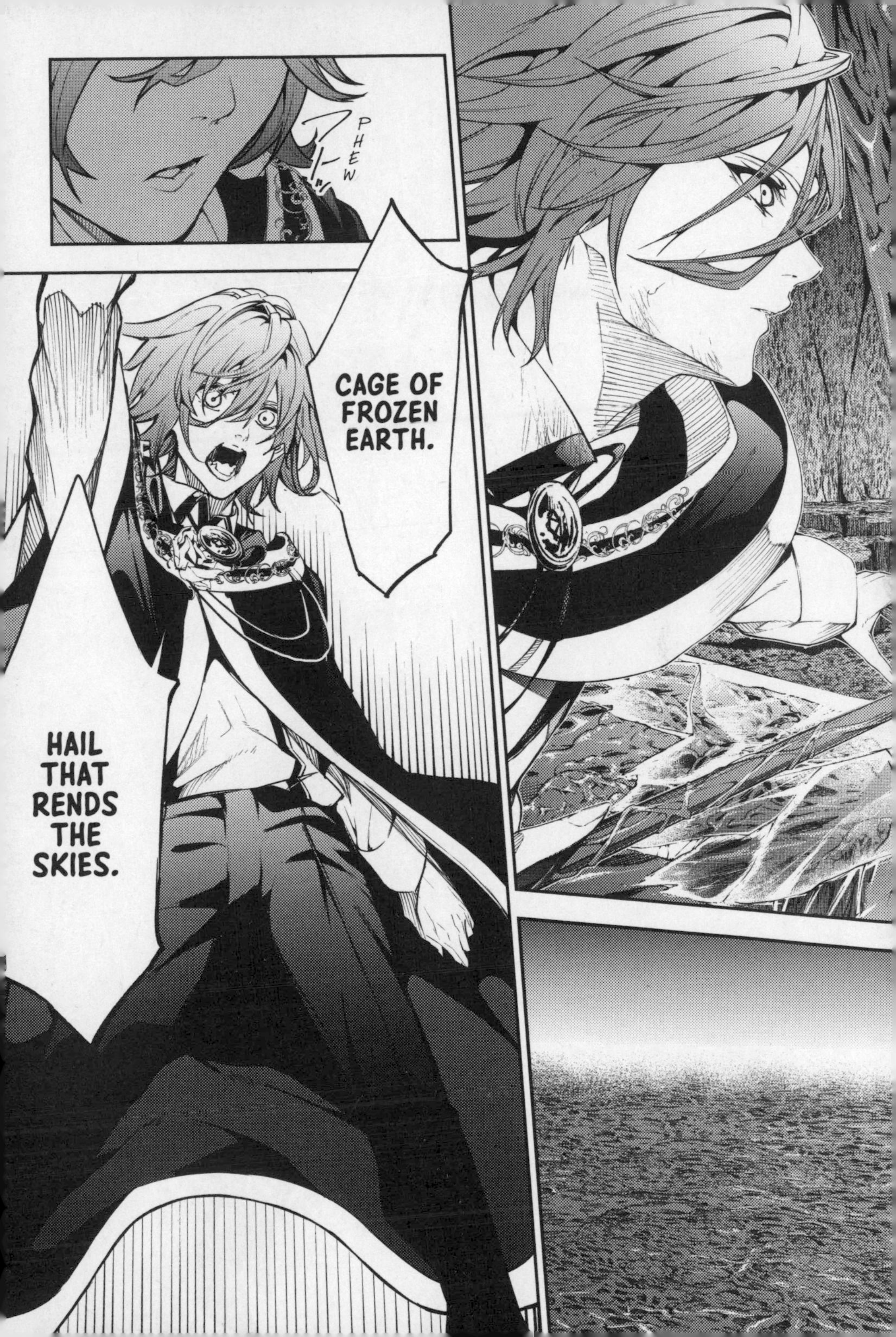
PHEW
CAGE OF FROZEN EARTH.
HAIL THAT RENDS THE SKIES.

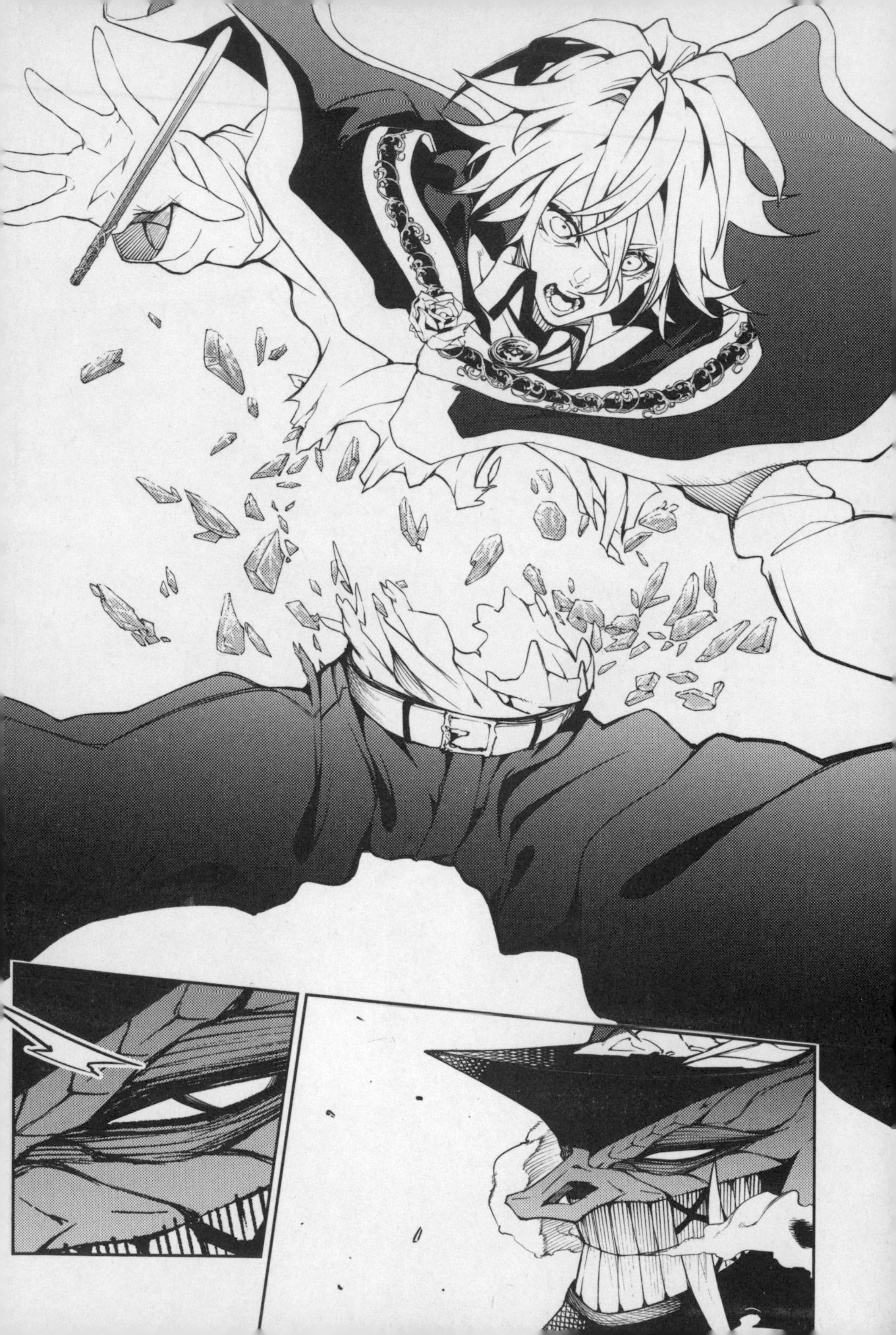

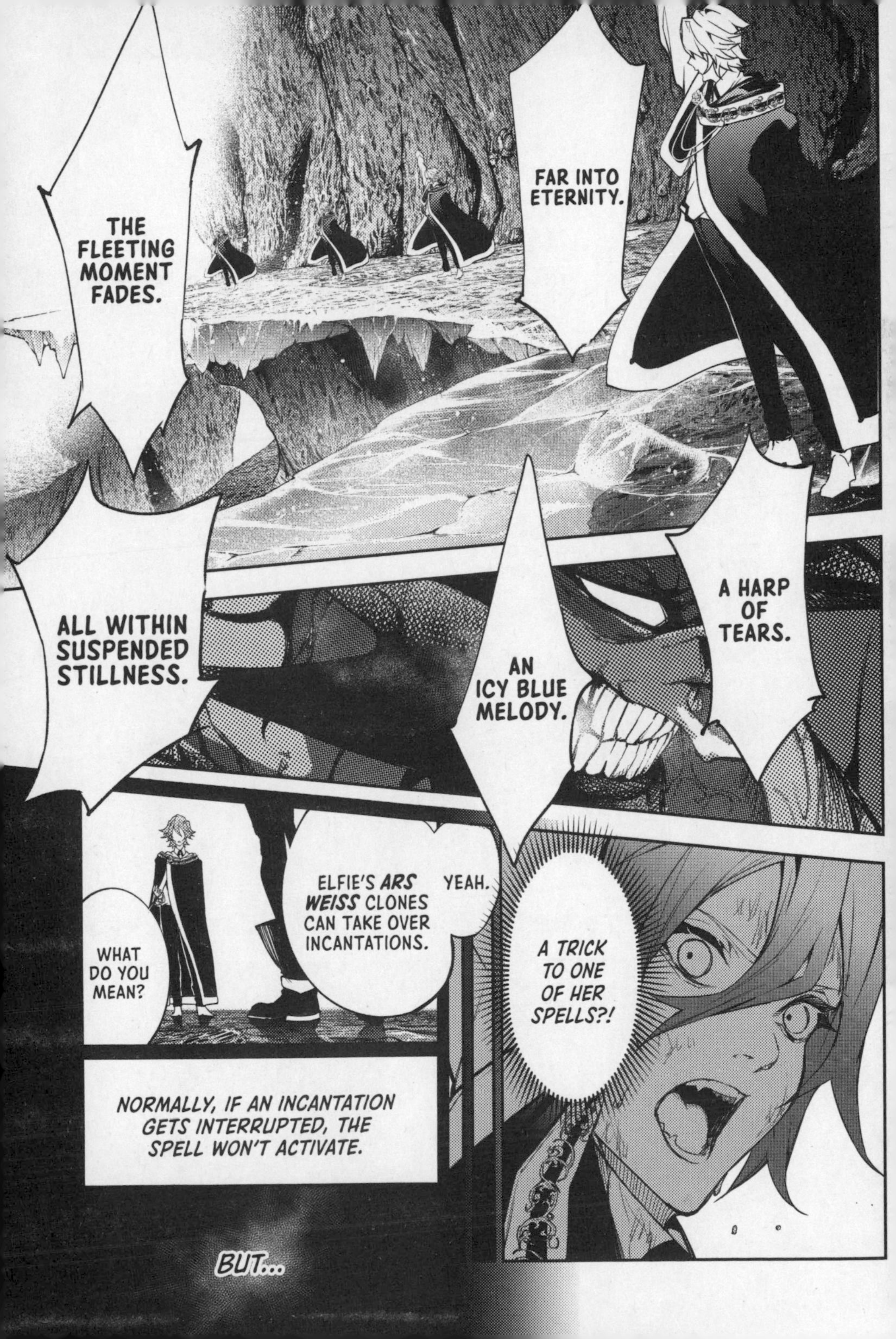
FAR INTO ETERNITY.
THE FLEETING MOMENT FADES.
A HARP OF TEARS.
AN ICY BLUE MELODY.
ALL WITHIN SUSPENDED STILLNESS.
A TRICK TO ONE OF HER SPELLS?!
YEAH.
ELFIE'S *ARS WEISS* CLONES CAN TAKE OVER INCANTATIONS.
WHAT DO YOU MEAN?
NORMALLY, IF AN INCANTATION GETS INTERRUPTED, THE SPELL WON'T ACTIVATE.
BUT...

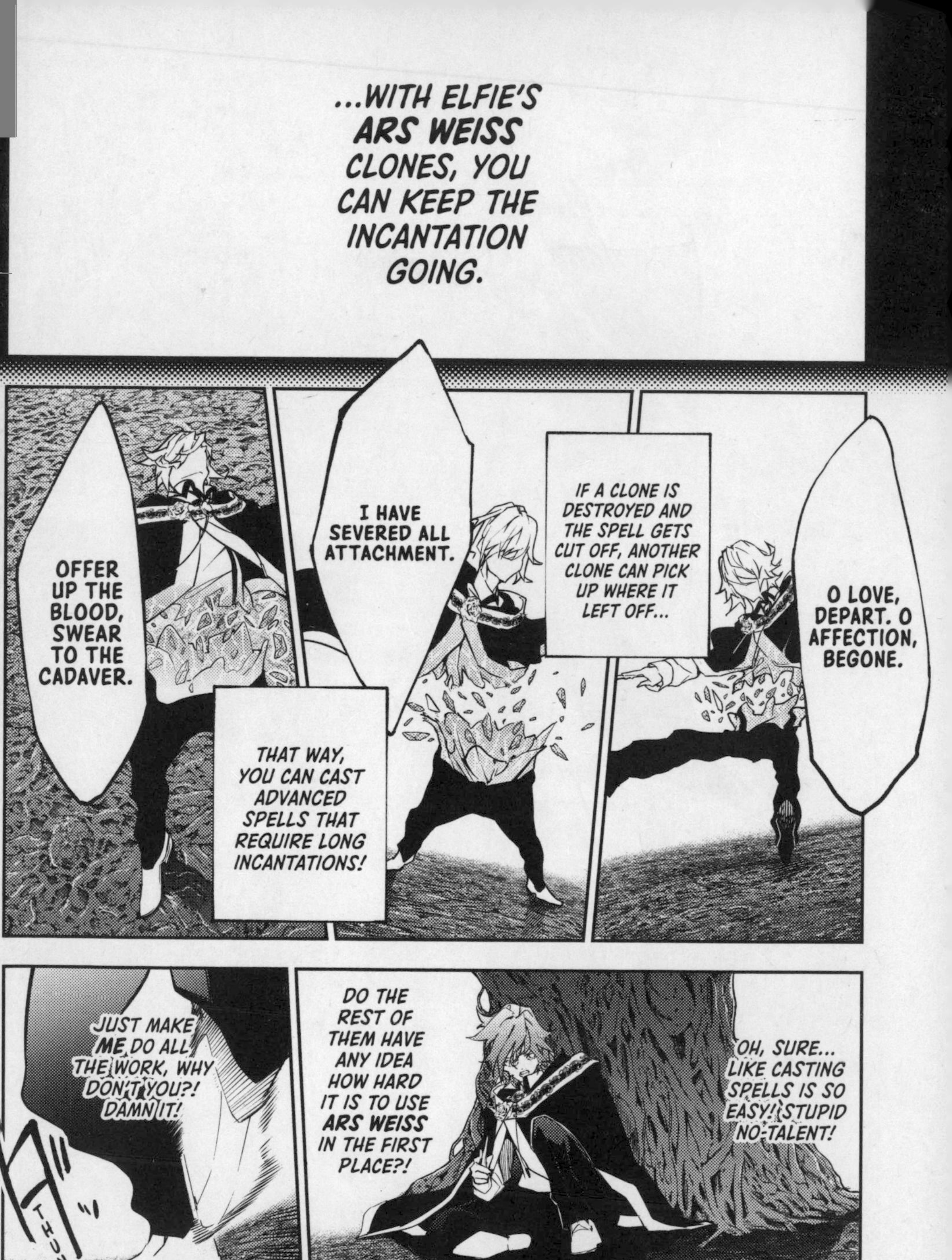
...WITH ELFIE'S ARS WEISS CLONES, YOU CAN KEEP THE INCANTATION GOING.
O LOVE, DEPART. O AFFECTION, BEGONE.
IF A CLONE IS DESTROYED AND THE SPELL GETS CUT OFF, ANOTHER CLONE CAN PICK UP WHERE IT LEFT OFF...
I HAVE SEVERED ALL ATTACHMENT.
THAT WAY, YOU CAN CAST ADVANCED SPELLS THAT REQUIRE LONG INCANTATIONS!
OFFER UP THE BLOOD, SWEAR TO THE CADAVER.
OH, SURE... LIKE CASTING SPELLS IS SO EASY! STUPID NO-TALENT!
DO THE REST OF THEM HAVE ANY IDEA HOW HARD IT IS TO USE ARS WEISS IN THE FIRST PLACE?!
JUST MAKE ME DO ALL THE WORK, WHY DON'T YOU?! DAMN IT!
THUN

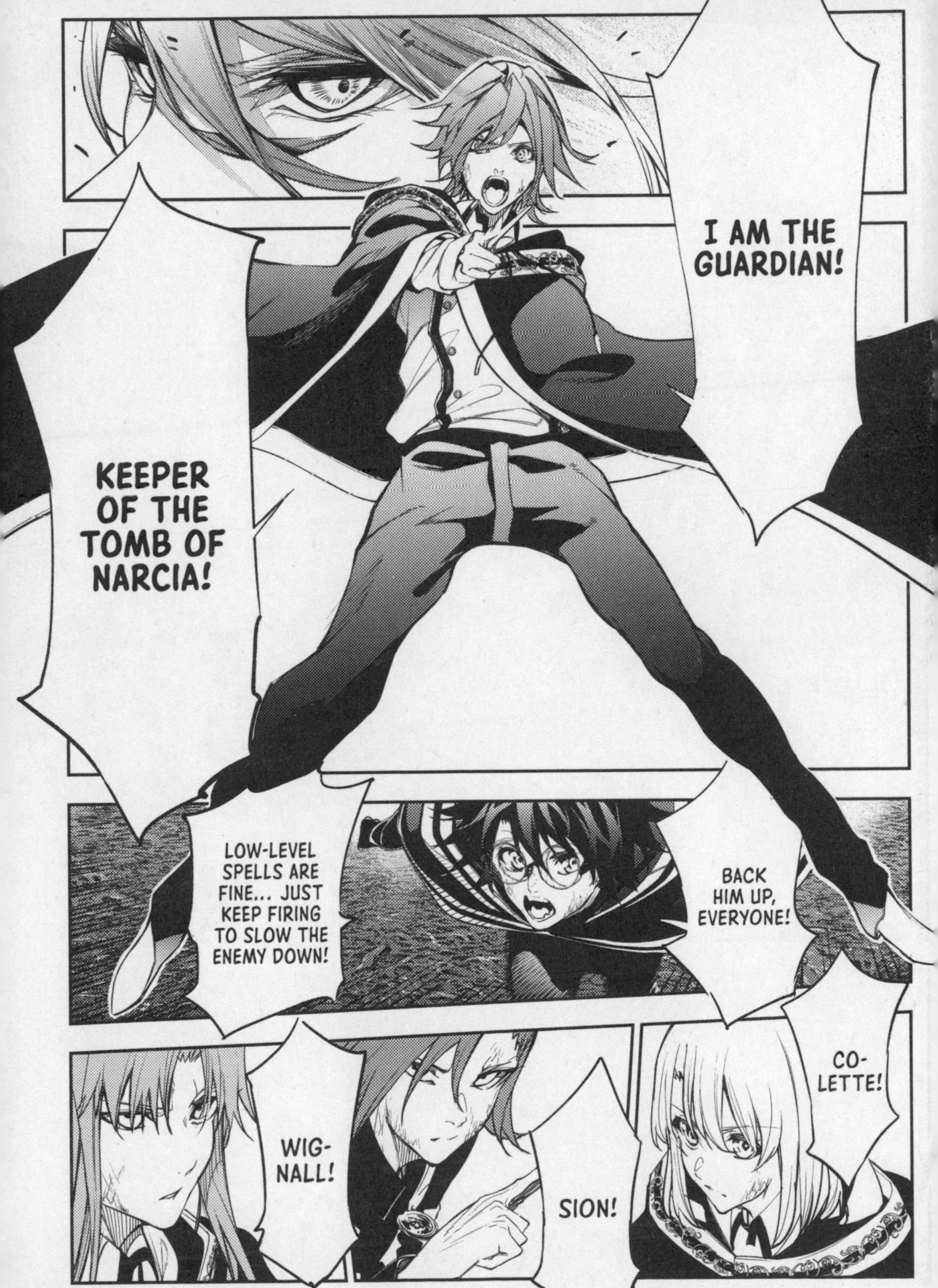
I AM THE GUARDIAN!
KEEPER OF THE TOMB OF NARCIA!
BACK HIM UP, EVERYONE!
LOW-LEVEL SPELLS ARE FINE... JUST KEEP FIRING TO SLOW THE ENEMY DOWN!
CO-LETTE!
SION!
WIG-NALL!

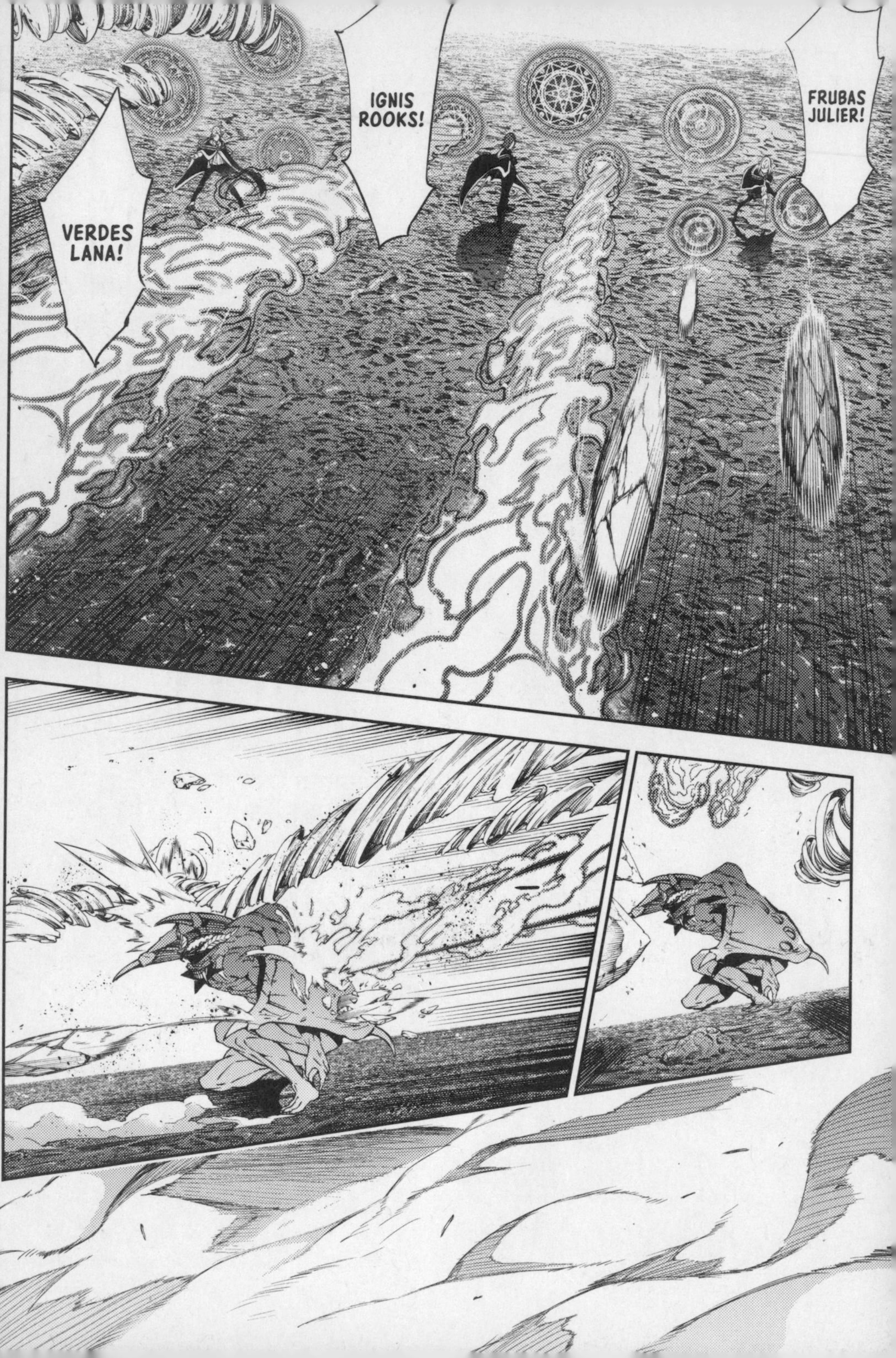
FRUBAS JULIER!
IGNIS ROOKS!
VERDES LANA!

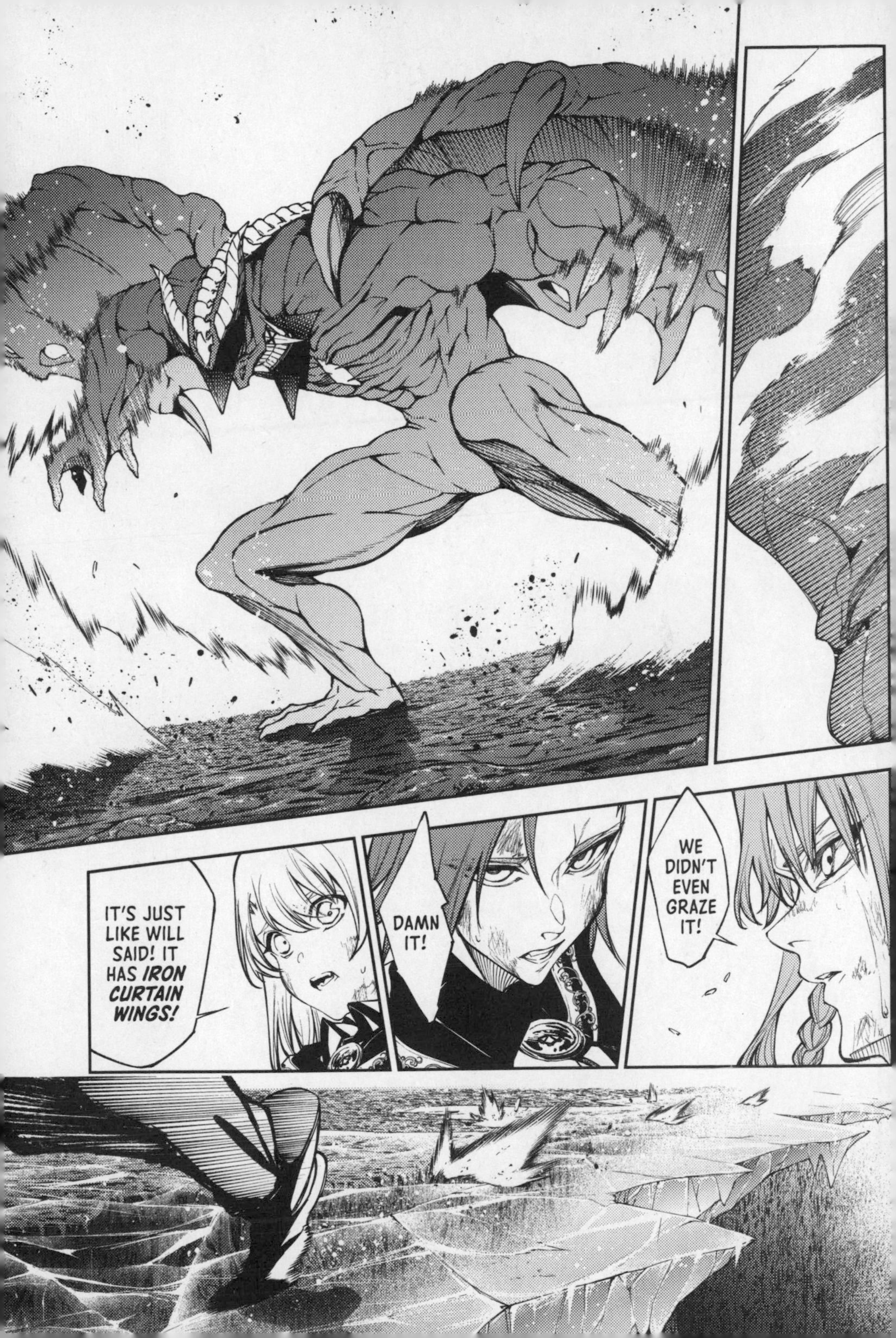
WE DIDN'T EVEN GRAZE IT!
DAMN IT!
IT'S JUST LIKE WILL SAID! IT HAS IRON CURTAIN WINGS!

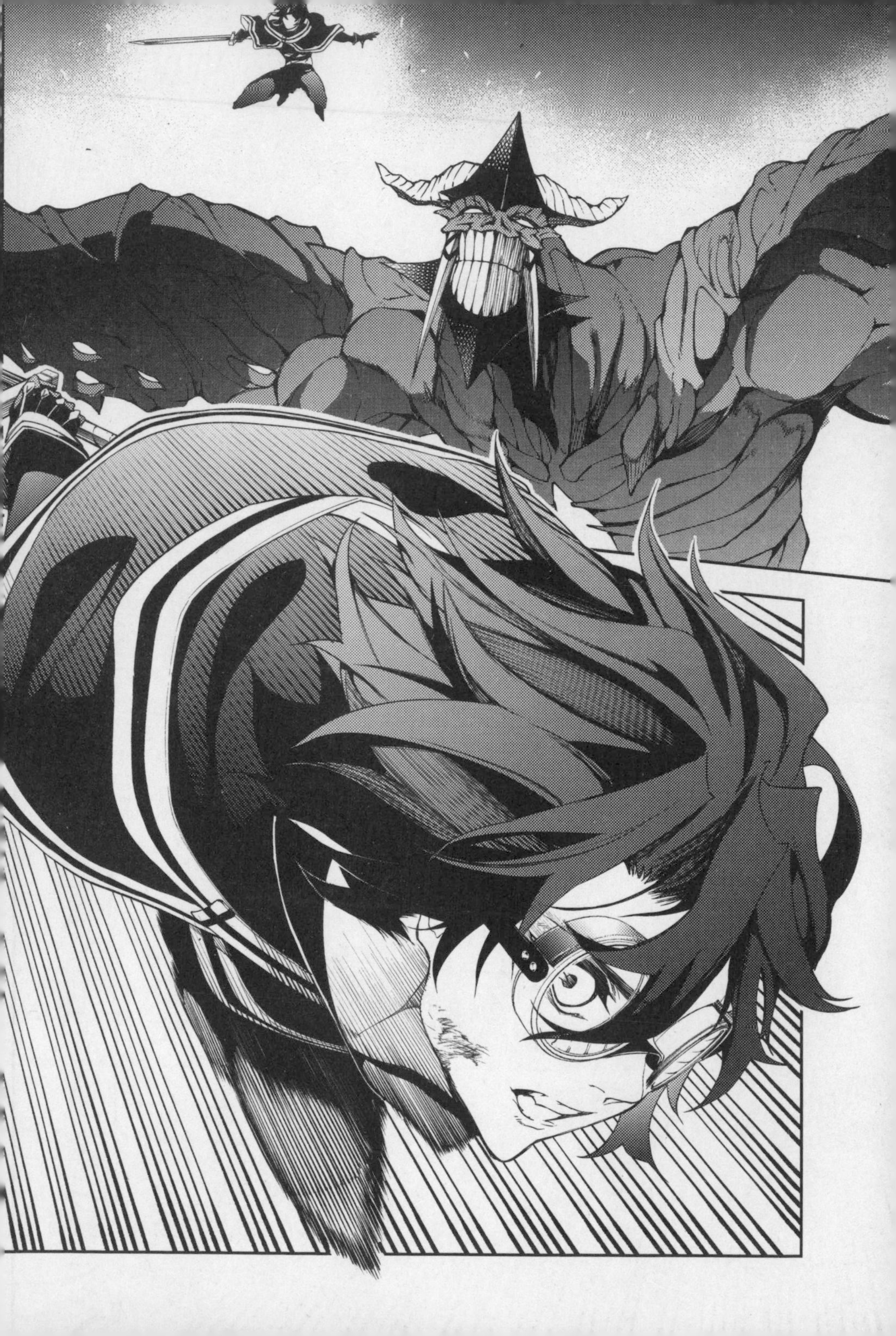

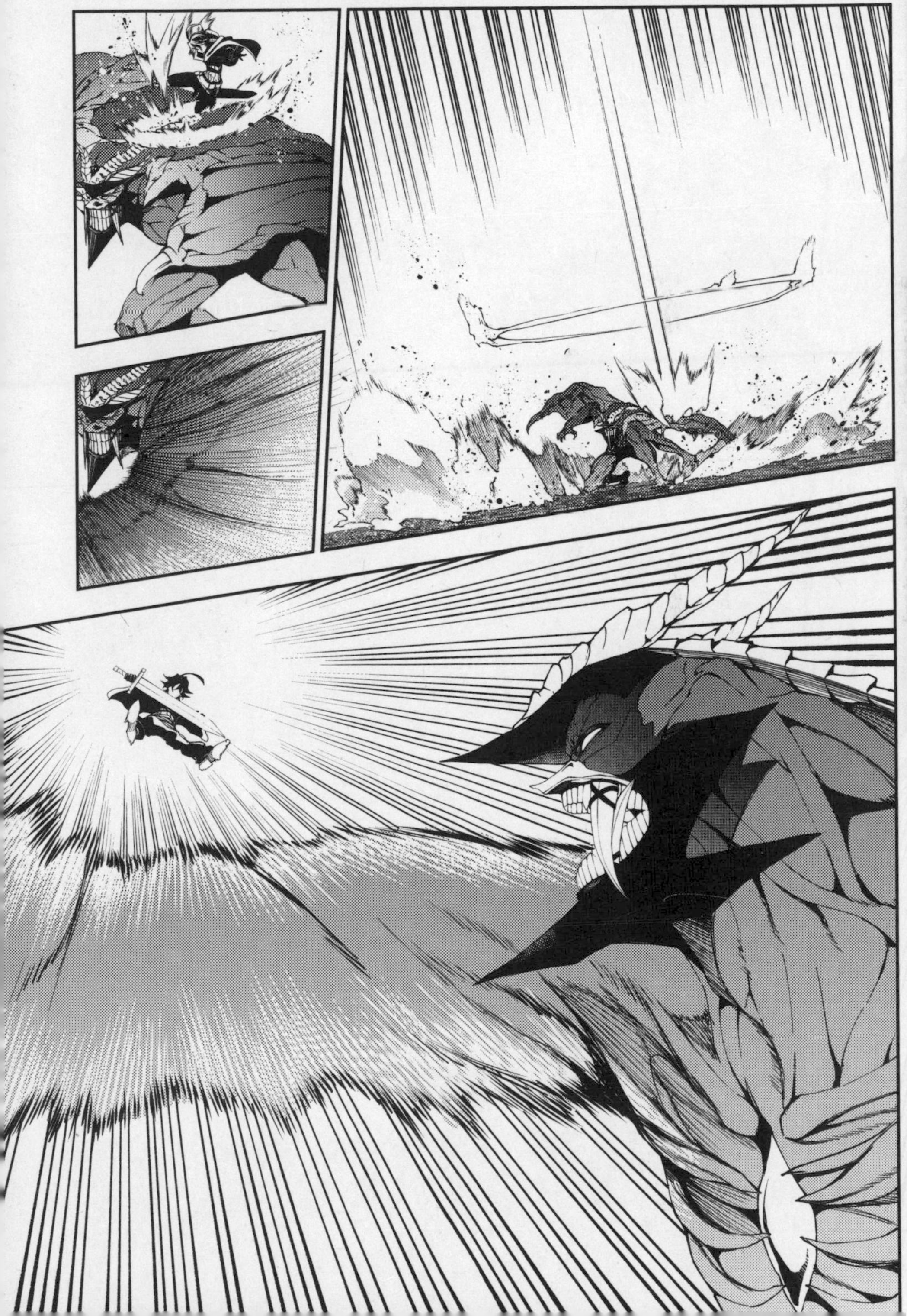

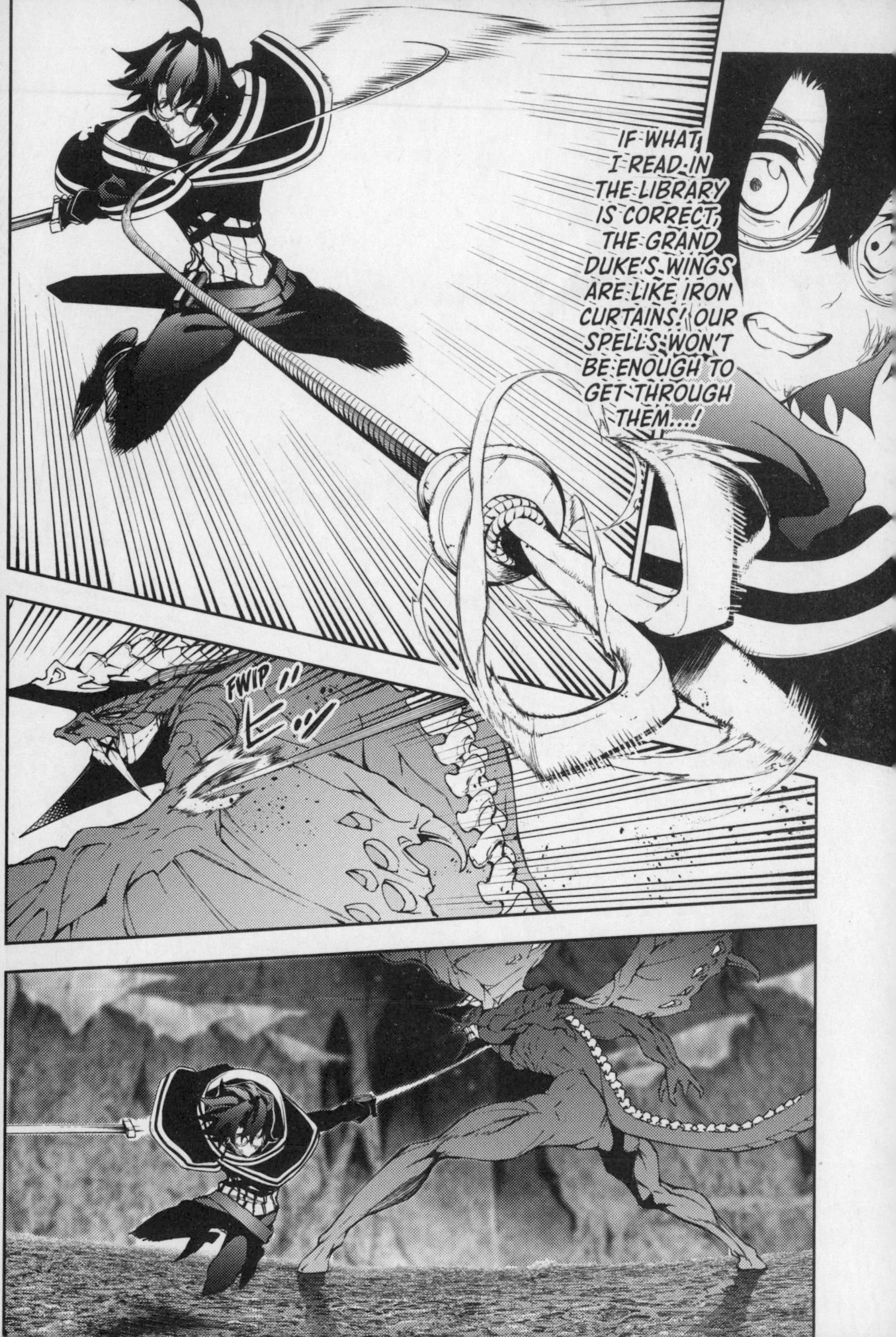
IF WHAT I READ IN THE LIBRARY IS CORRECT, THE GRAND DUKE'S WINGS ARE LIKE IRON CURTAINS! OUR SPELLS WON'T BE ENOUGH TO GET THROUGH THEM...!
FWIP
ヒッ

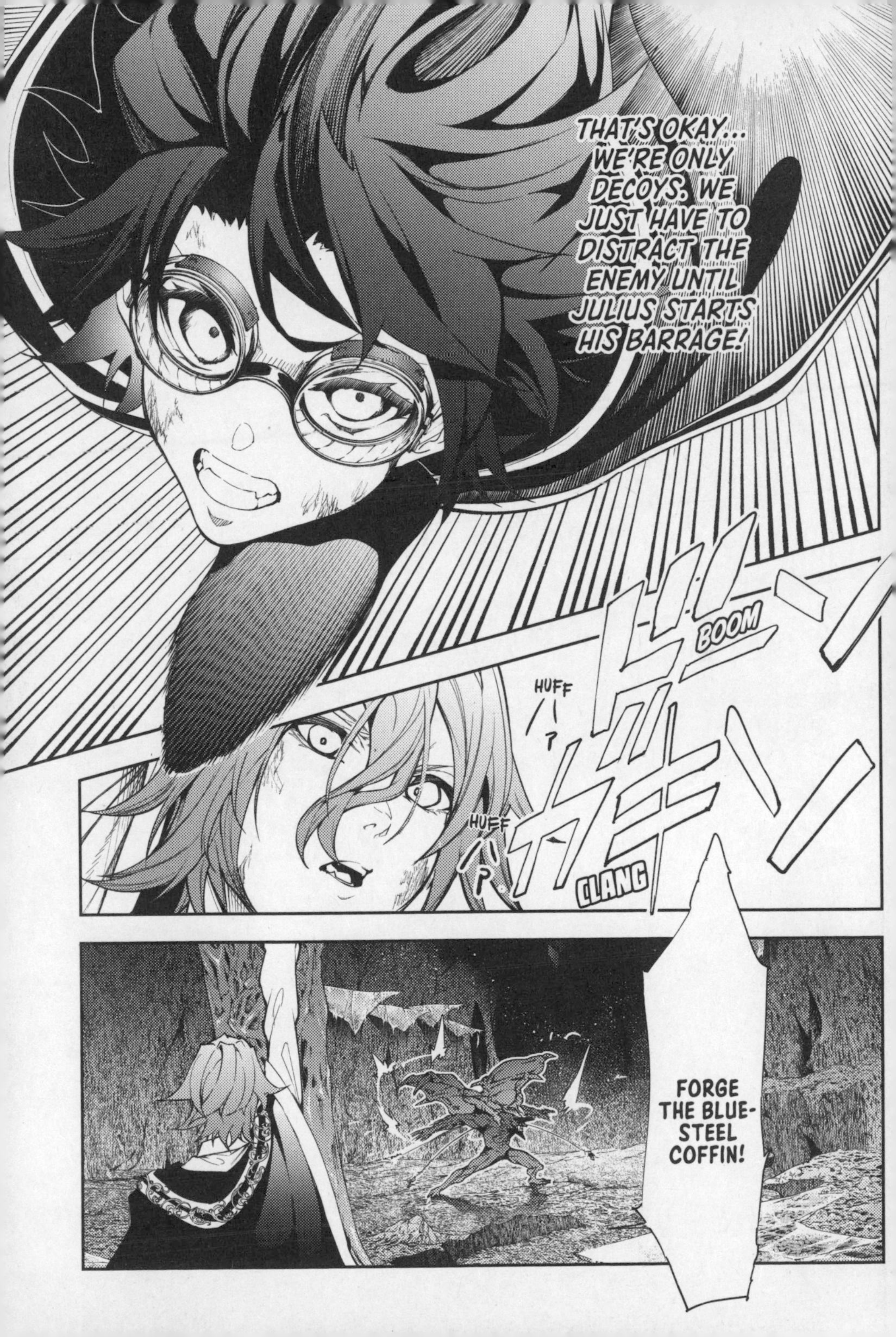
THAT'S OKAY... WE'RE ONLY DECOYS. WE JUST HAVE TO DISTRACT THE ENEMY UNTIL JULIUS STARTS HIS BARRAGE!
BOOM
HUFF
HUFF
CLANG
FORGE THE BLUE-STEEL COFFIN!

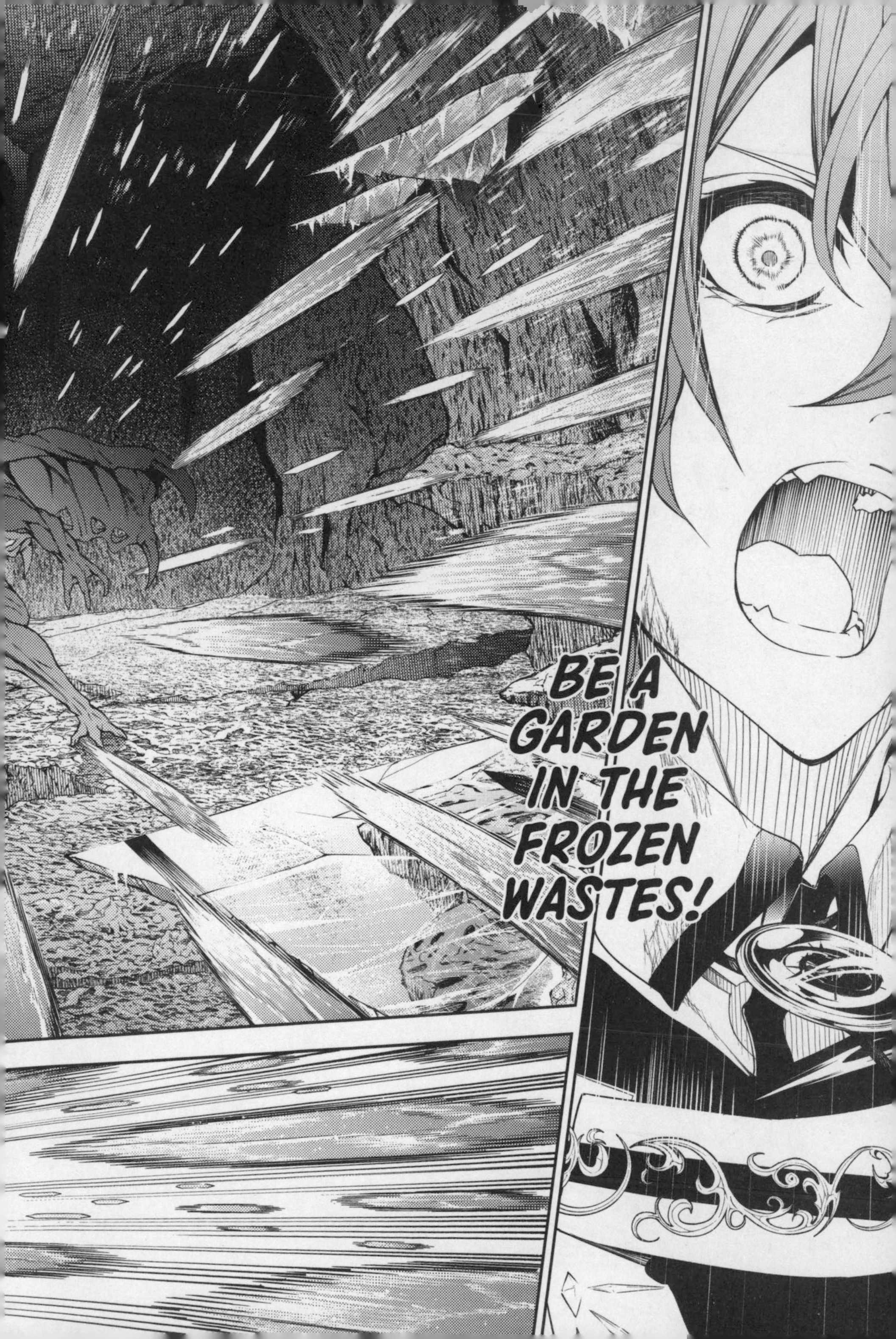
BE A GARDEN IN THE FROZEN WASTES!

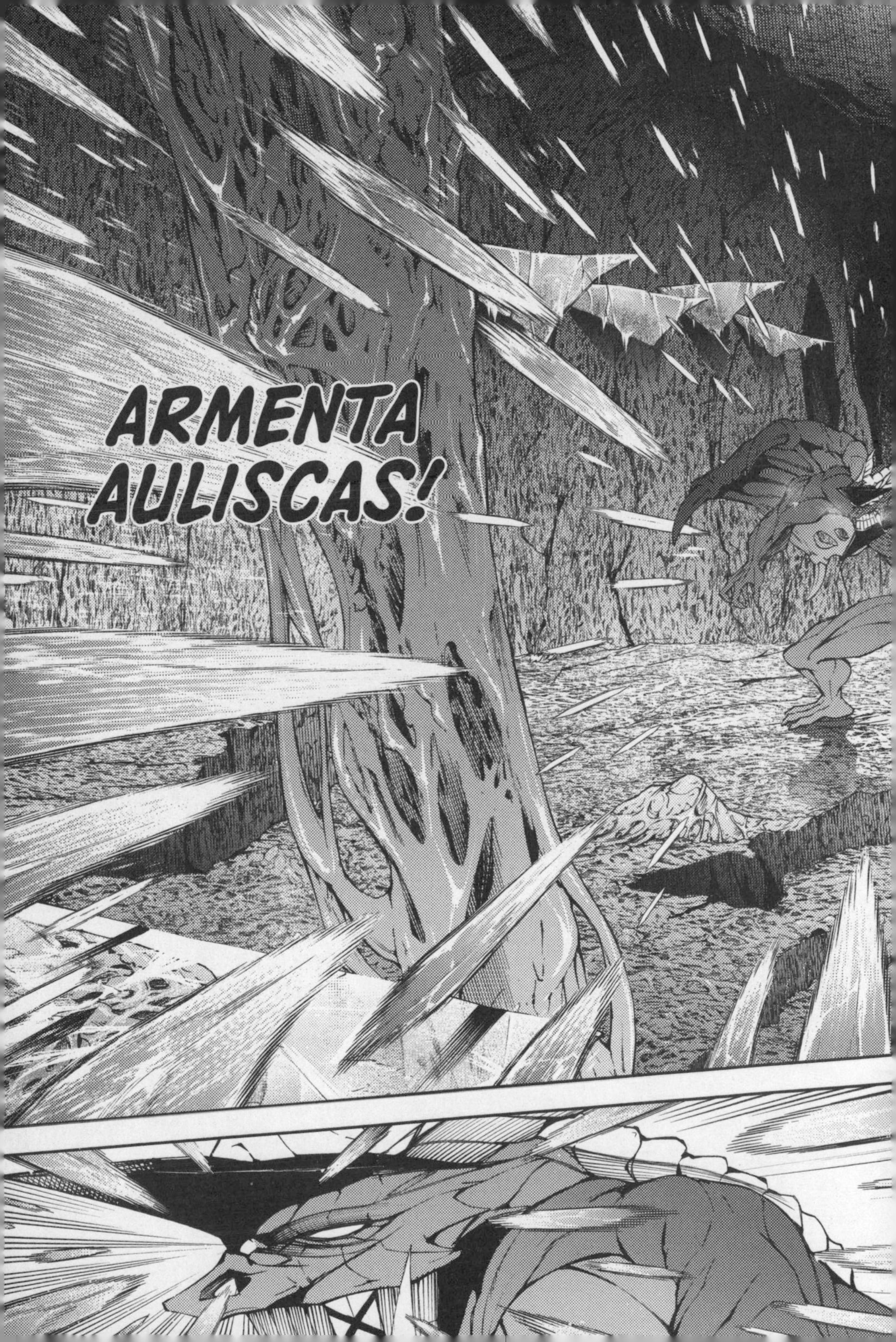
ARMENTA AULISCAS!

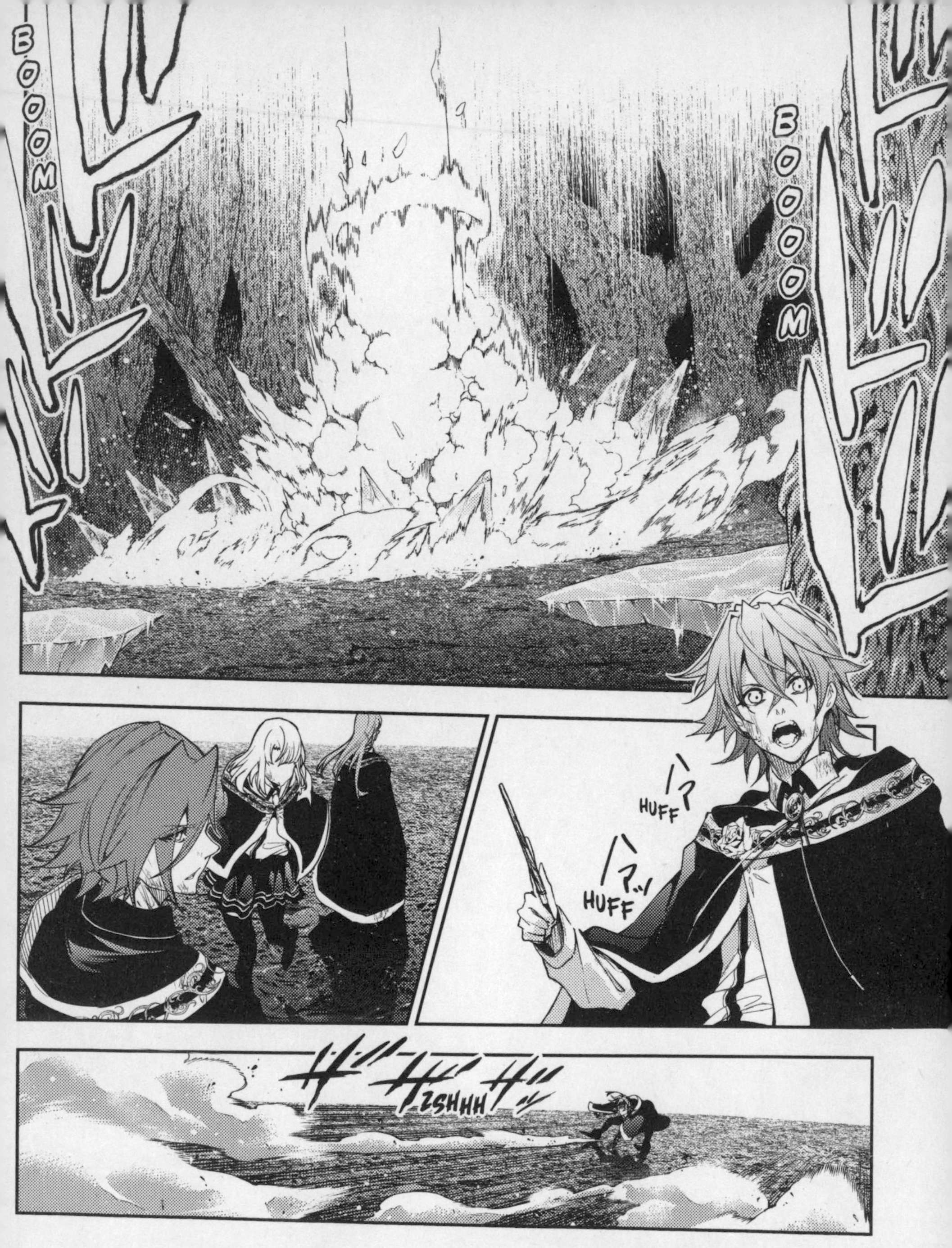
BOOOOOM
BOOOM
HUFF
HUFF
ZSHHH

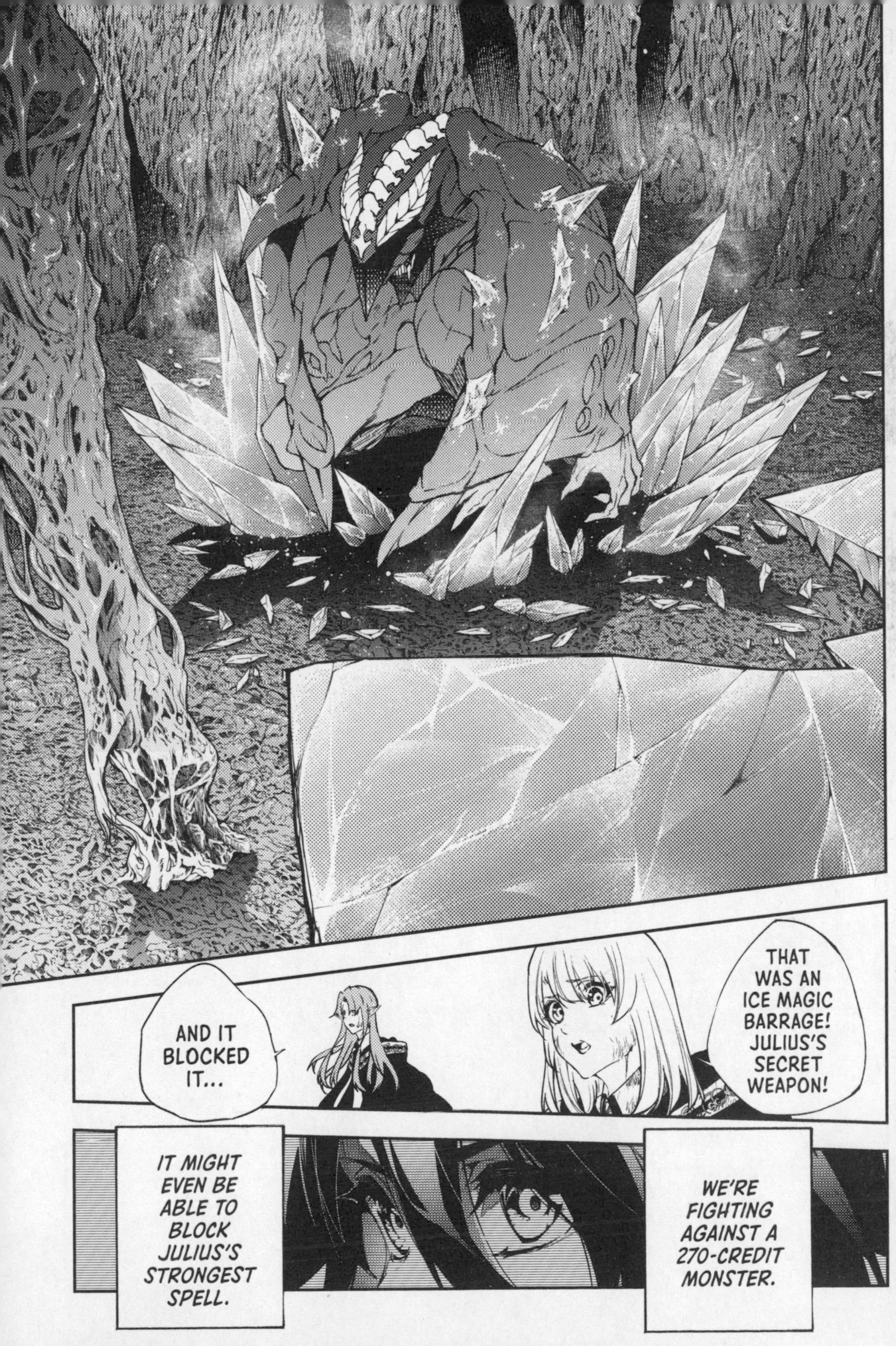
THAT WAS AN ICE MAGIC BARRAGE! JULIUS'S SECRET WEAPON!
AND IT BLOCKED IT...
WE'RE FIGHTING AGAINST A 270-CREDIT MONSTER.
IT MIGHT EVEN BE ABLE TO BLOCK JULIUS'S STRONGEST SPELL.

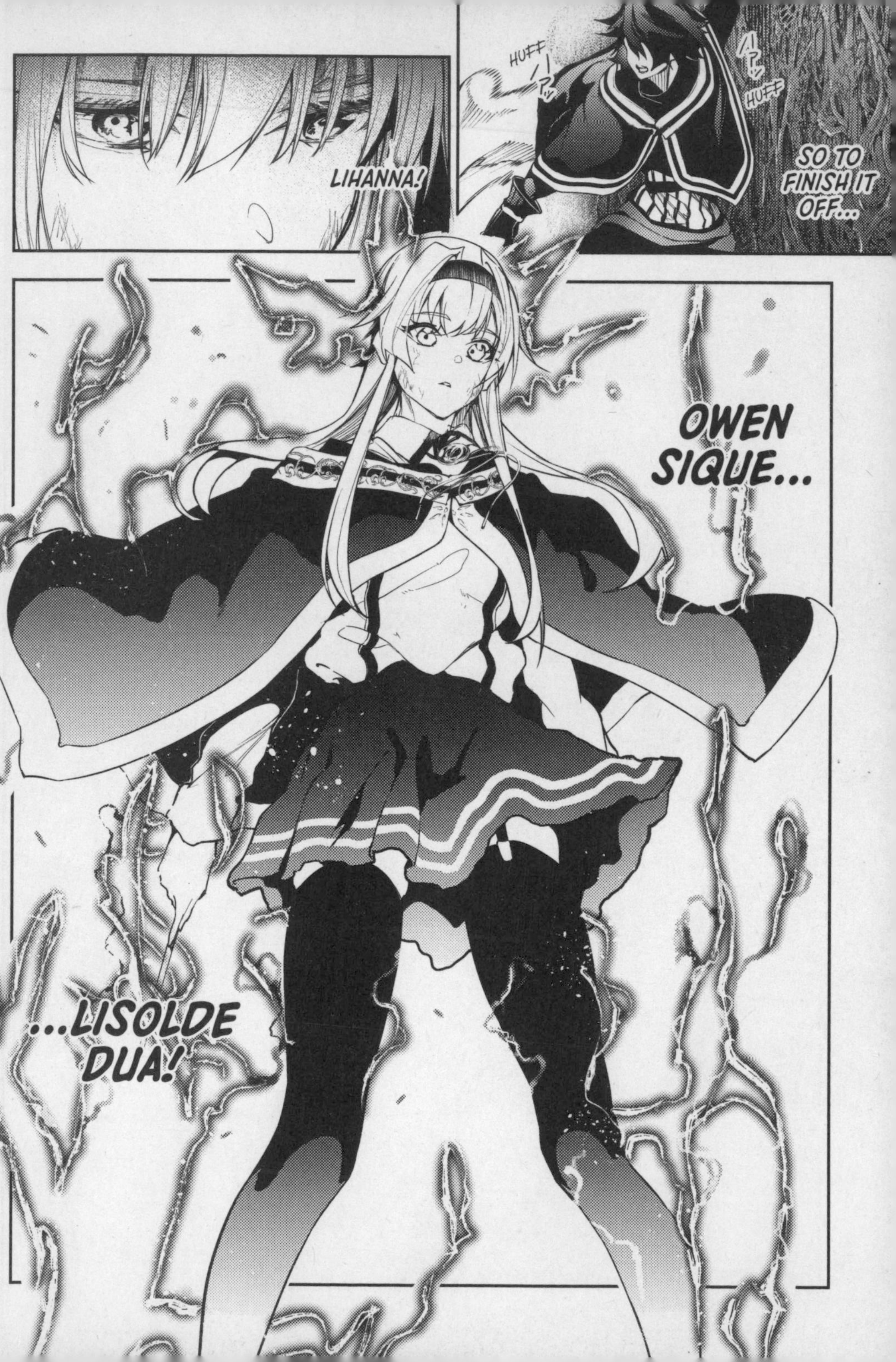
HUFF
HUFF
SO TO FINISH IT OFF...
LIHANNA!
OWEN SIQUE...
...LISOLDE DUA!

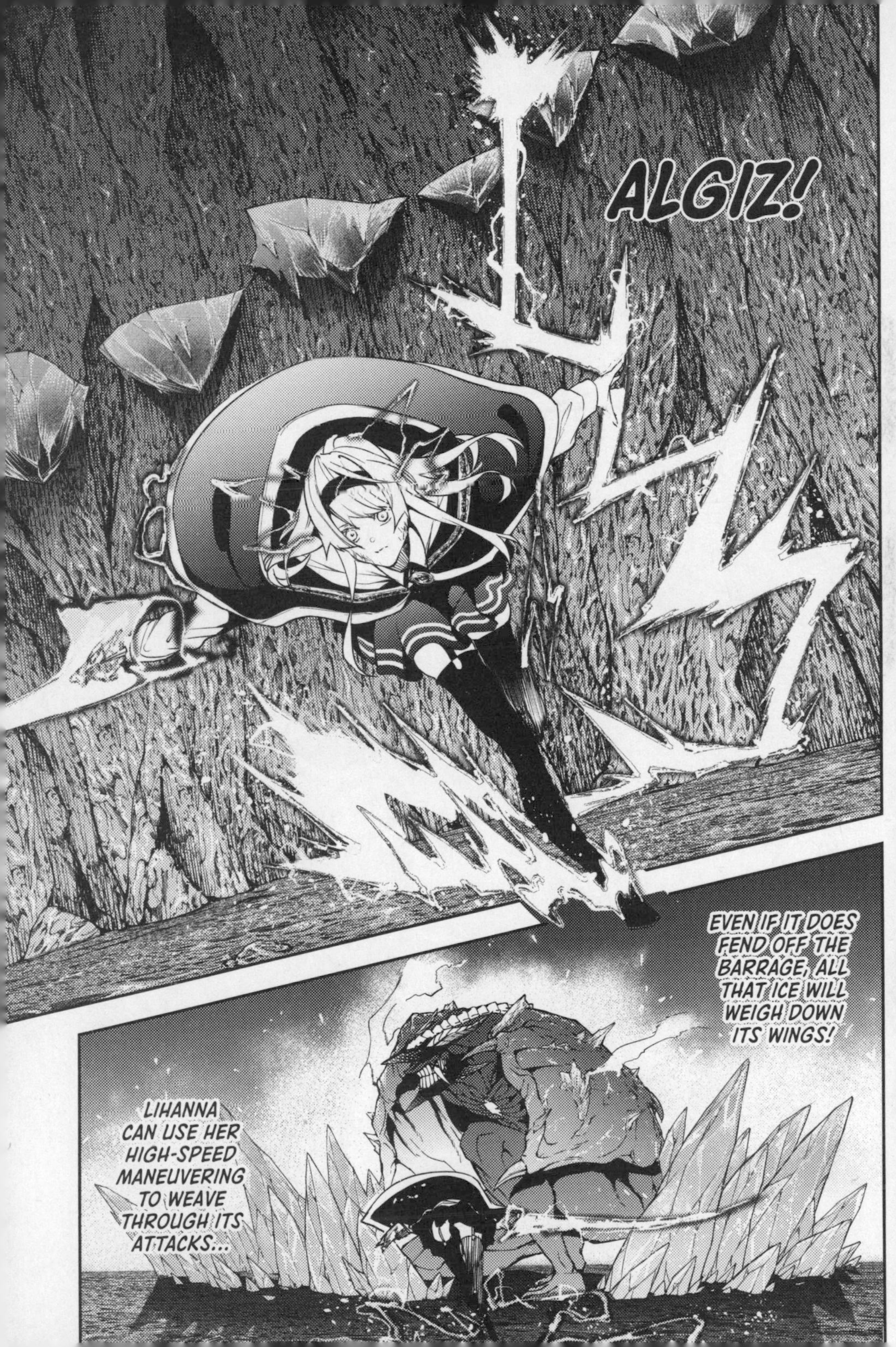
ALGIZ!
EVEN IF IT DOES FEND OFF THE BARRAGE, ALL THAT ICE WILL WEIGH DOWN ITS WINGS!
LIHANNA CAN USE HER HIGH-SPEED MANEUVERING TO WEAVE THROUGH ITS ATTACKS...

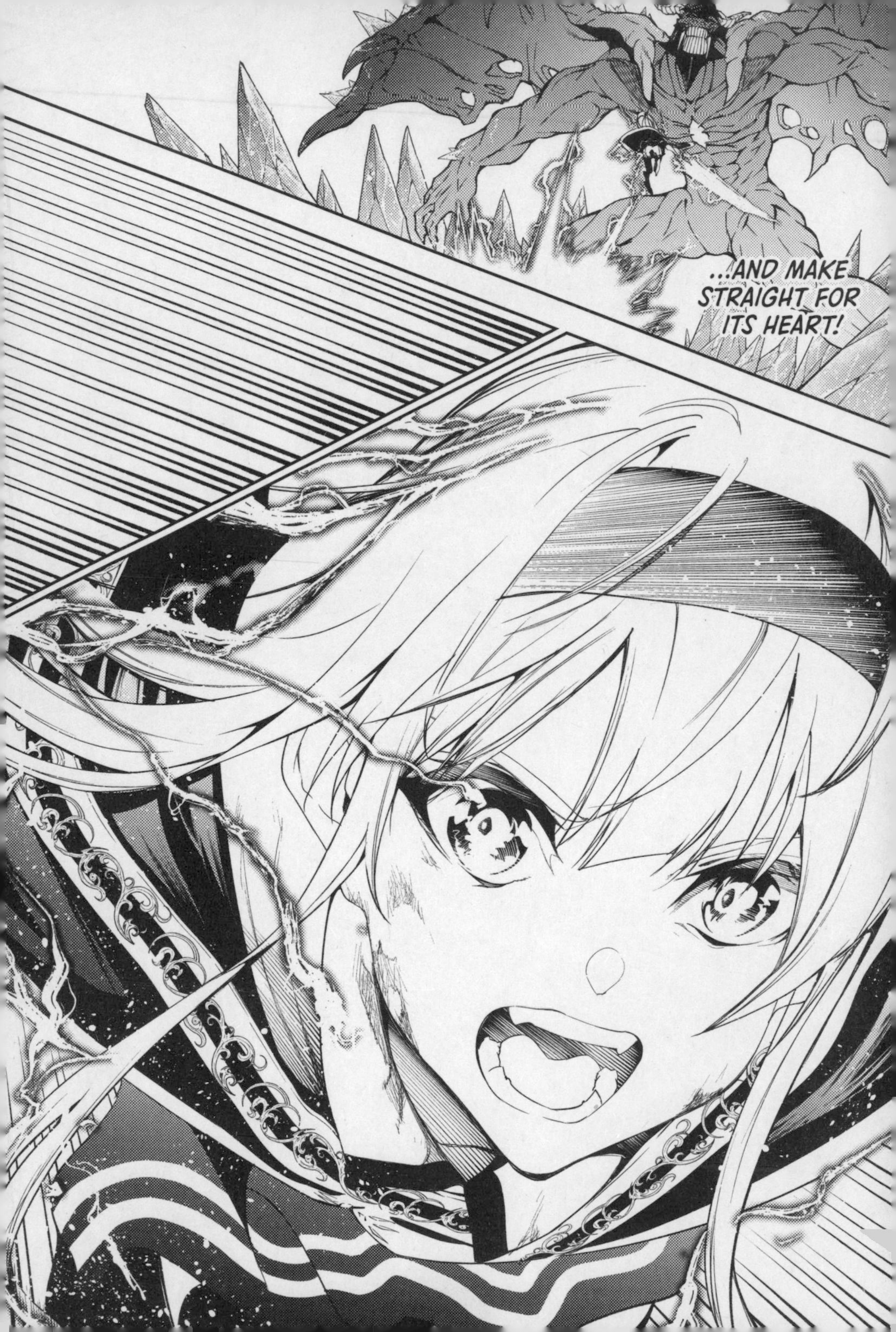
...AND MAKE STRAIGHT FOR ITS HEART!

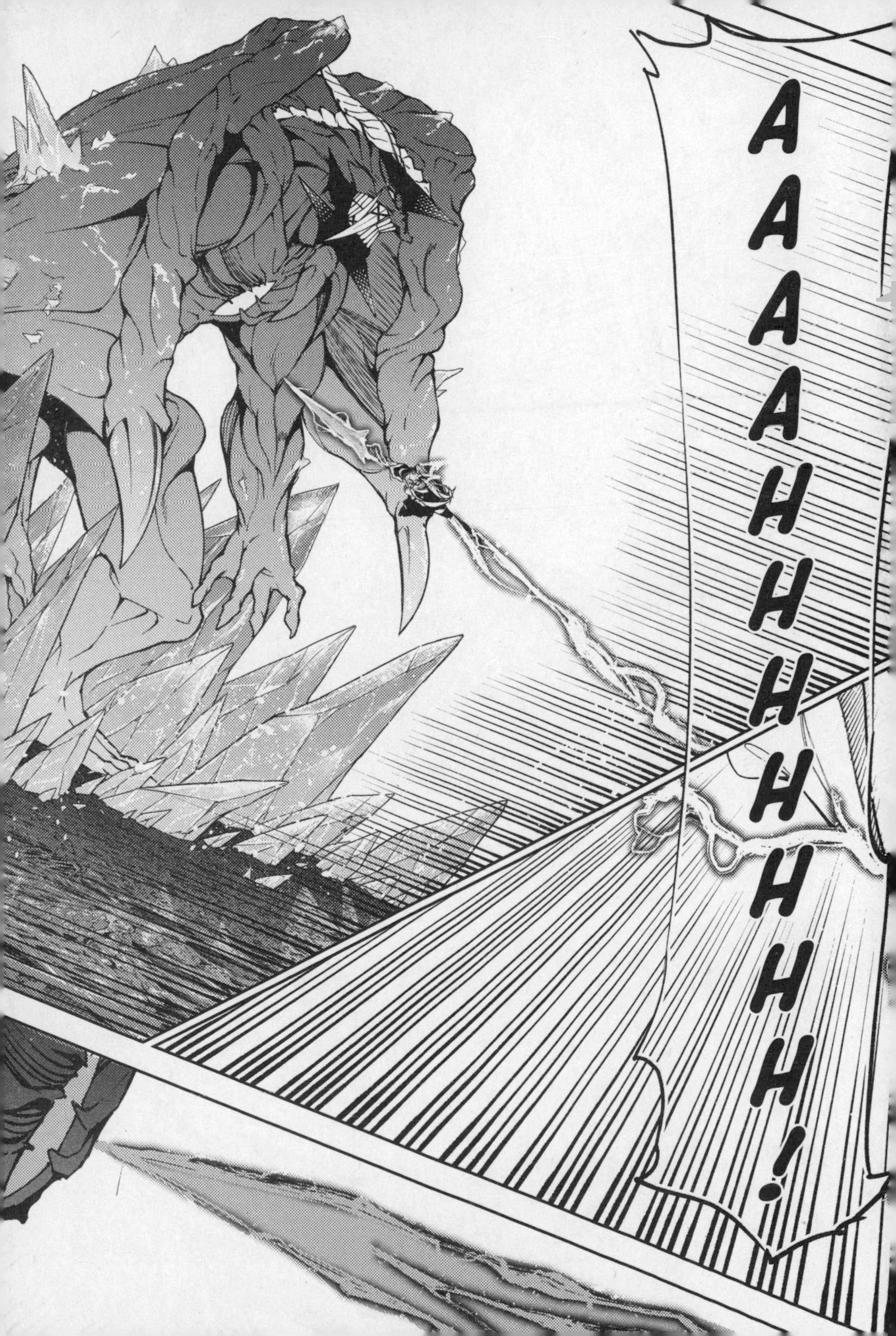
AAAAHHHHHHHH!

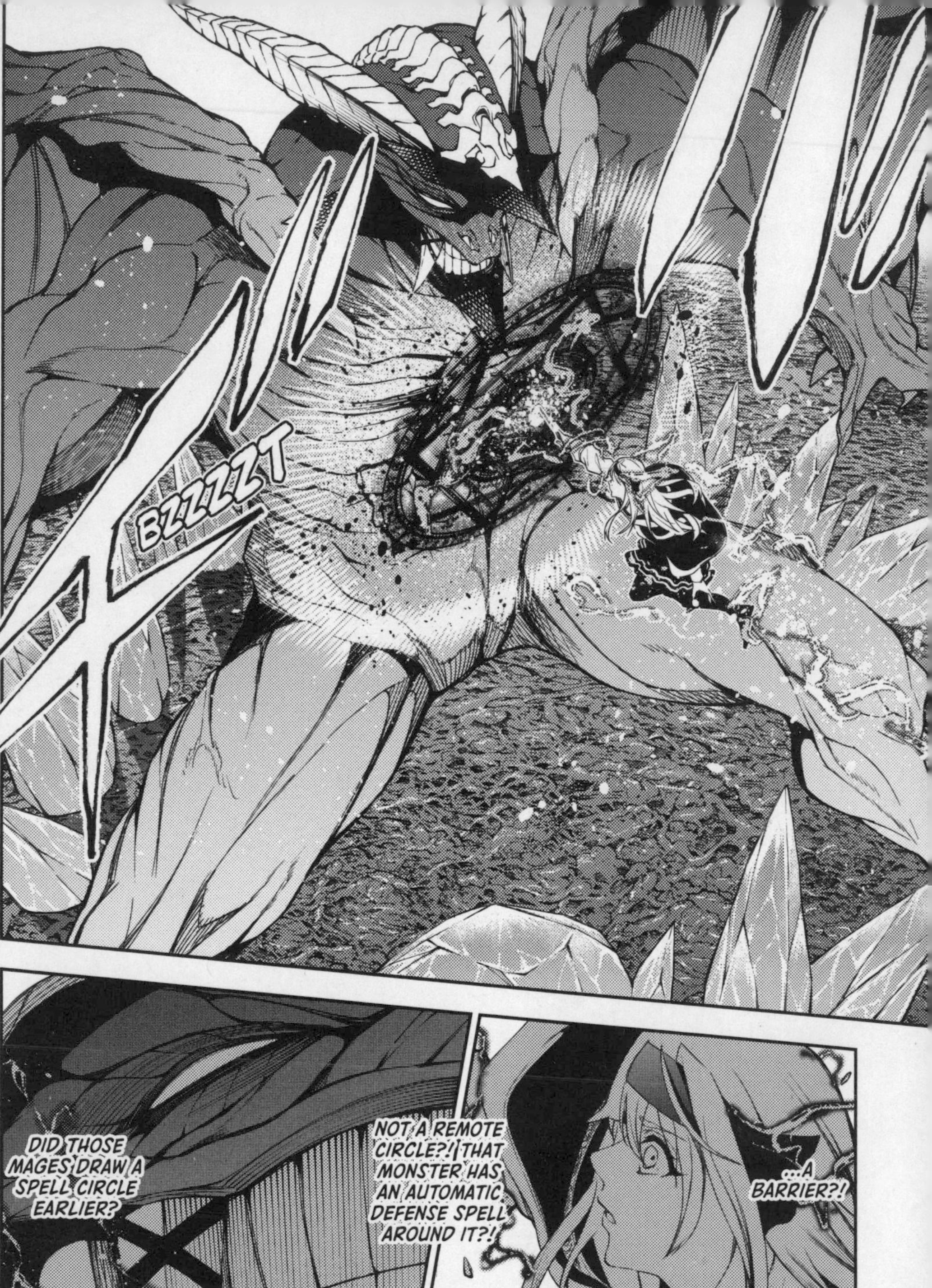
BZZZZZT
...A BARRIER?!
NOT A REMOTE CIRCLE?! THAT MONSTER HAS AN AUTOMATIC DEFENSE SPELL AROUND IT?!
DID THOSE MAGES DRAW A SPELL CIRCLE EARLIER?

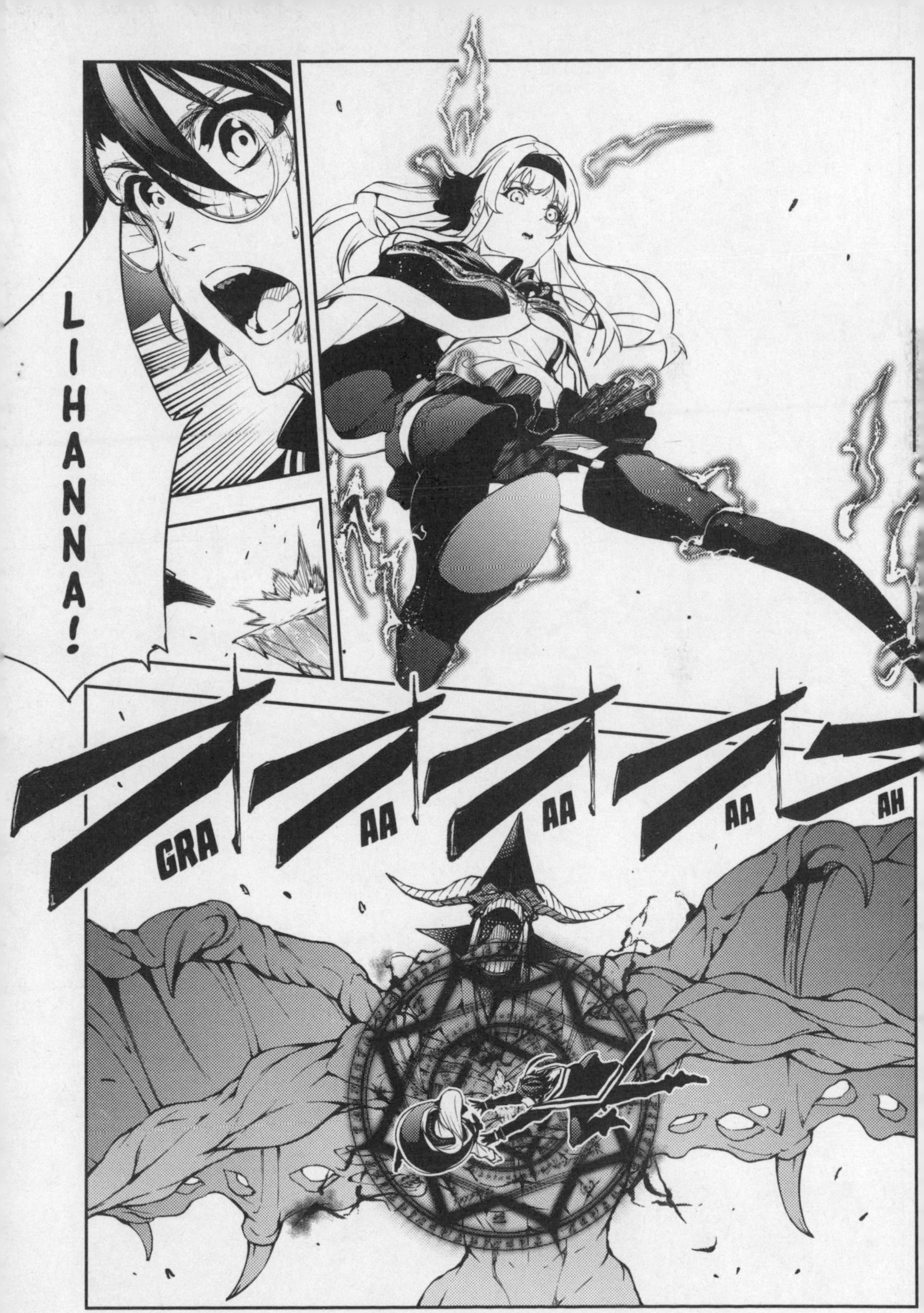
LIHANNA!
GRA AA AA AA AH

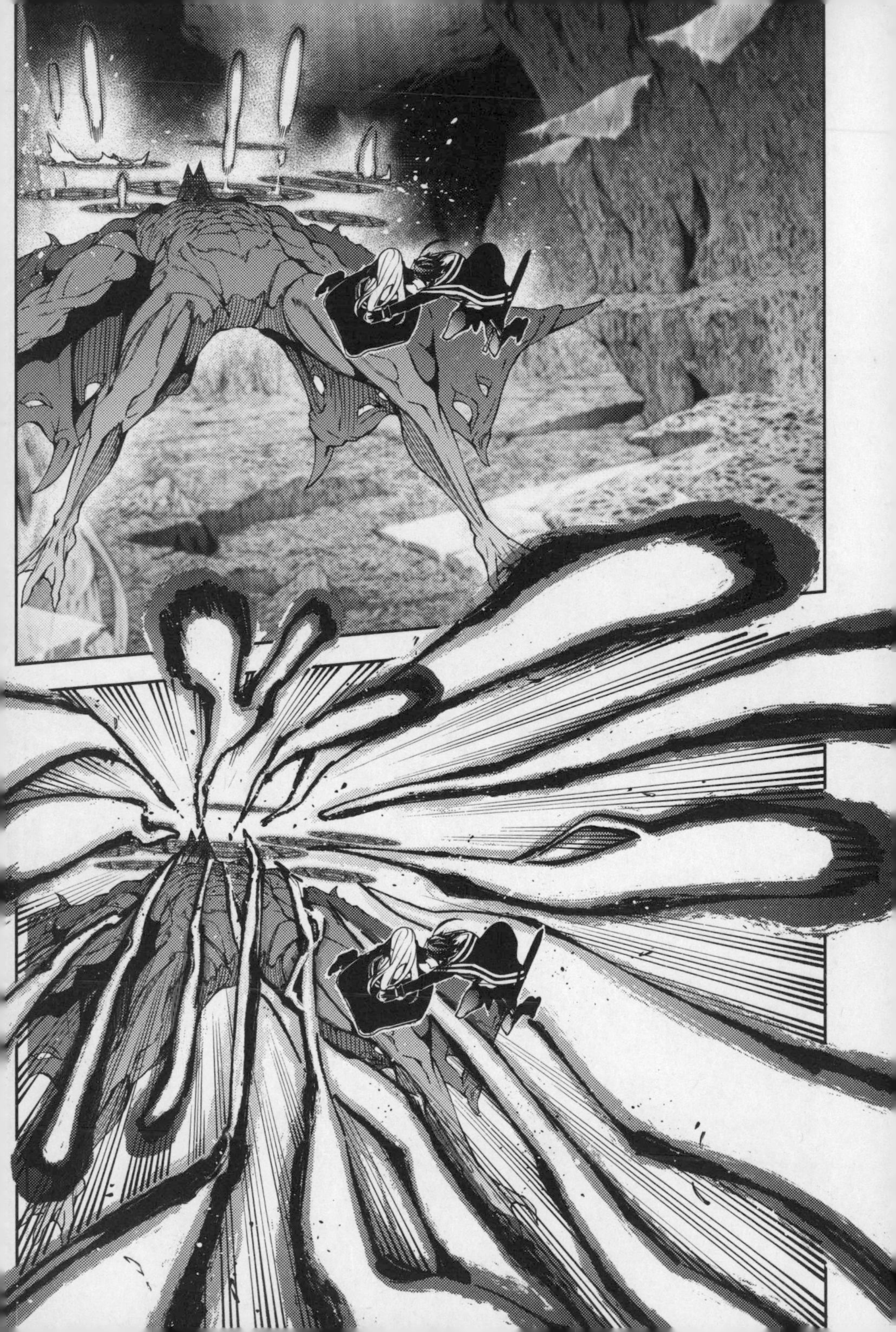

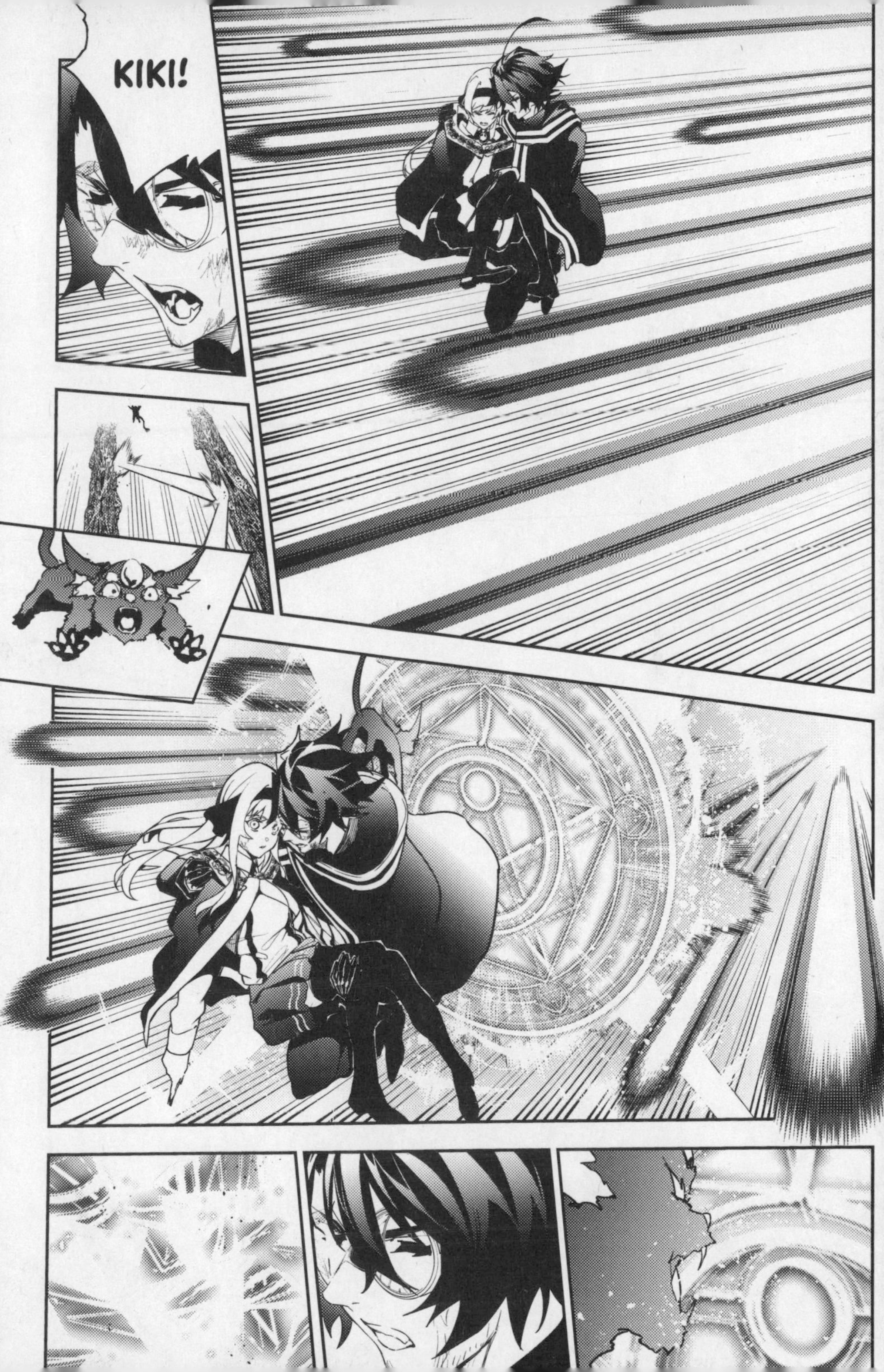
KIKI!

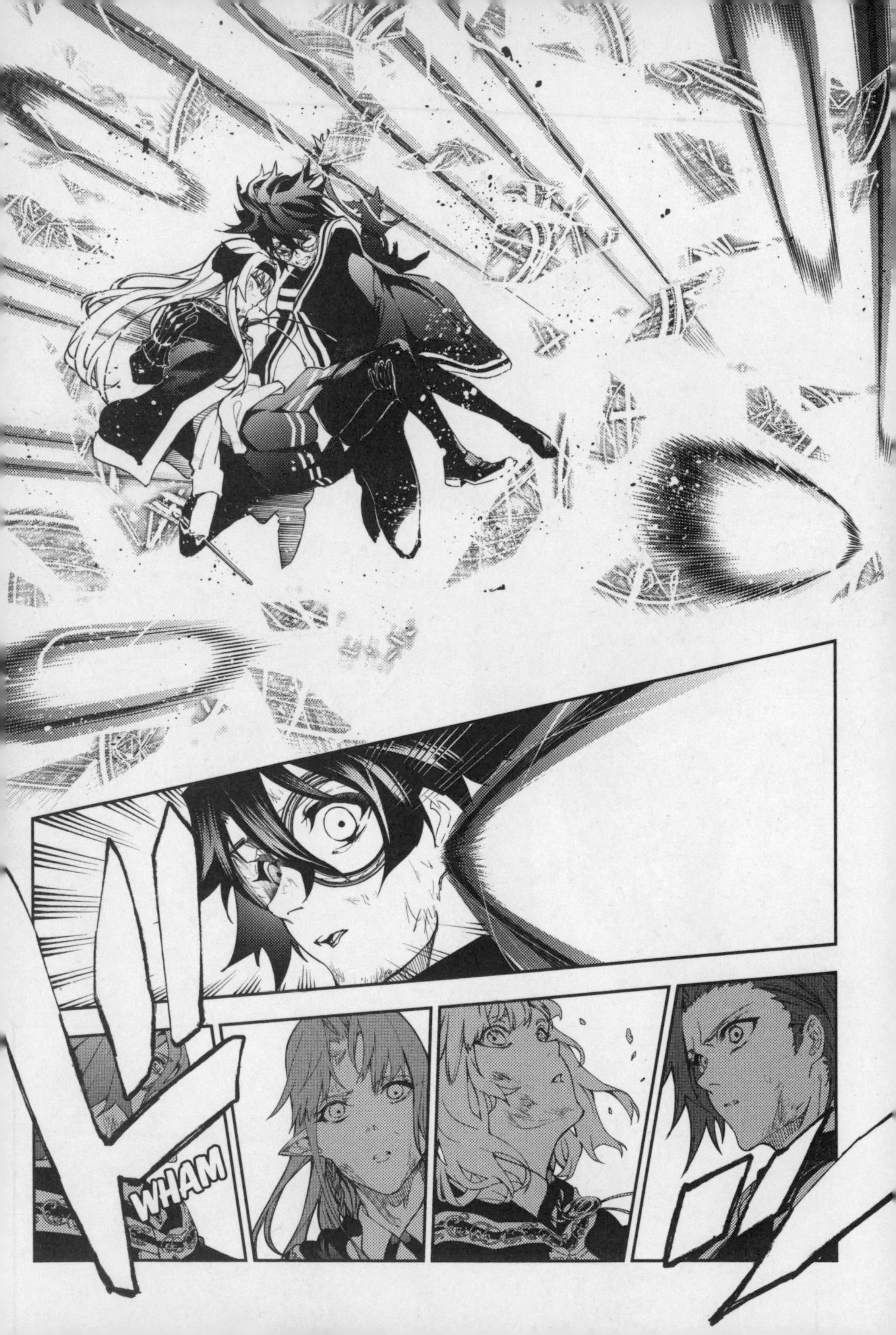
WHAM

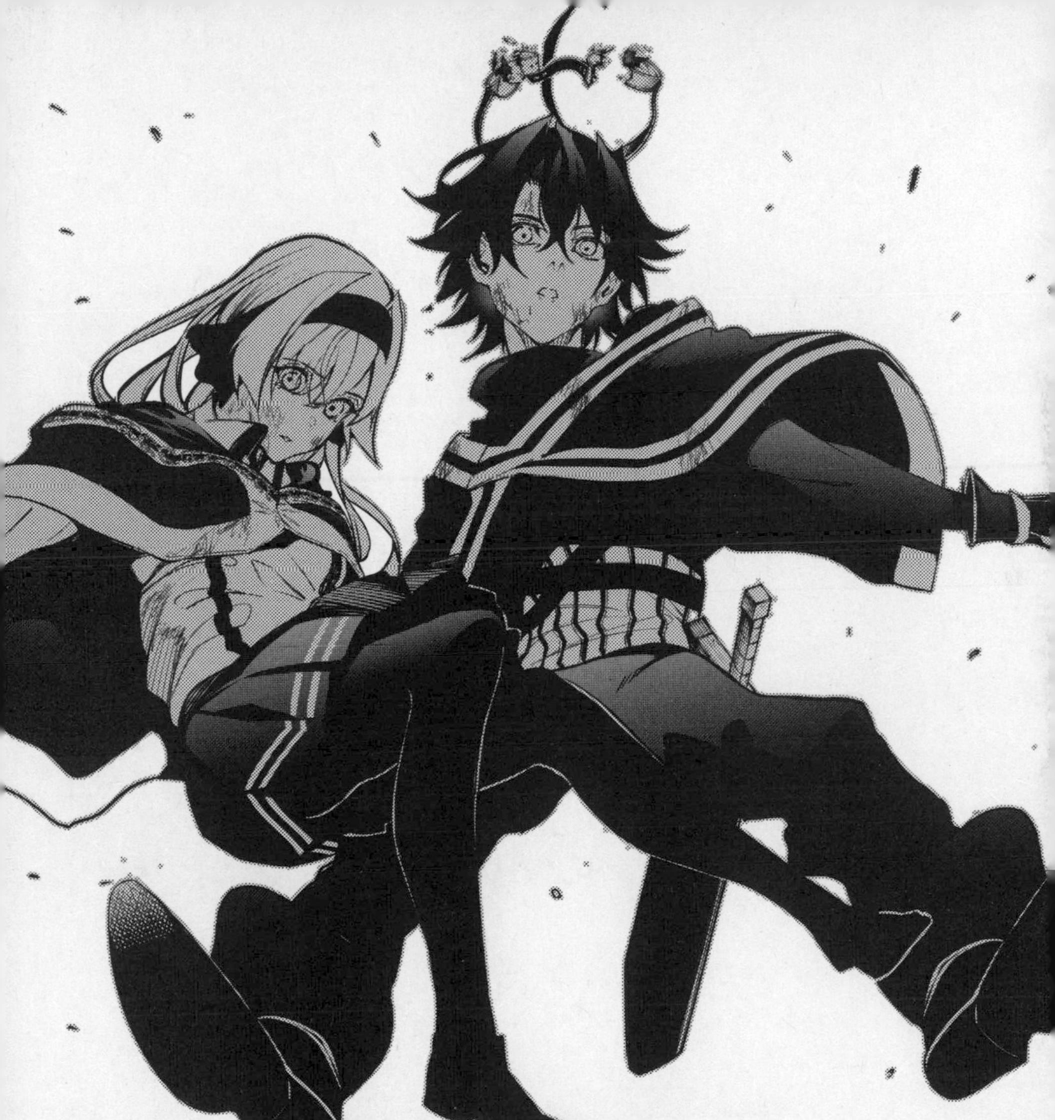
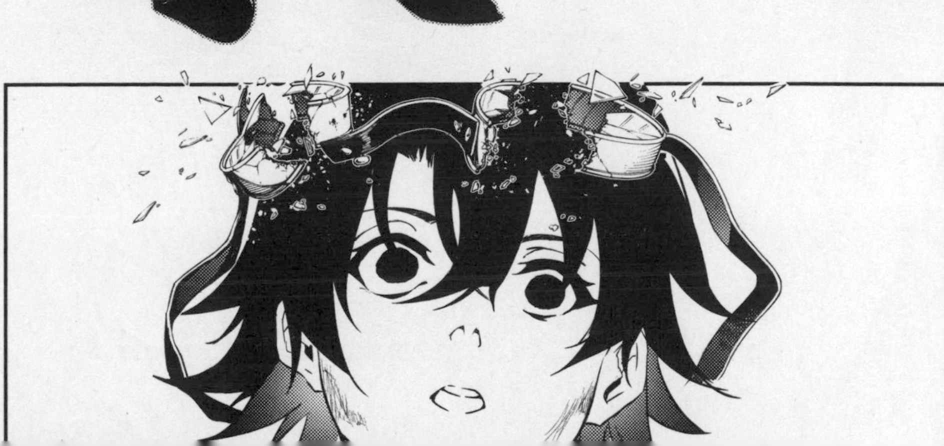

Wistoria
Wand and Sword

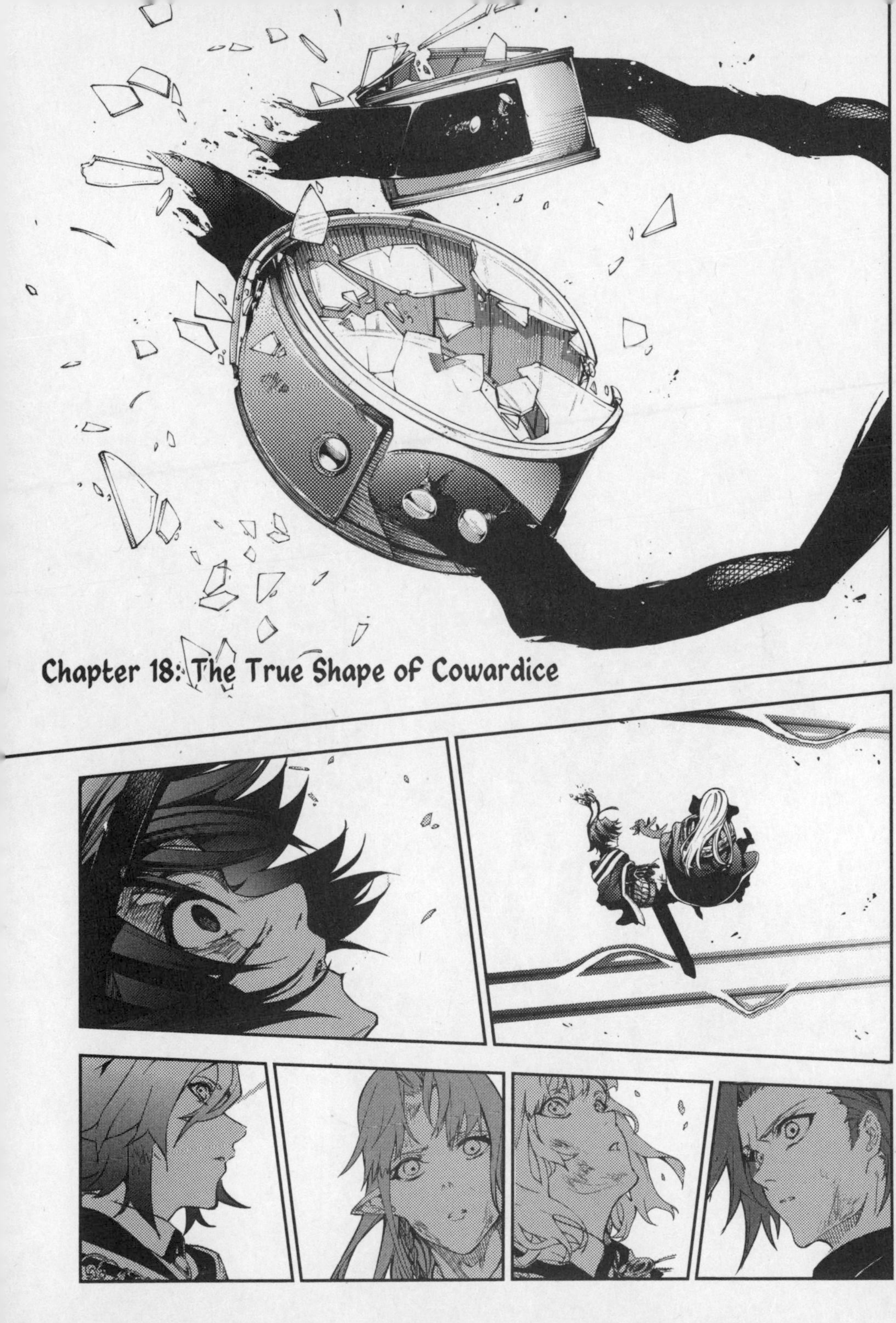
Chapter 18: The True Shape of Cowardice

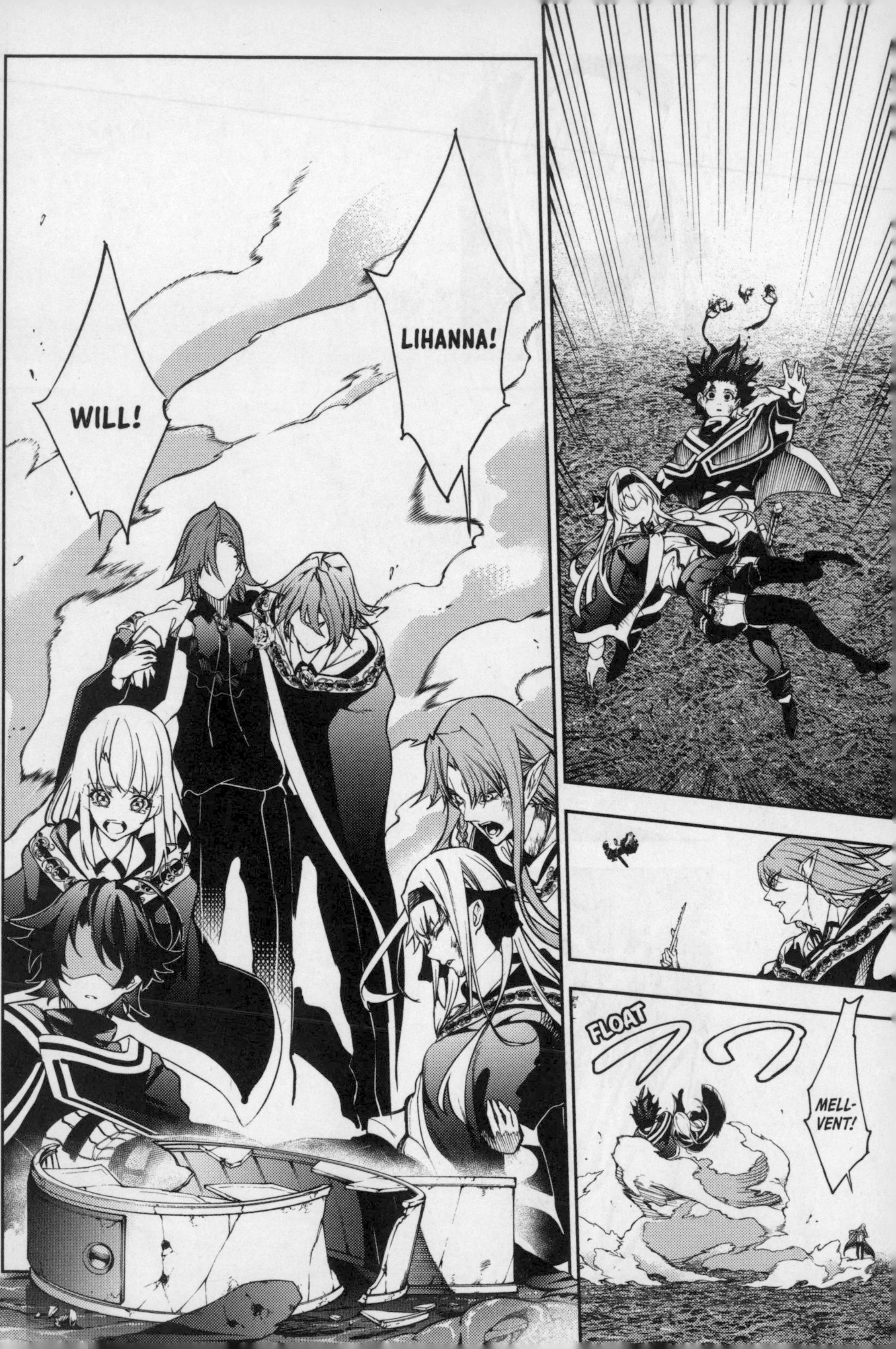
MELL-VENT!
FLOAT
LIHANNA!
WILL!

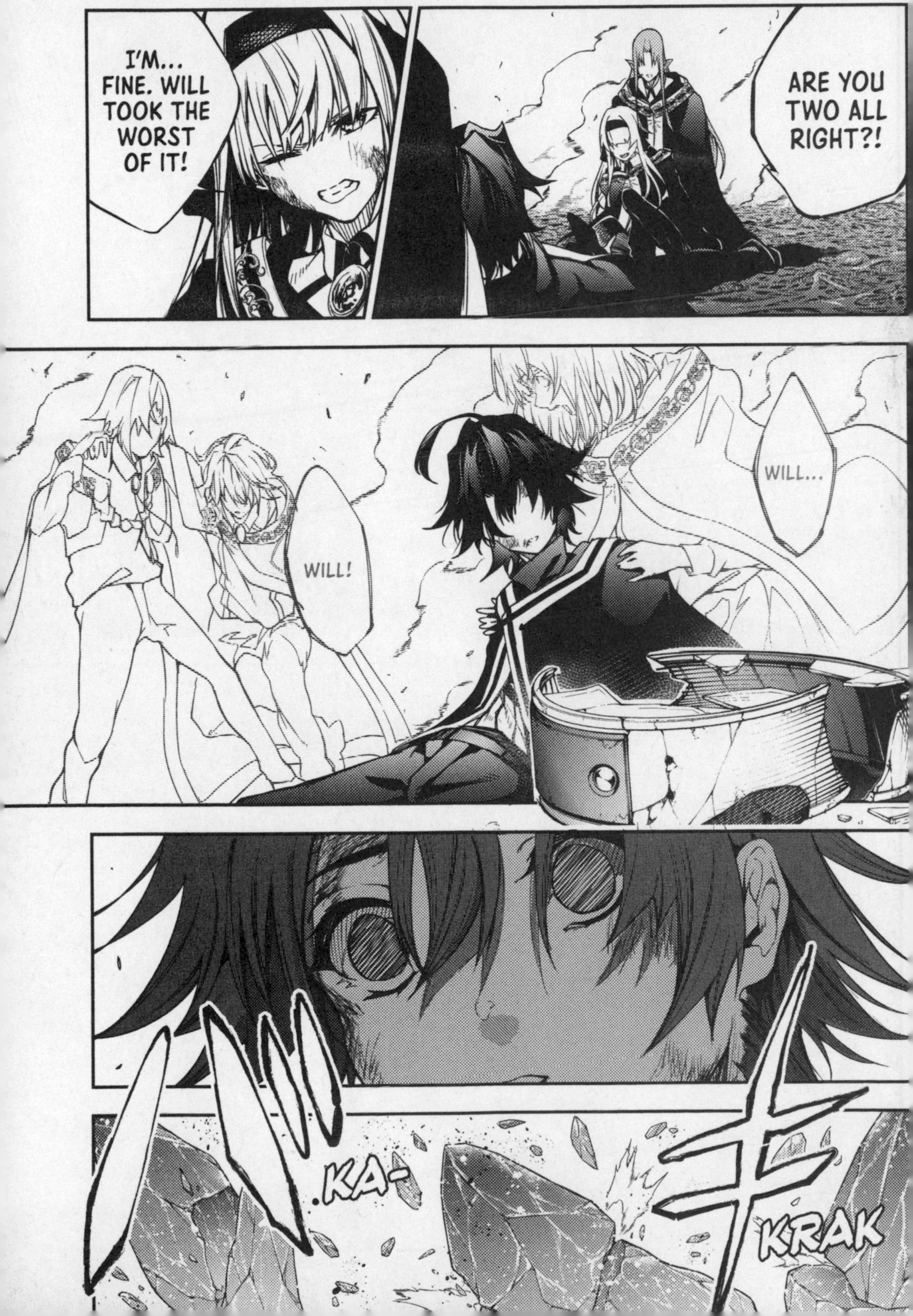
ARE YOU TWO ALL RIGHT?!
I'M... FINE. WILL TOOK THE WORST OF IT!
WILL...
WILL!
KA-
KRAK

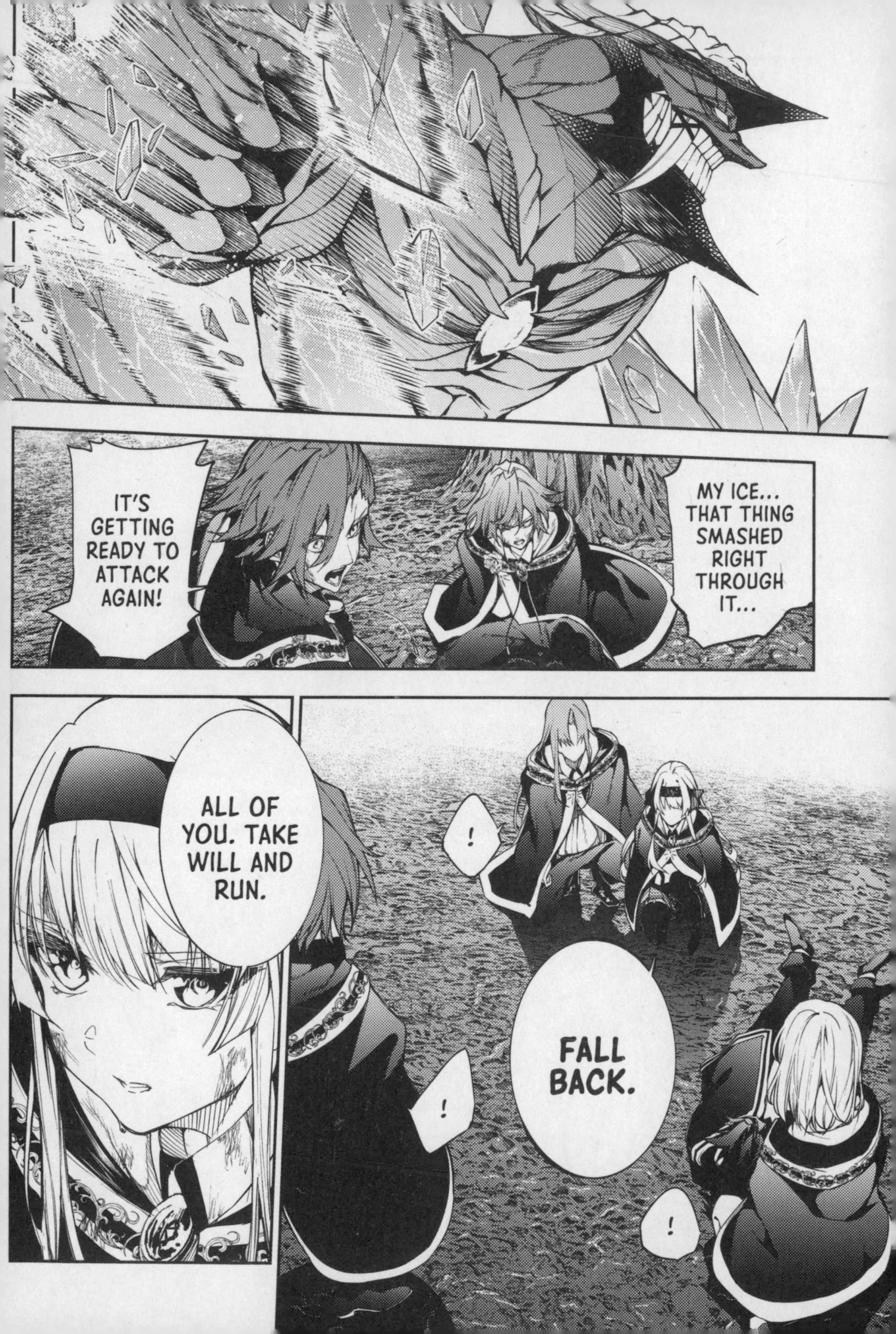
MY ICE... THAT THING SMASHED RIGHT THROUGH IT...
IT'S GETTING READY TO ATTACK AGAIN!
!
FALL BACK.
!
!
ALL OF YOU. TAKE WILL AND RUN.

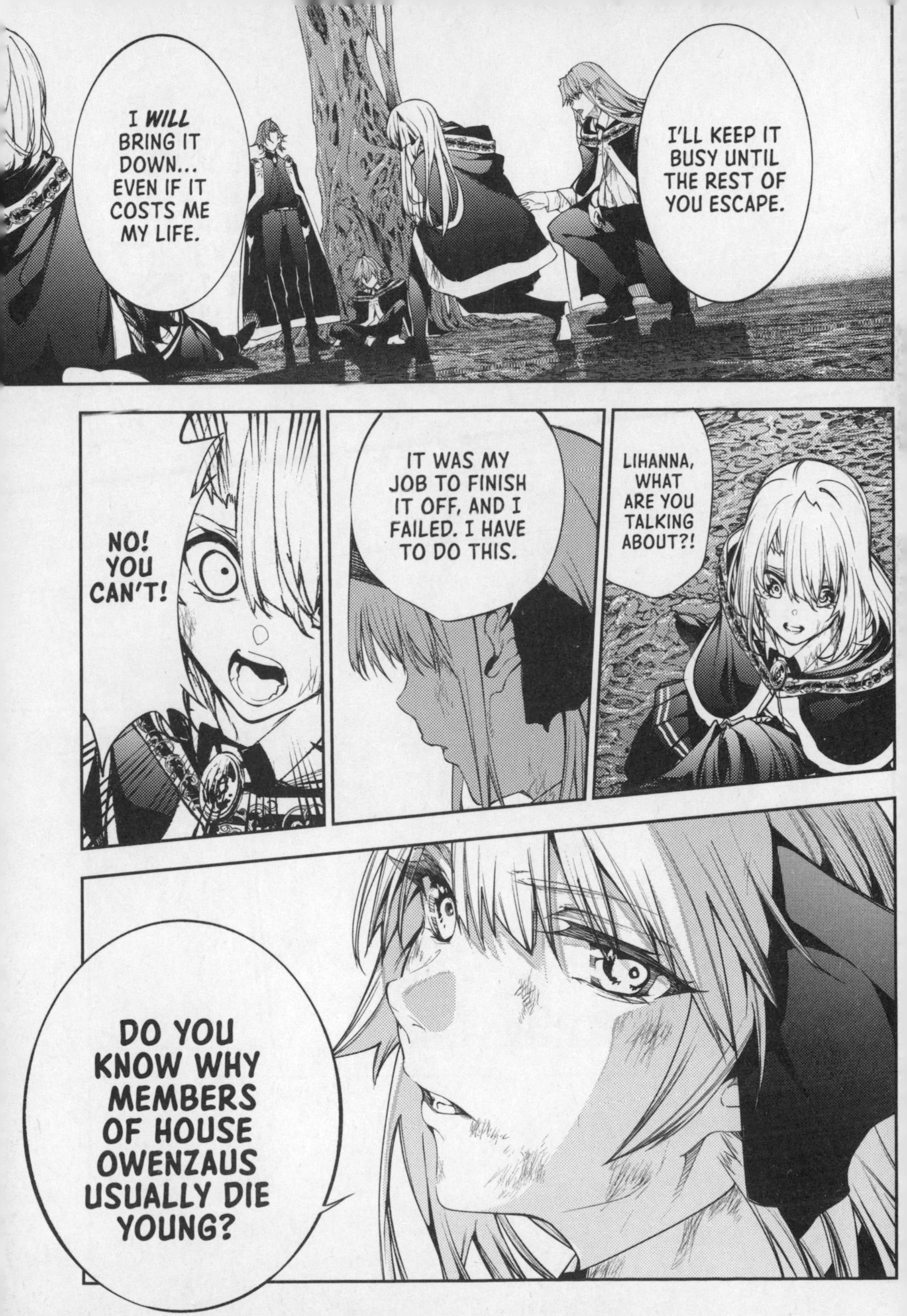
I'LL KEEP IT BUSY UNTIL THE REST OF YOU ESCAPE.
I *WILL* BRING IT DOWN... EVEN IF IT COSTS ME MY LIFE.
LIHANNA, WHAT ARE YOU TALKING ABOUT?!
IT WAS MY JOB TO FINISH IT OFF, AND I FAILED. I HAVE TO DO THIS.
NO! YOU CAN'T!
DO YOU KNOW WHY MEMBERS OF HOUSE OWENZAUS USUALLY DIE YOUNG?

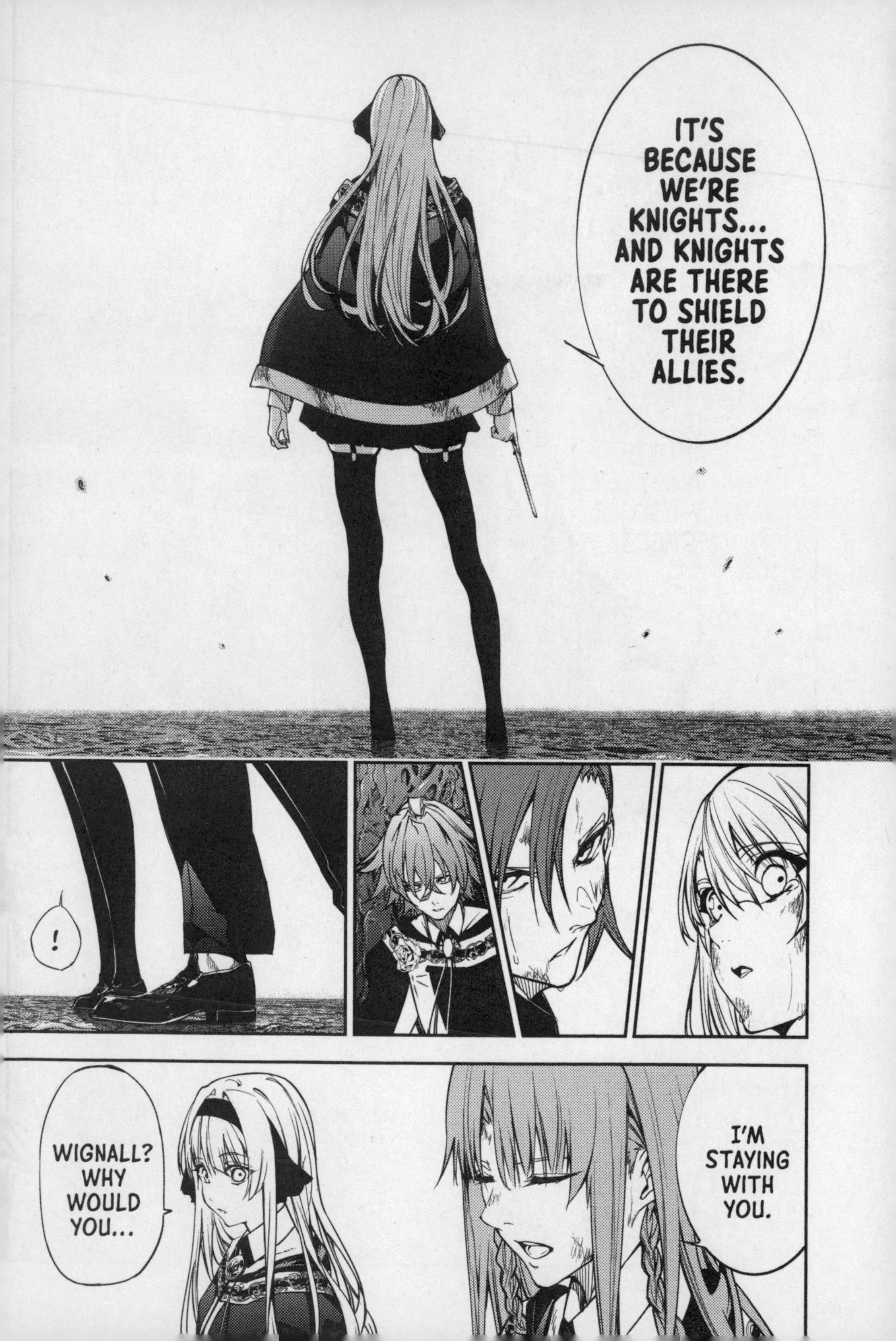
IT'S BECAUSE WE'RE KNIGHTS... AND KNIGHTS ARE THERE TO SHIELD THEIR ALLIES.
!
I'M STAYING WITH YOU.
WIGNALL? WHY WOULD YOU...

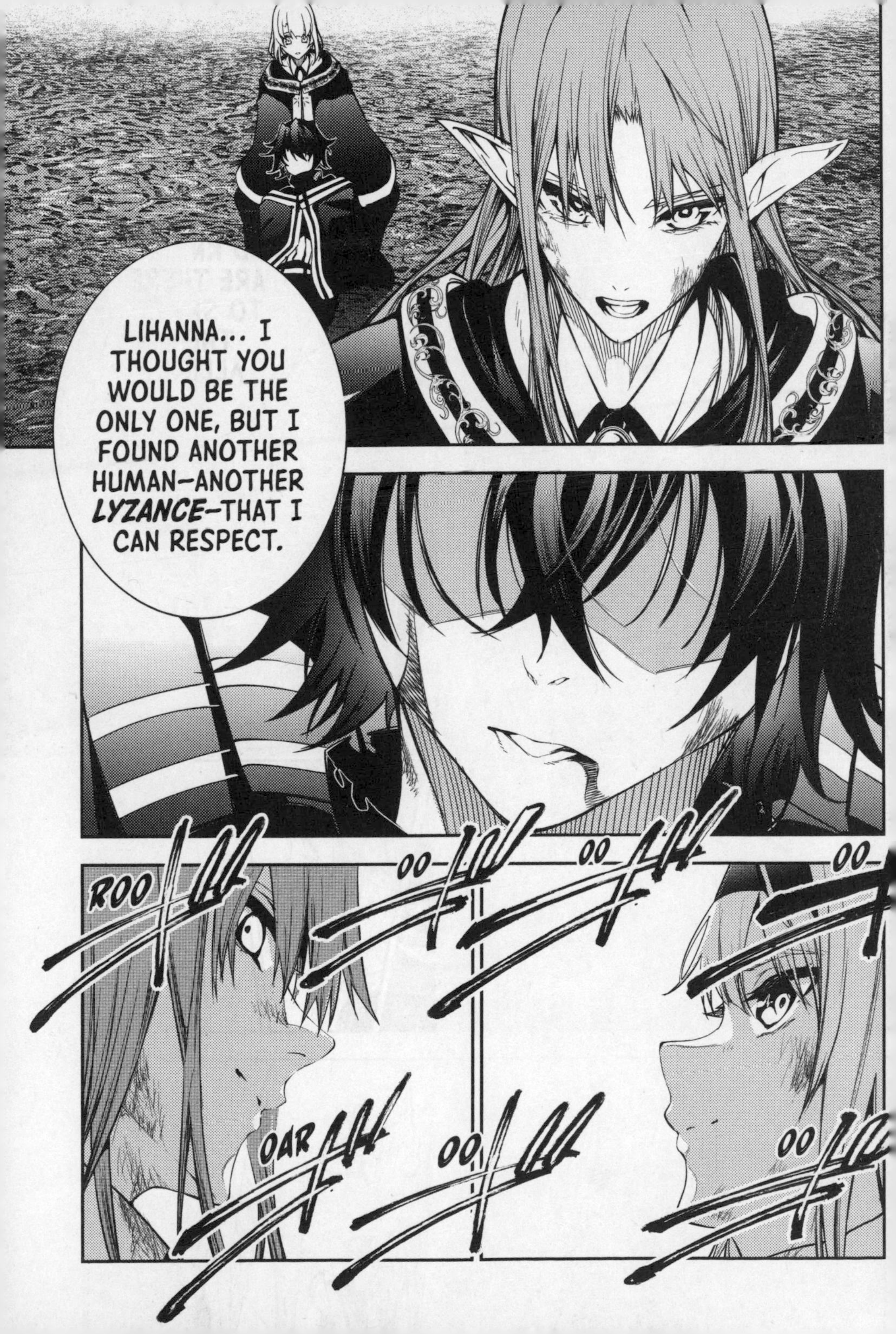
LIHANNA... I THOUGHT YOU WOULD BE THE ONLY ONE, BUT I FOUND ANOTHER HUMAN—ANOTHER *LYZANCE*—THAT I CAN RESPECT.
ROO
OO
OO
OO
OAR
OO
OO

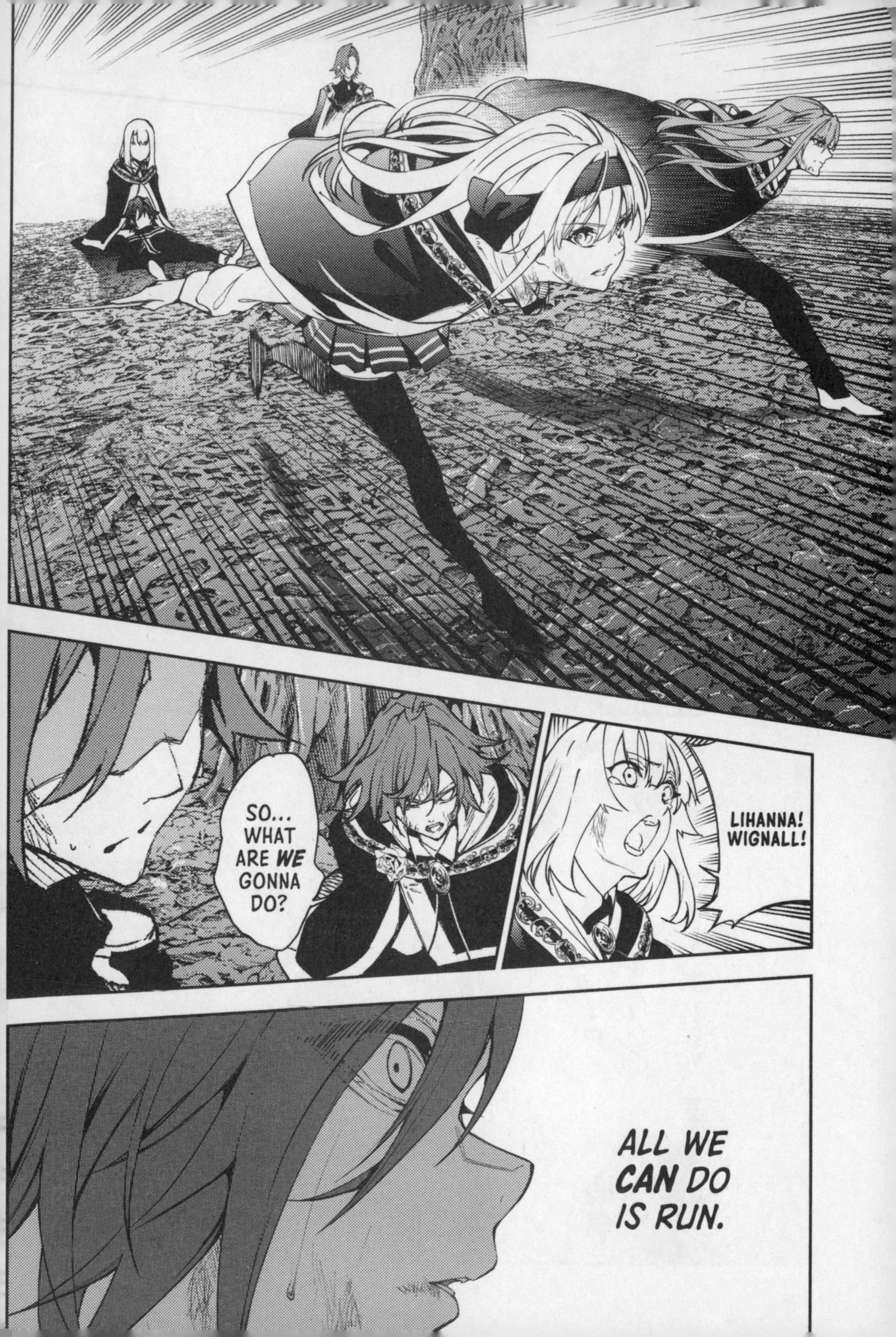
LIHANNA! WIGNALL!
SO... WHAT ARE WE GONNA DO?
ALL WE CAN DO IS RUN.

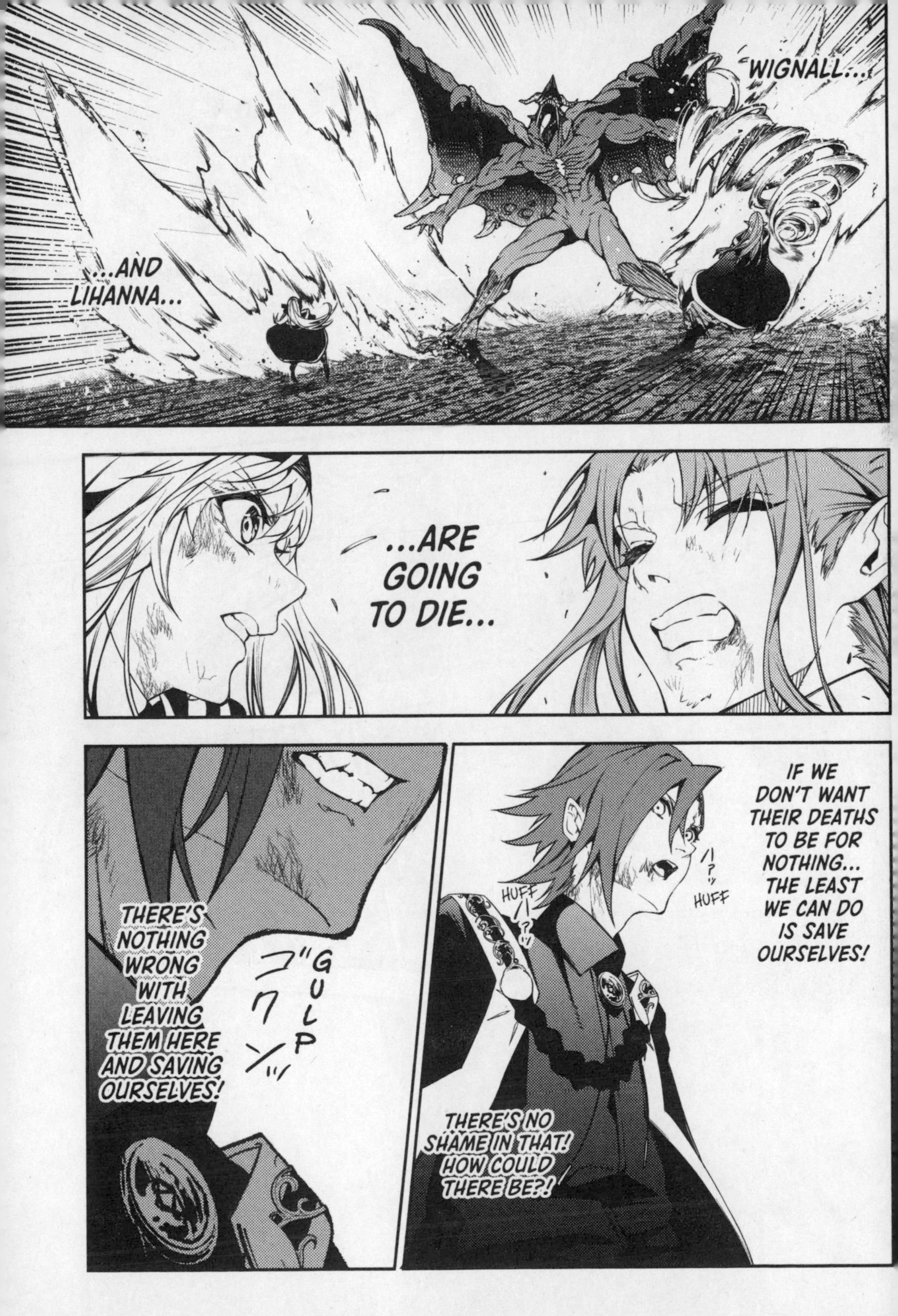
WIGNALL...
...AND LIHANNA...
...ARE GOING TO DIE...
IF WE DON'T WANT THEIR DEATHS TO BE FOR NOTHING... THE LEAST WE CAN DO IS SAVE OURSELVES!
HUFF
HUFF
THERE'S NO SHAME IN THAT! HOW COULD THERE BE?!
THERE'S NOTHING WRONG WITH LEAVING THEM HERE AND SAVING OURSELVES!
GULP

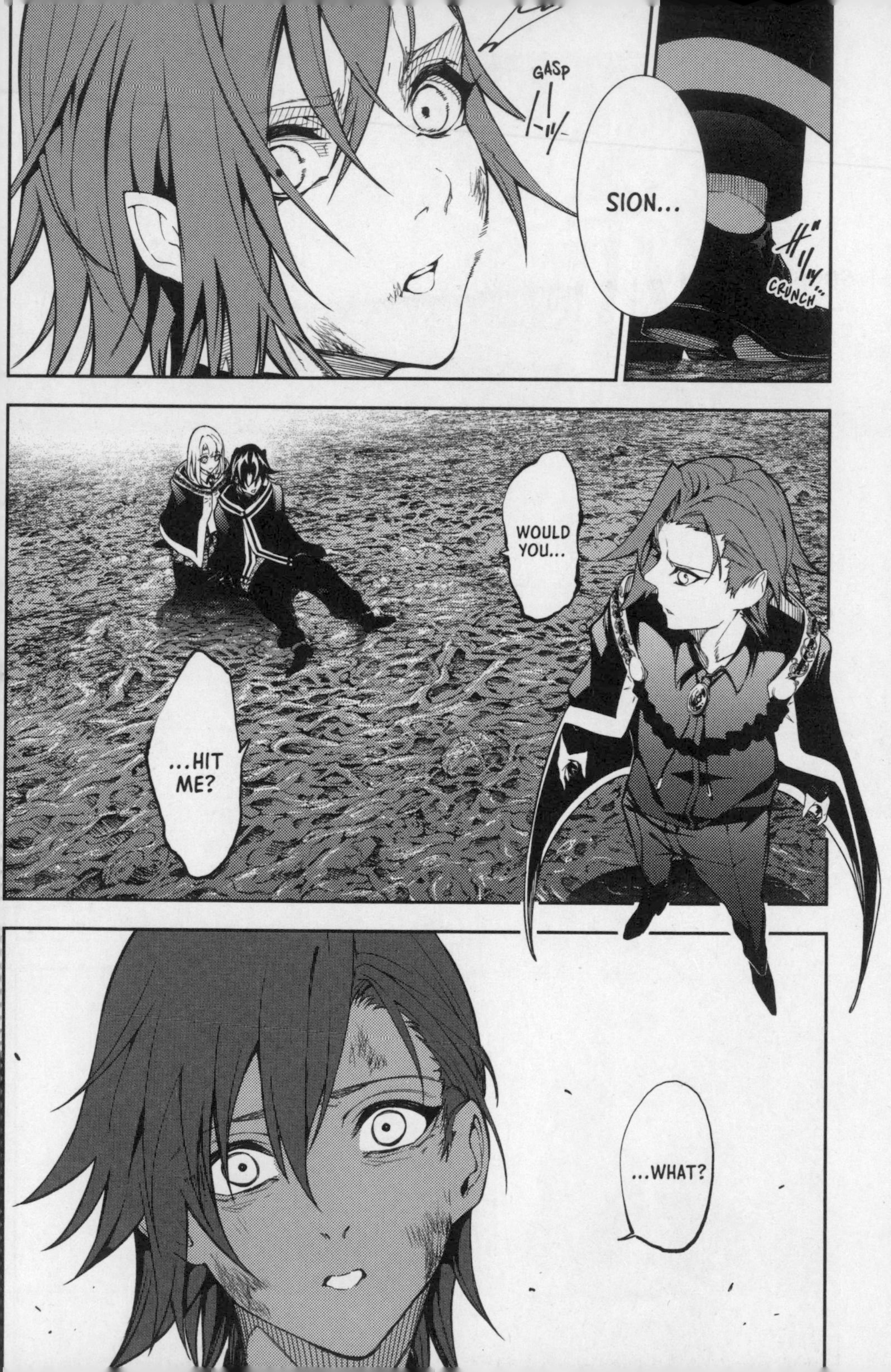

CRUNCH
GASP
SION...
WOULD YOU...
...HIT ME?
...WHAT?

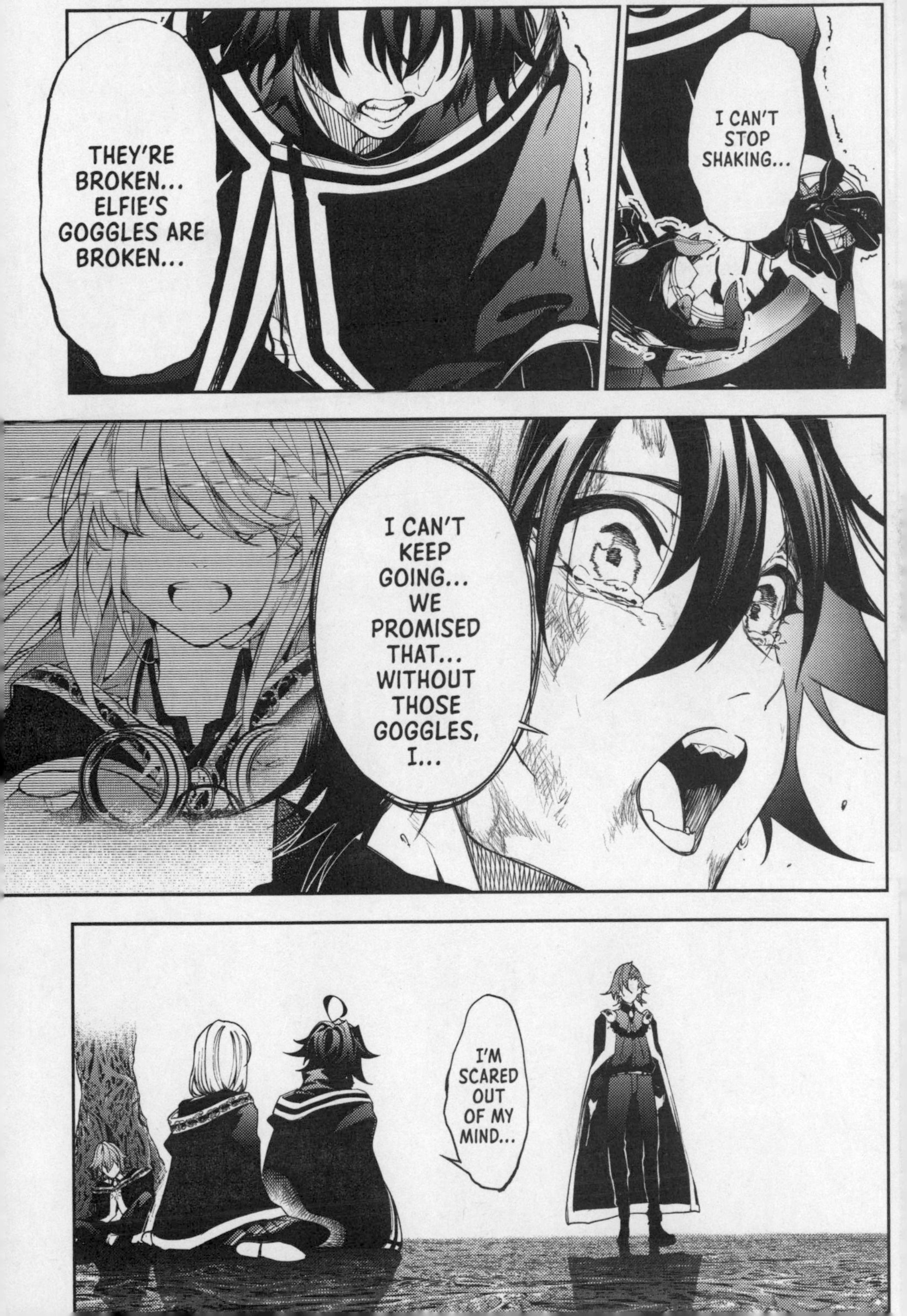
I CAN'T STOP SHAKING...
THEY'RE BROKEN... ELFIE'S GOGGLES ARE BROKEN...
I CAN'T KEEP GOING... WE PROMISED THAT... WITHOUT THOSE GOGGLES, I...
I'M SCARED OUT OF MY MIND...

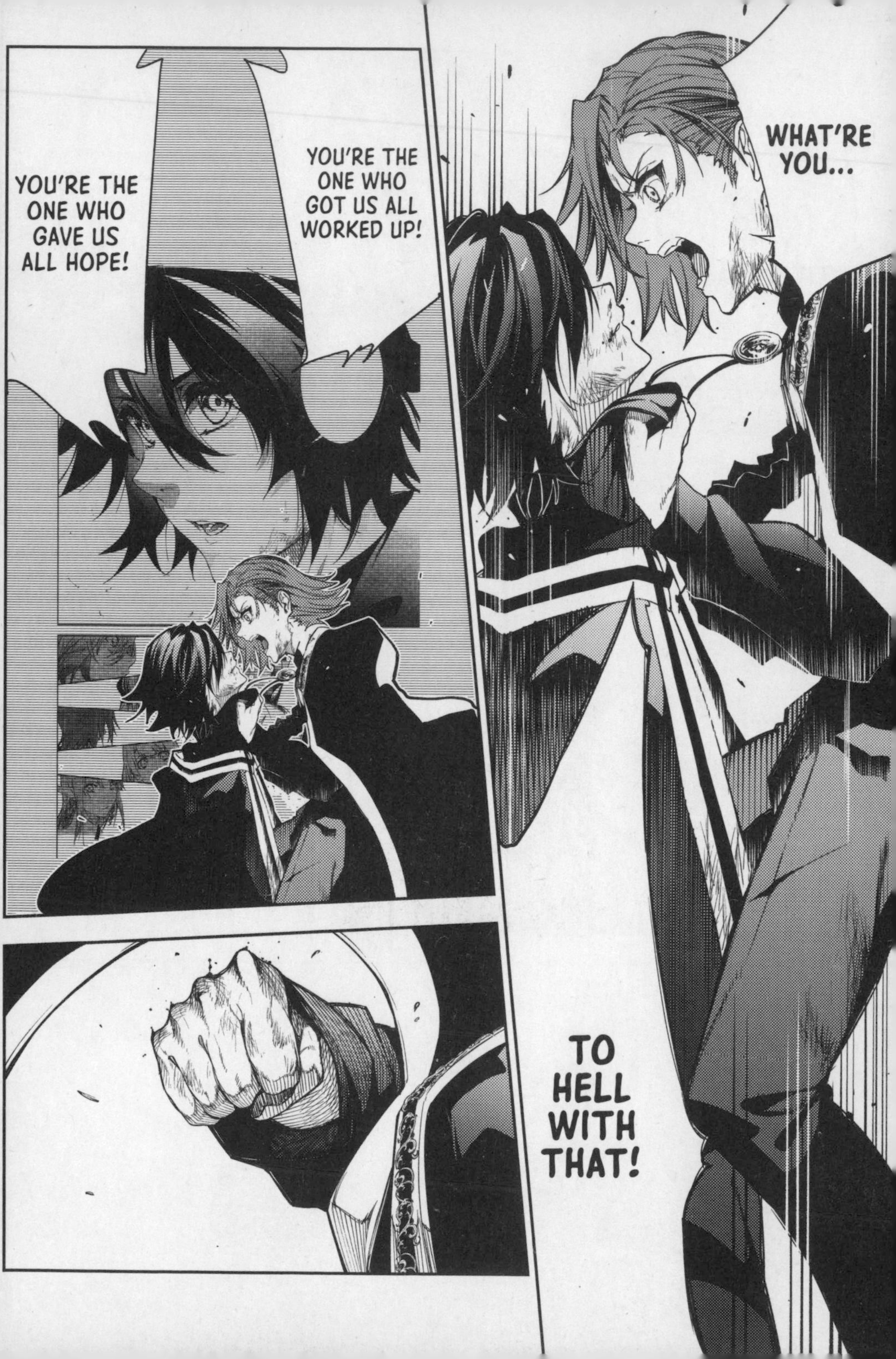
WHAT'RE YOU...
TO HELL WITH THAT!
YOU'RE THE ONE WHO GOT US ALL WORKED UP!
YOU'RE THE ONE WHO GAVE US ALL HOPE!

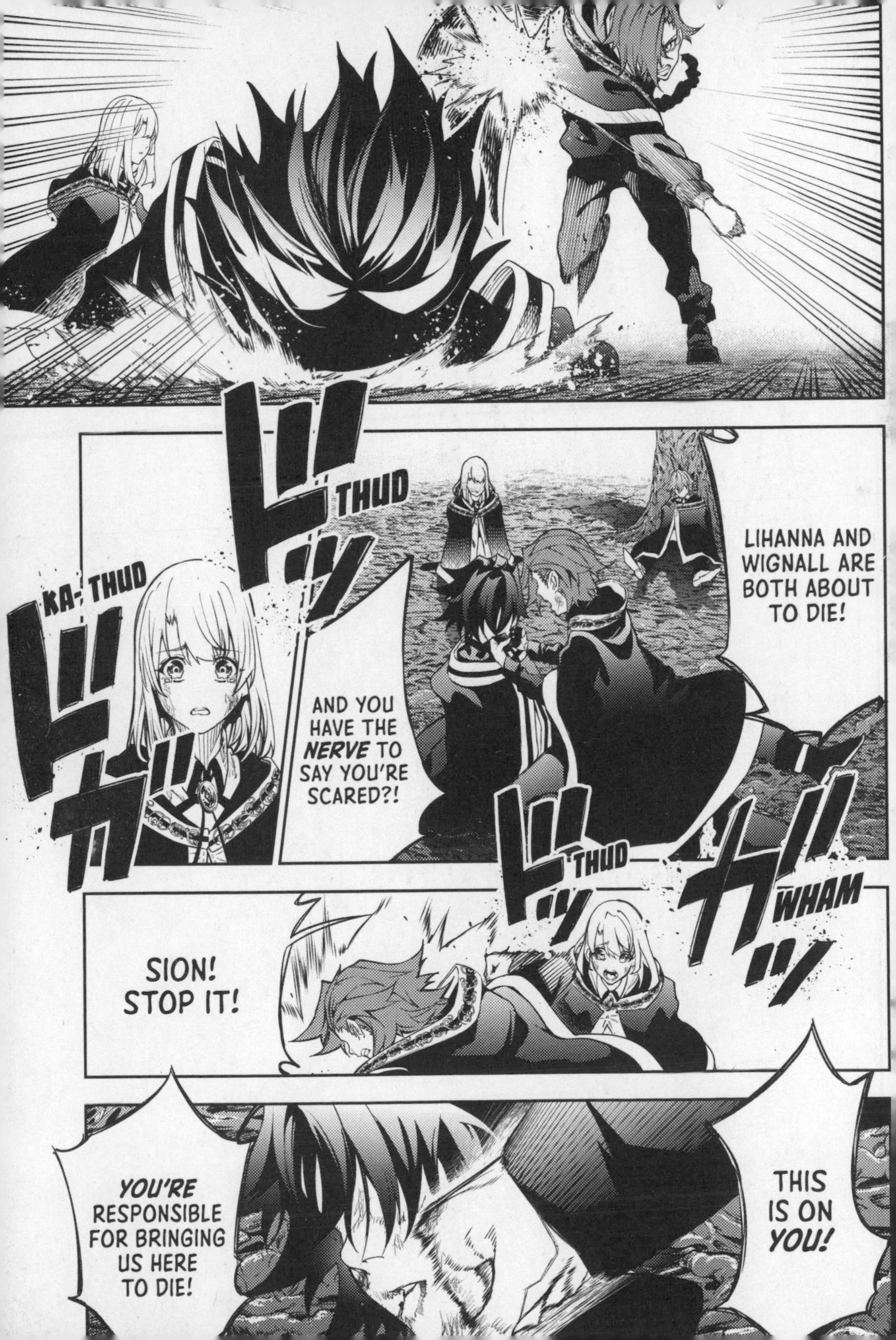

ドッ THUD
LIHANNA AND WIGNALL ARE BOTH ABOUT TO DIE!
AND YOU HAVE THE *NERVE* TO SAY YOU'RE SCARED?!
ドガッ KA-THUD
ガッ WHAM
ドッ THUD
SION! STOP IT!
THIS IS ON *YOU!*
YOU'RE RESPONSIBLE FOR BRINGING US HERE TO DIE!

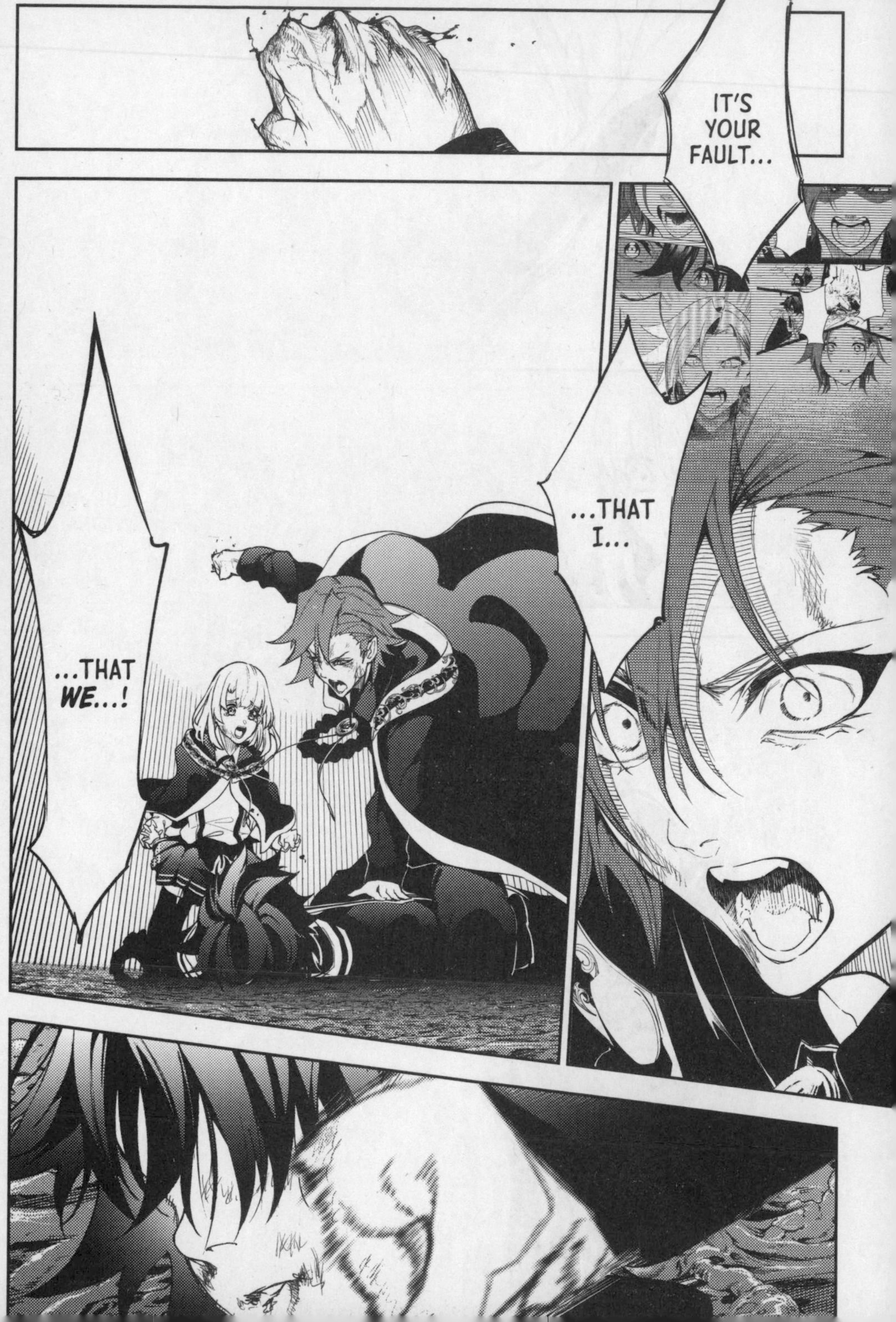
IT'S YOUR FAULT...
...THAT I...
...THAT *WE*...!

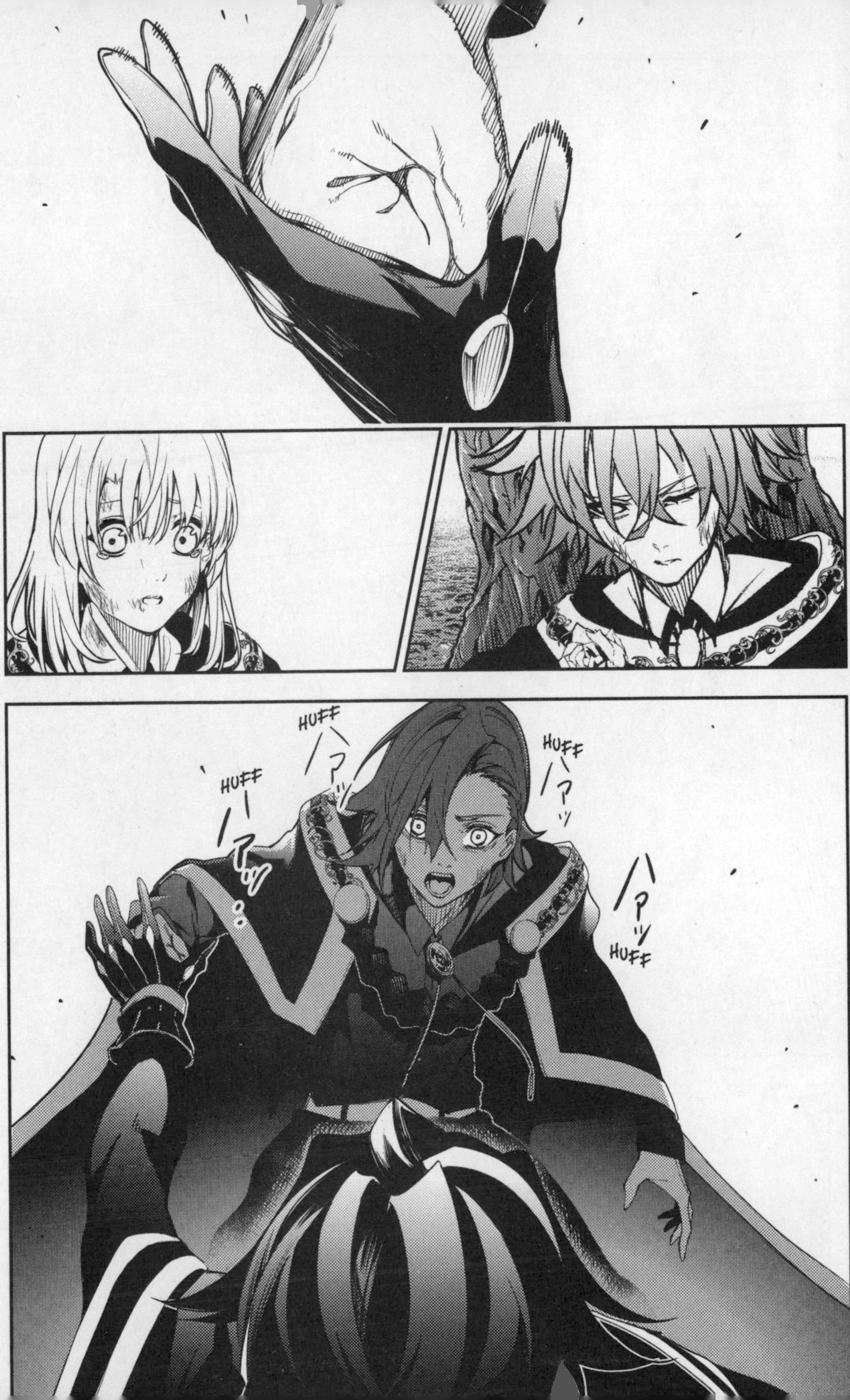
ハァッ
HUFF
HUFF
ハァッ
HUFF
ハァッ
HUFF
ハァッ

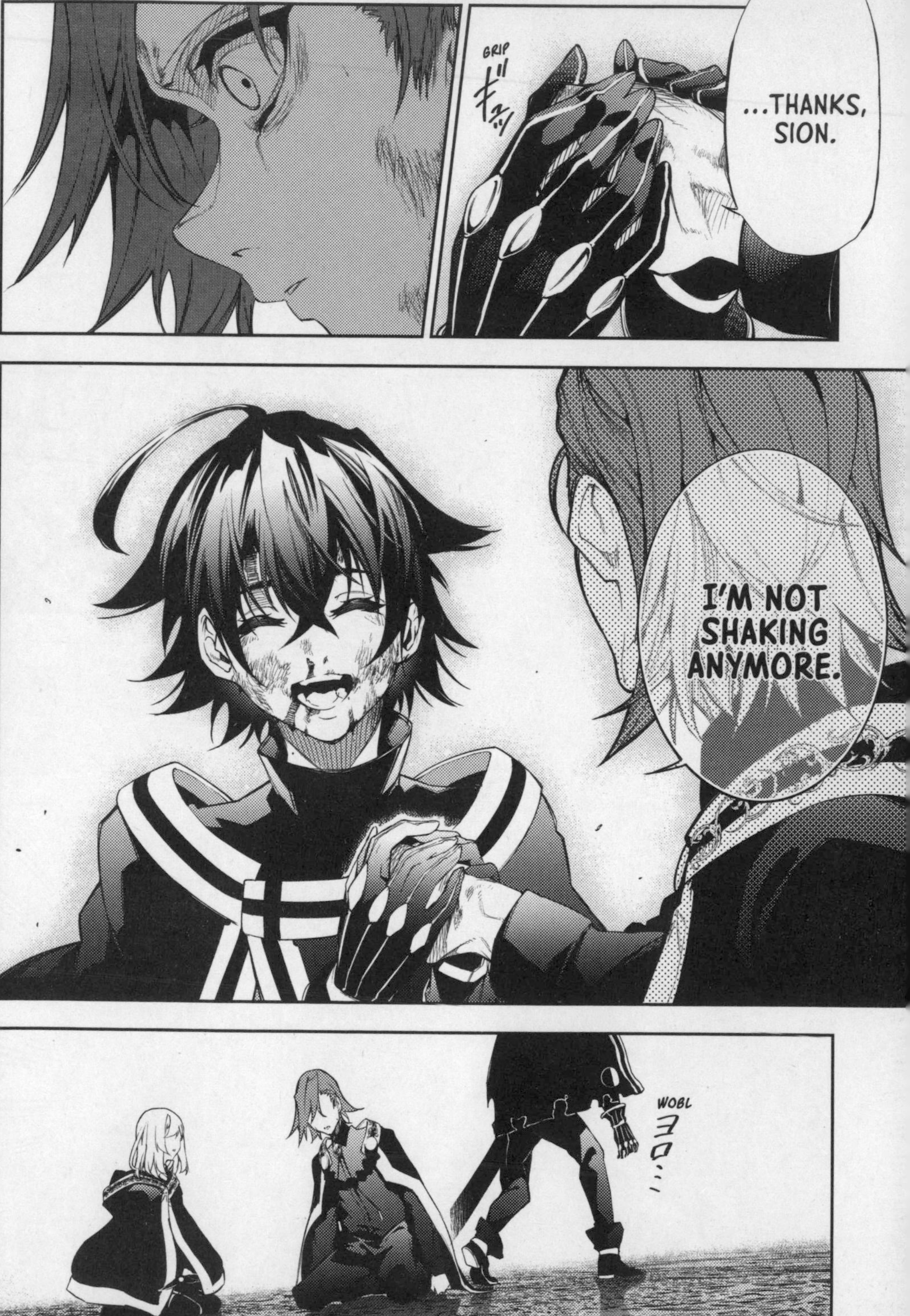
...THANKS, SION.
GRIP
I'M NOT SHAKING ANYMORE.
WOBL

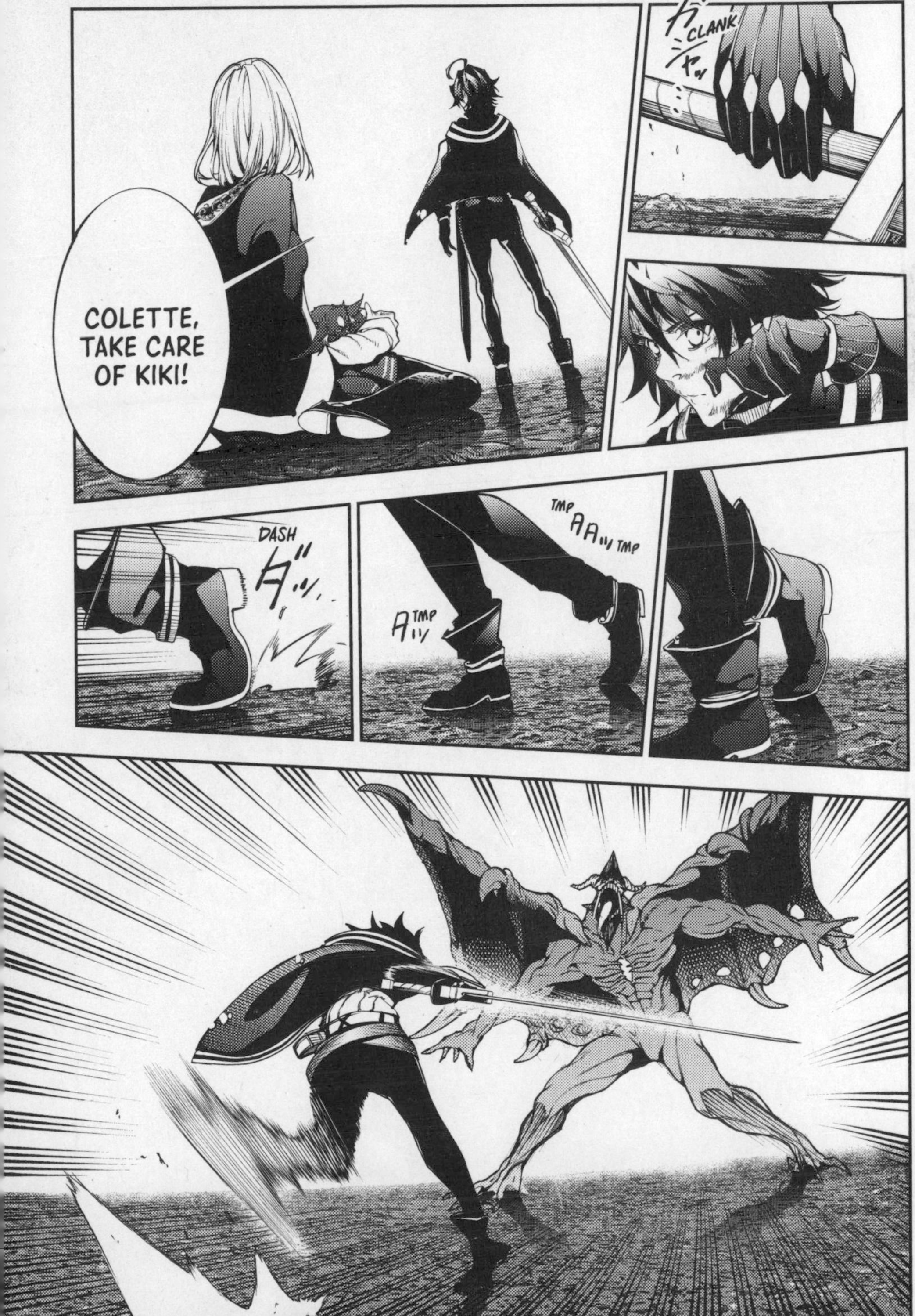
CLANK
COLETTE, TAKE CARE OF KIKI!
TMP
TMP
TMP
DASH

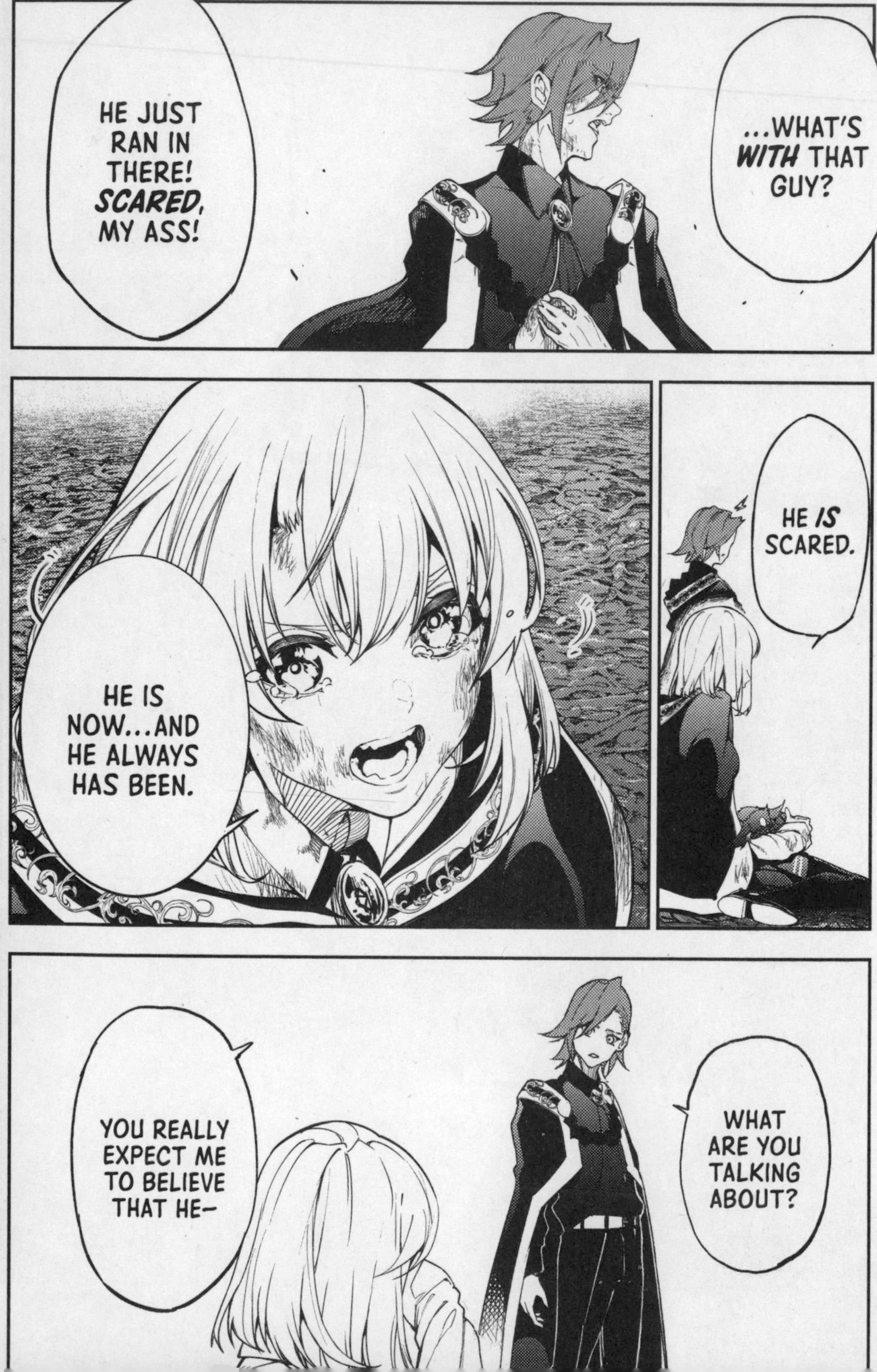
...WHAT'S *WITH* THAT GUY?
HE JUST RAN IN THERE! *SCARED*, MY ASS!
HE *IS* SCARED.
HE IS NOW...AND HE ALWAYS HAS BEEN.
WHAT ARE YOU TALKING ABOUT?
YOU REALLY EXPECT ME TO BELIEVE THAT HE–

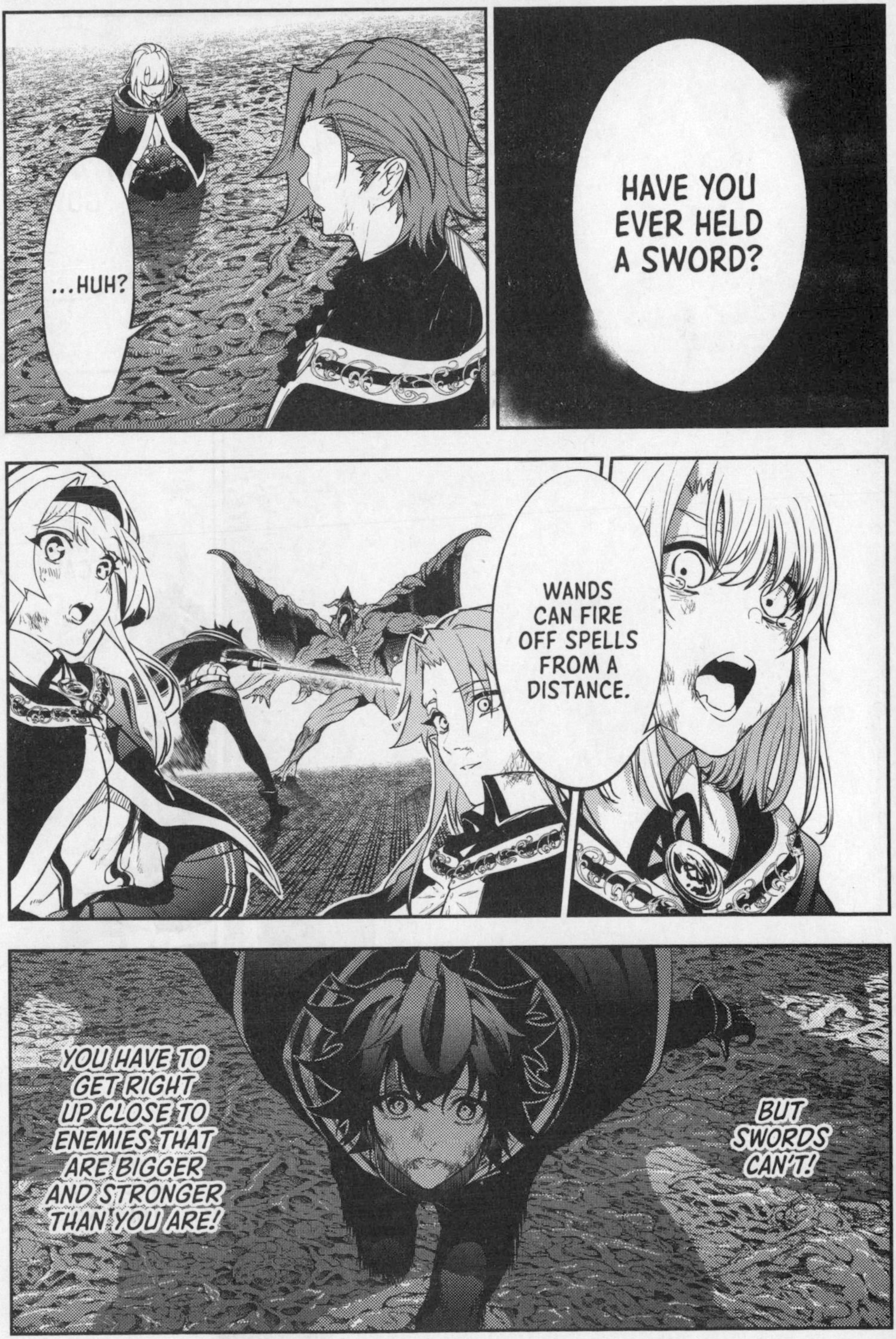
HAVE YOU EVER HELD A SWORD?
...HUH?
WANDS CAN FIRE OFF SPELLS FROM A DISTANCE.
BUT SWORDS CAN'T!
YOU HAVE TO GET RIGHT UP CLOSE TO ENEMIES THAT ARE BIGGER AND STRONGER THAN YOU ARE!

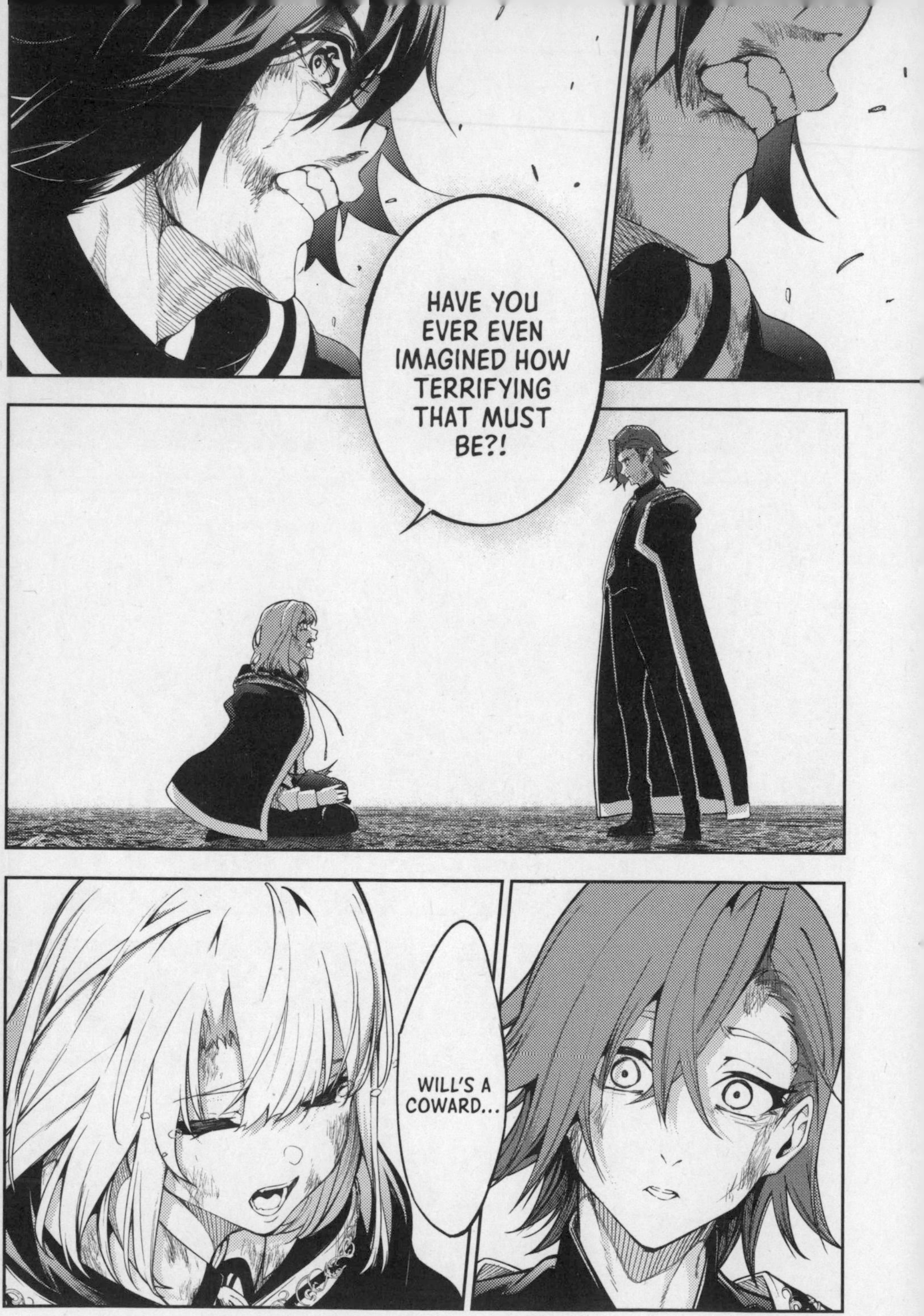
HAVE YOU EVER EVEN IMAGINED HOW TERRIFYING THAT MUST BE?!
WILL'S A COWARD...

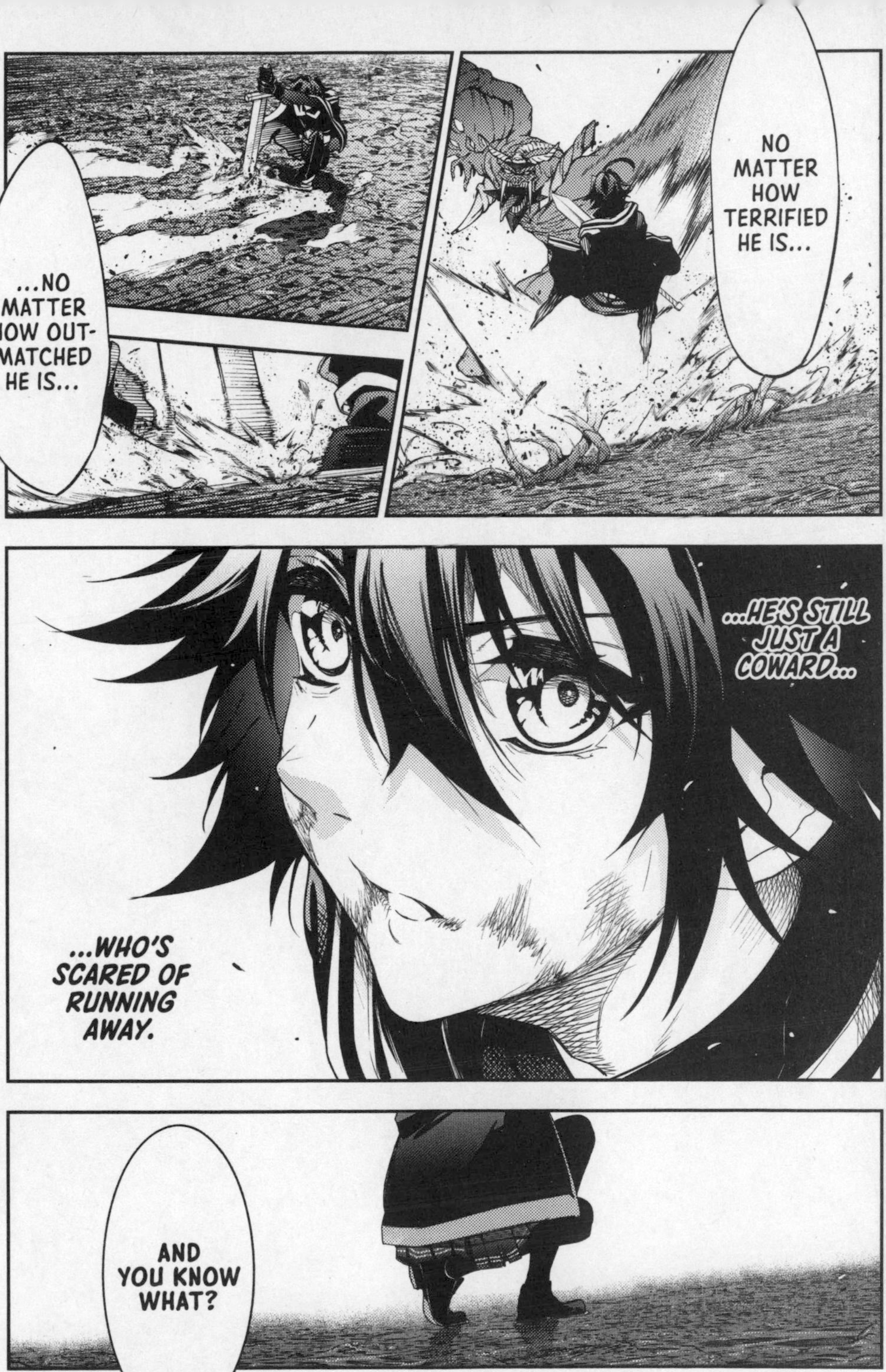

NO MATTER HOW TERRIFIED HE IS...
...NO MATTER HOW OUT-MATCHED HE IS...
...HE'S STILL JUST A COWARD...
...WHO'S SCARED OF RUNNING AWAY.
AND YOU KNOW WHAT?

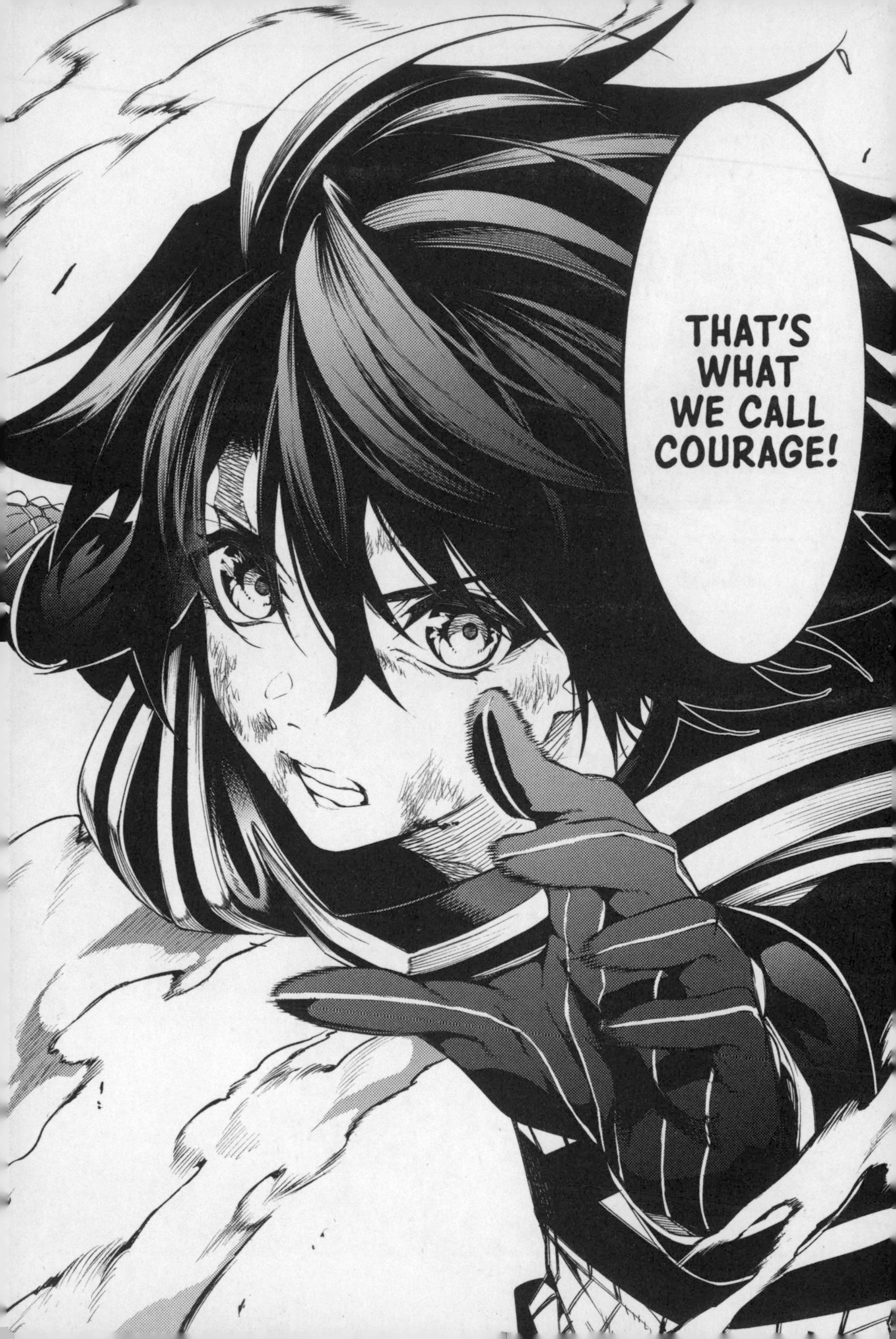
THAT'S WHAT WE CALL COURAGE!

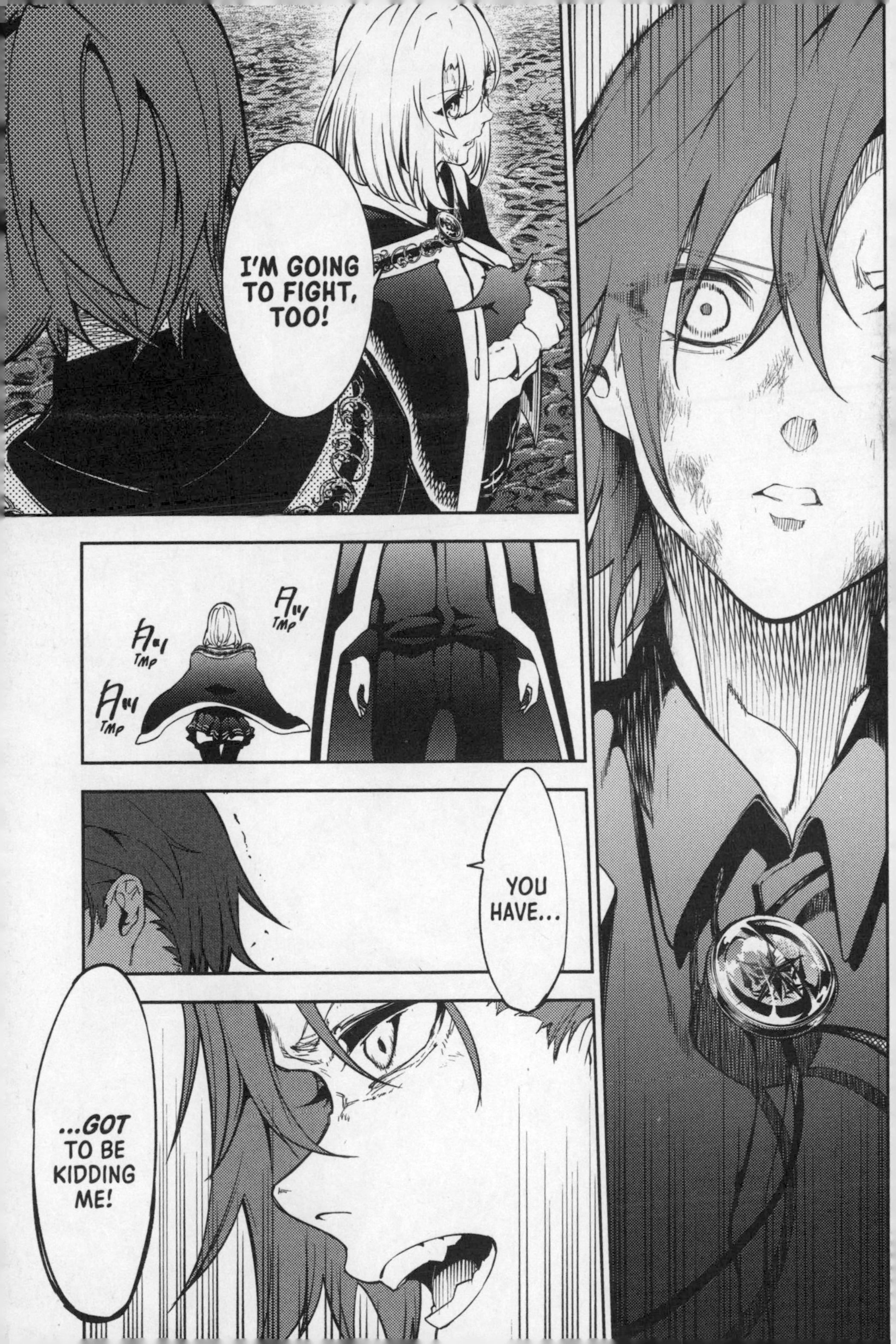
I'M GOING TO FIGHT, TOO!
TMP
TMP
TMP
YOU HAVE...
...GOT TO BE KIDDING ME!

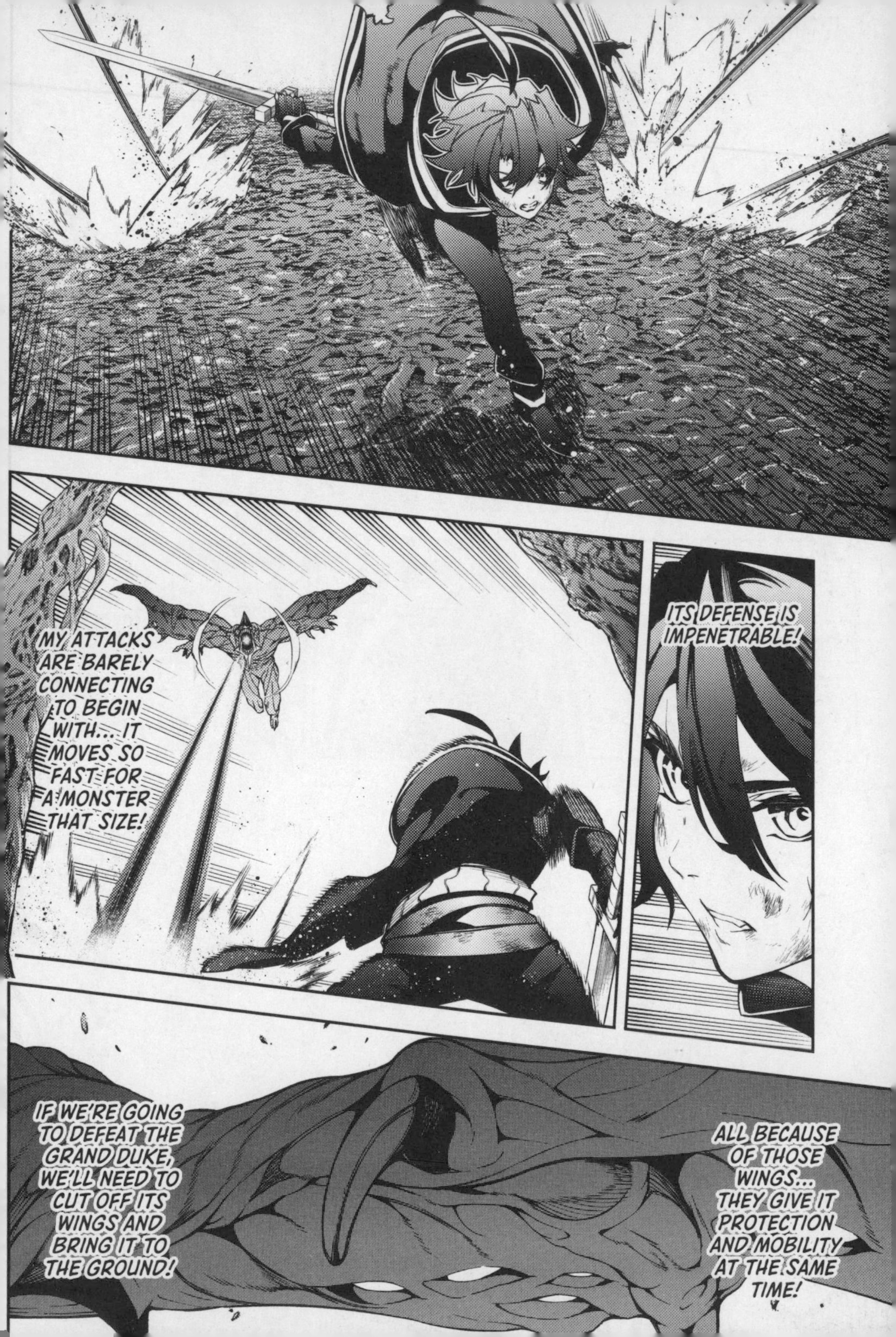
ITS DEFENSE IS IMPENETRABLE!
MY ATTACKS ARE BARELY CONNECTING TO BEGIN WITH... IT MOVES SO FAST FOR A MONSTER THAT SIZE!
ALL BECAUSE OF THOSE WINGS... THEY GIVE IT PROTECTION AND MOBILITY AT THE SAME TIME!
IF WE'RE GOING TO DEFEAT THE GRAND DUKE, WE'LL NEED TO CUT OFF ITS WINGS AND BRING IT TO THE GROUND!

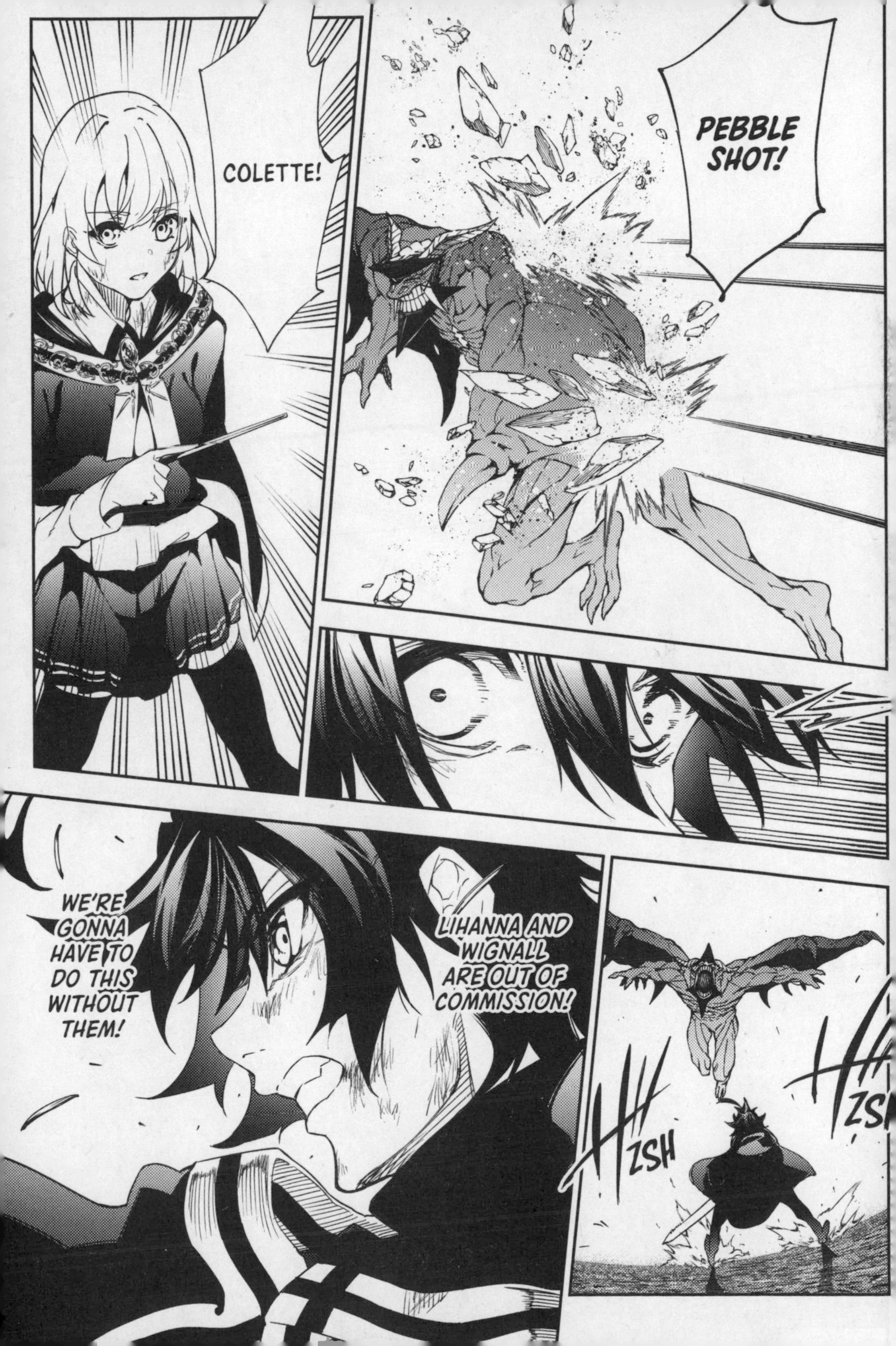
PEBBLE SHOT!
COLETTE!
ZS
ZSH
LIHANNA AND WIGNALL ARE OUT OF COMMISSION!
WE'RE GONNA HAVE TO DO THIS WITHOUT THEM!

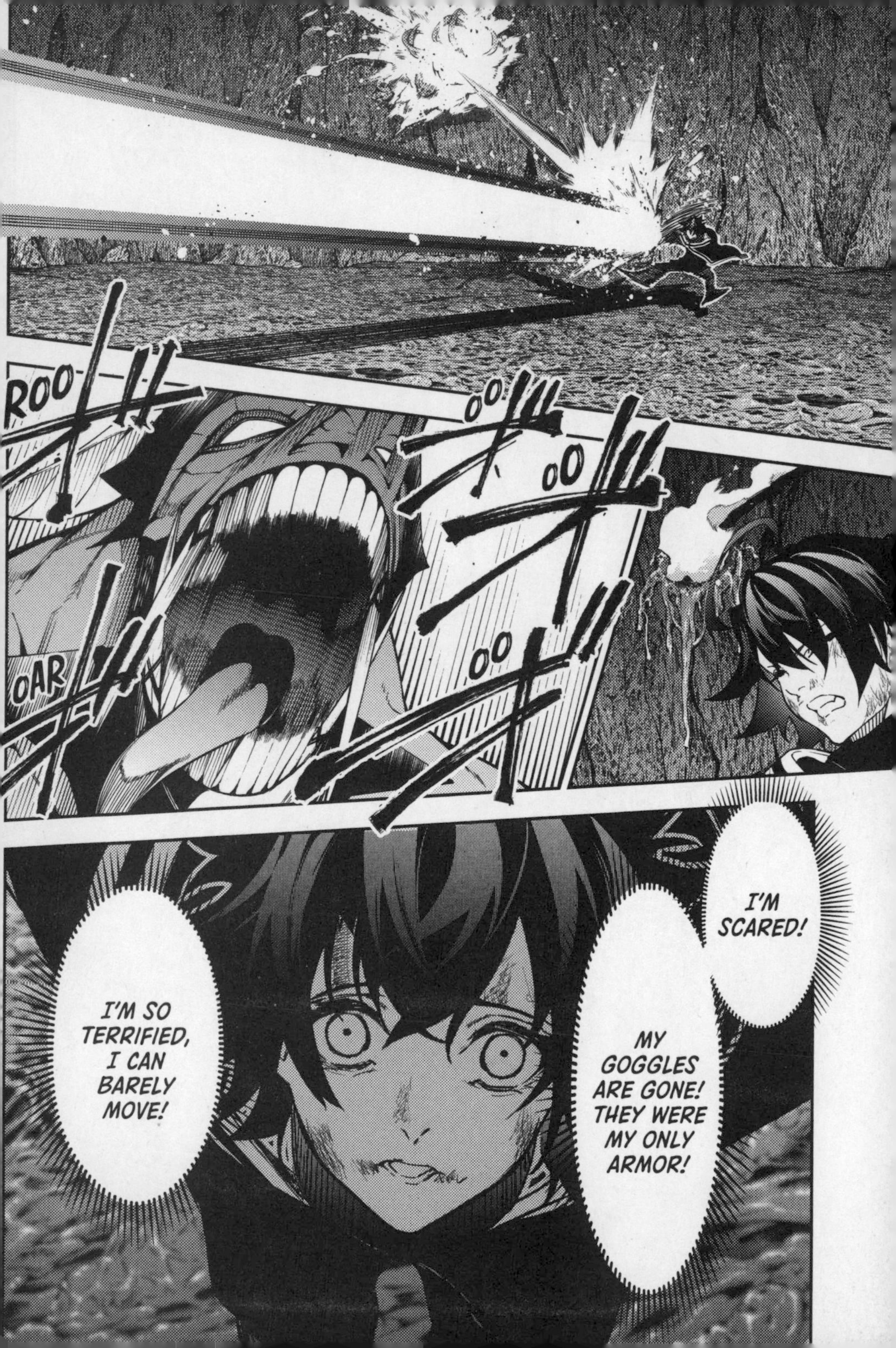
ROO
OO
OO
OO
OAR
I'M SCARED!
MY GOGGLES ARE GONE! THEY WERE MY ONLY ARMOR!
I'M SO TERRIFIED, I CAN BARELY MOVE!

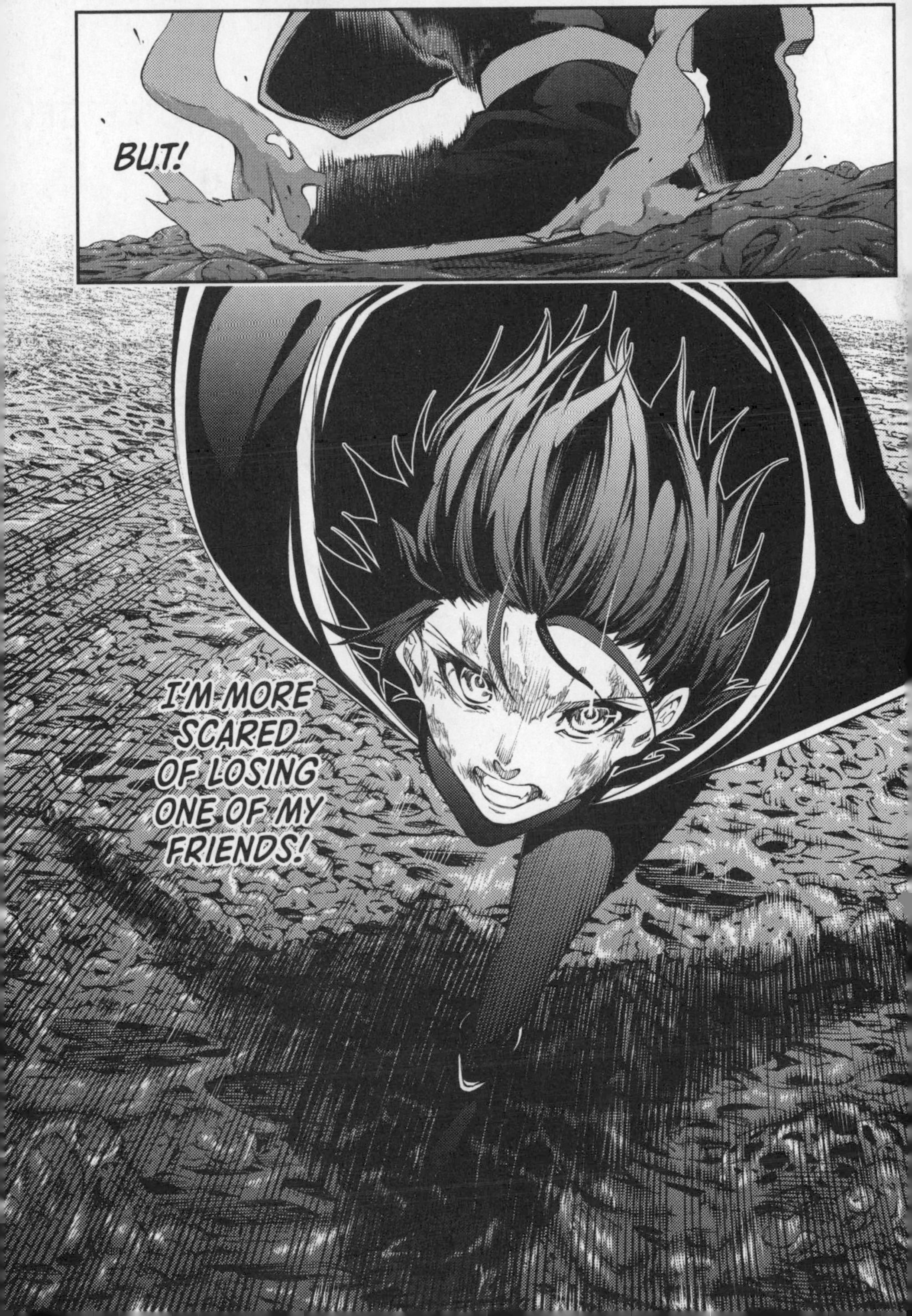
BUT!
I'M MORE SCARED OF LOSING ONE OF MY FRIENDS!

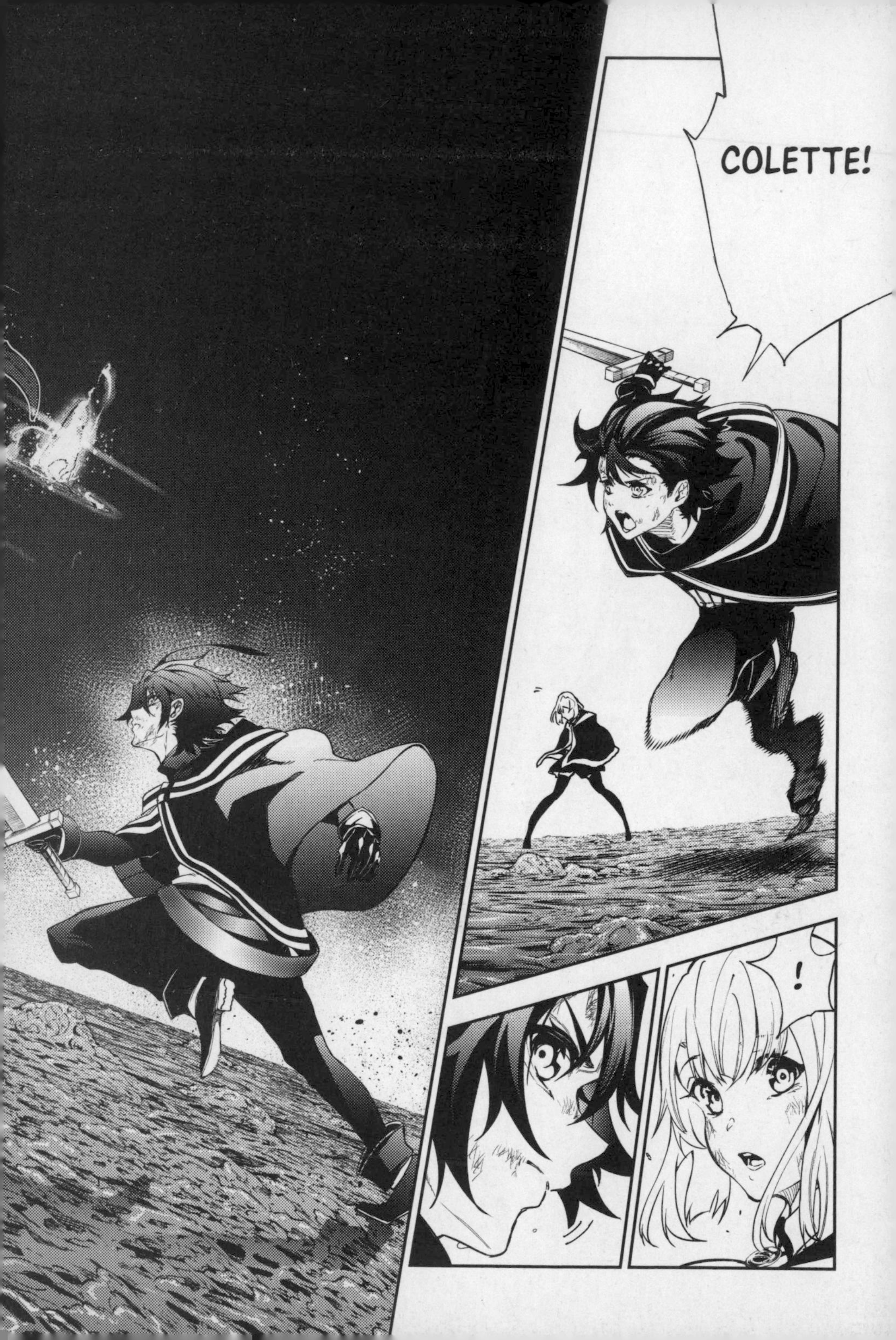
COLETTE!
!

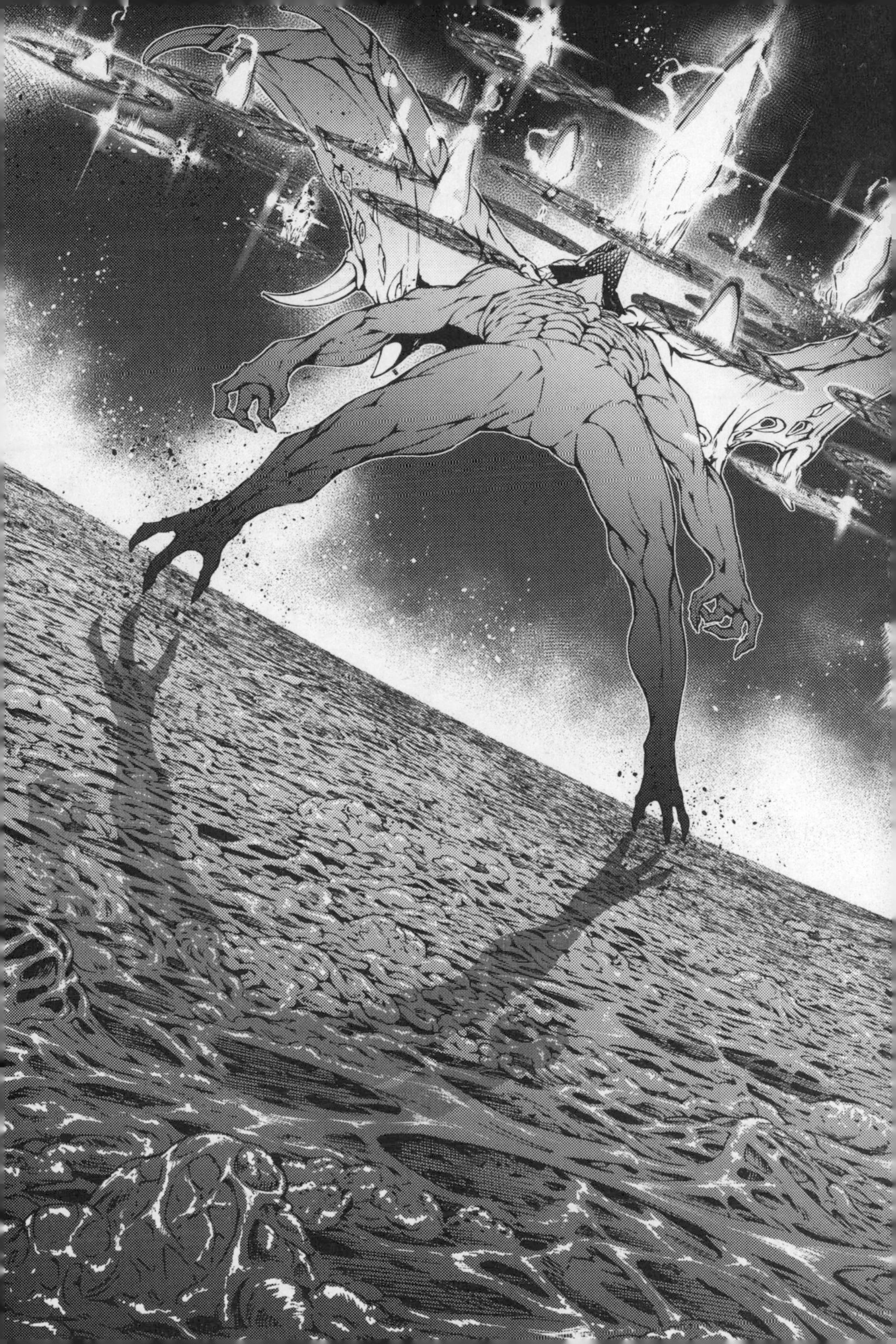

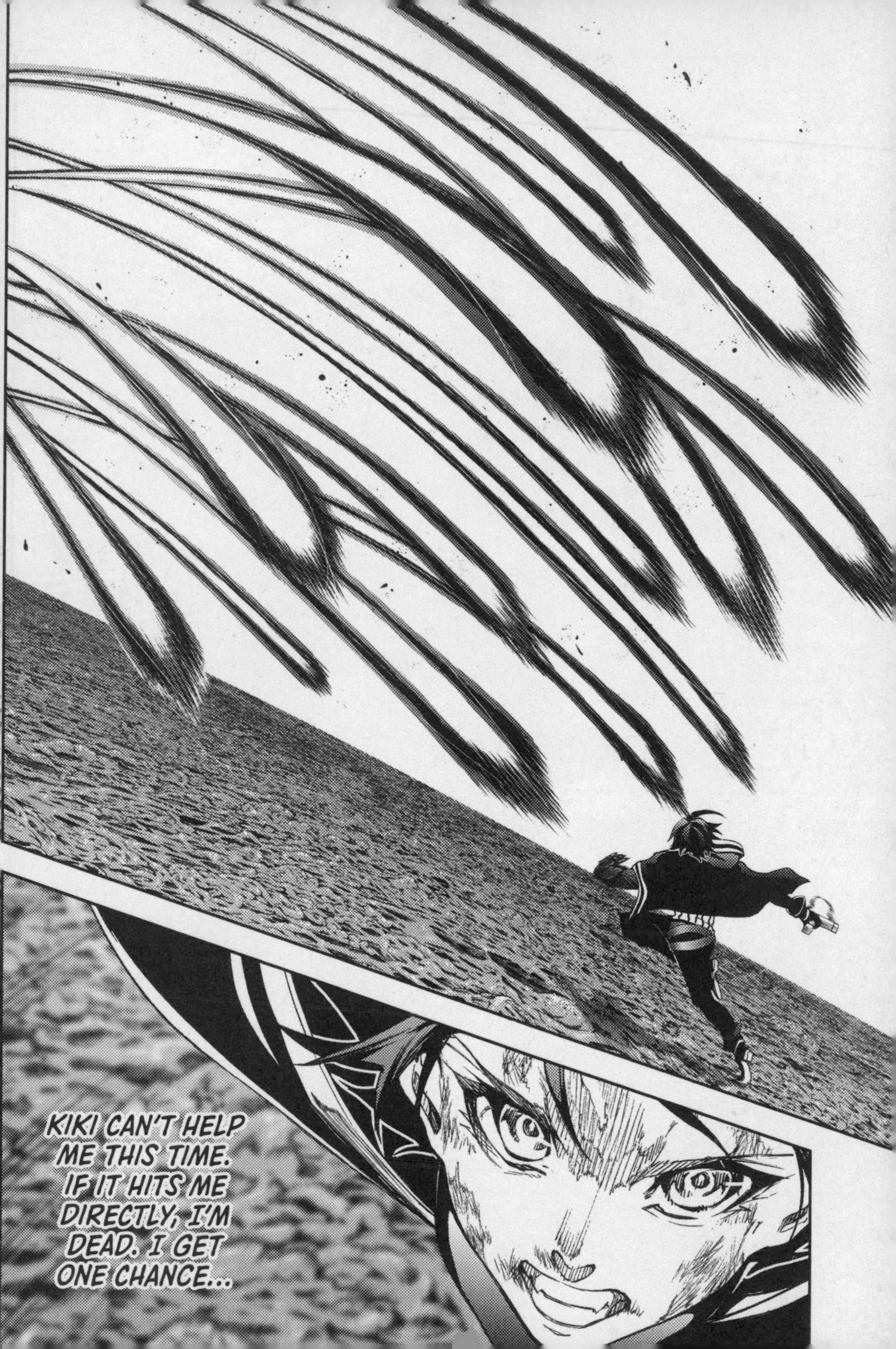
KIKI CAN'T HELP ME THIS TIME. IF IT HITS ME DIRECTLY, I'M DEAD. I GET ONE CHANCE...

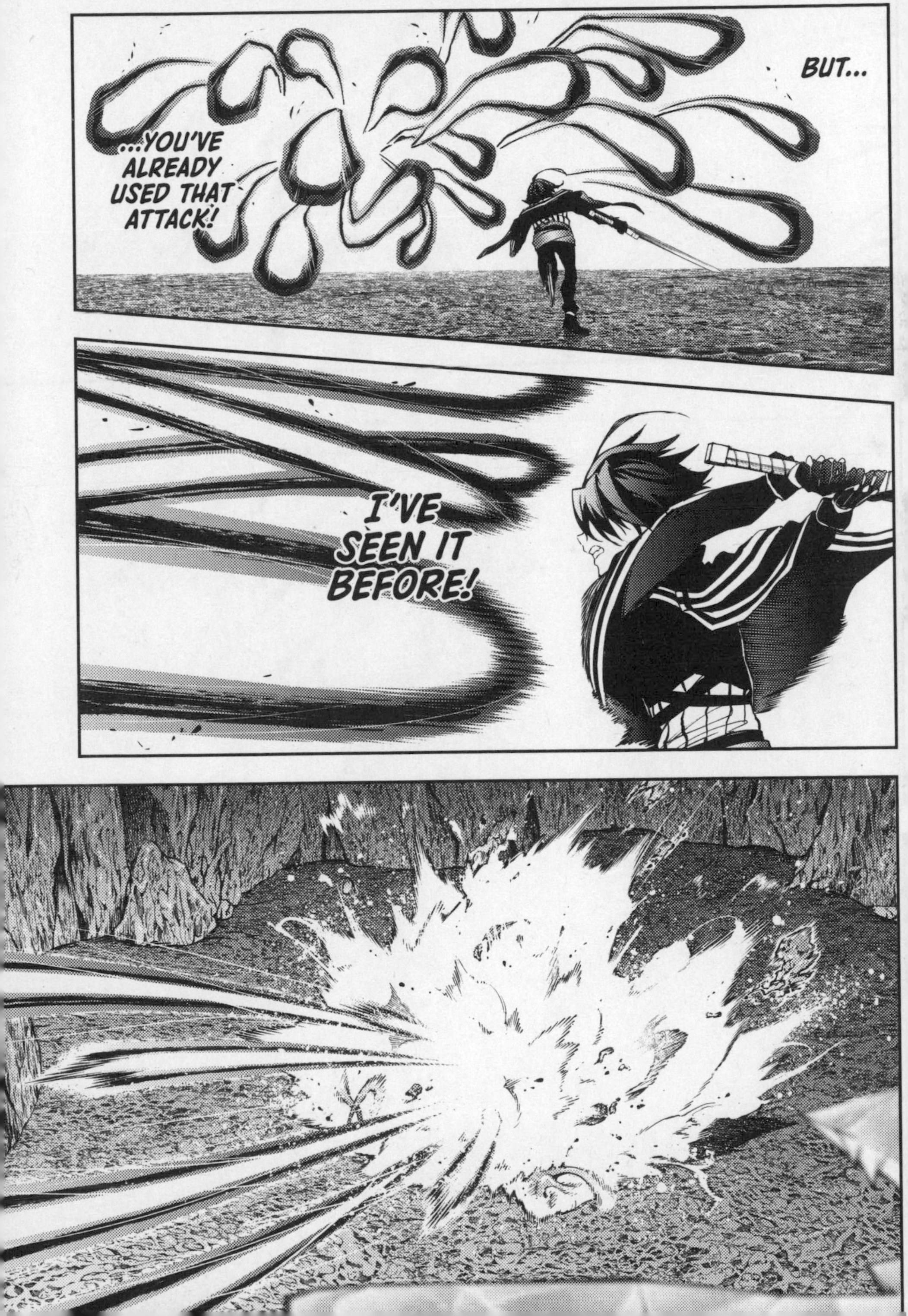
BUT...
...YOU'VE ALREADY USED THAT ATTACK!
I'VE SEEN IT BEFORE!

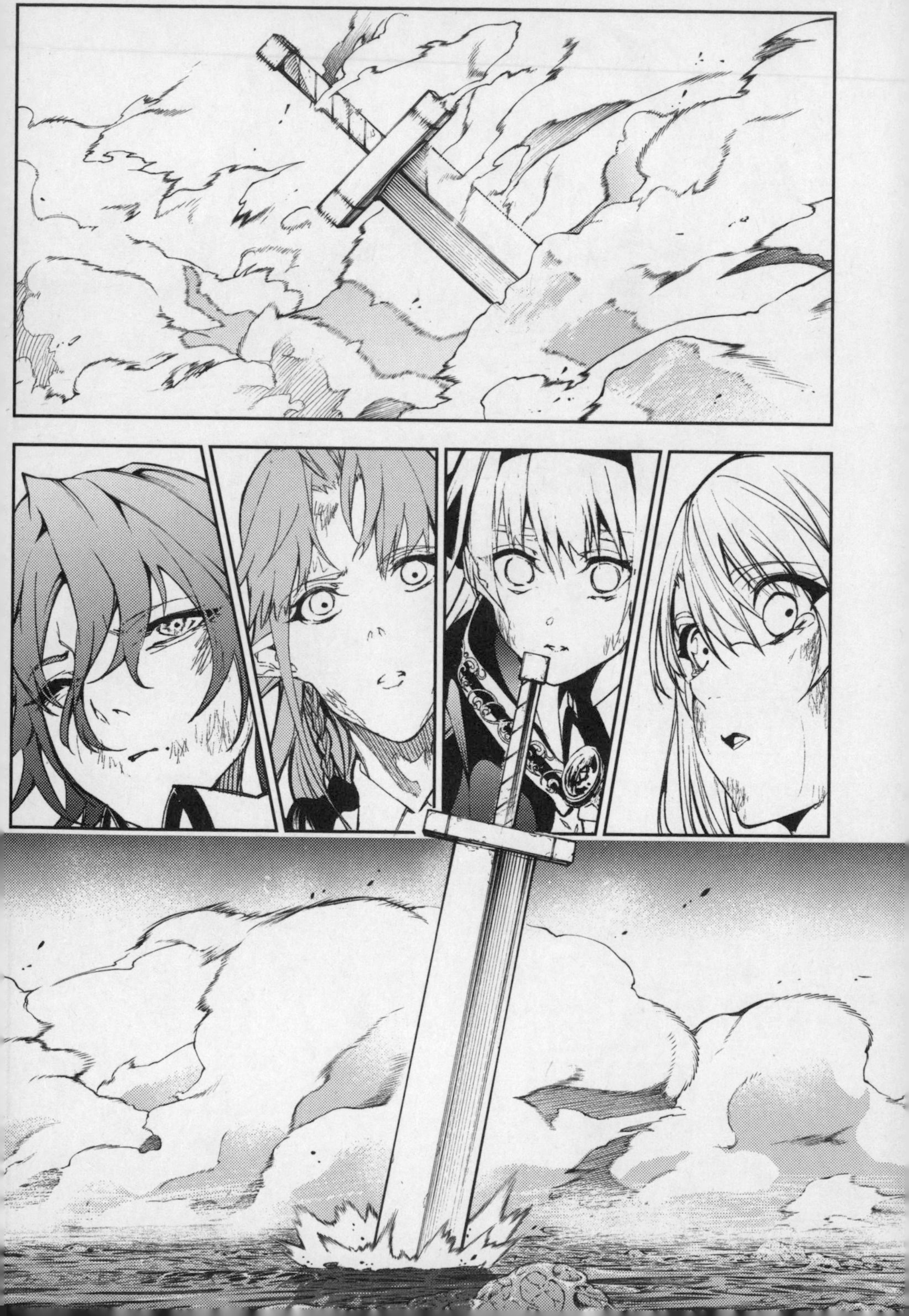

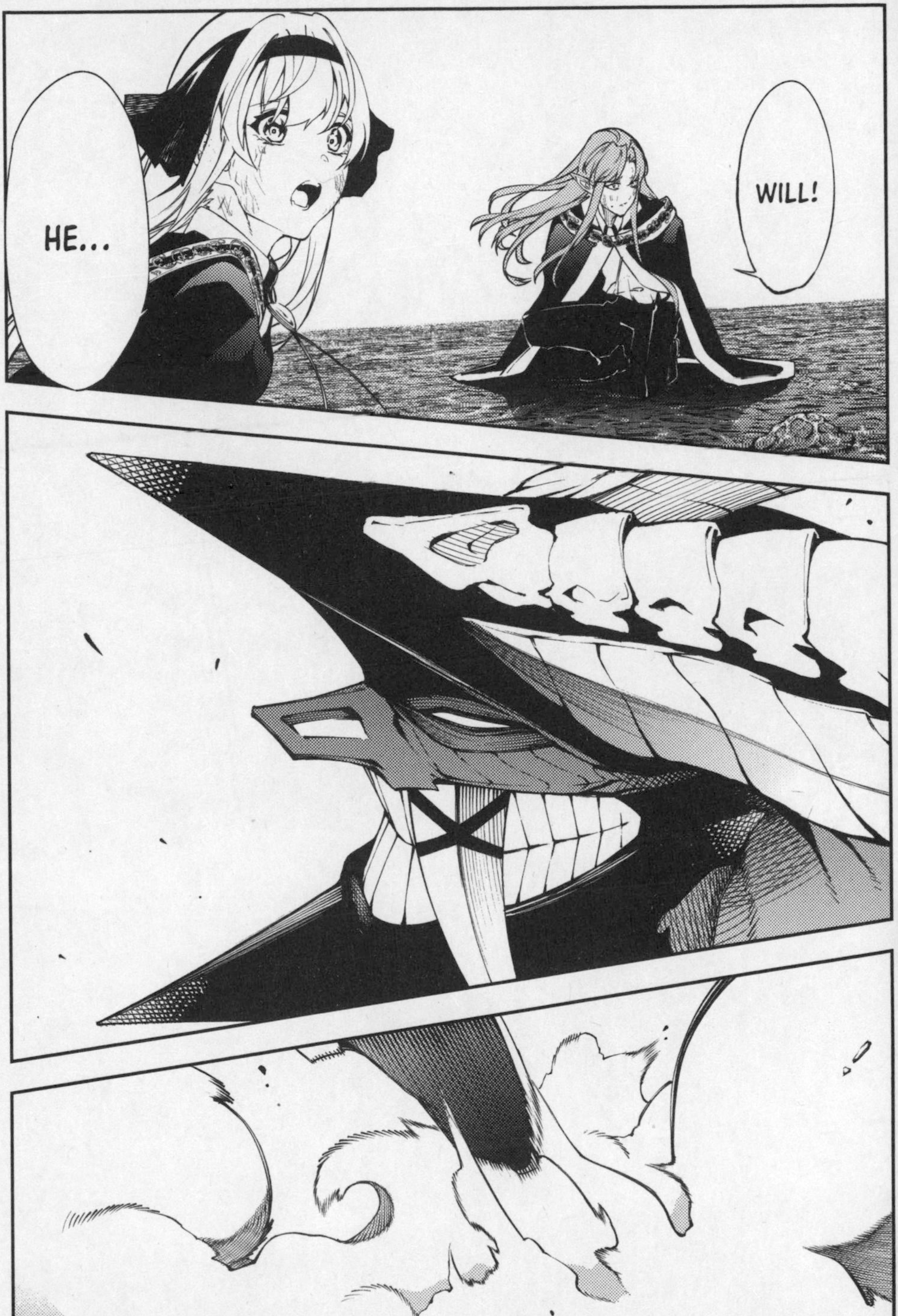
WILL!
HE...

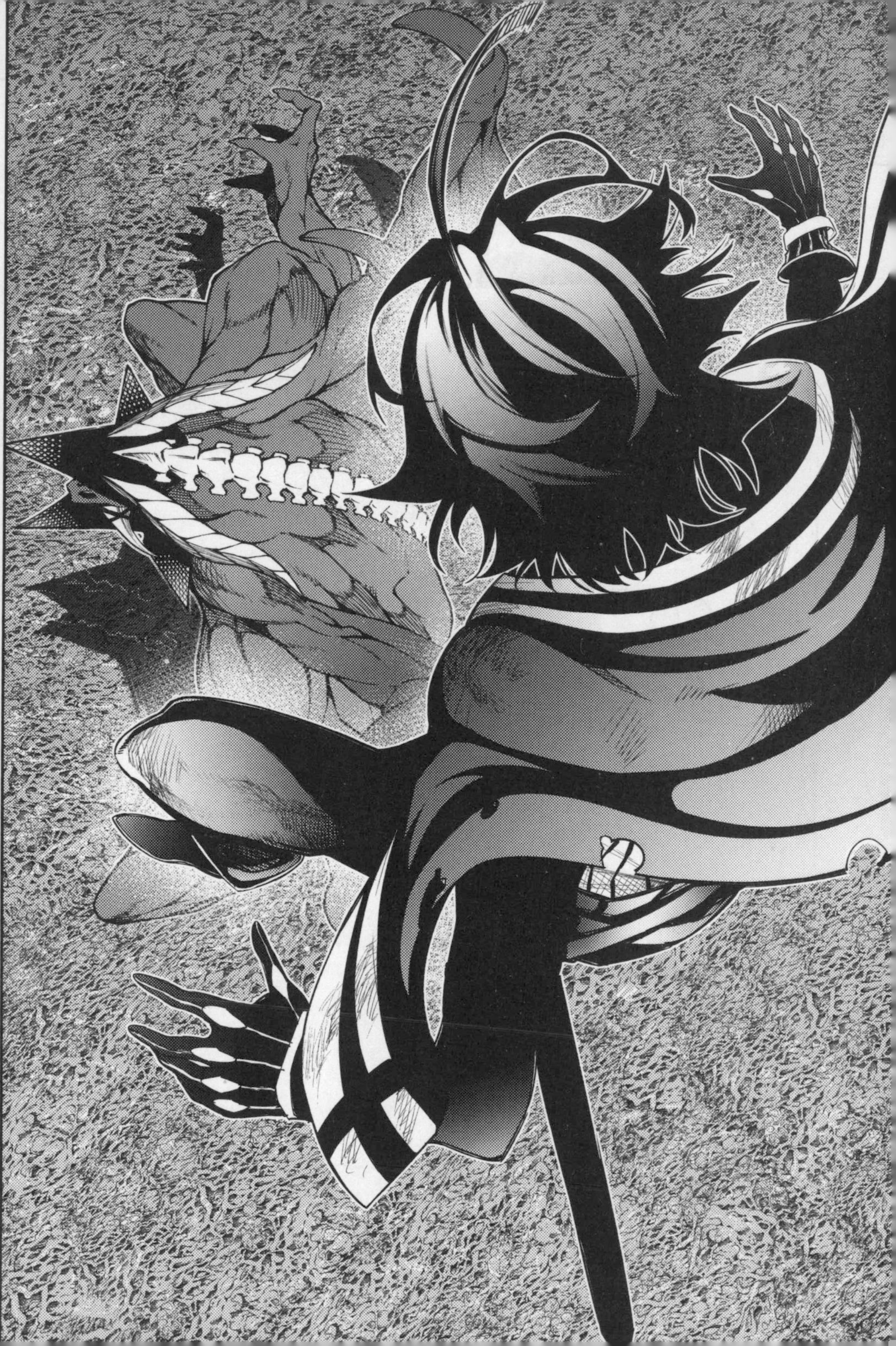

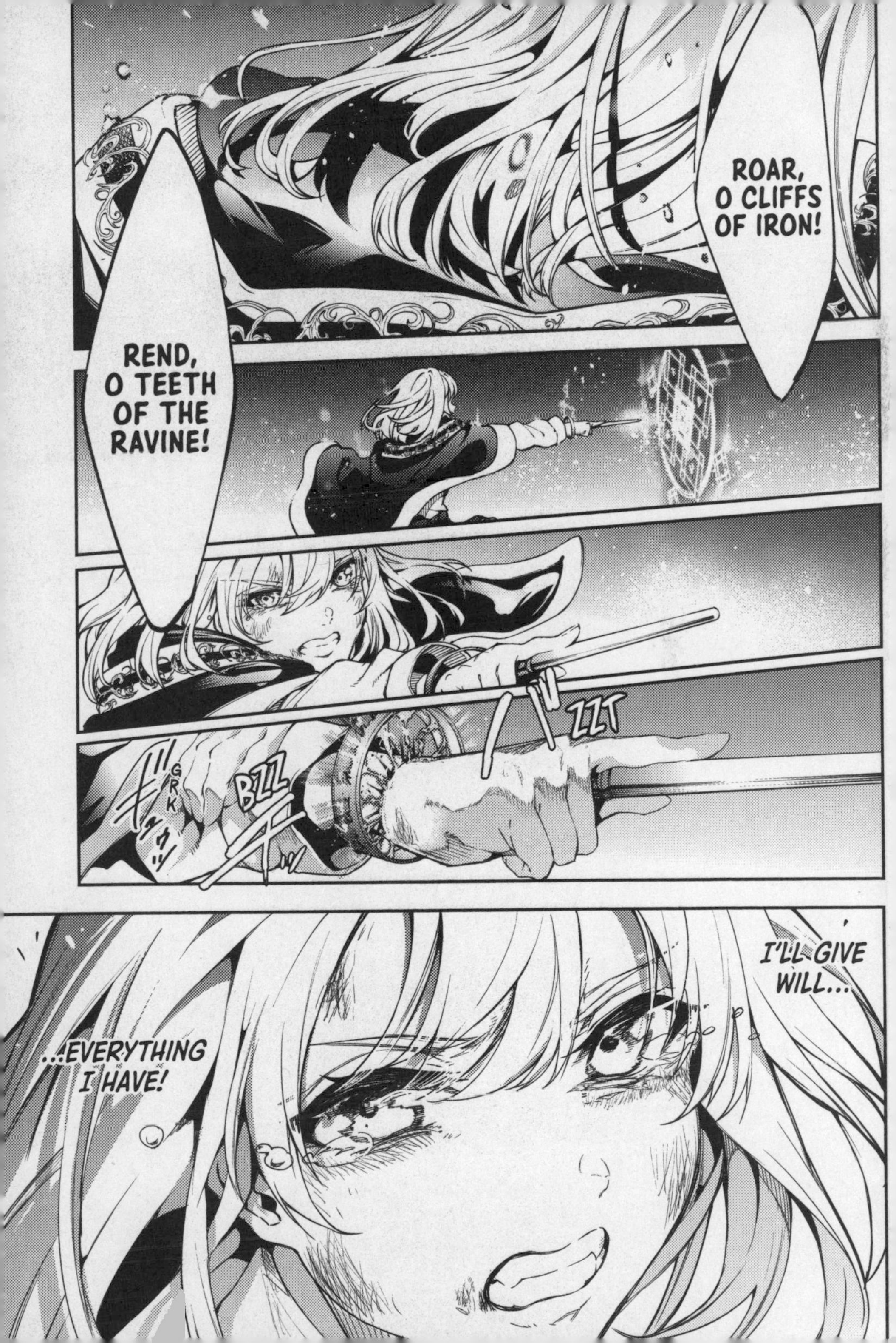
ROAR, O CLIFFS OF IRON!
REND, O TEETH OF THE RAVINE!
ZZT
BZZ
GRK
I'LL GIVE WILL...
...EVERYTHING I HAVE!

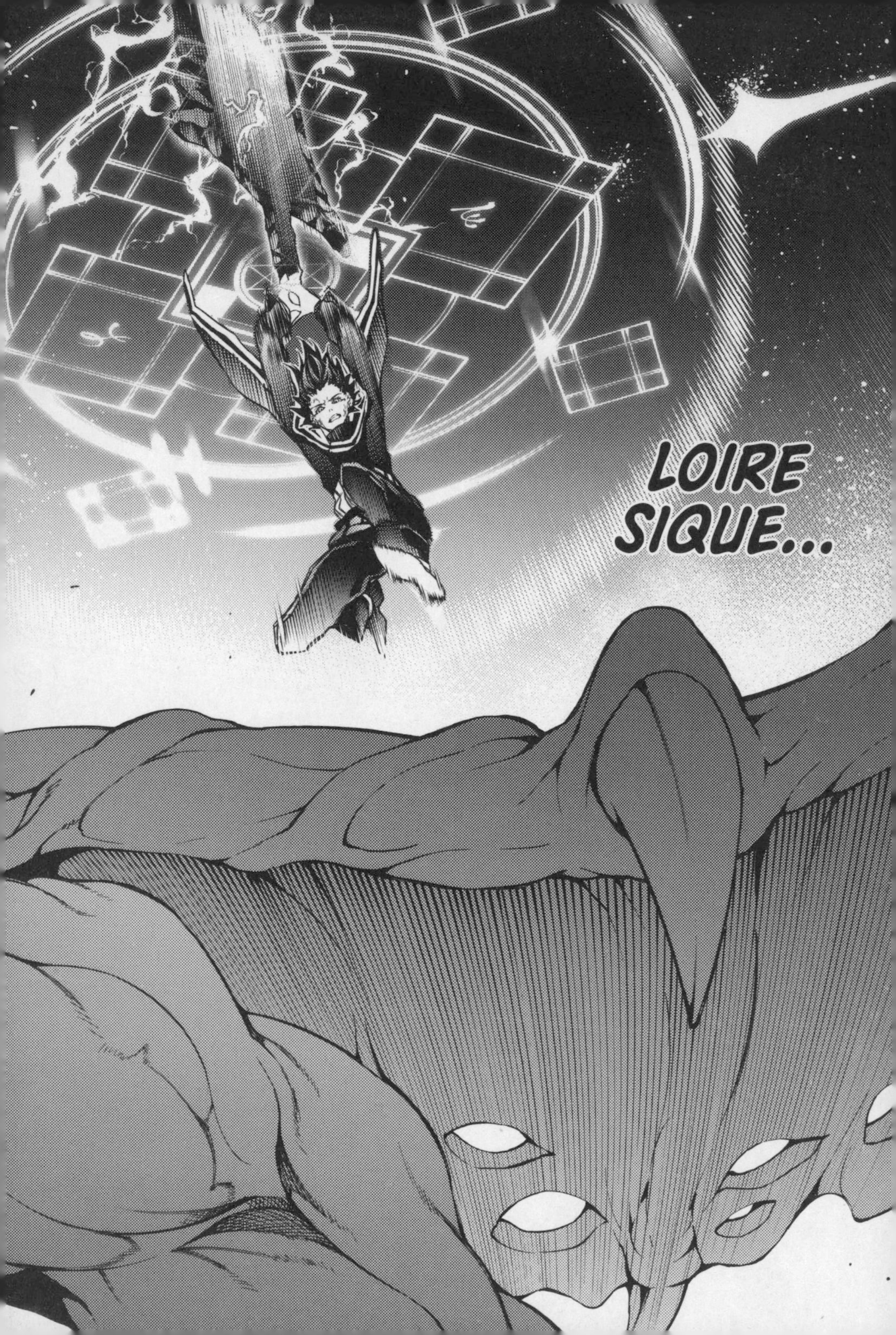
LOIRE SIQUE...

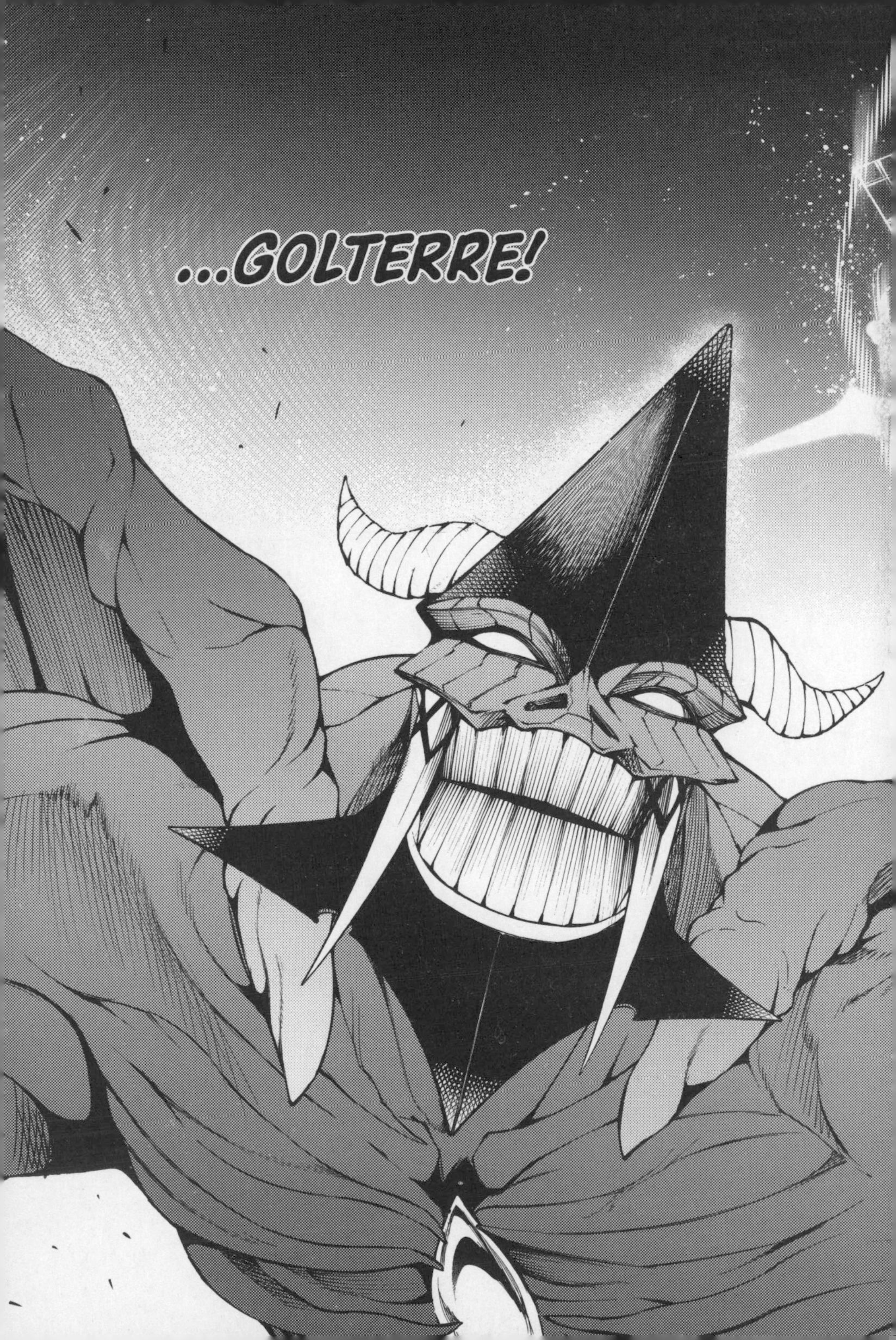
...GOLTERRE!

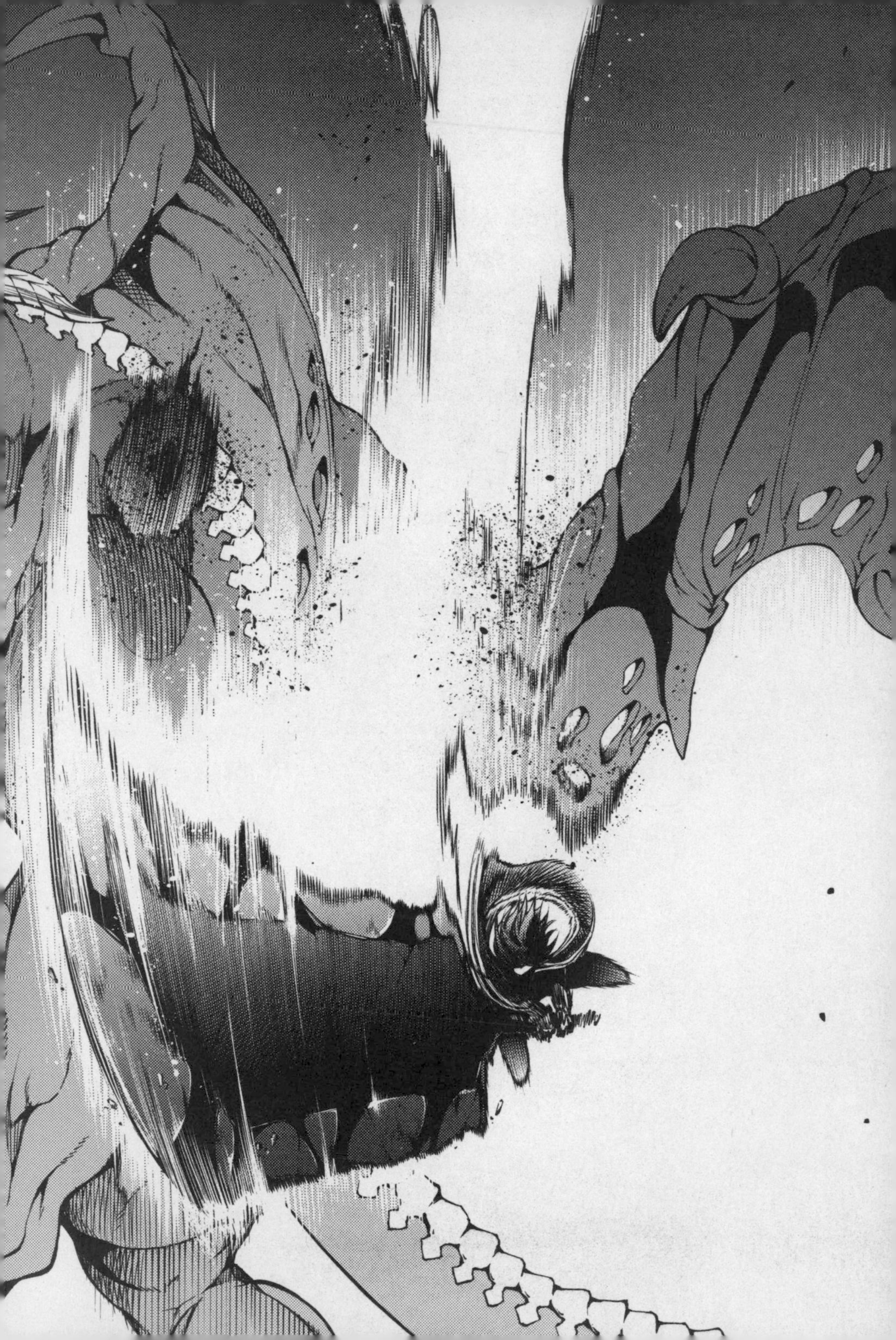

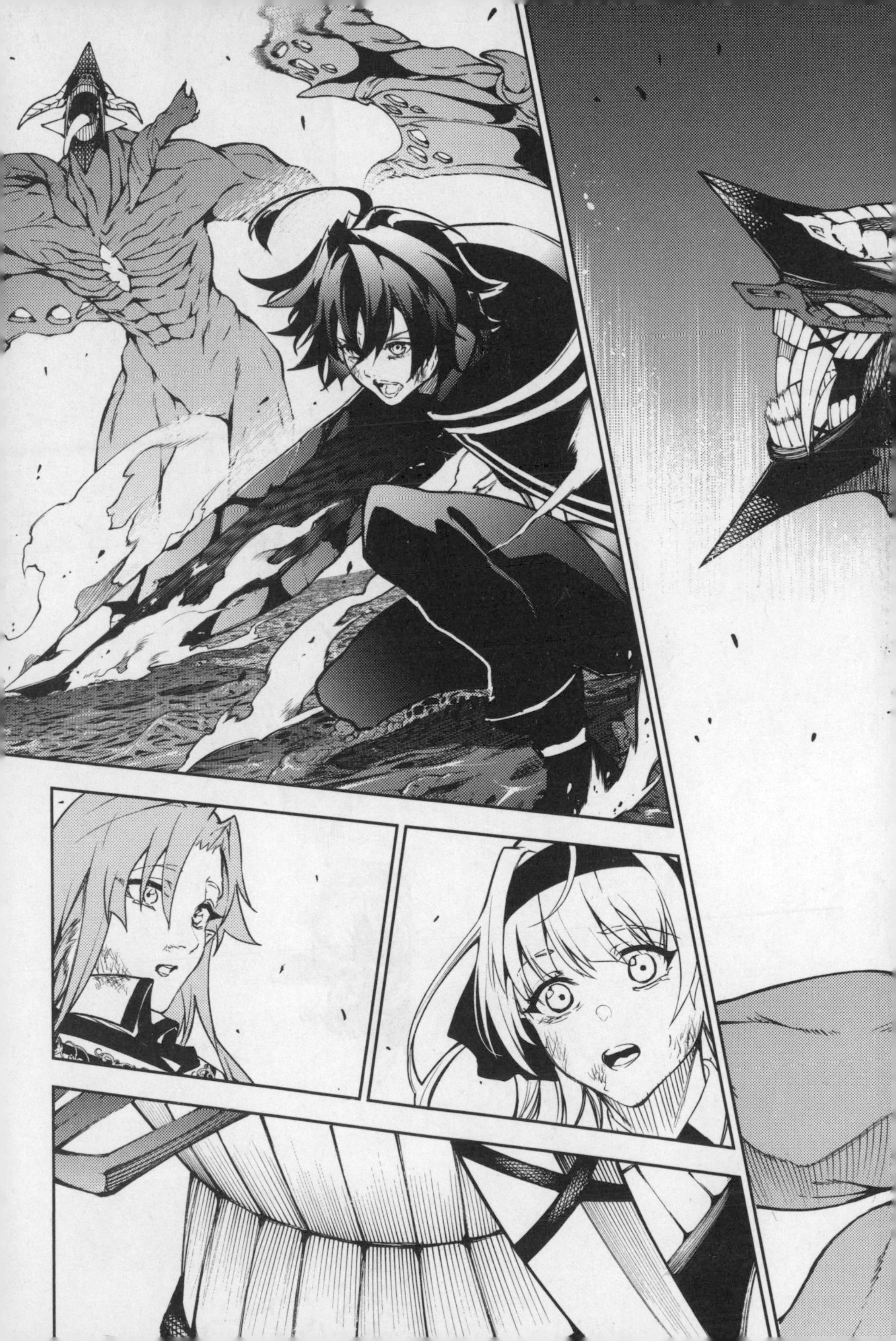

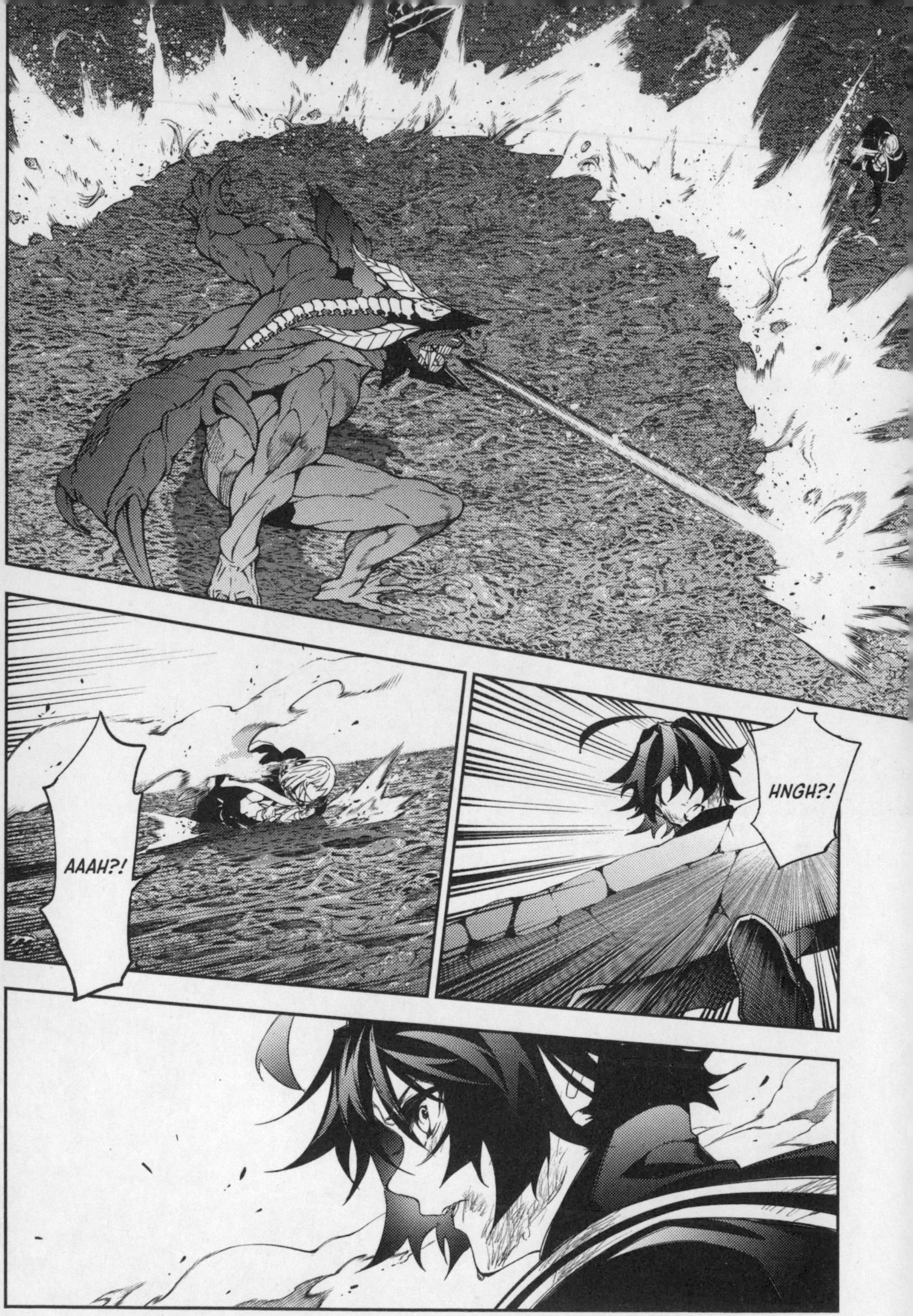
HNGH?!
AAAH?!

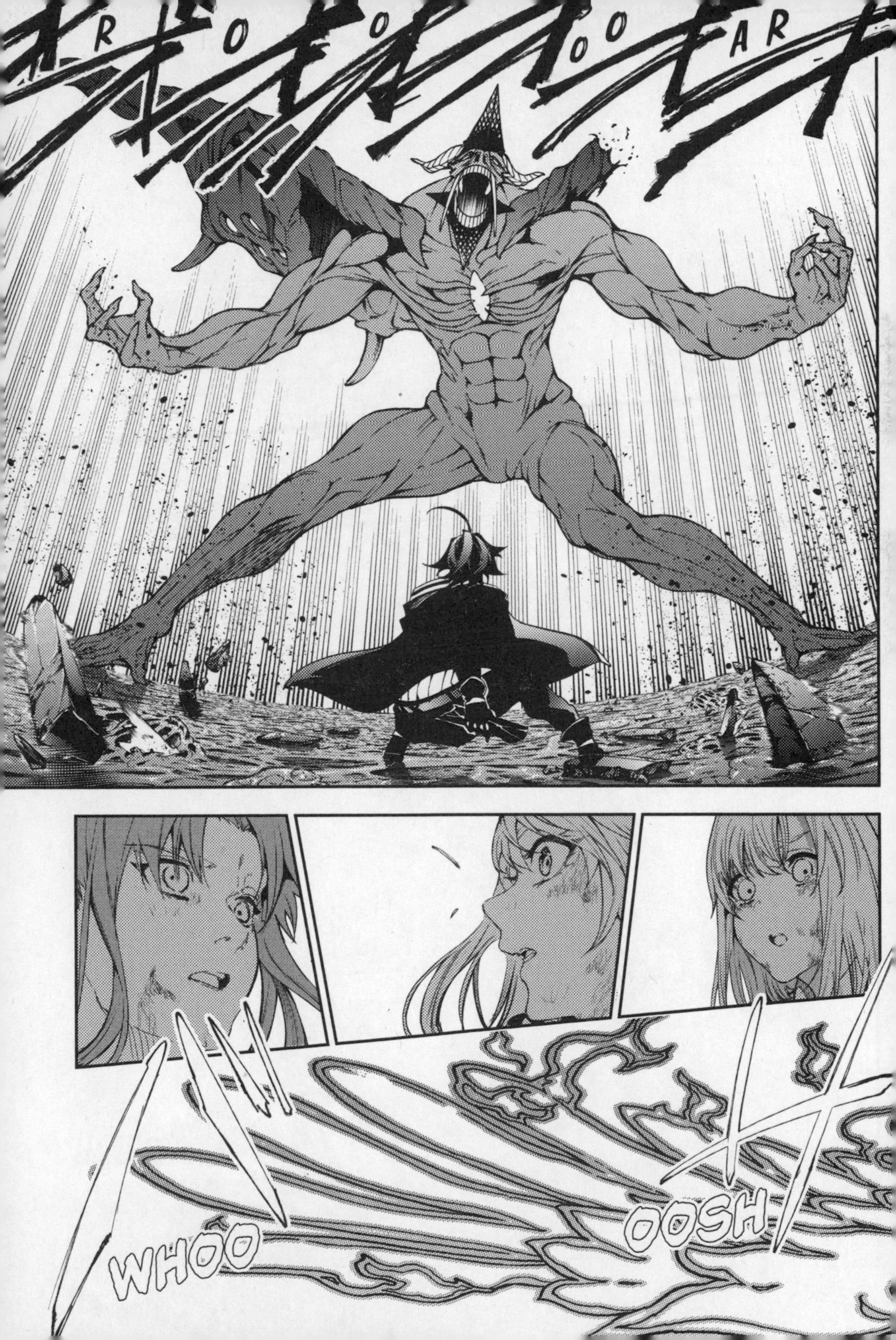
ROOOOAR
WHOO
OOSH

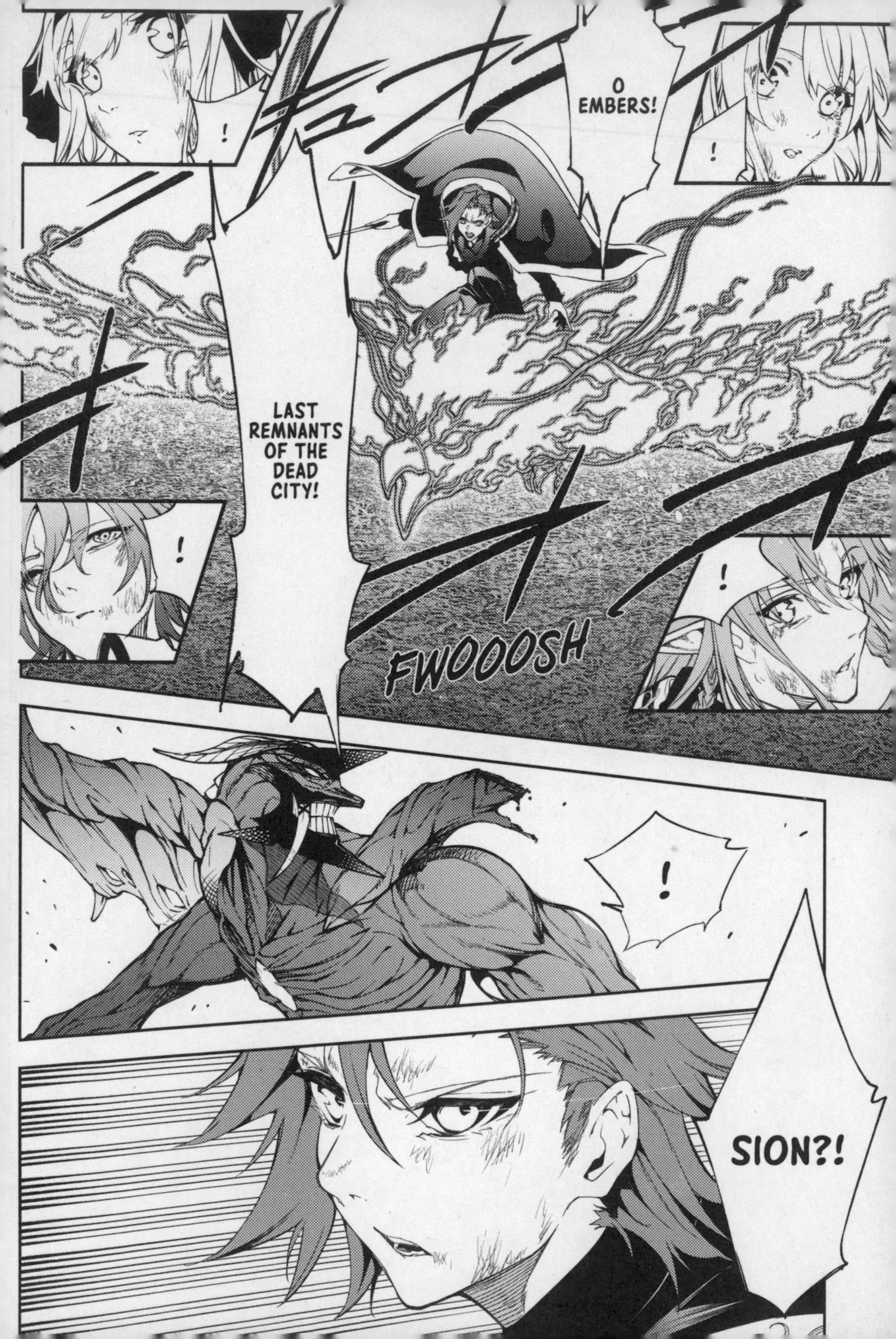
!
O EMBERS!
!
LAST REMNANTS OF THE DEAD CITY!
FWOOOSH
!
!
!
SION?!

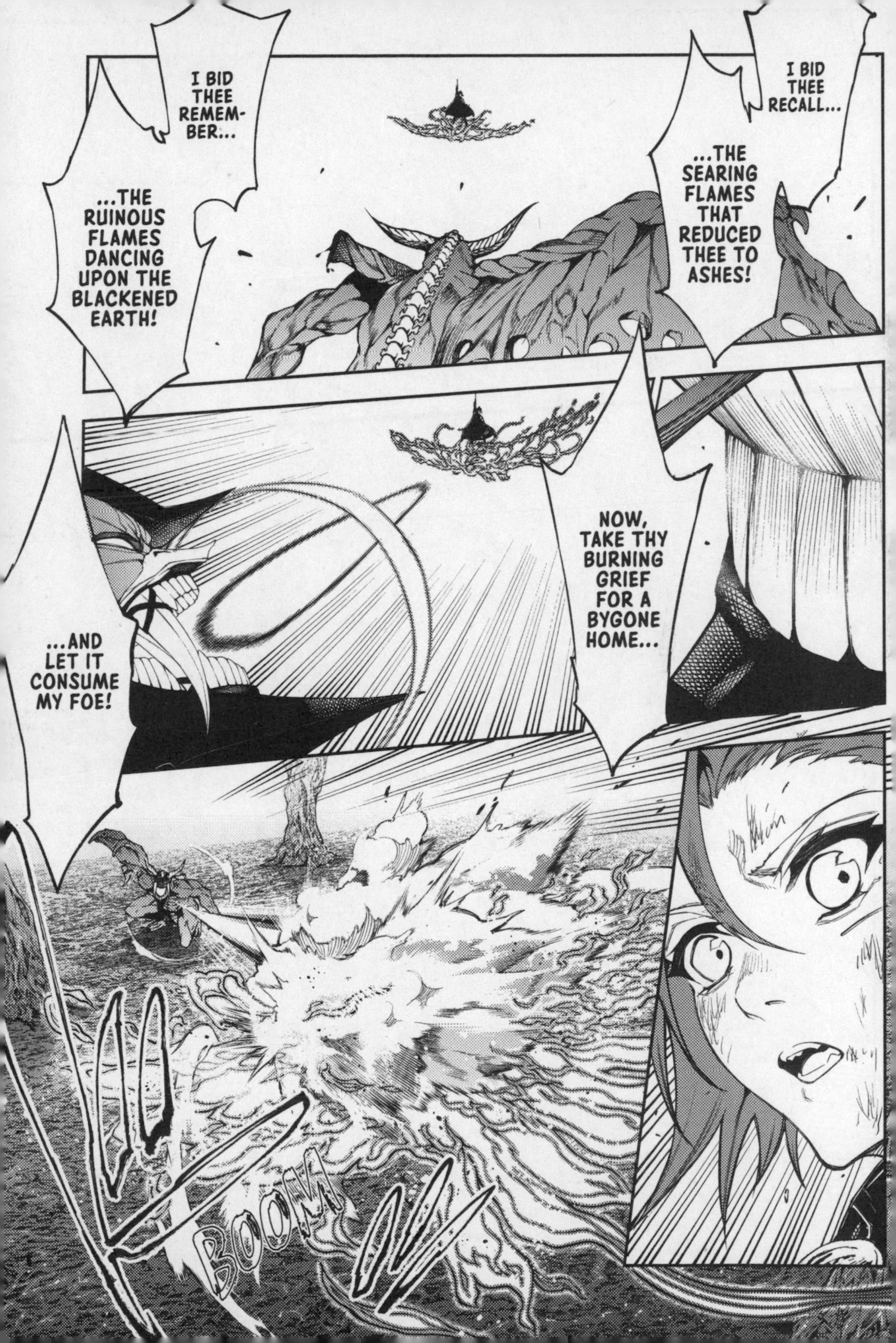
I BID THEE RECALL...
...THE SEARING FLAMES THAT REDUCED THEE TO ASHES!
I BID THEE REMEMBER...
...THE RUINOUS FLAMES DANCING UPON THE BLACKENED EARTH!
NOW, TAKE THY BURNING GRIEF FOR A BYGONE HOME...
...AND LET IT CONSUME MY FOE!
BOOM

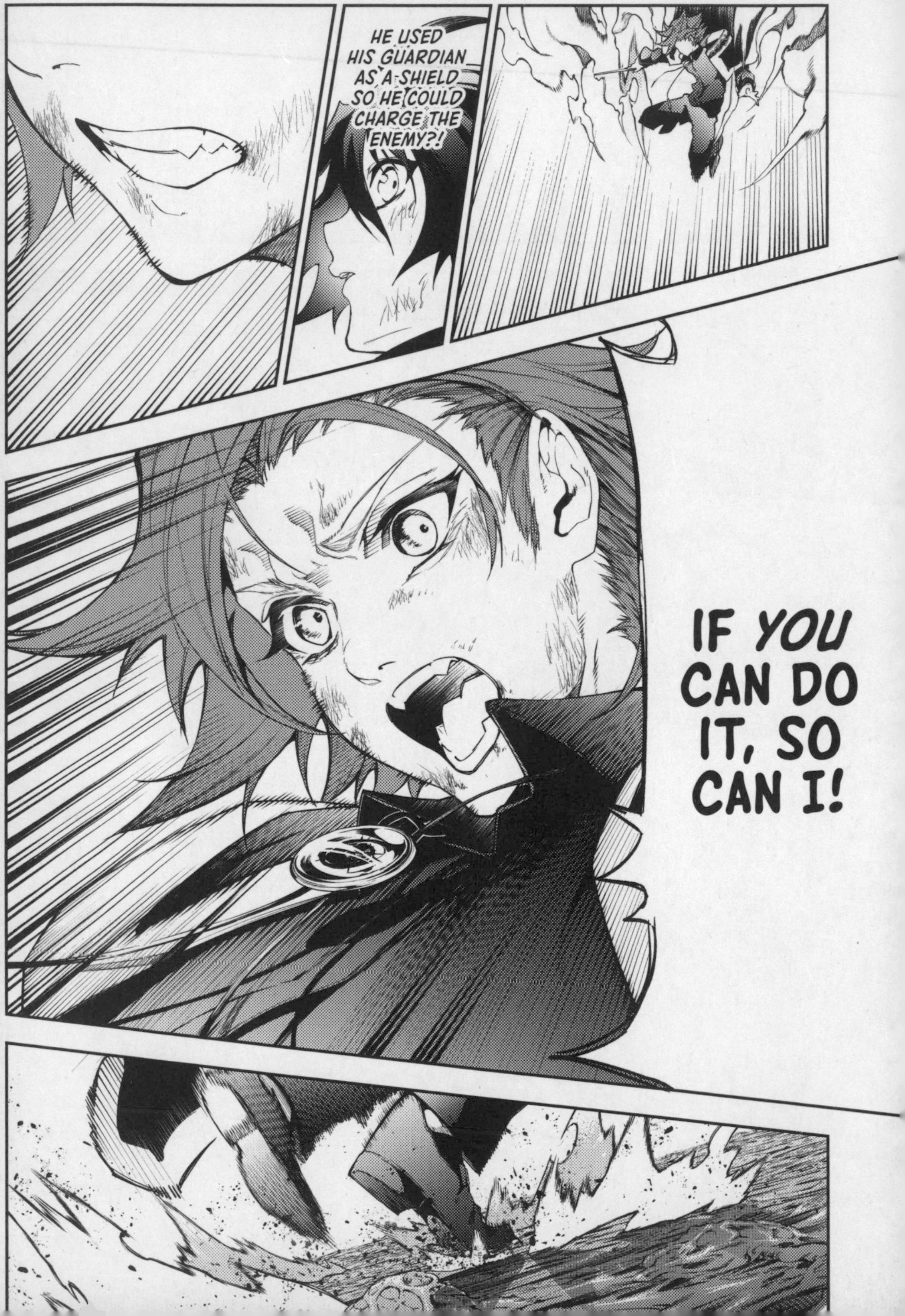
HE USED HIS GUARDIAN AS A SHIELD SO HE COULD CHARGE THE ENEMY?!
IF *YOU* CAN DO IT, SO CAN I!

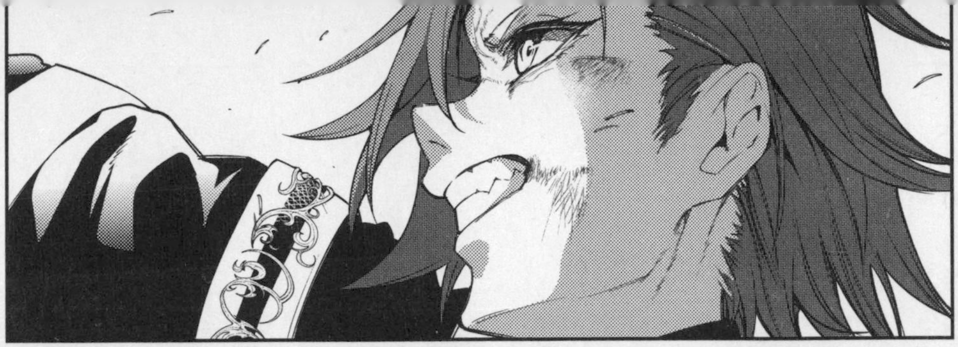

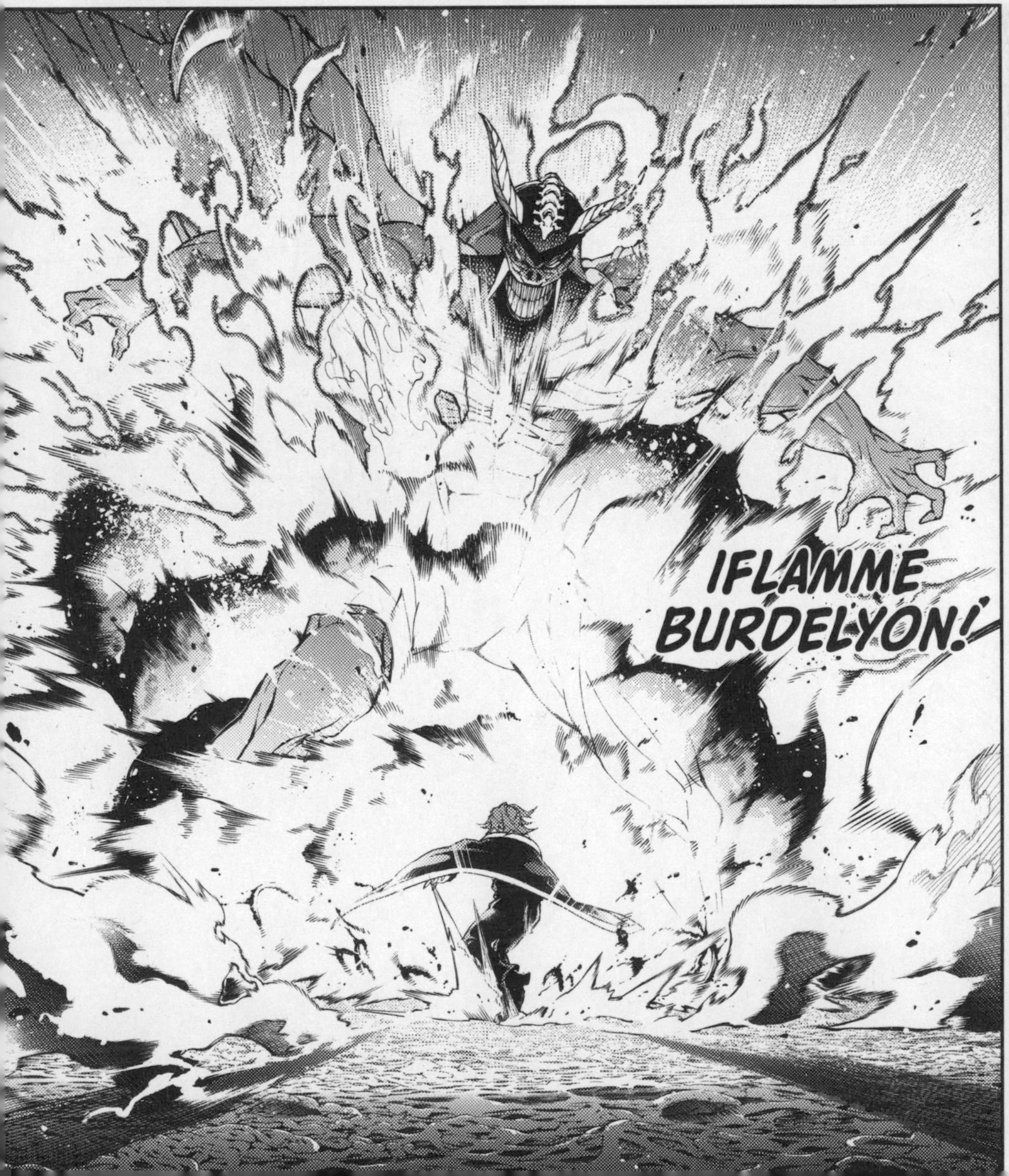
IFLAMME BURDELYON!

Wistoria
Wand and Sword

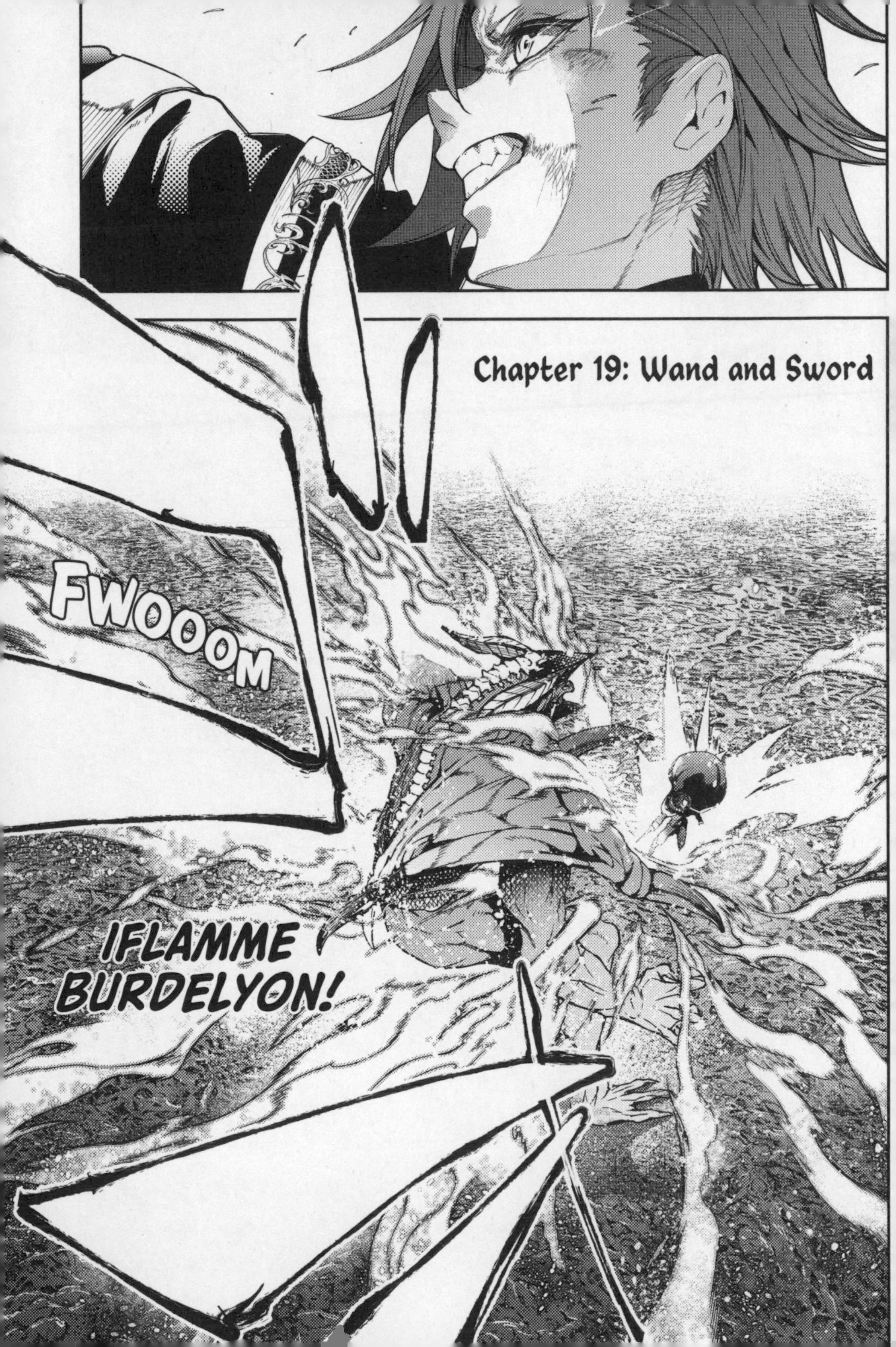
Chapter 19: Wand and Sword
FWOOOM
IFLAMME BURDELYON!

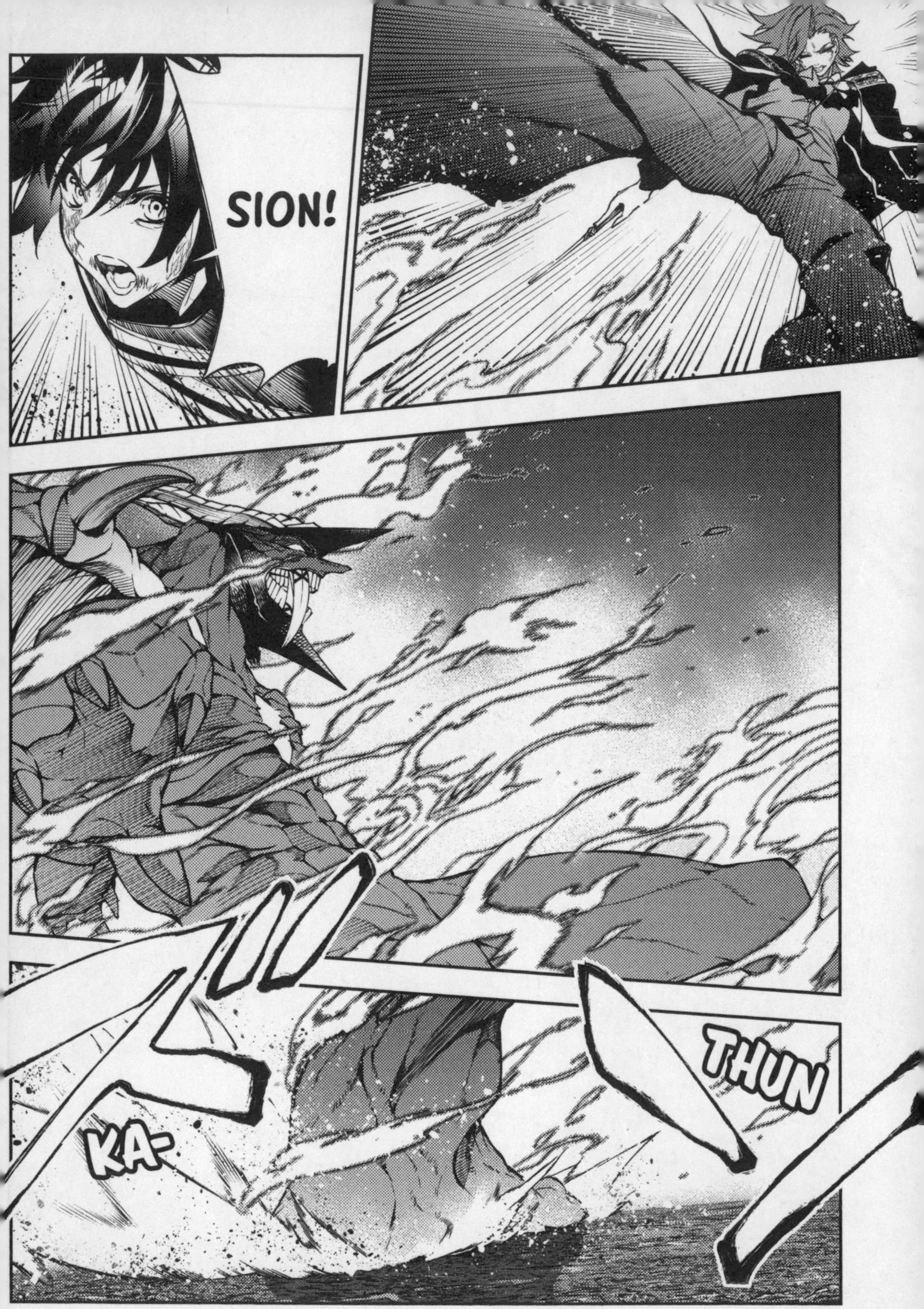
SION!
THUN
KA-

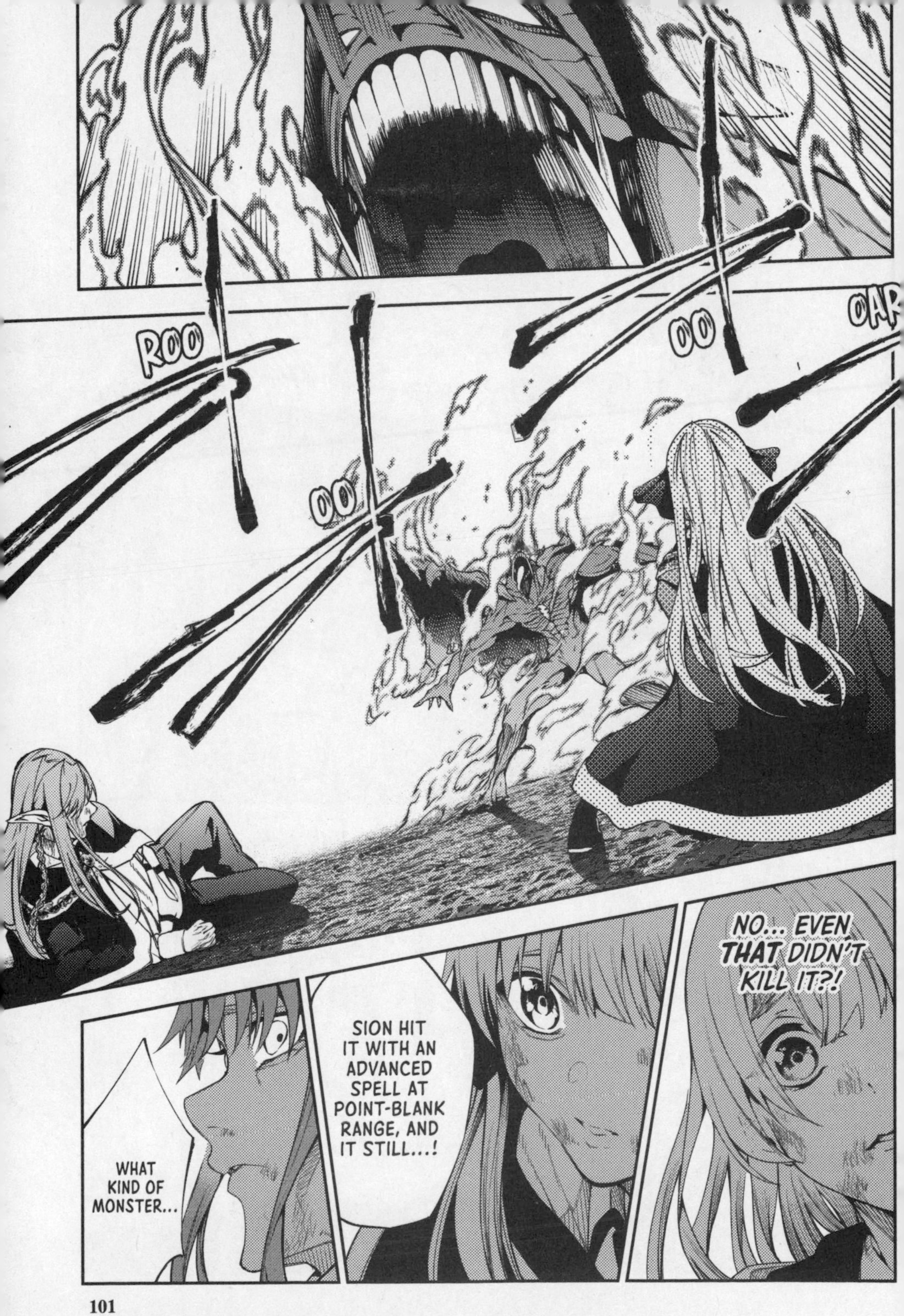
ROO
OO
OO
OAR
NO... EVEN THAT DIDN'T KILL IT?!
SION HIT IT WITH AN ADVANCED SPELL AT POINT-BLANK RANGE, AND IT STILL...!
WHAT KIND OF MONSTER...

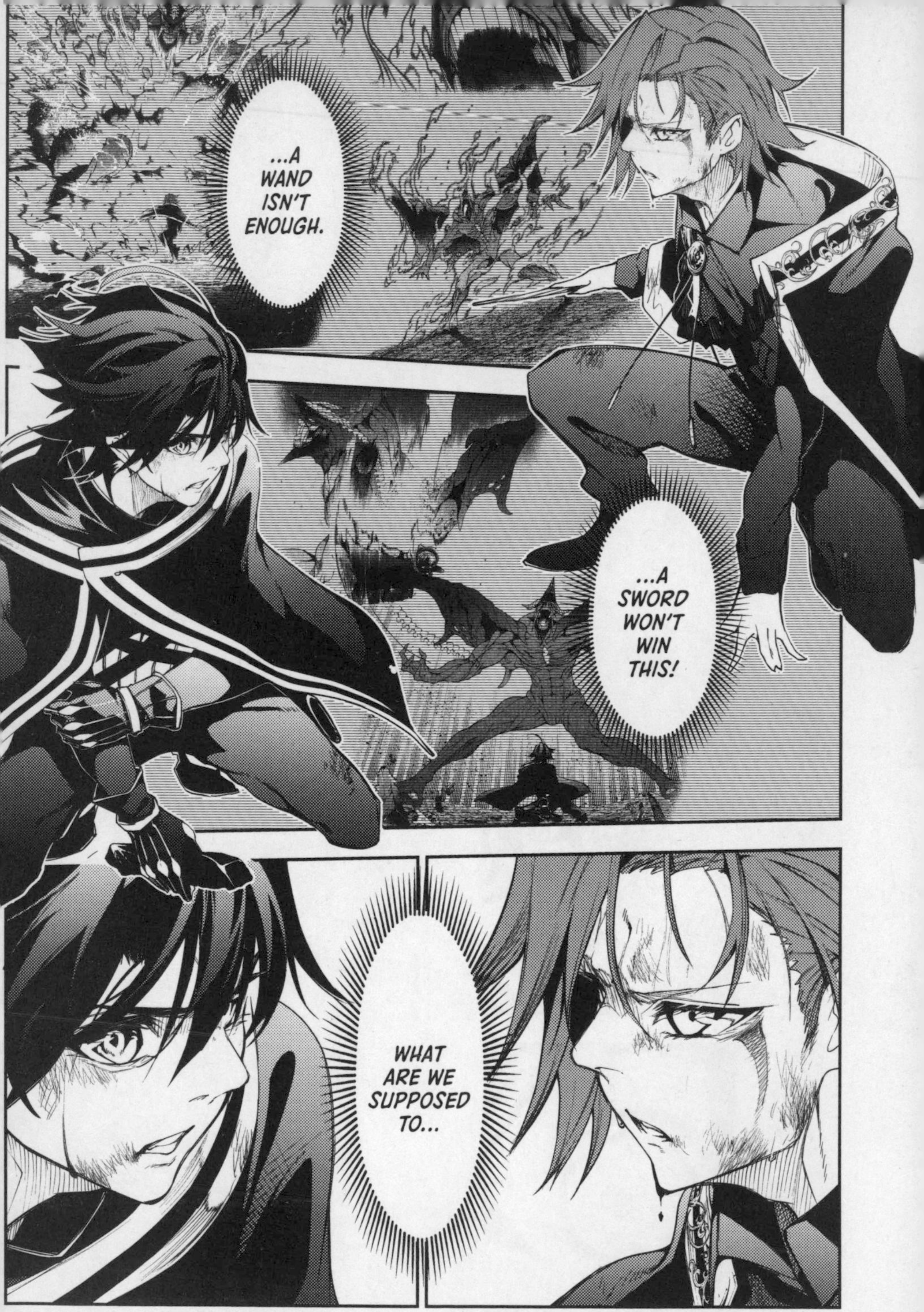
...A WAND ISN'T ENOUGH.
...A SWORD WON'T WIN THIS!
WHAT ARE WE SUPPOSED TO...

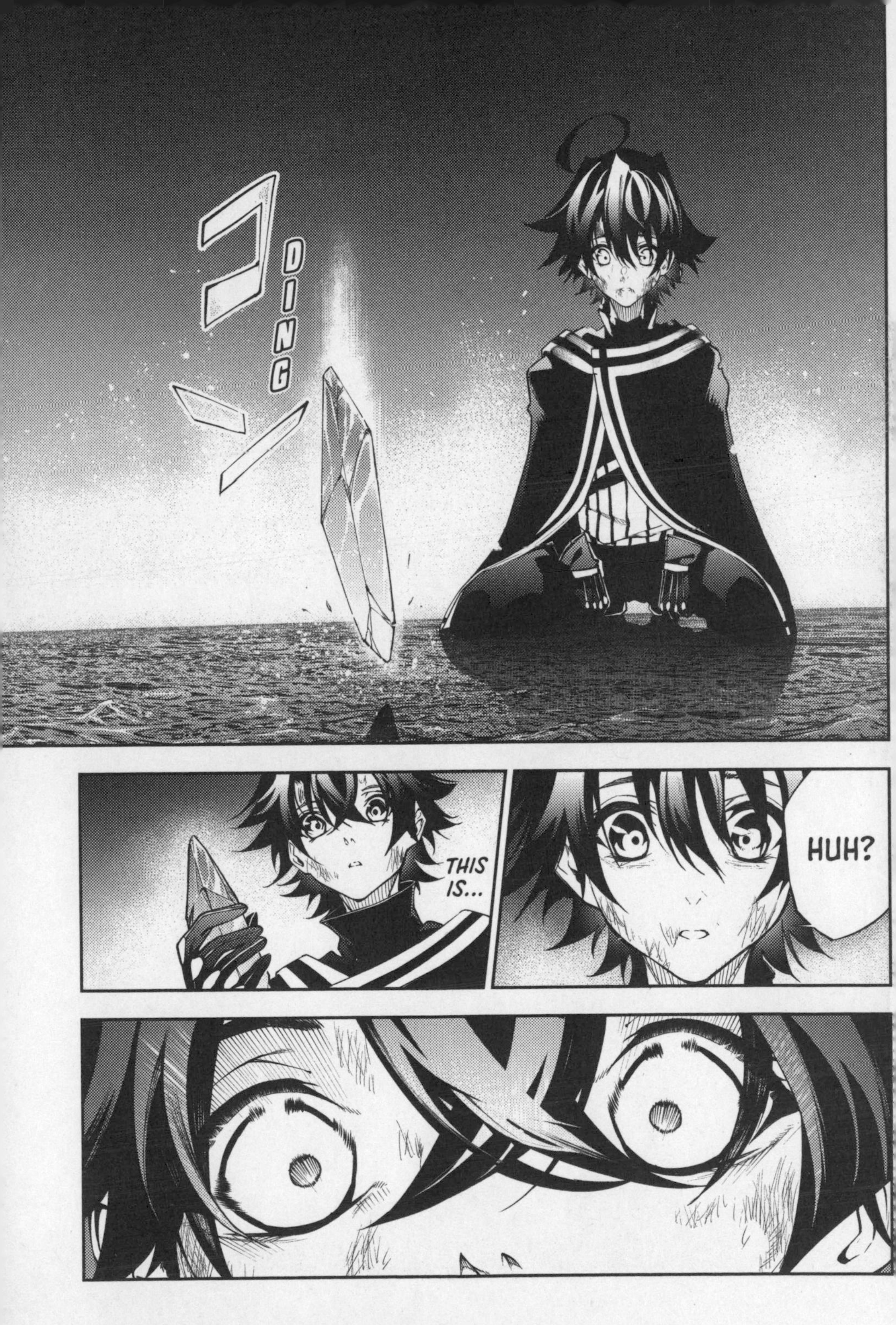
DING
HUH?
THIS IS...

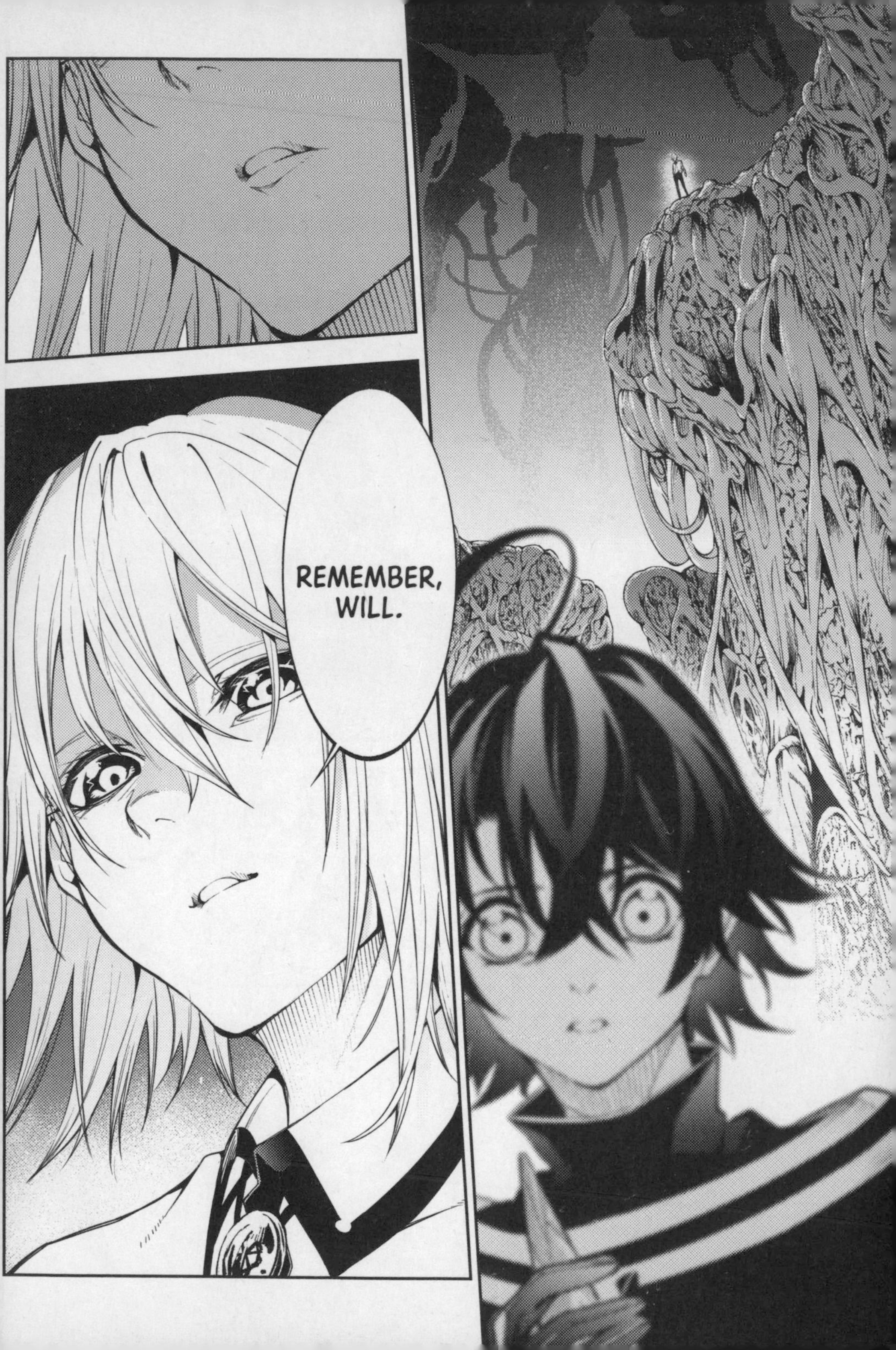
REMEMBER, WILL.

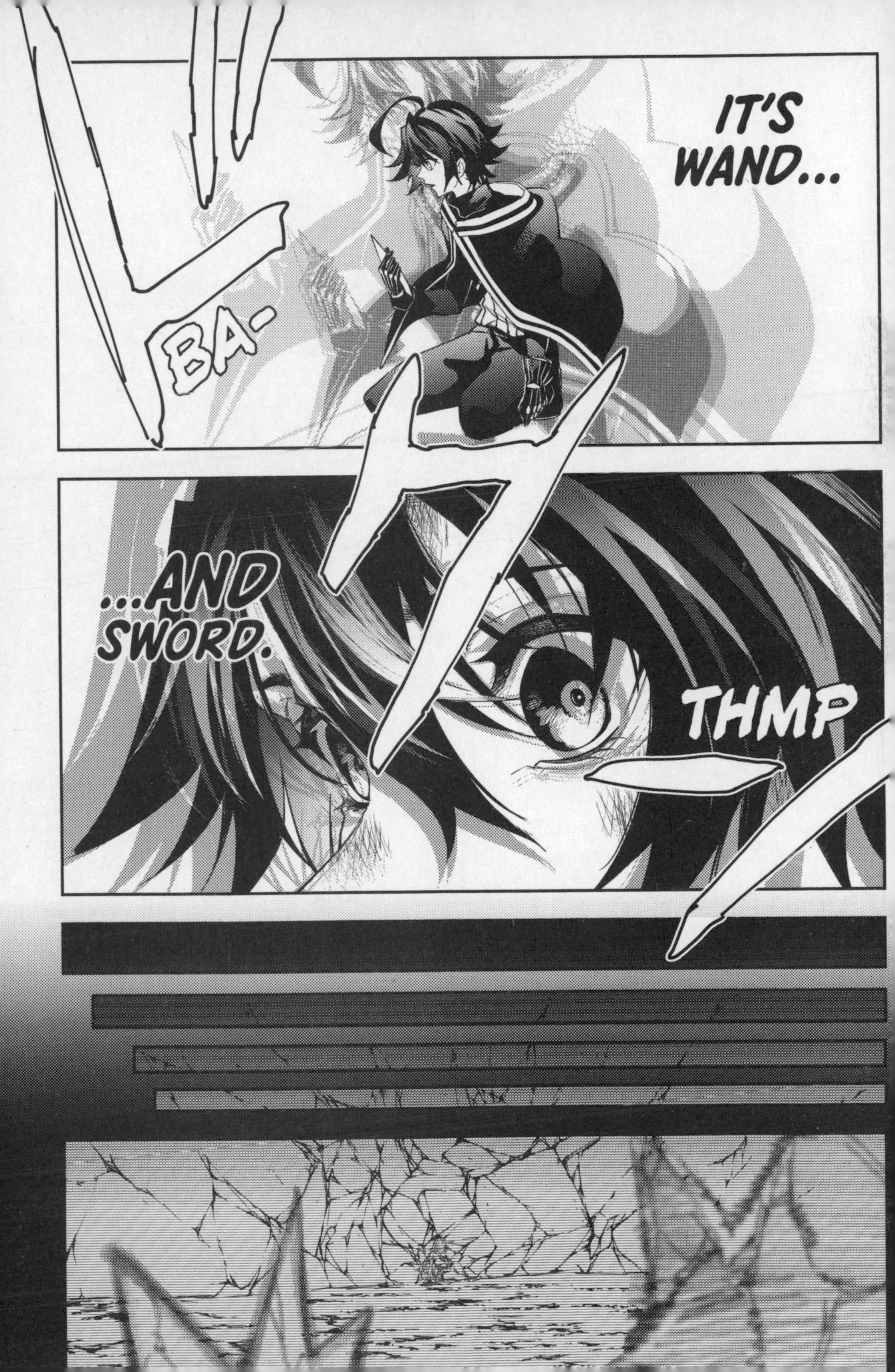
IT'S WAND...
BA-
THMP
...AND SWORD.

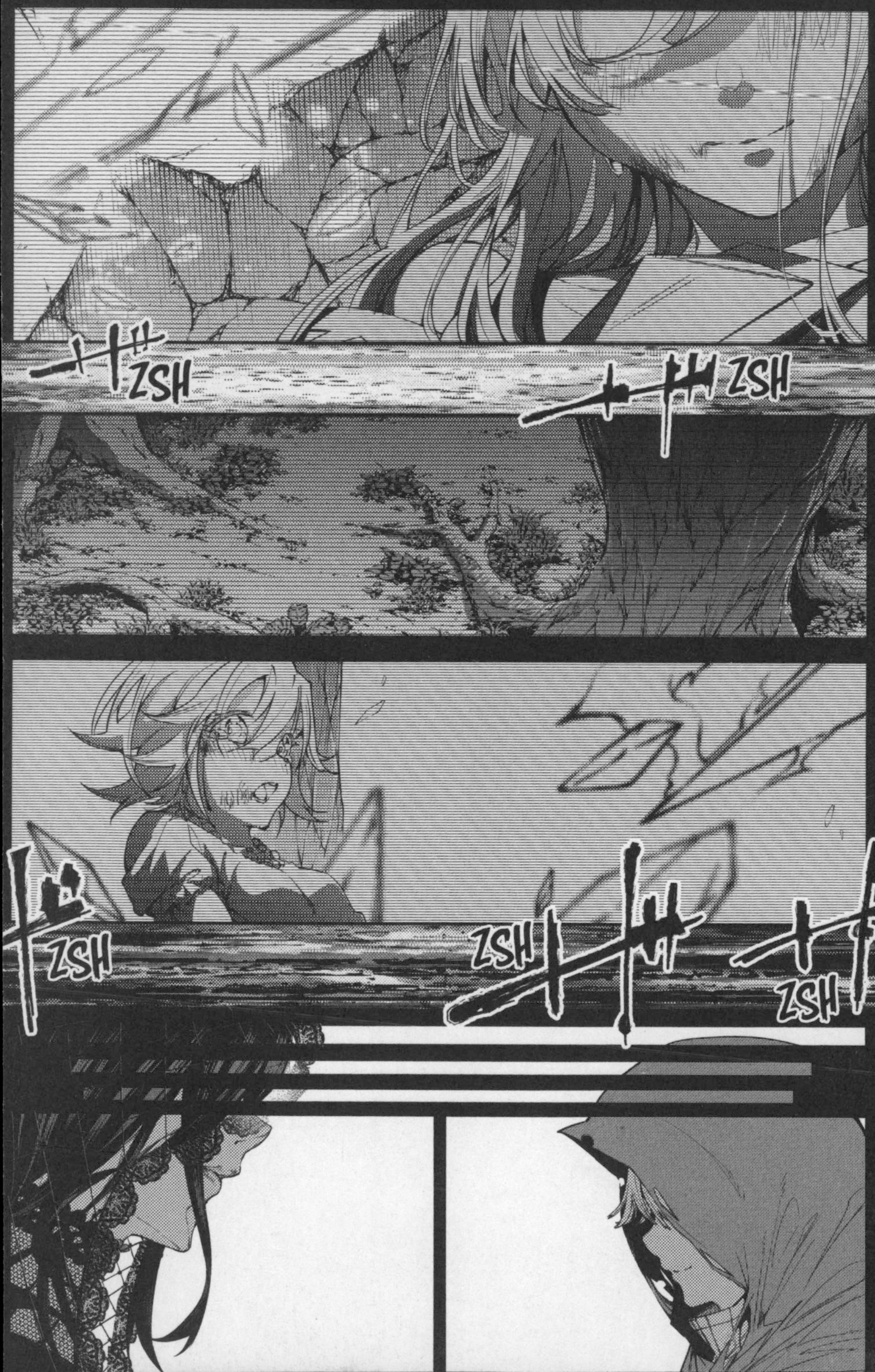
ZSH
ZSH
ZSH
ZSH
ZSH

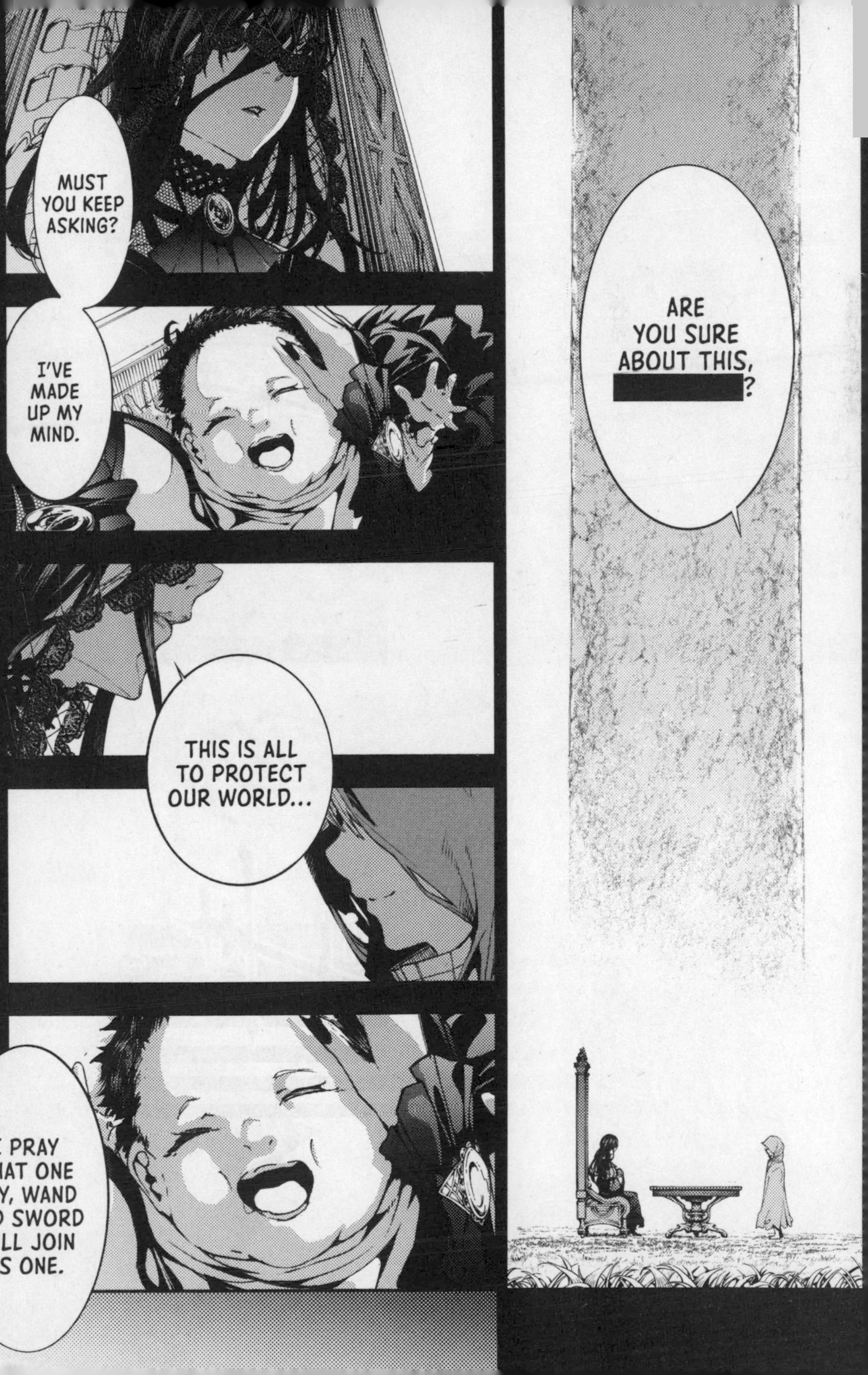
ARE YOU SURE ABOUT THIS, [redacted]?
MUST YOU KEEP ASKING?
I'VE MADE UP MY MIND.
THIS IS ALL TO PROTECT OUR WORLD...
I PRAY THAT ONE DAY, WAND AND SWORD WILL JOIN AS ONE.

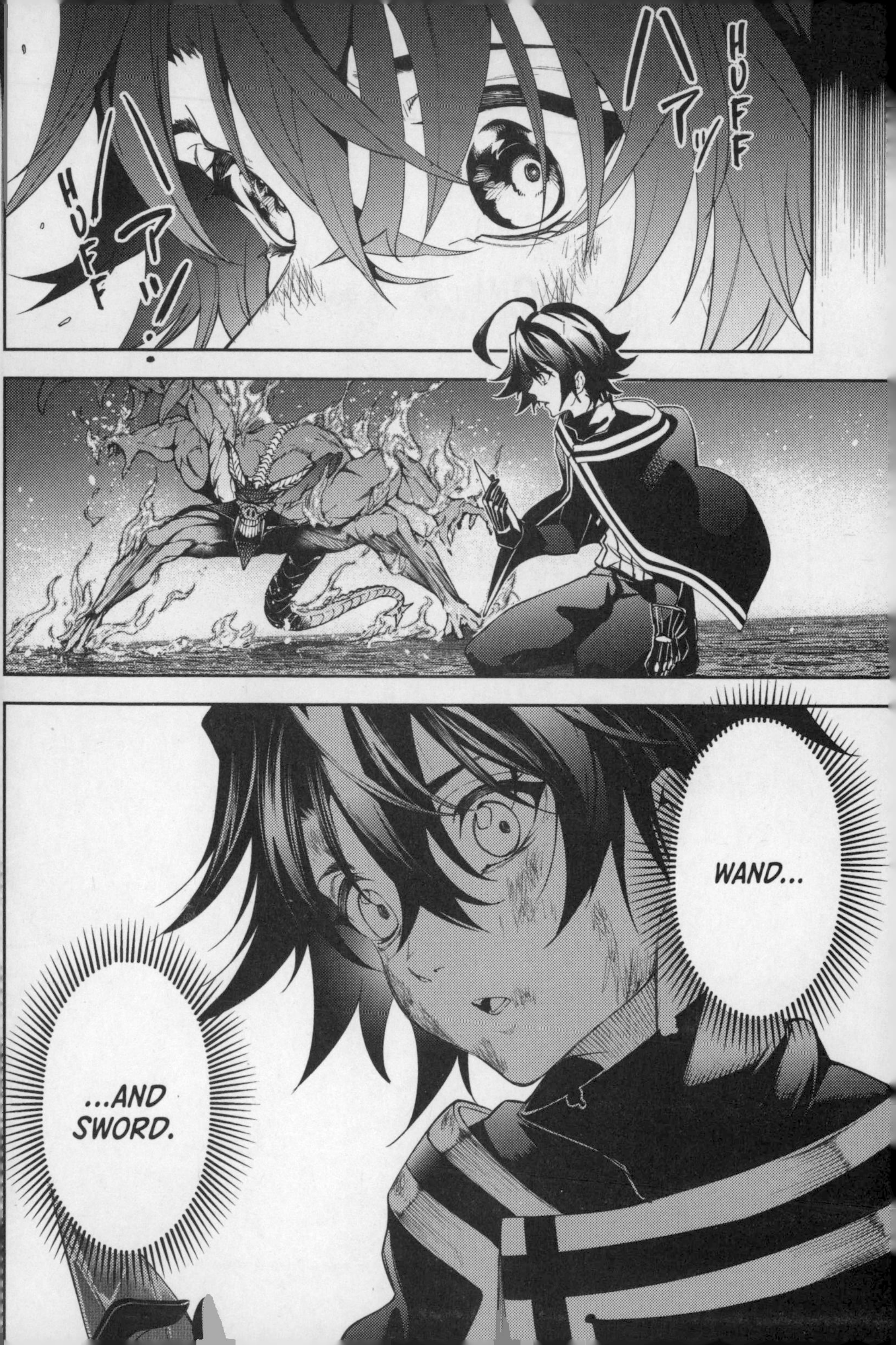

ハアッ
HUFF HUFF
HUFF HUFF
WAND...
...AND SWORD.

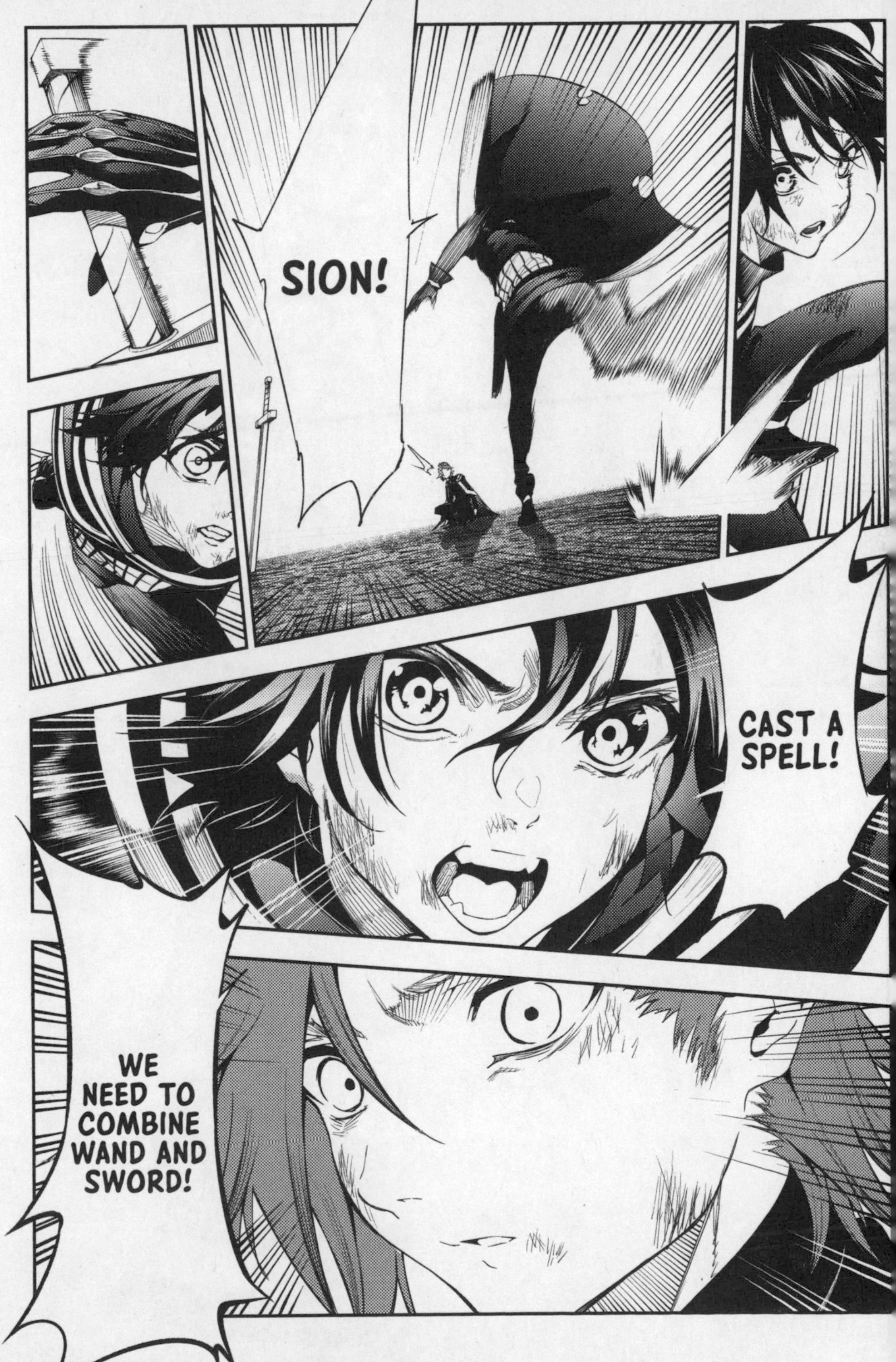
SION!
CAST A SPELL!
WE NEED TO COMBINE WAND AND SWORD!

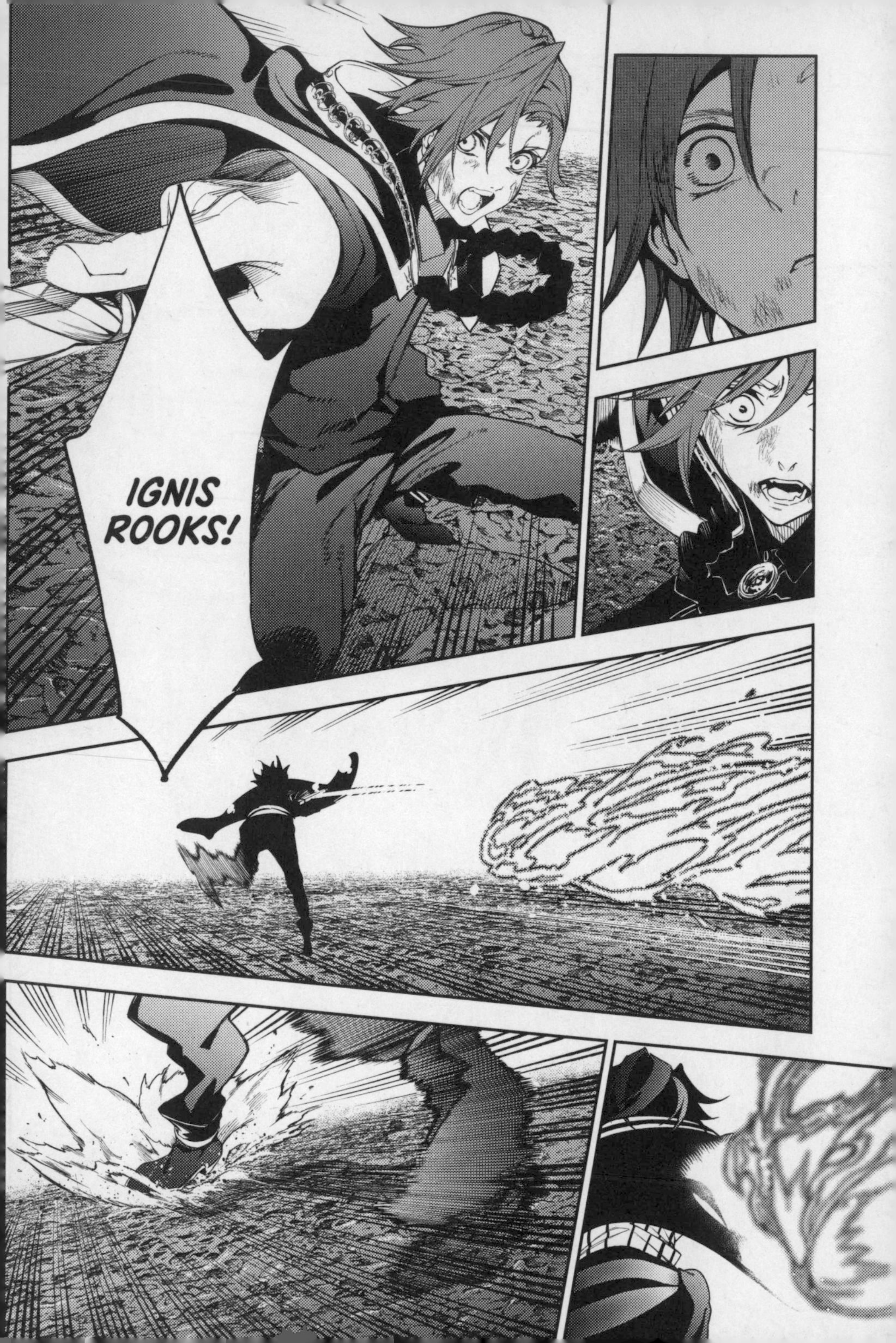
IGNIS ROOKS!

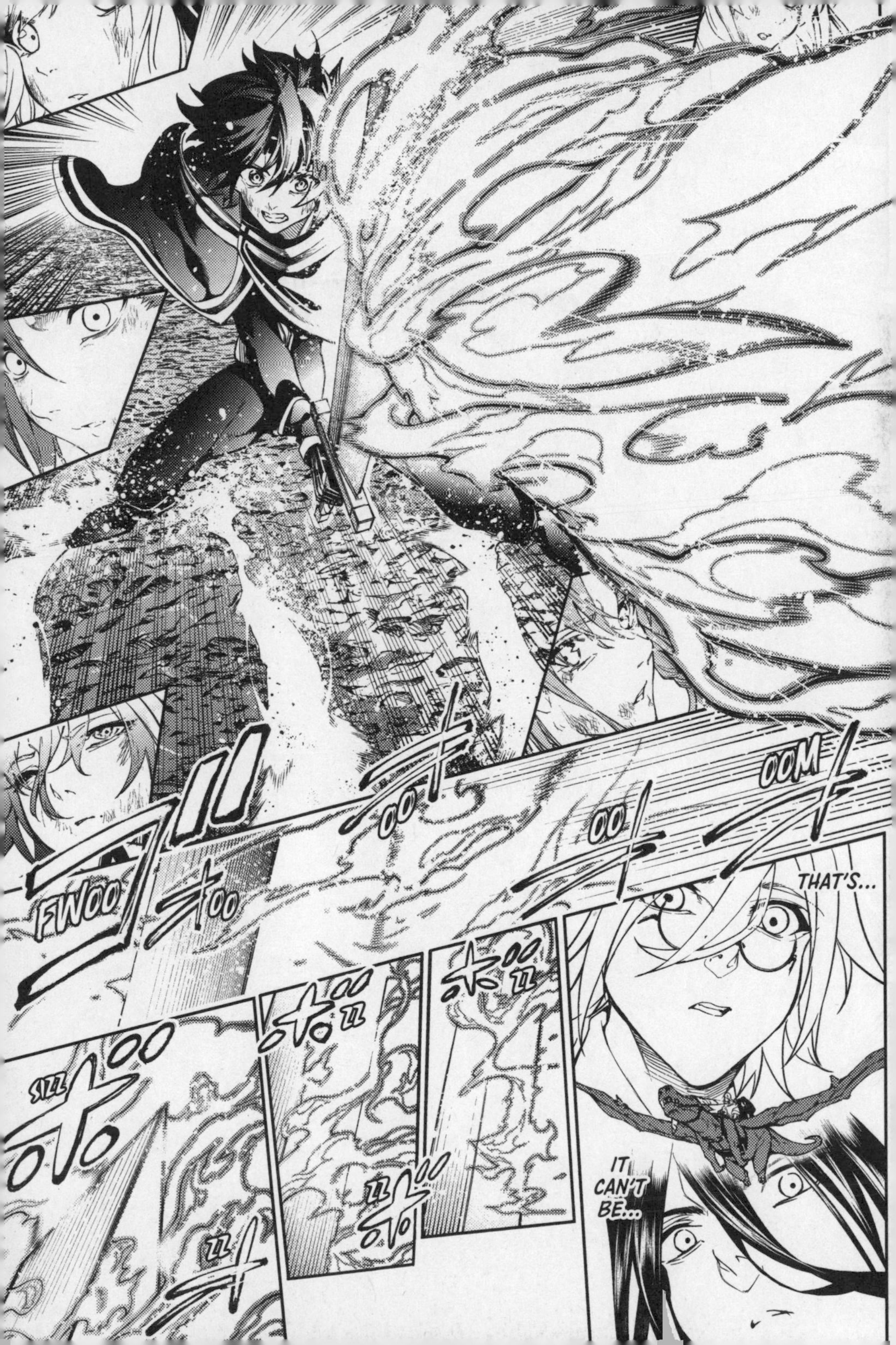
FWOO
OO
OO
OOM
THAT'S...
IT CAN'T BE...
ZZ
ZZ
SIZZ
ZZ

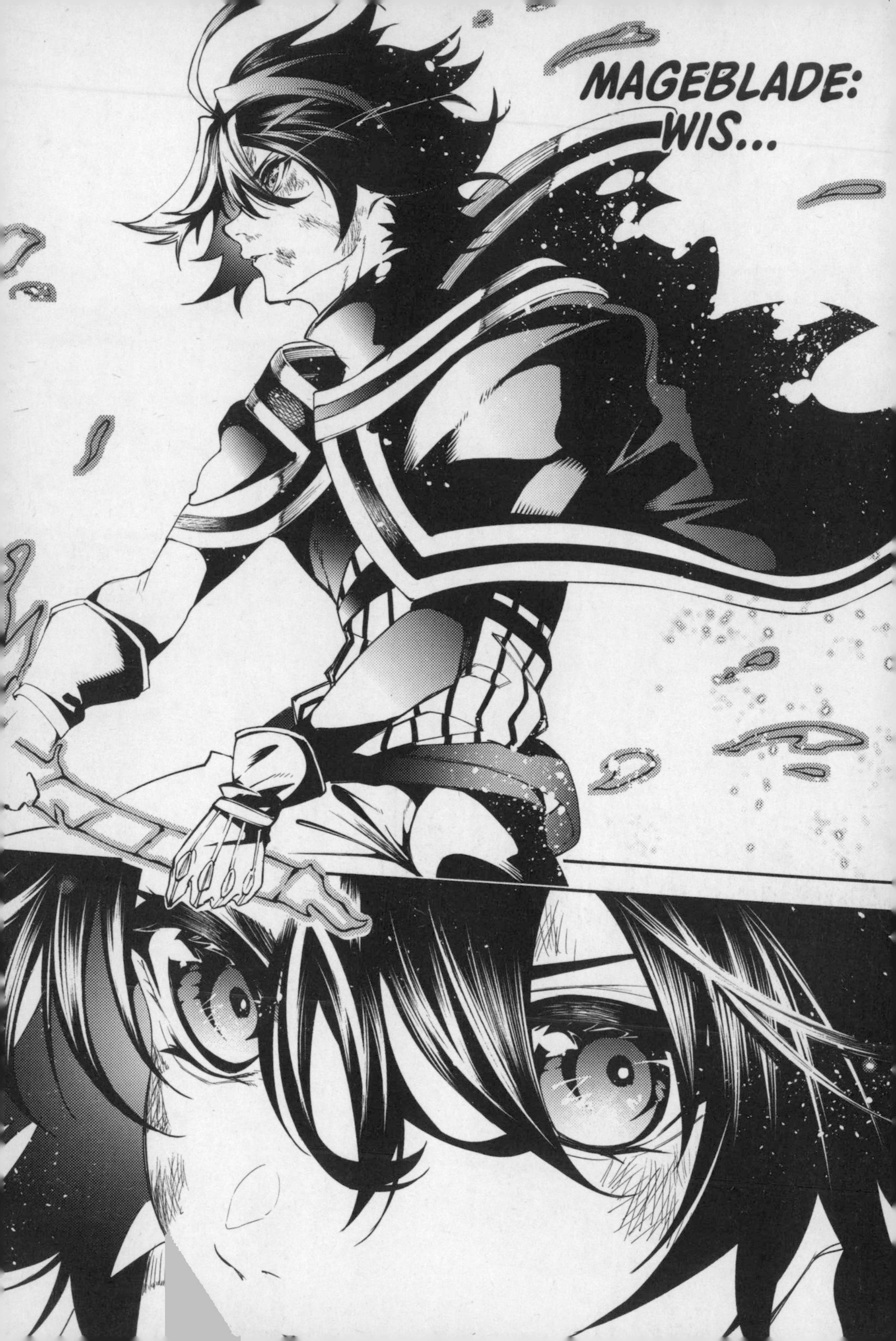
MAGEBLADE: WIS...

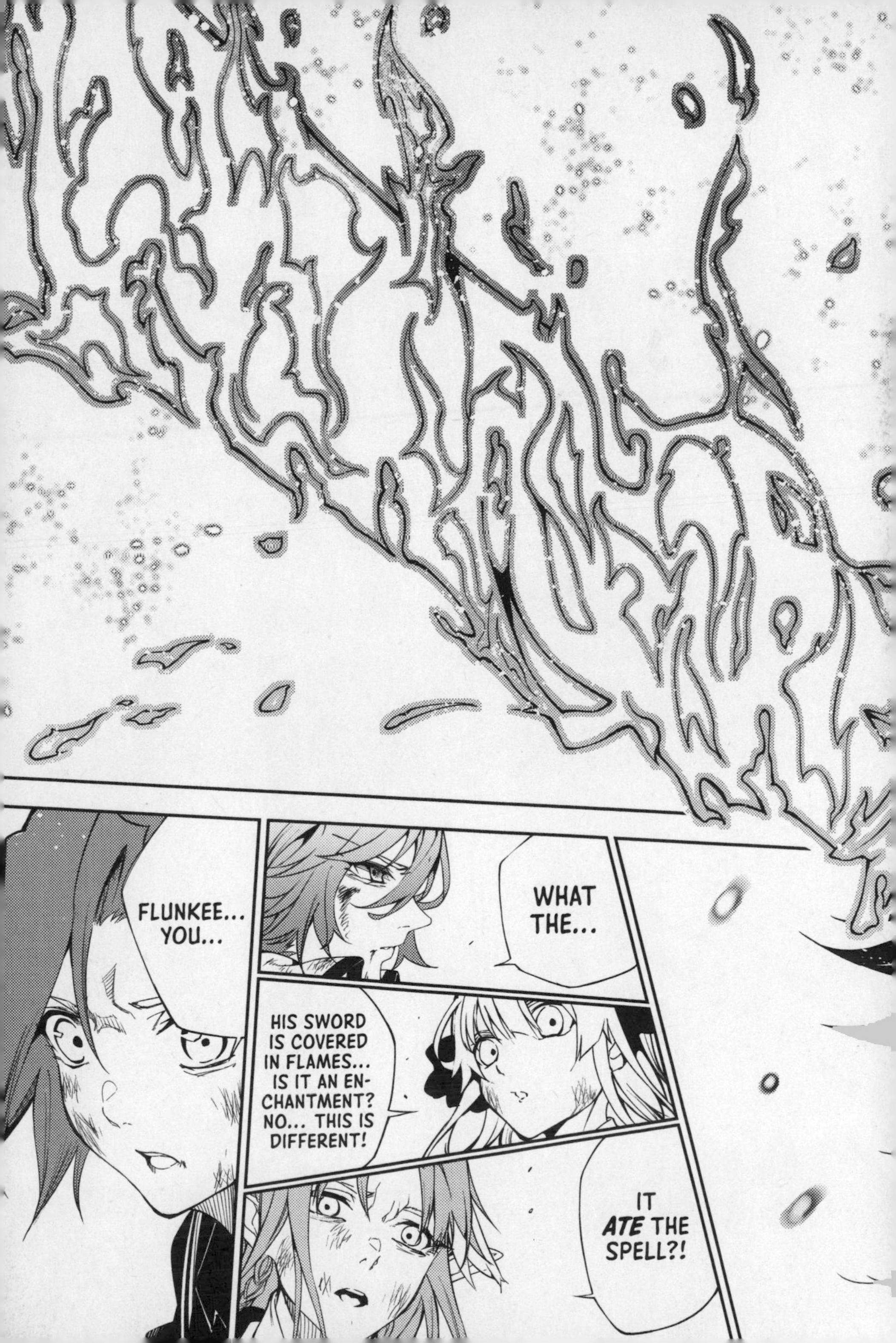
WHAT THE...
HIS SWORD IS COVERED IN FLAMES... IS IT AN EN-CHANTMENT? NO... THIS IS DIFFERENT!
IT ATE THE SPELL?!
FLUNKEE... YOU...

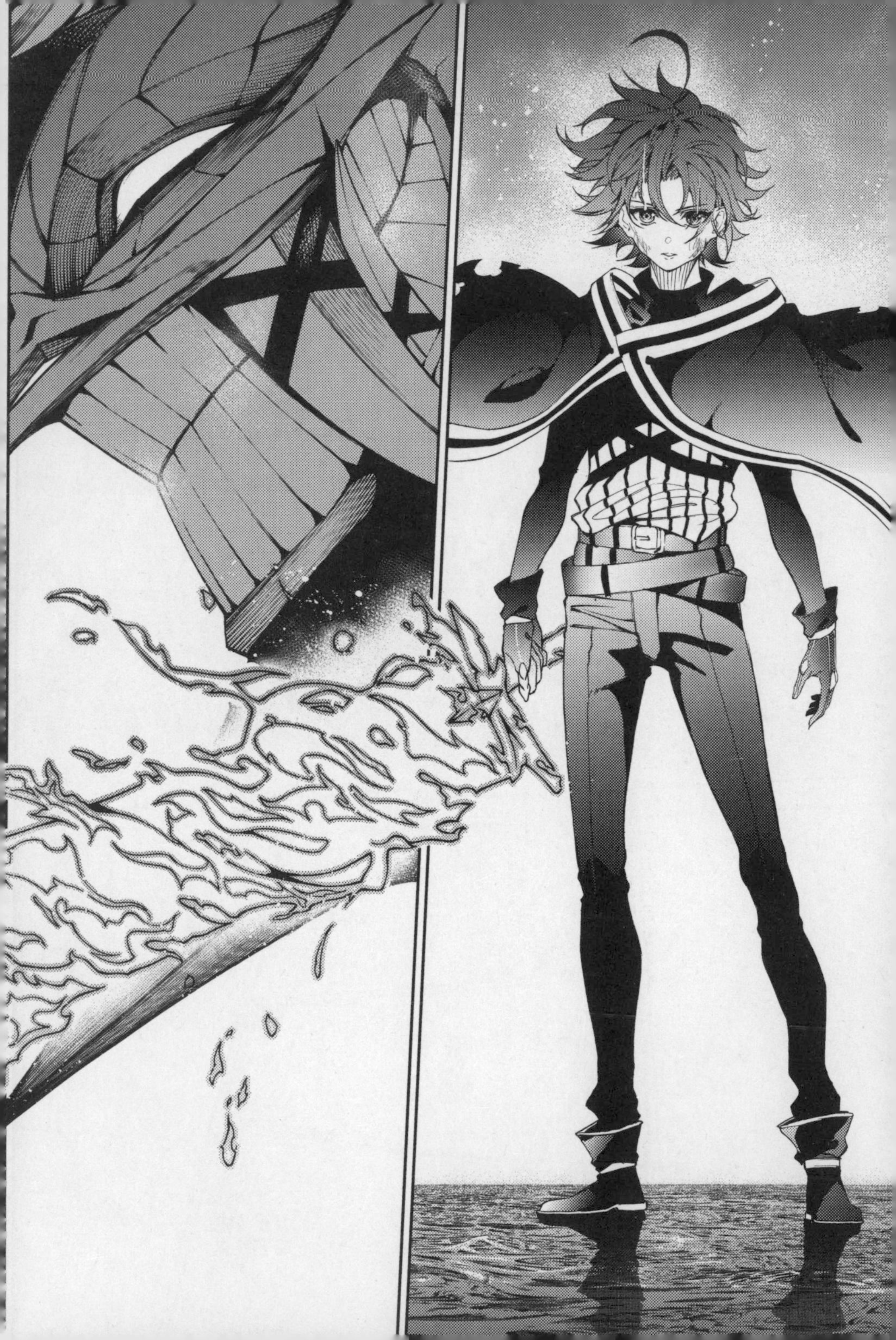

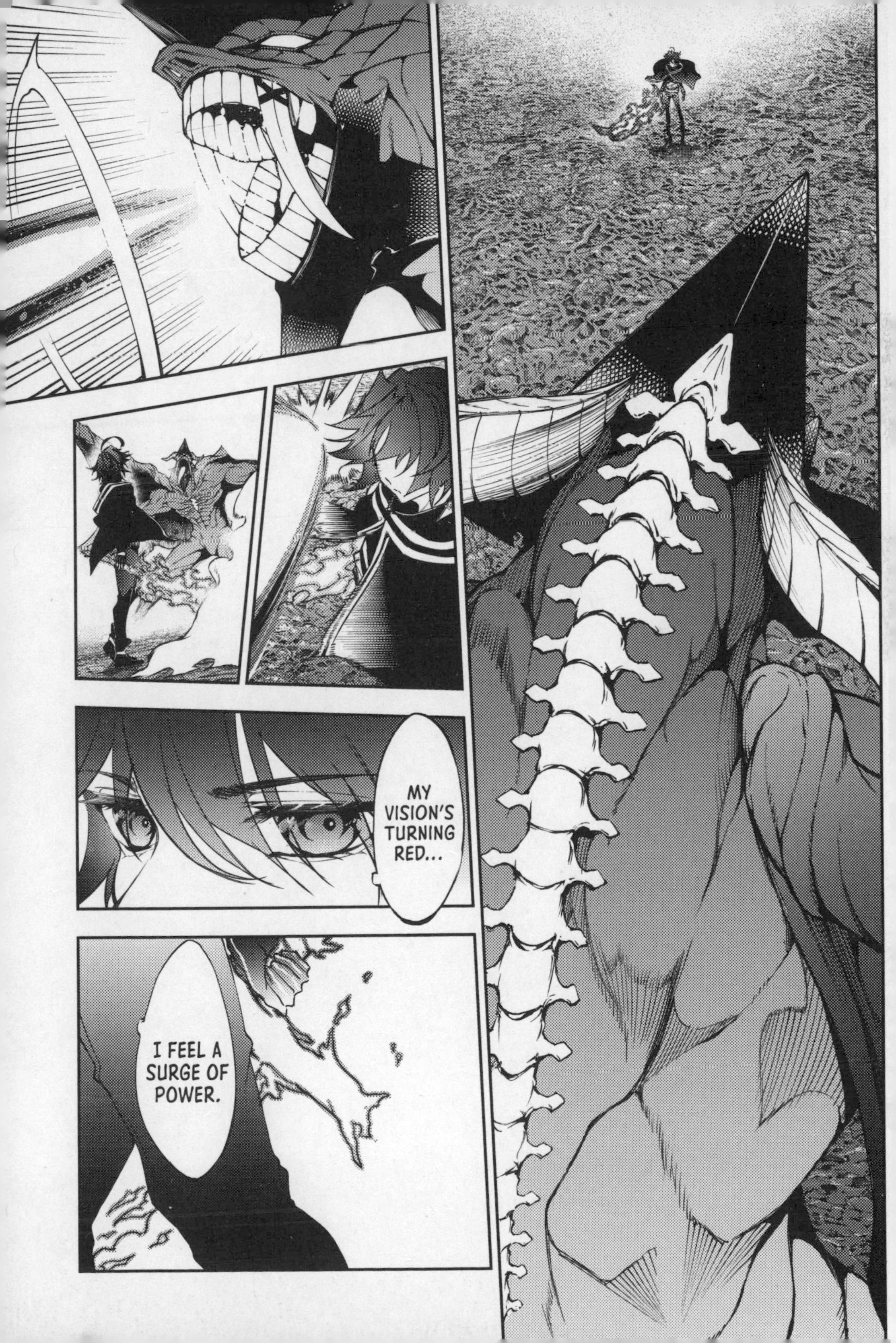
MY VISION'S TURNING RED...
I FEEL A SURGE OF POWER.

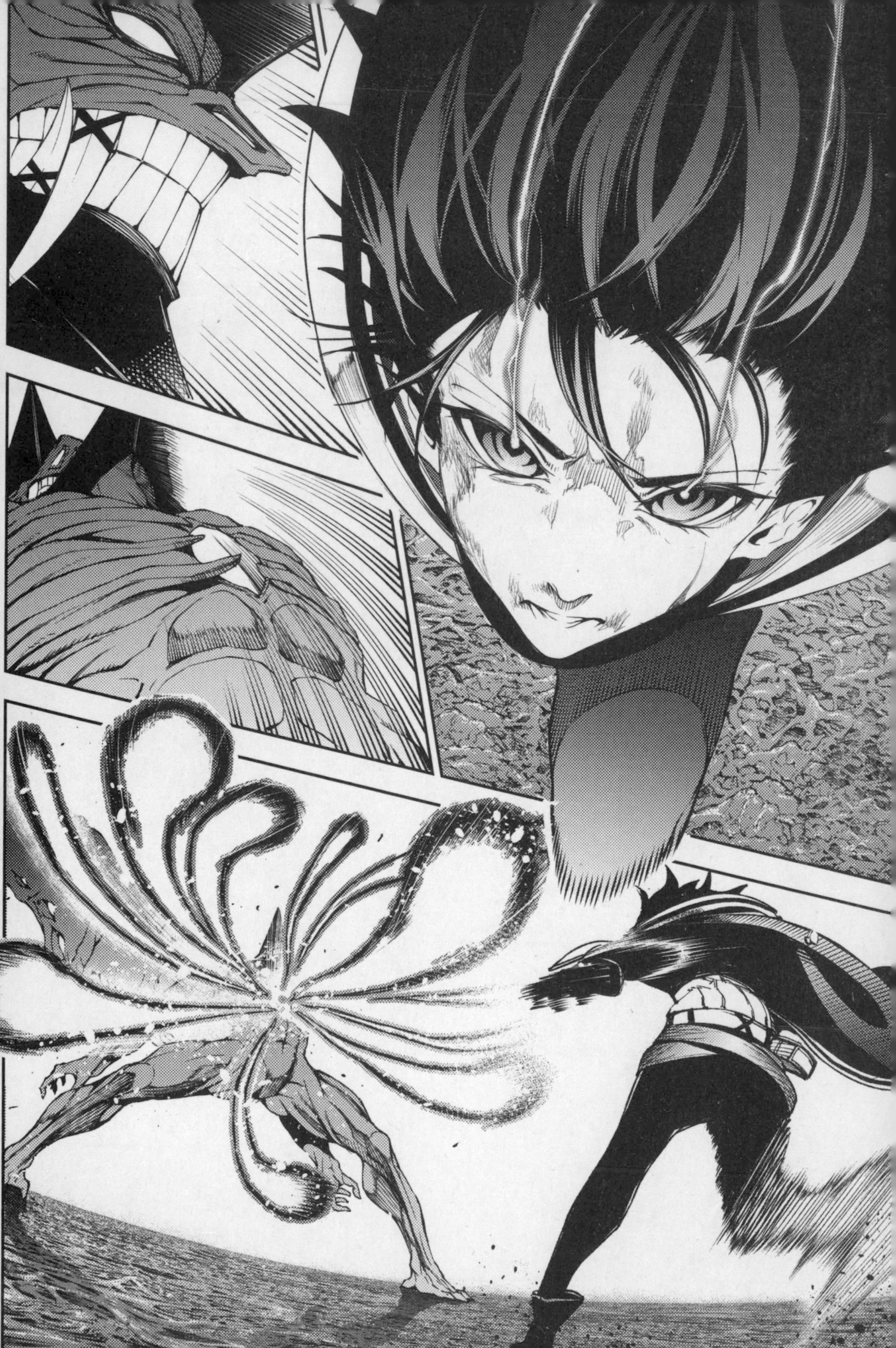

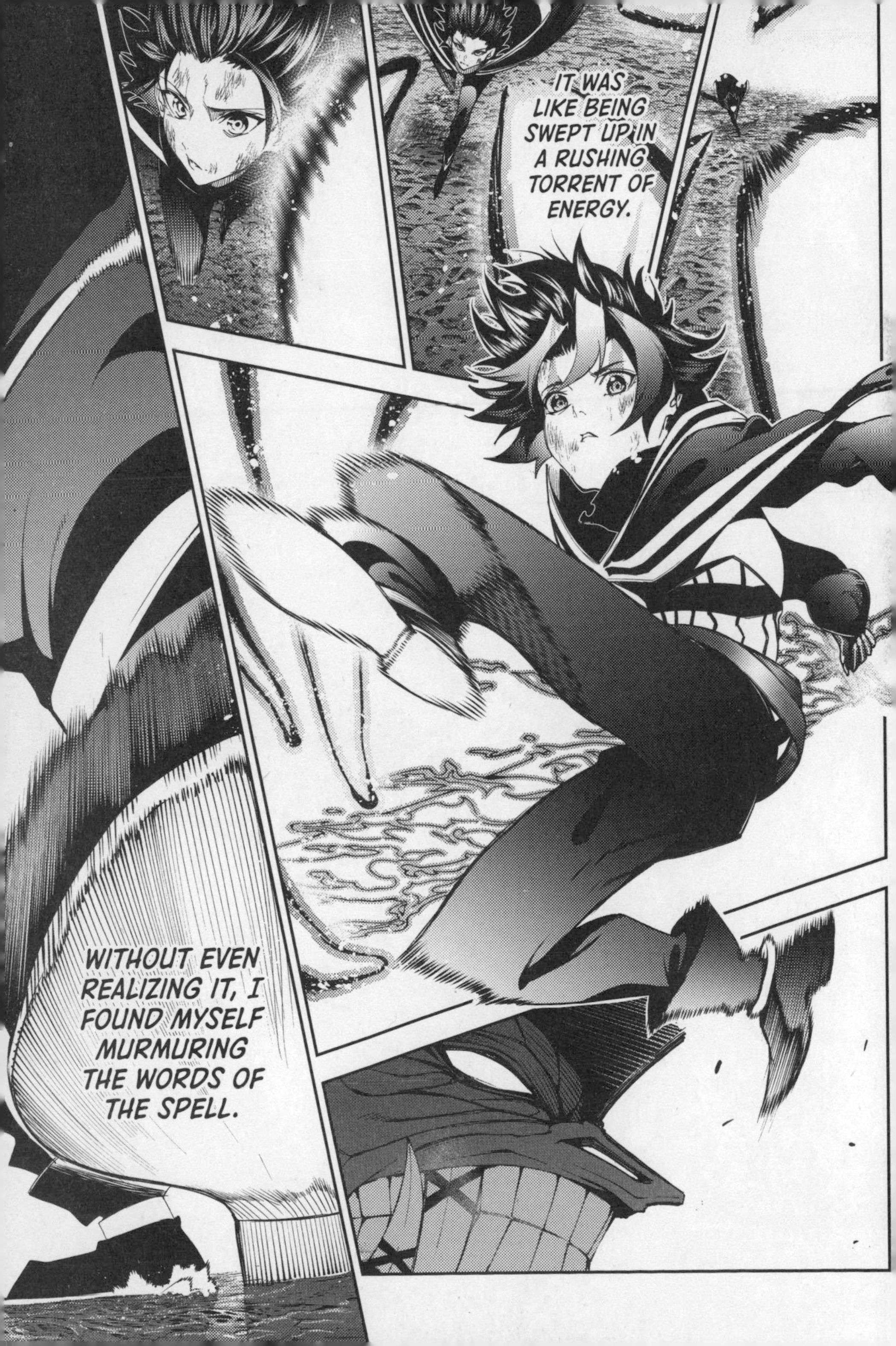
IT WAS LIKE BEING SWEPT UP IN A RUSHING TORRENT OF ENERGY.
WITHOUT EVEN REALIZING IT, I FOUND MYSELF MURMURING THE WORDS OF THE SPELL.

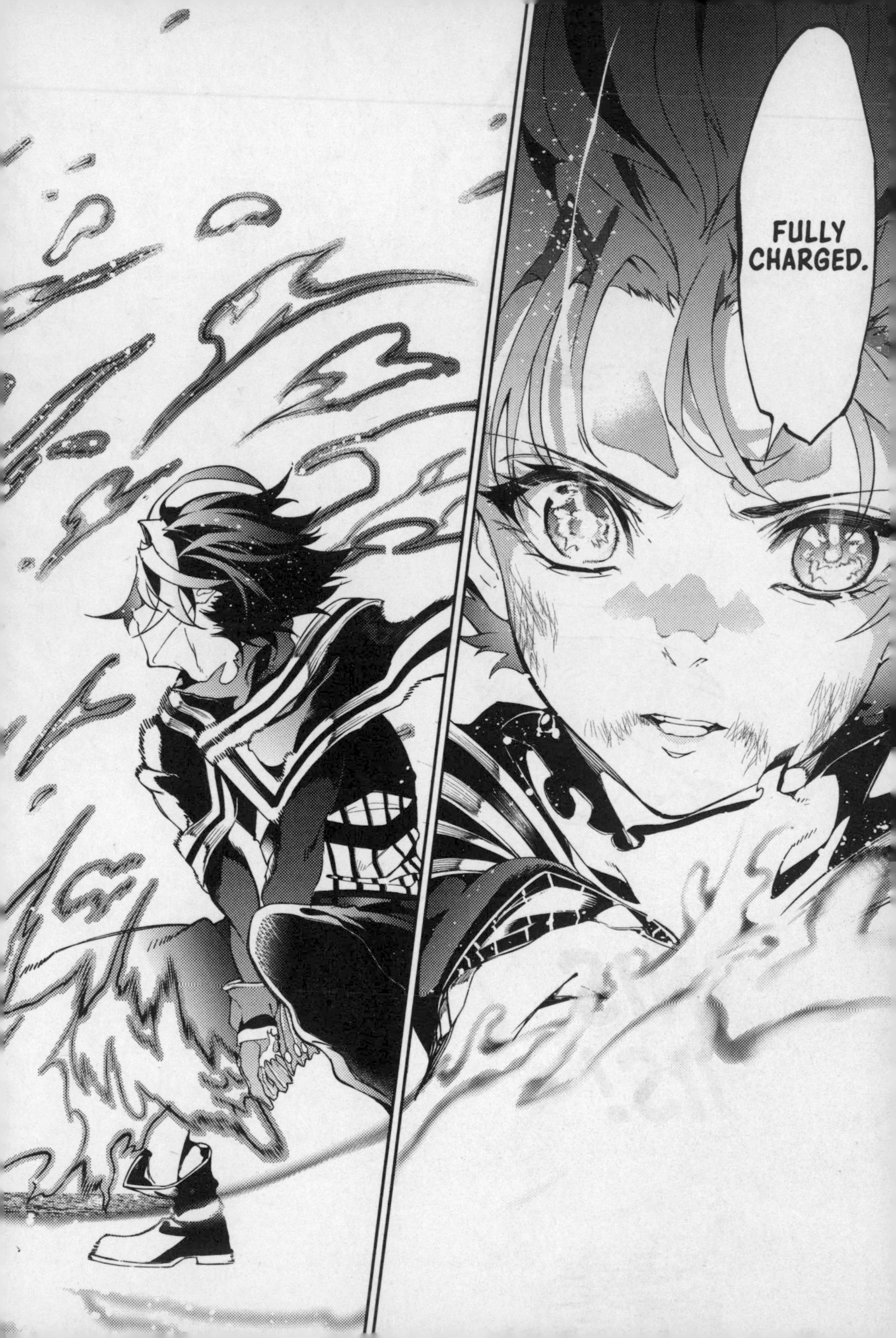
FULLY CHARGED.

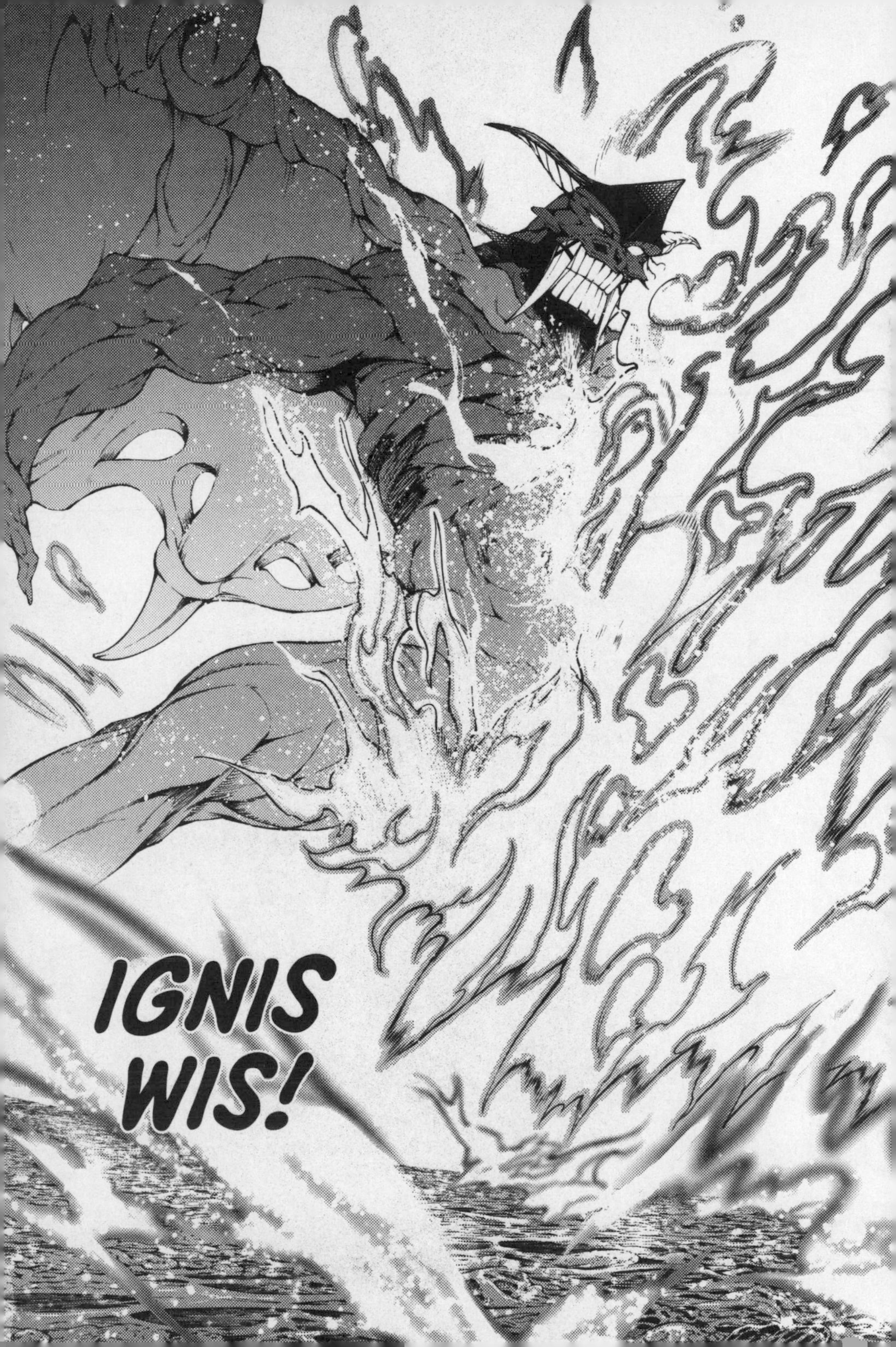
IGNIS WIS!

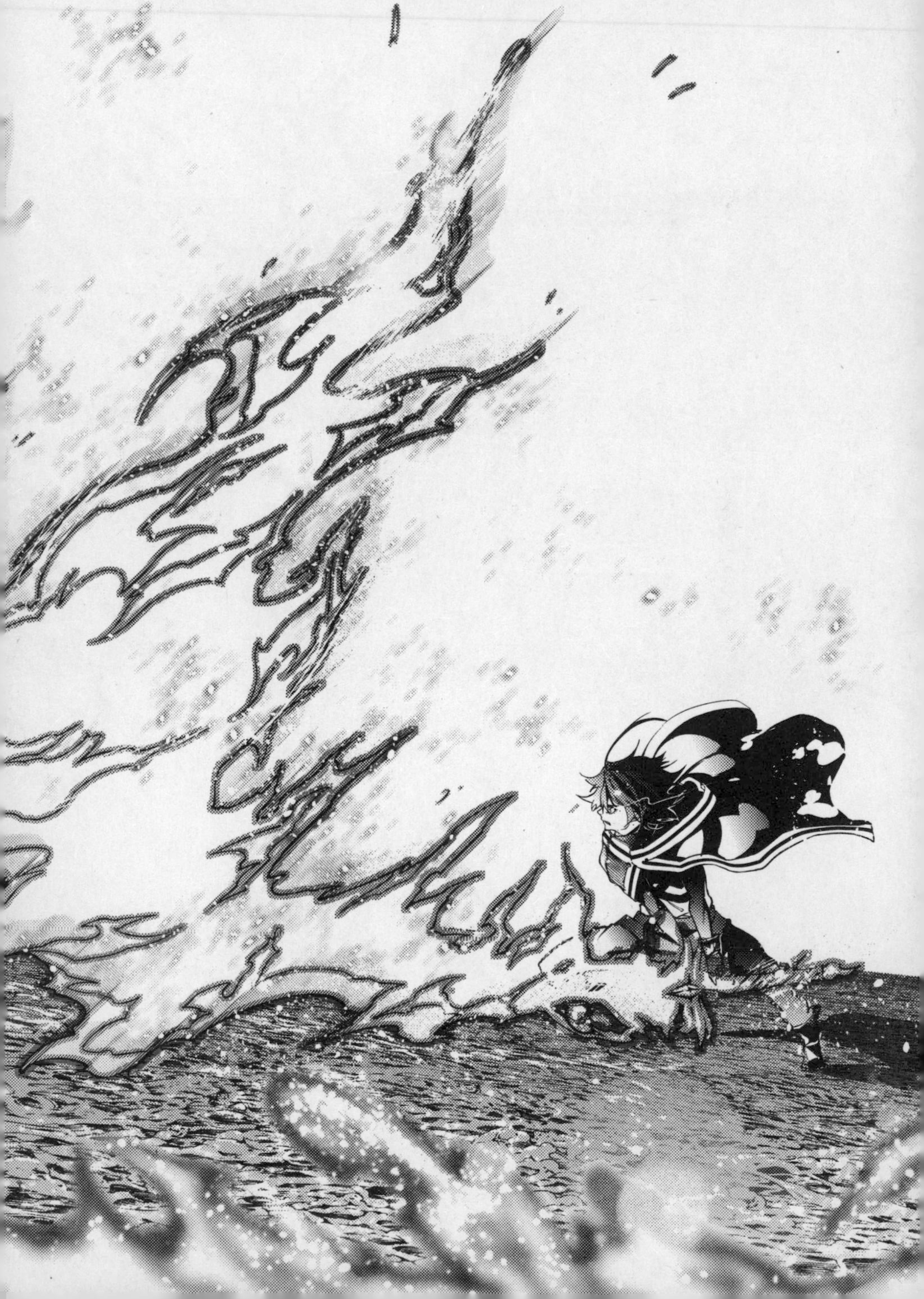

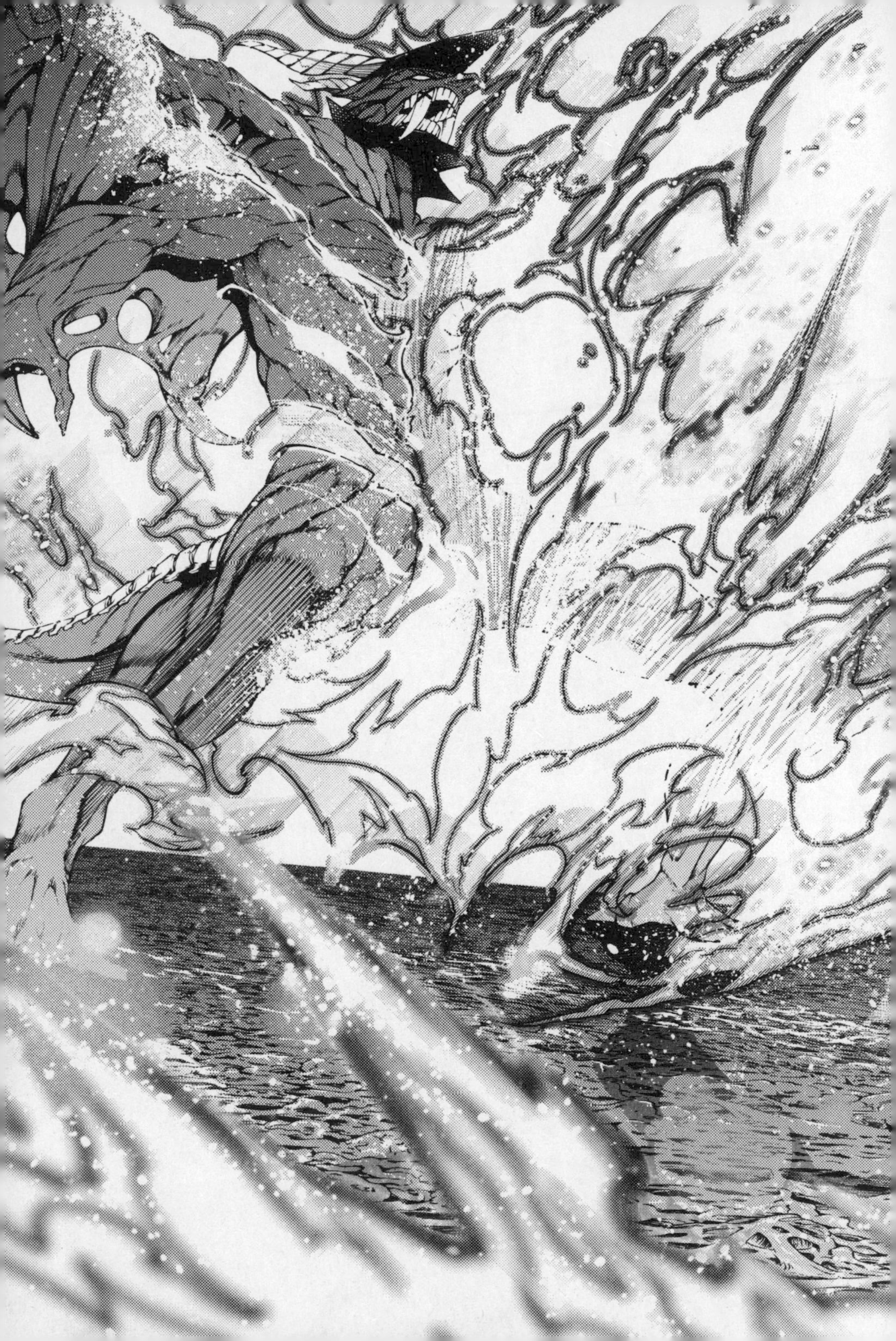

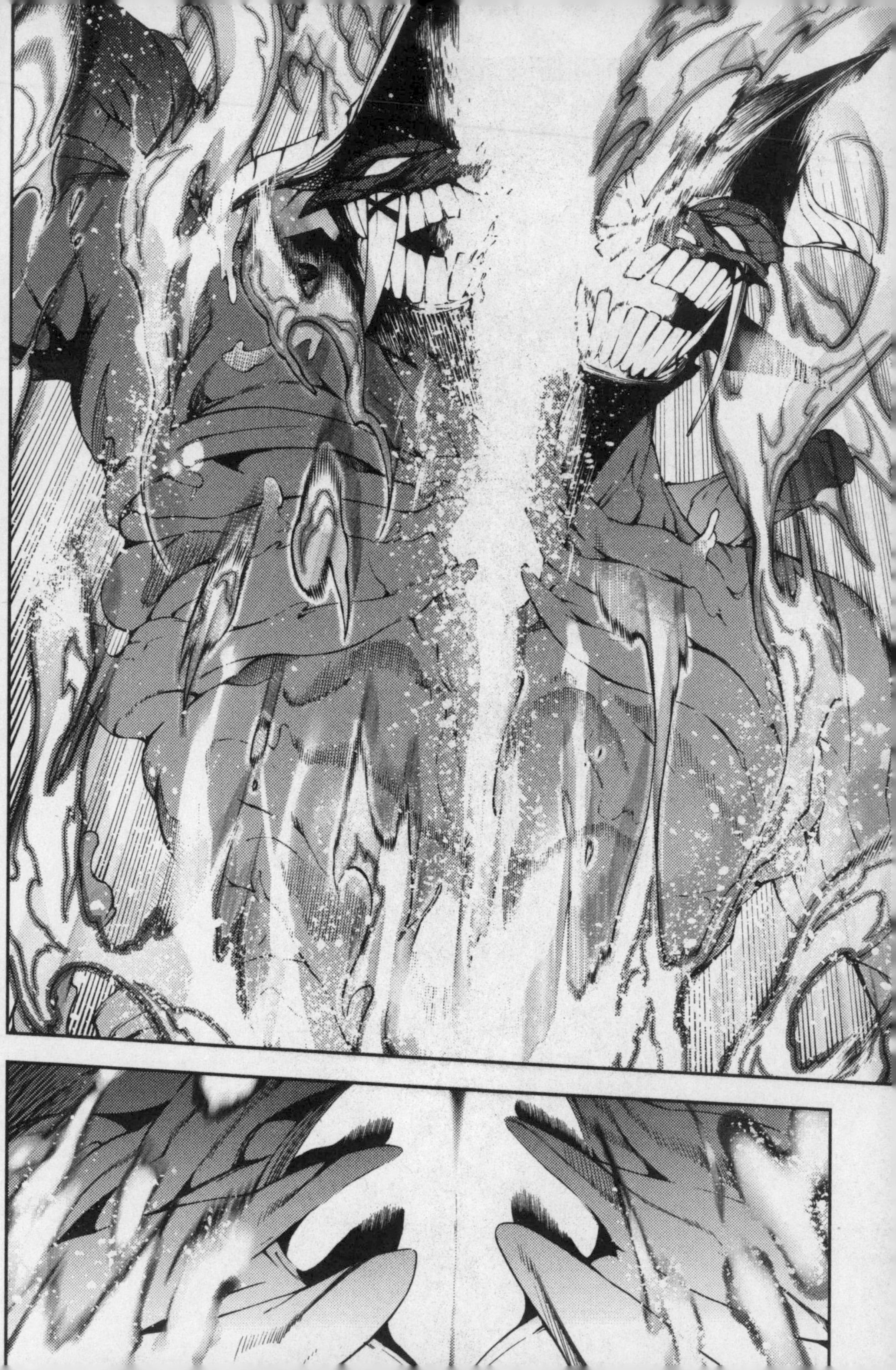

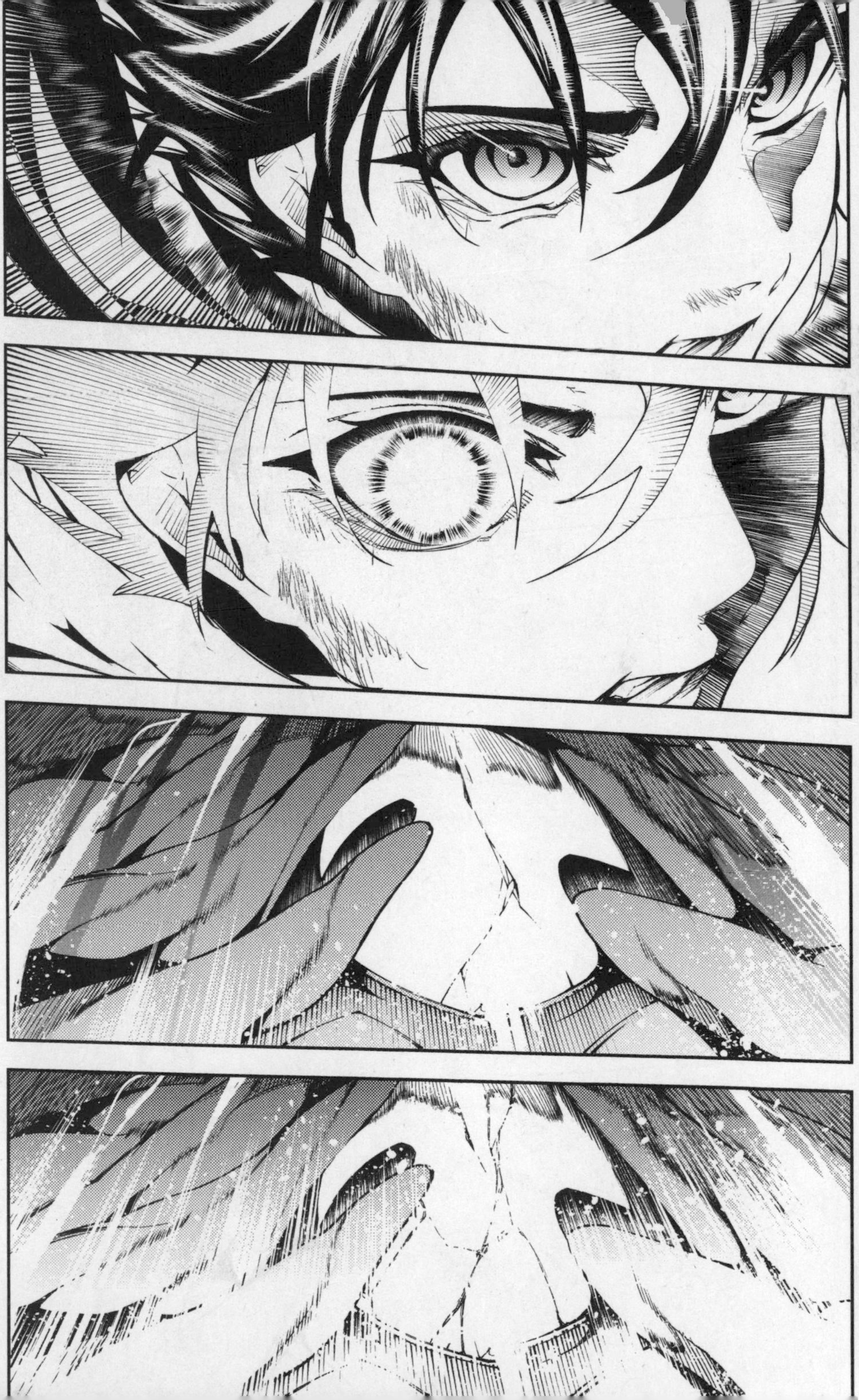

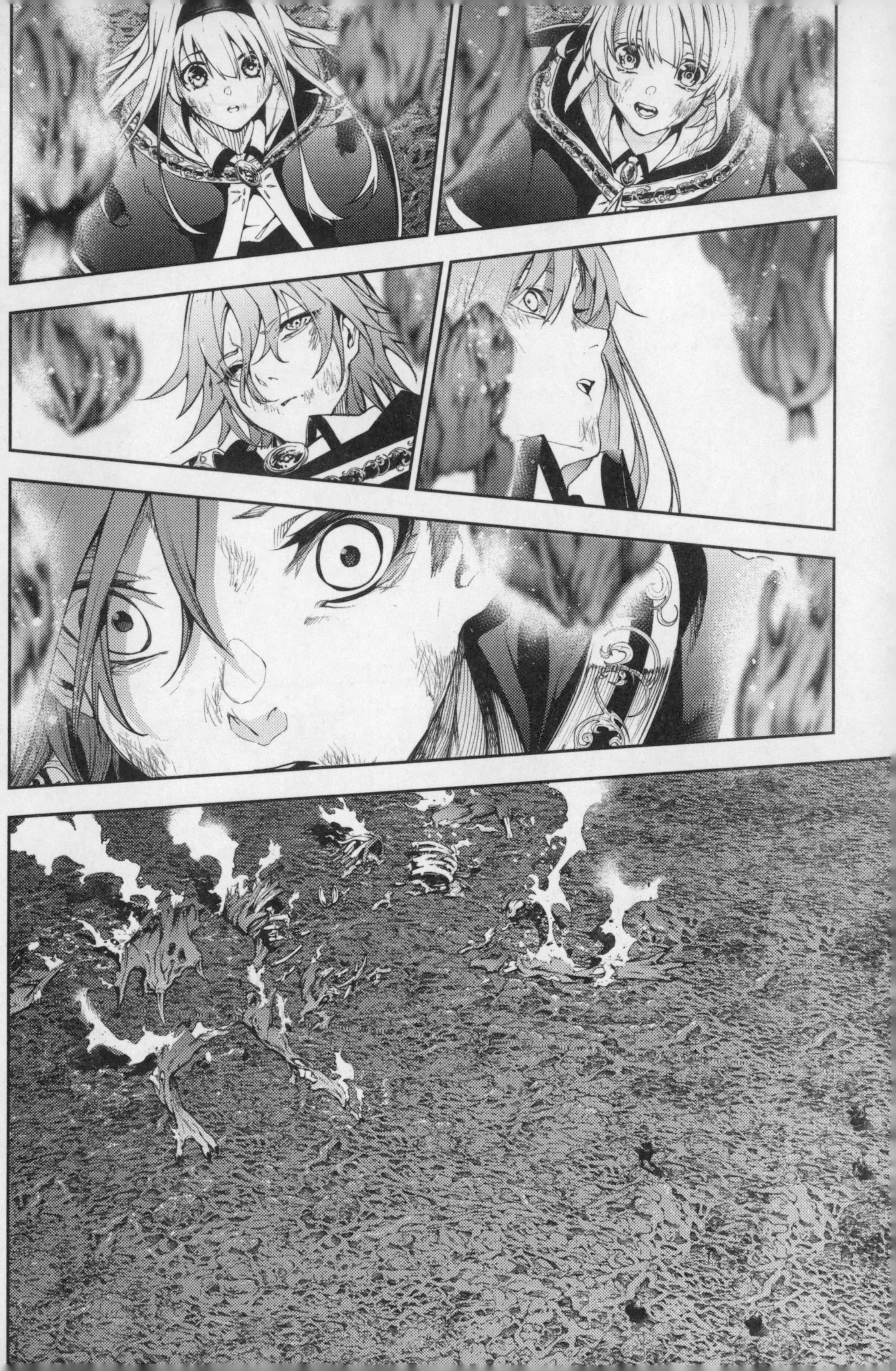

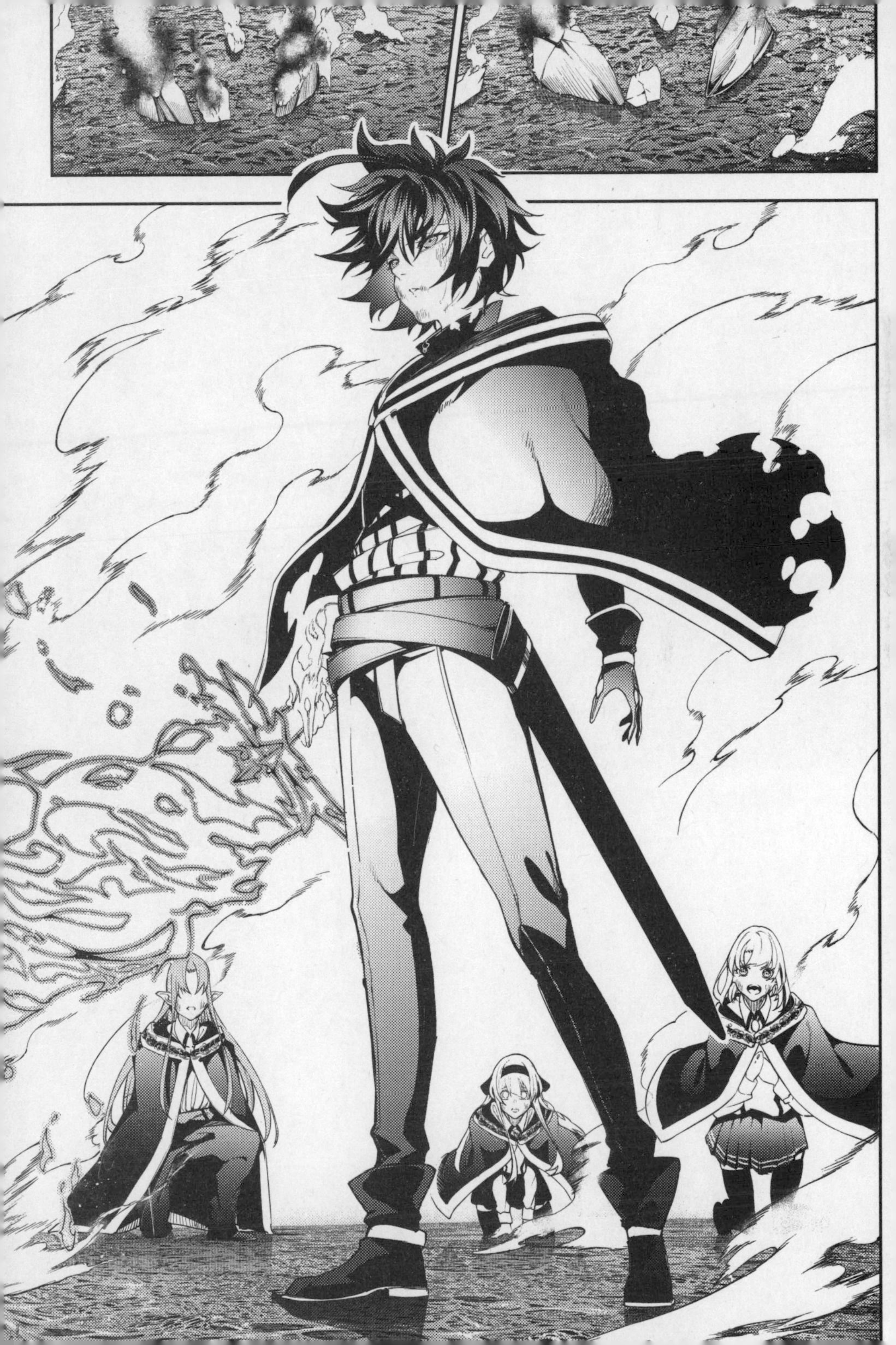

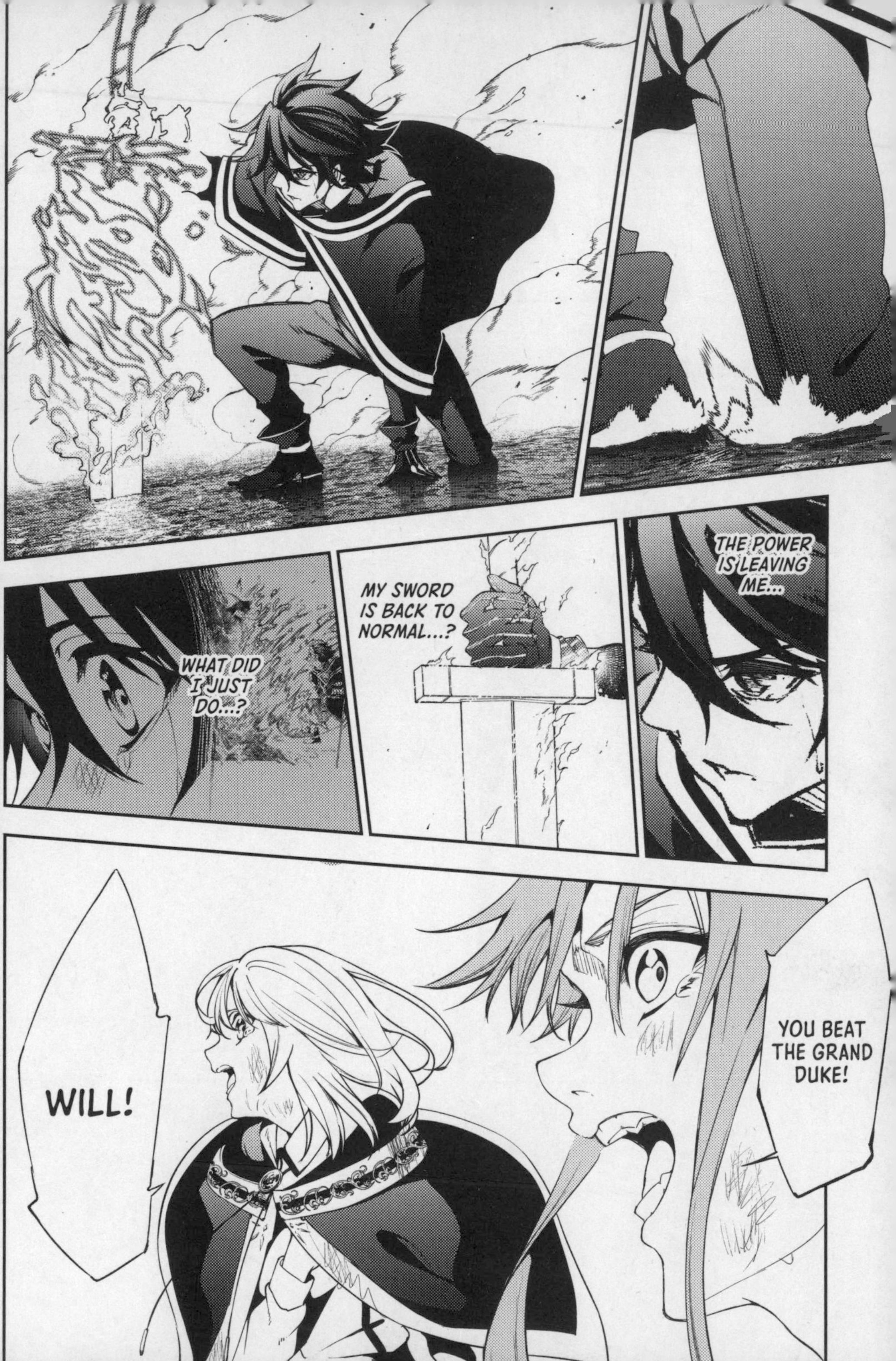
THE POWER IS LEAVING ME...
MY SWORD IS BACK TO NORMAL...?
WHAT DID I JUST DO...?
YOU BEAT THE GRAND DUKE!
WILL!

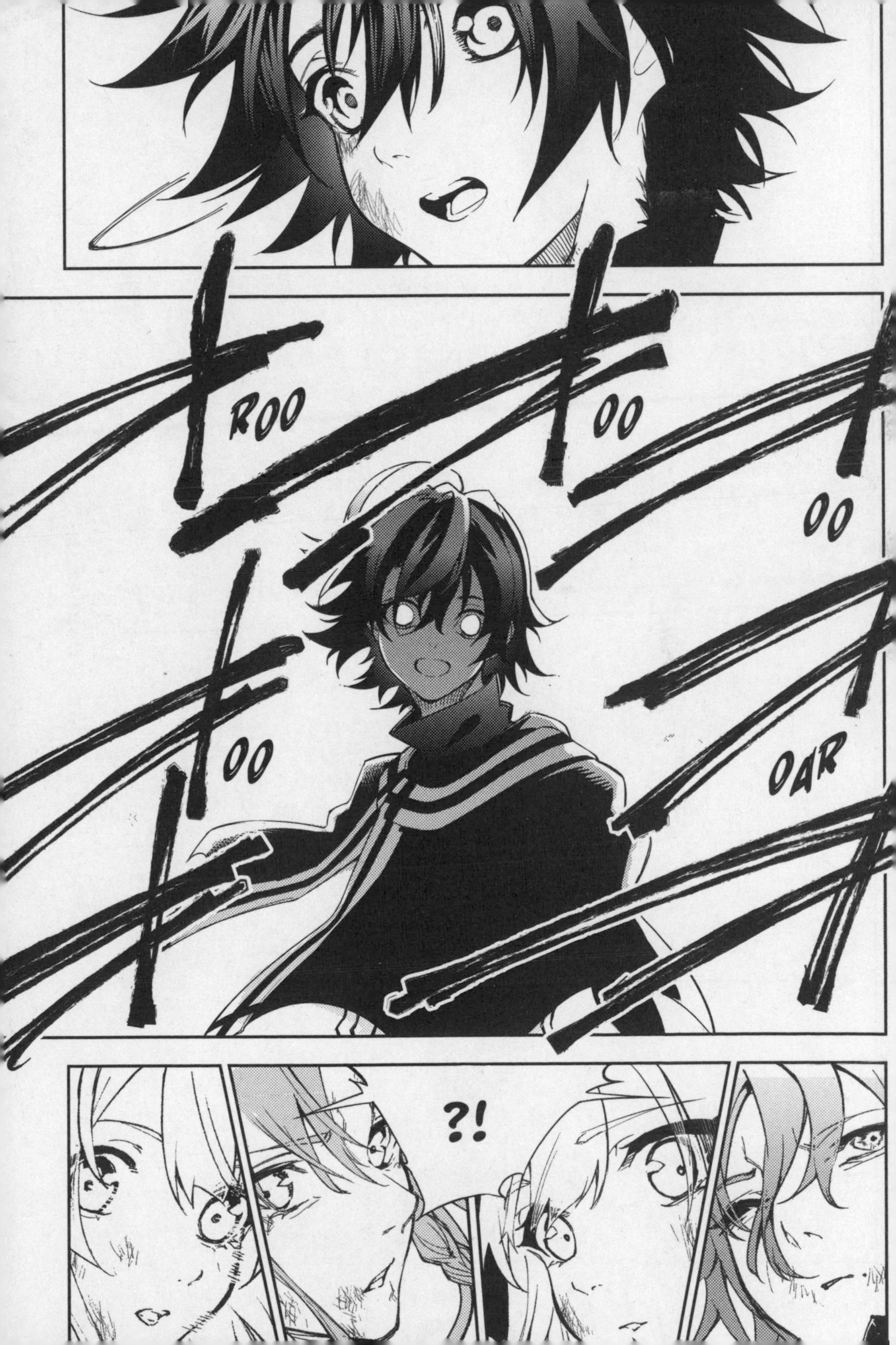
ROO
OO
OO
OO
OAR
?!

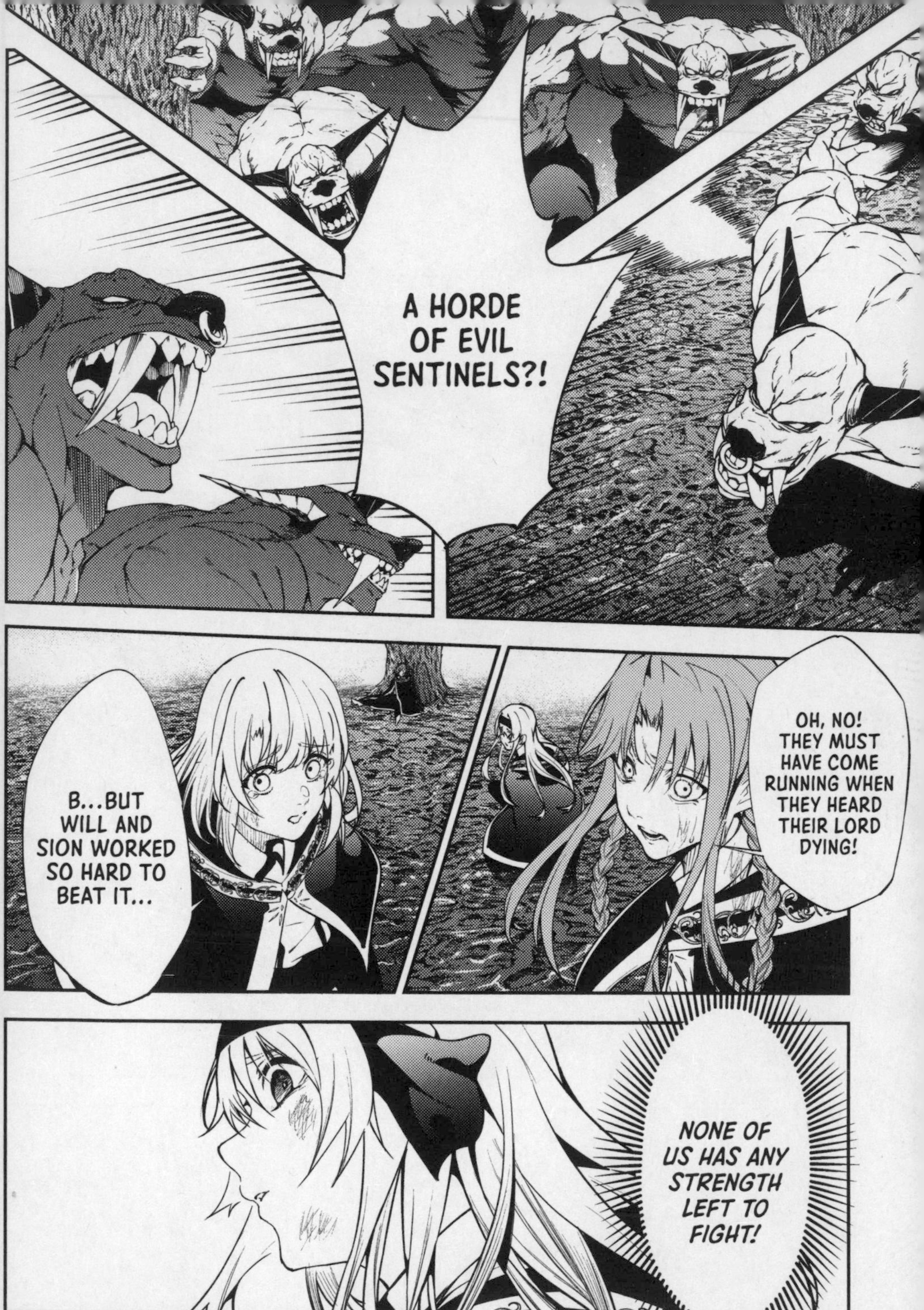
A HORDE OF EVIL SENTINELS?!
OH, NO! THEY MUST HAVE COME RUNNING WHEN THEY HEARD THEIR LORD DYING!
B...BUT WILL AND SION WORKED SO HARD TO BEAT IT...
NONE OF US HAS ANY STRENGTH LEFT TO FIGHT!

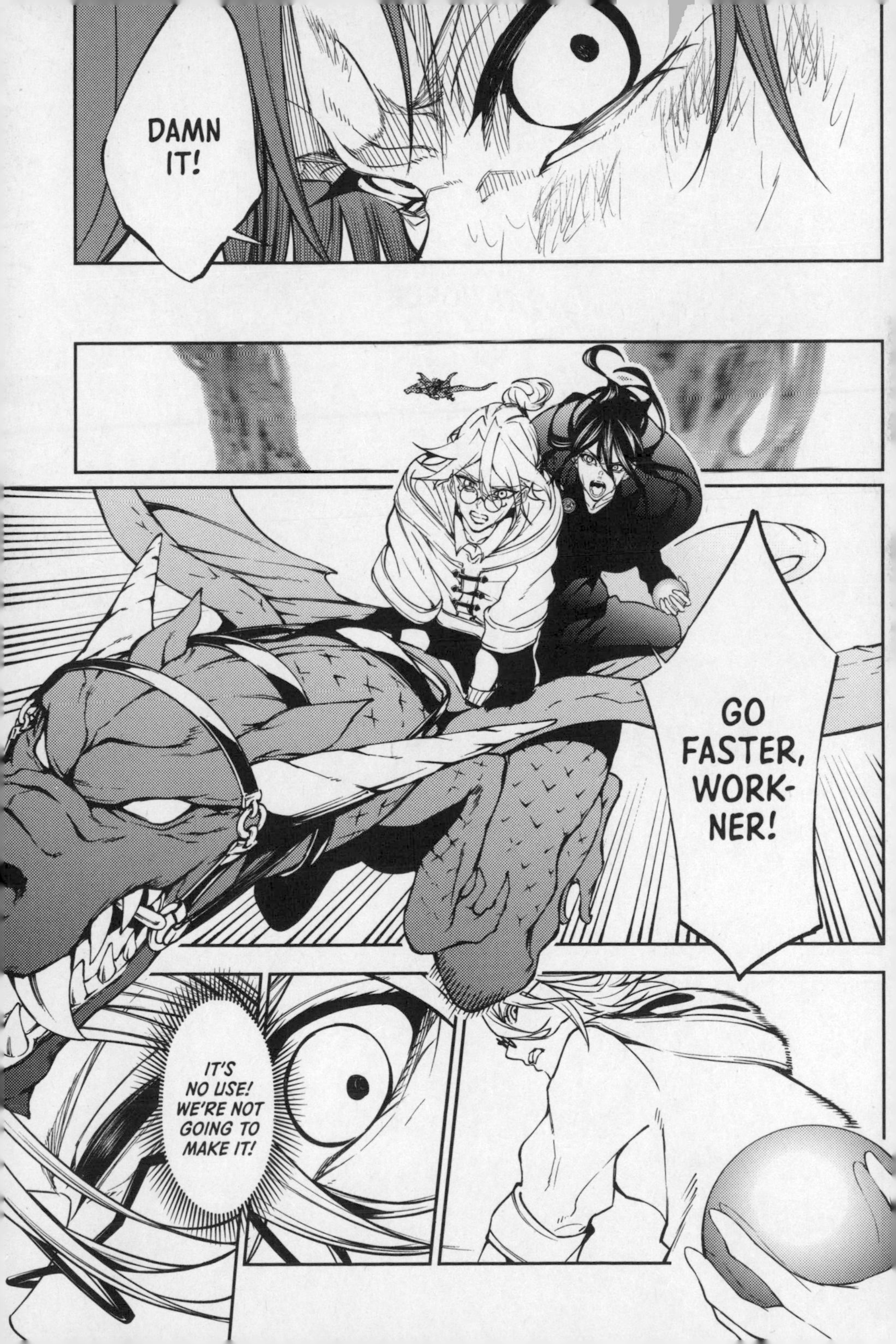
DAMN IT!
GO FASTER, WORK-NER!
IT'S NO USE! WE'RE NOT GOING TO MAKE IT!

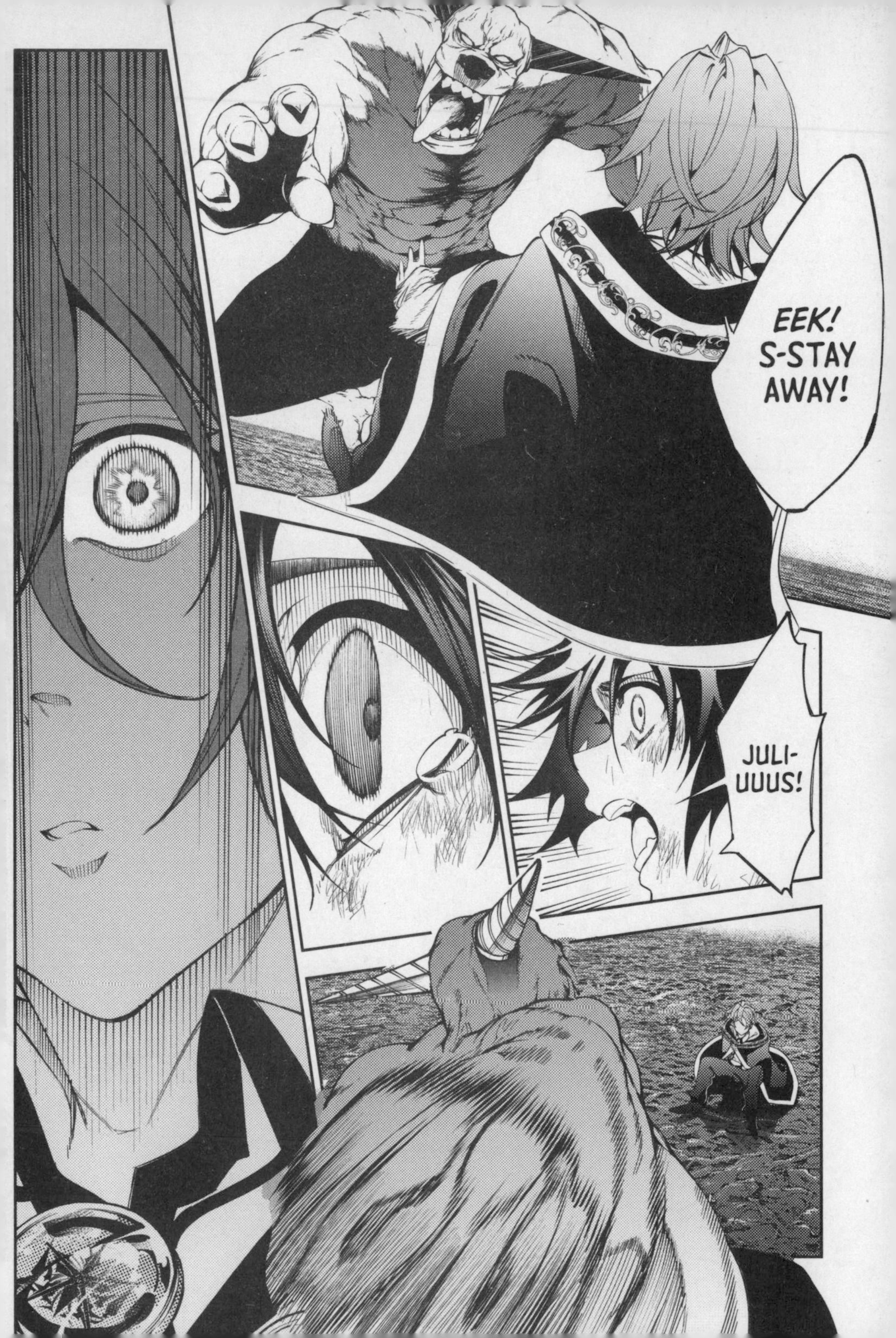
EEK! S-STAY AWAY!
JULI-UUUS!

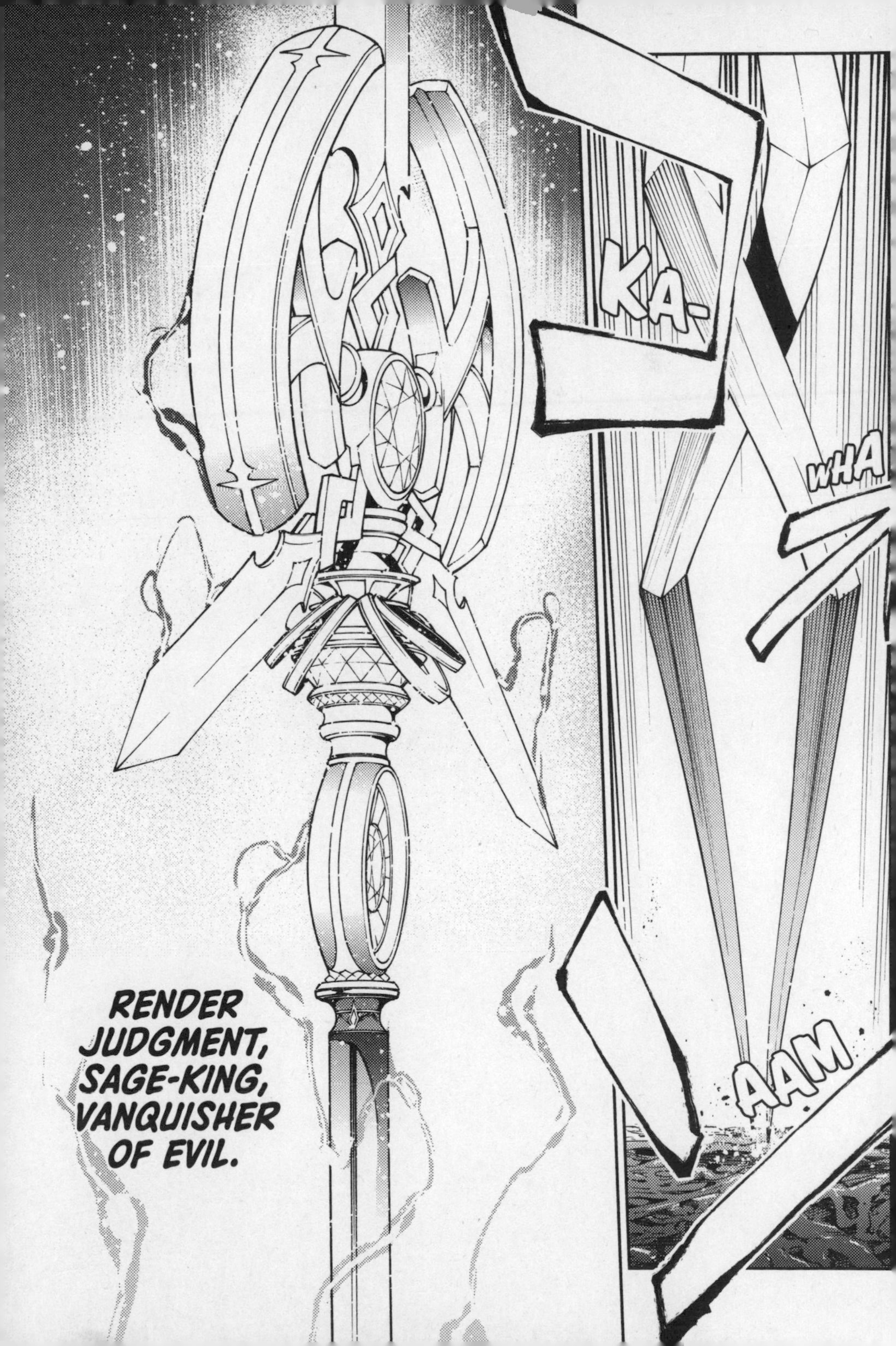
KA-
WHA
AAM
RENDER JUDGMENT, SAGE-KING, VANQUISHER OF EVIL.

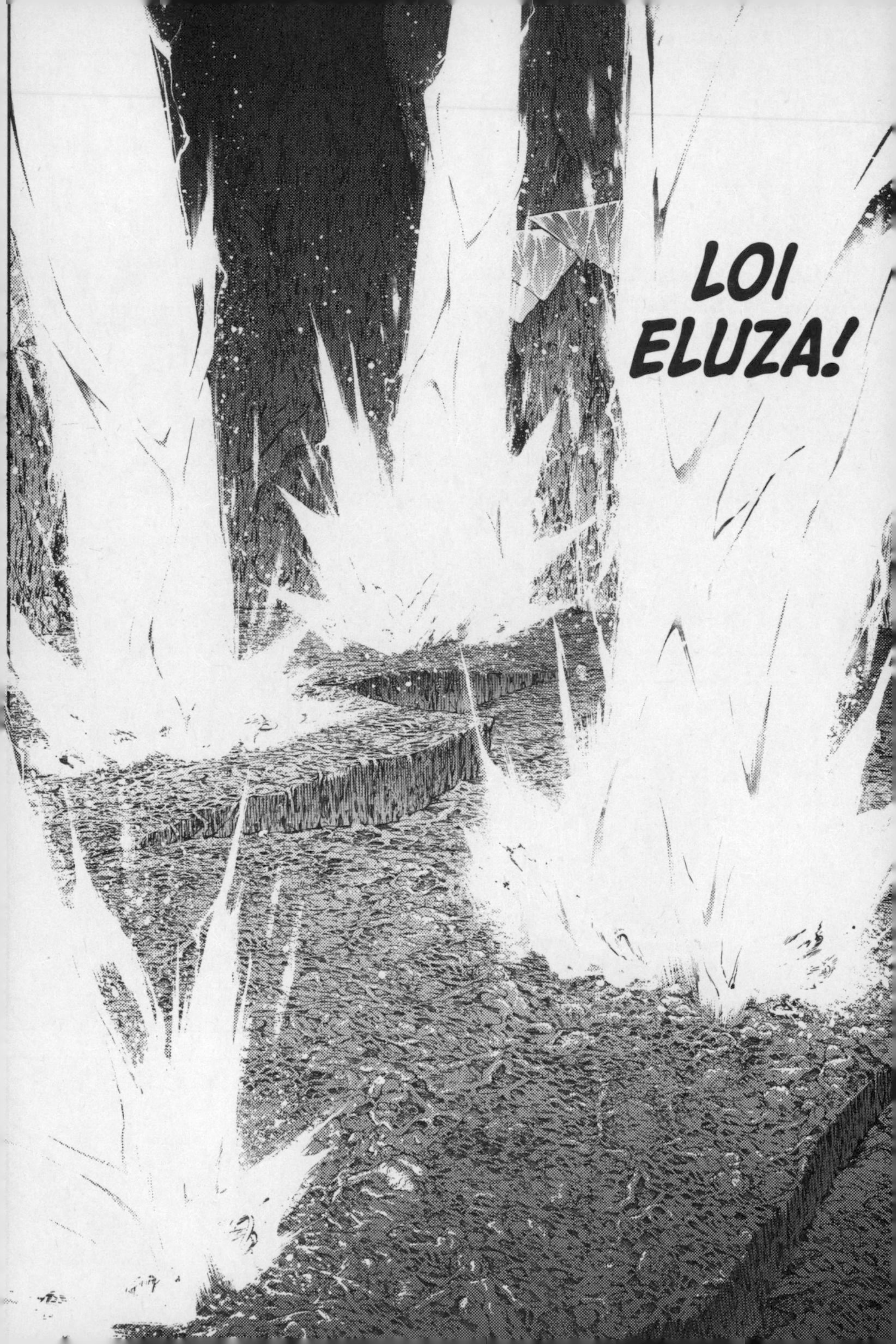
LOI
ELUZA!

AN ADVANCED ANNIHILATION SPELL?

WHA...

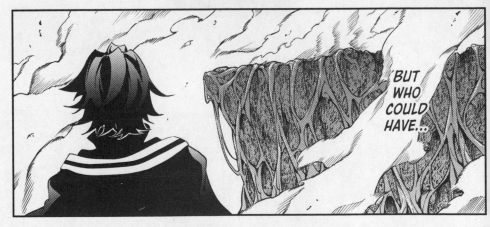

BUT WHO COULD HAVE...

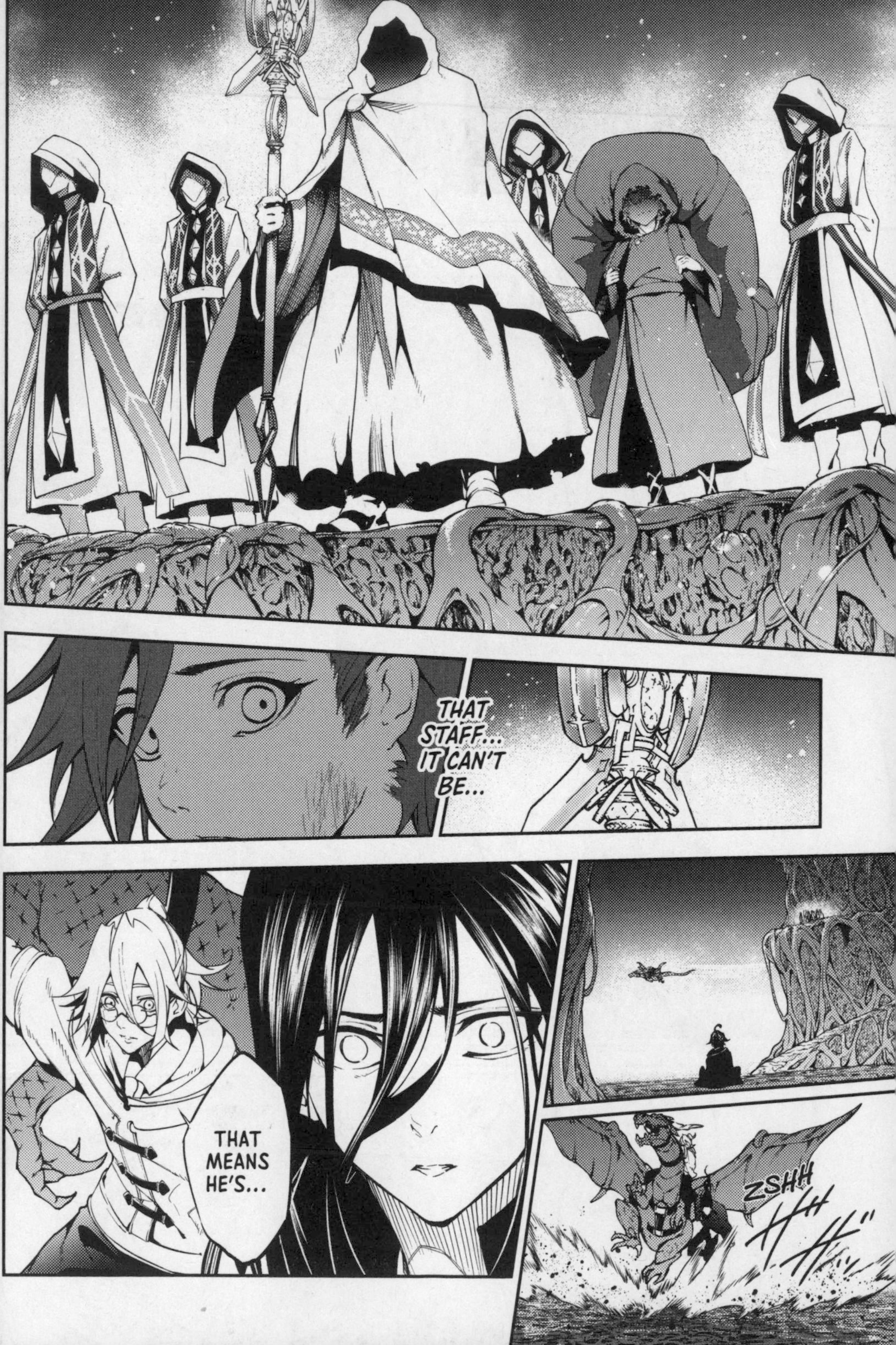
THAT STAFF... IT CAN'T BE...
ZSHH
THAT MEANS HE'S...

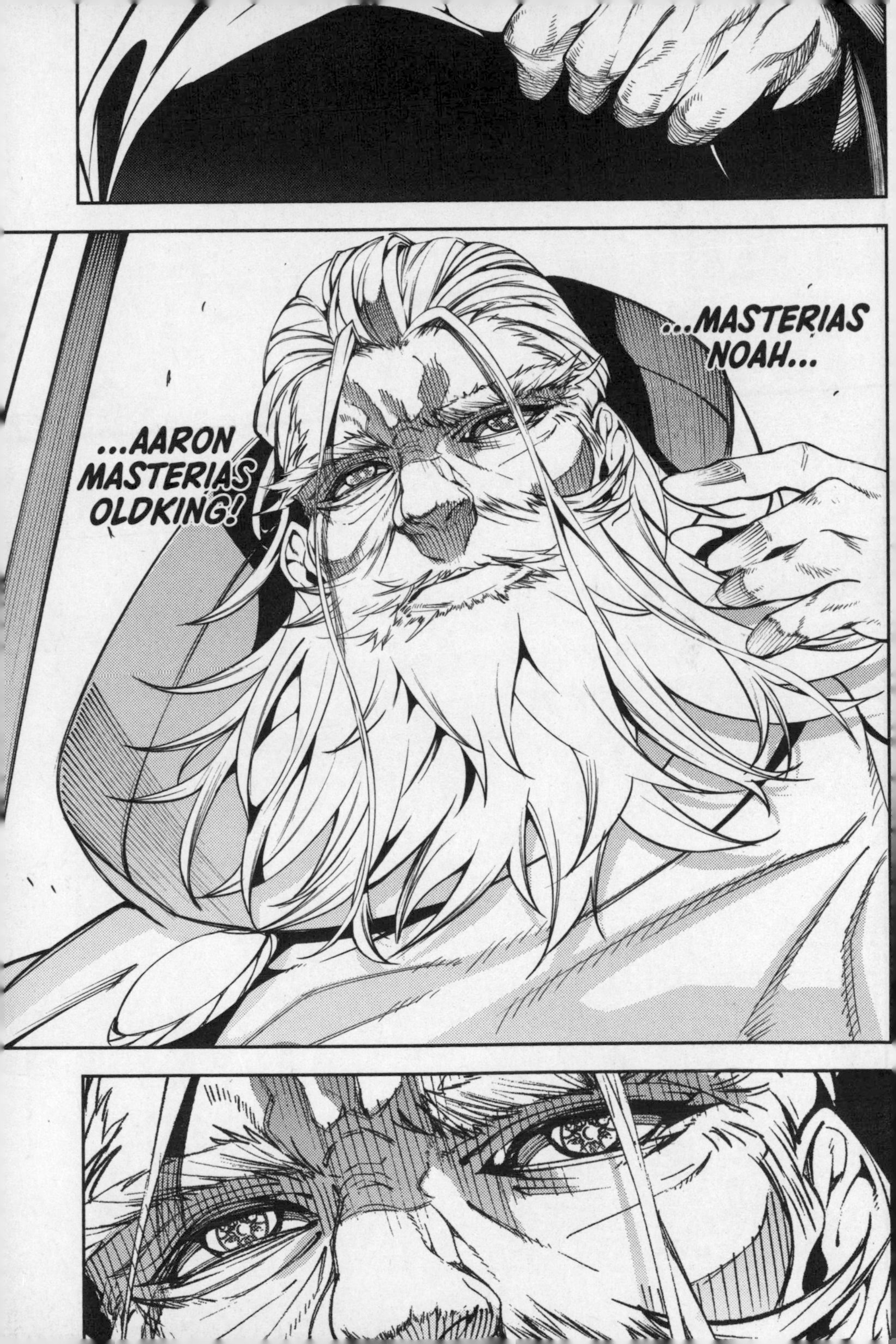
...MASTERIAS NOAH...
...AARON MASTERIAS OLDKING!

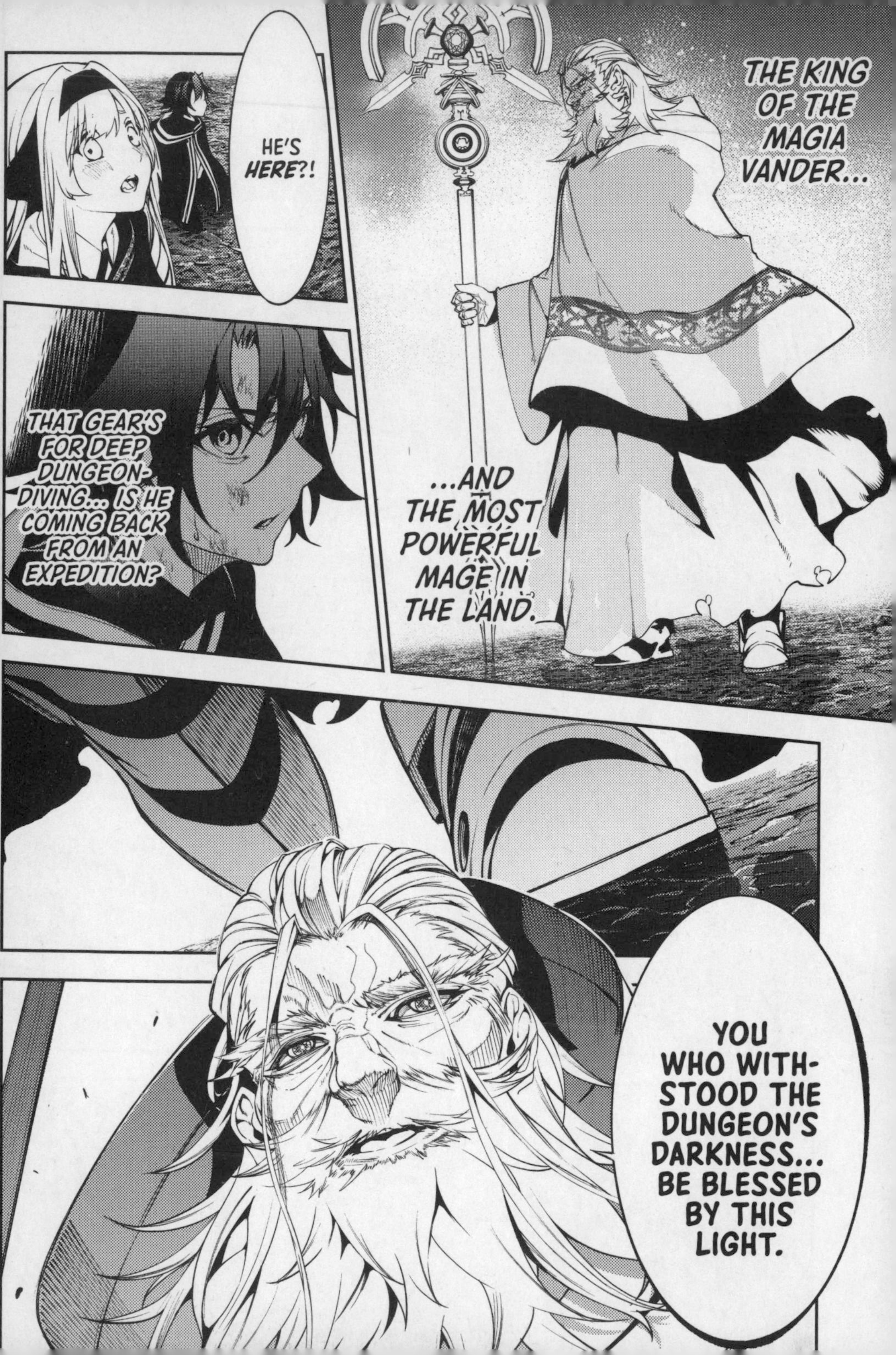
THE KING OF THE MAGIA VANDER...
...AND THE MOST POWERFUL MAGE IN THE LAND.
HE'S HERE?!
THAT GEAR'S FOR DEEP DUNGEON-DIVING... IS HE COMING BACK FROM AN EXPEDITION?
YOU WHO WITH-STOOD THE DUNGEON'S DARKNESS... BE BLESSED BY THIS LIGHT.

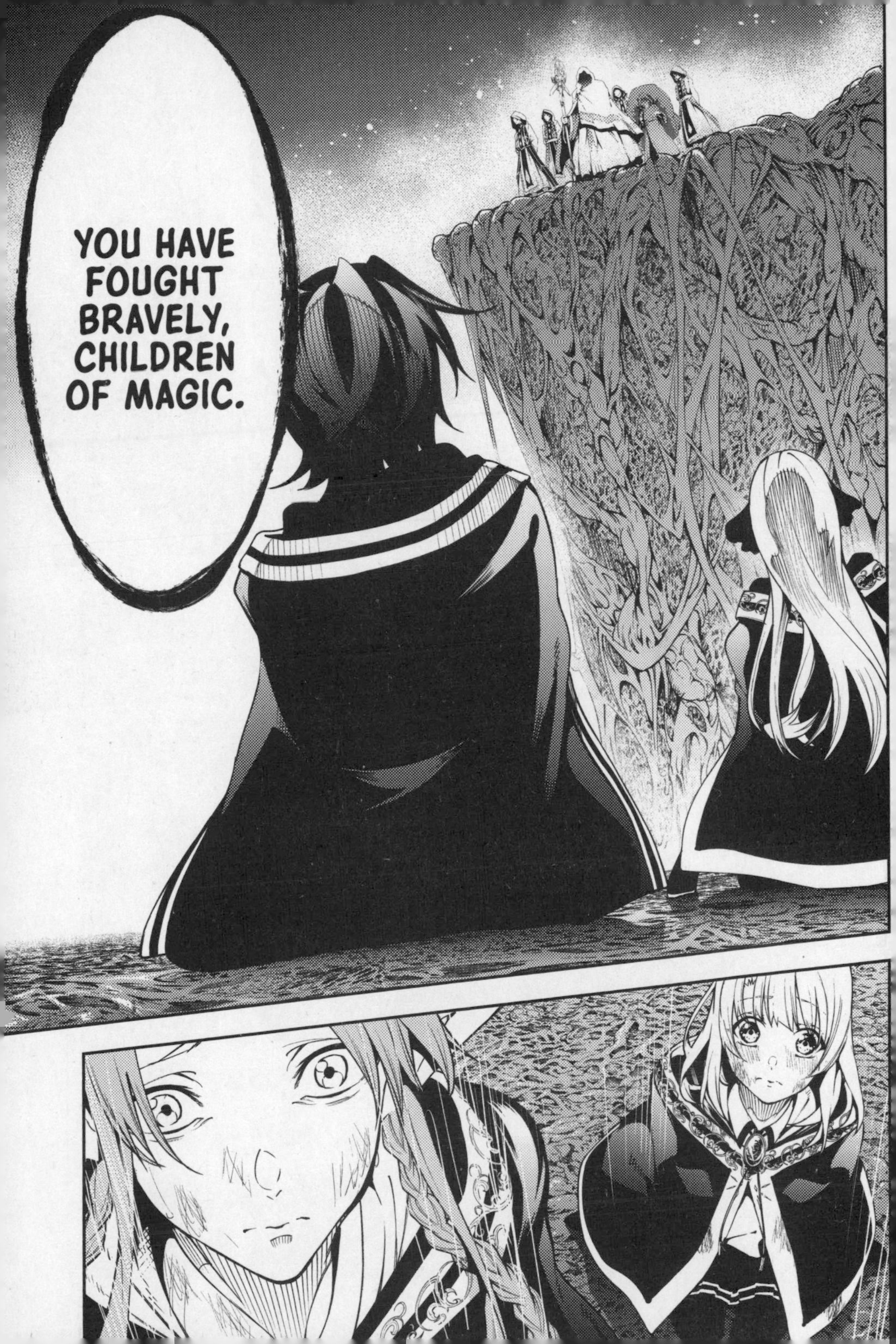
YOU HAVE FOUGHT BRAVELY, CHILDREN OF MAGIC.

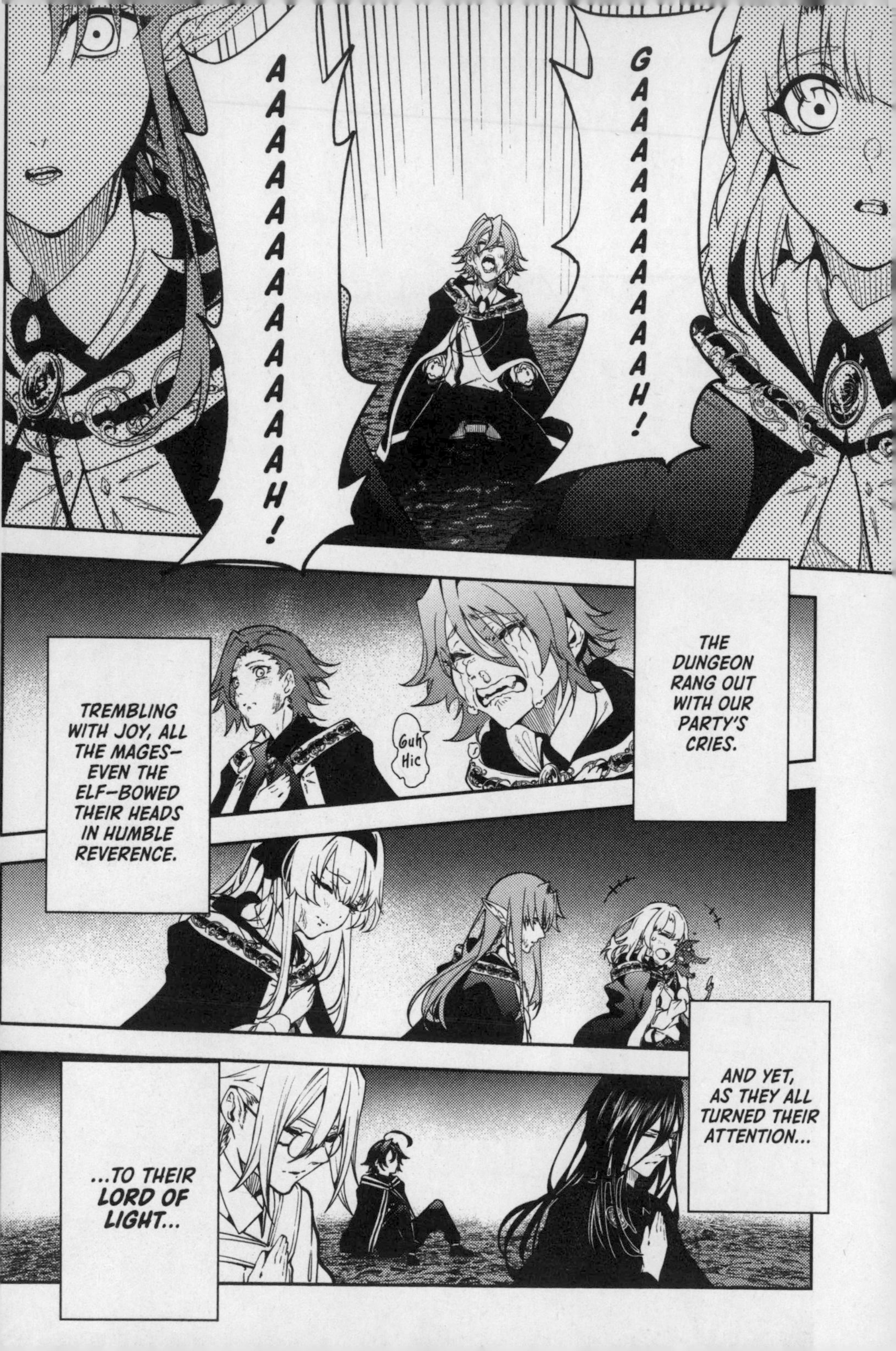

GAAAAAAAAAAH!
AAAAAAAAAAAAH!
THE DUNGEON RANG OUT WITH OUR PARTY'S CRIES.
Guh Hic
TREMBLING WITH JOY, ALL THE MAGES—EVEN THE ELF—BOWED THEIR HEADS IN HUMBLE REVERENCE.
AND YET, AS THEY ALL TURNED THEIR ATTENTION...
...TO THEIR LORD OF LIGHT...

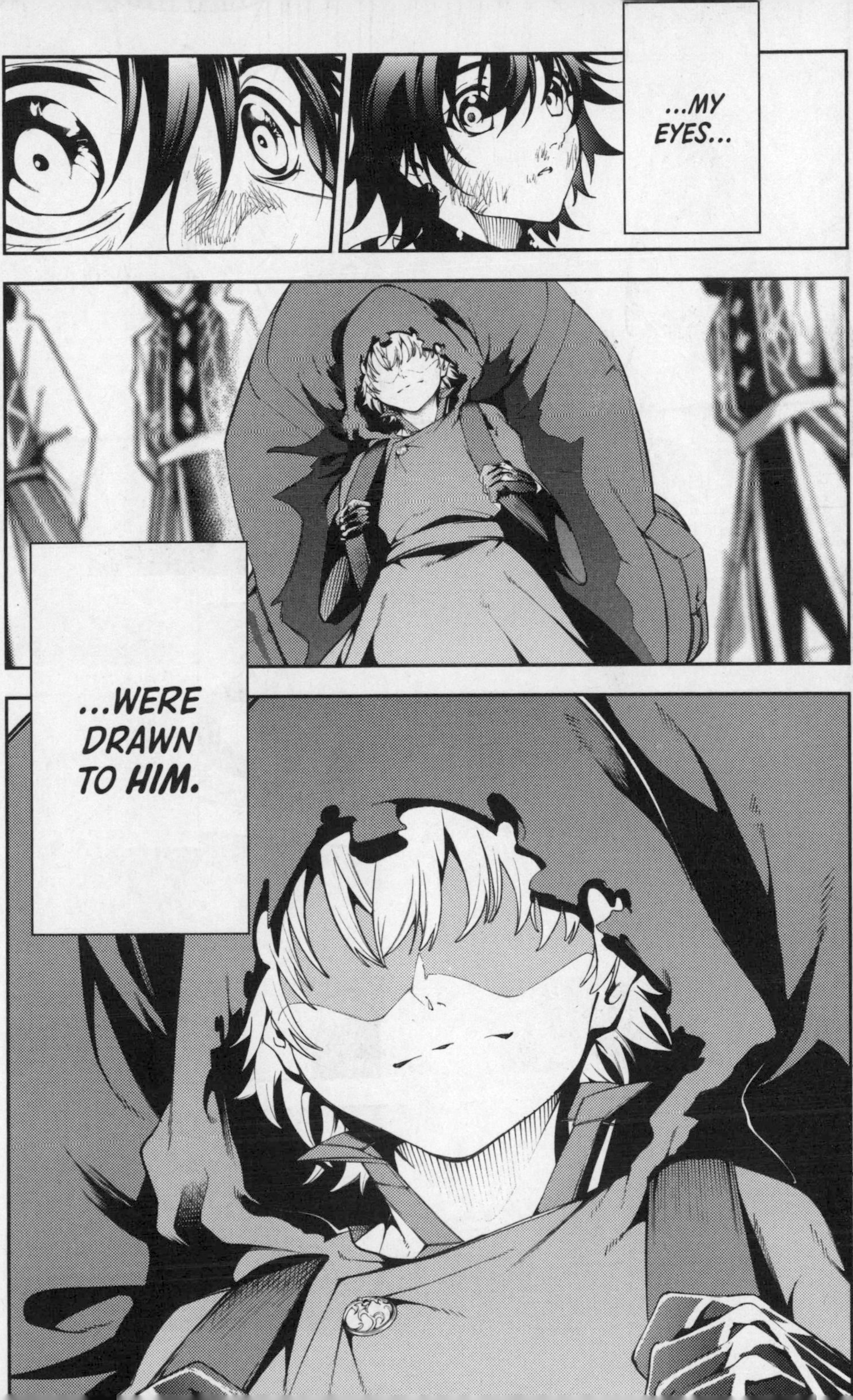
...MY EYES...
...WERE DRAWN TO HIM.

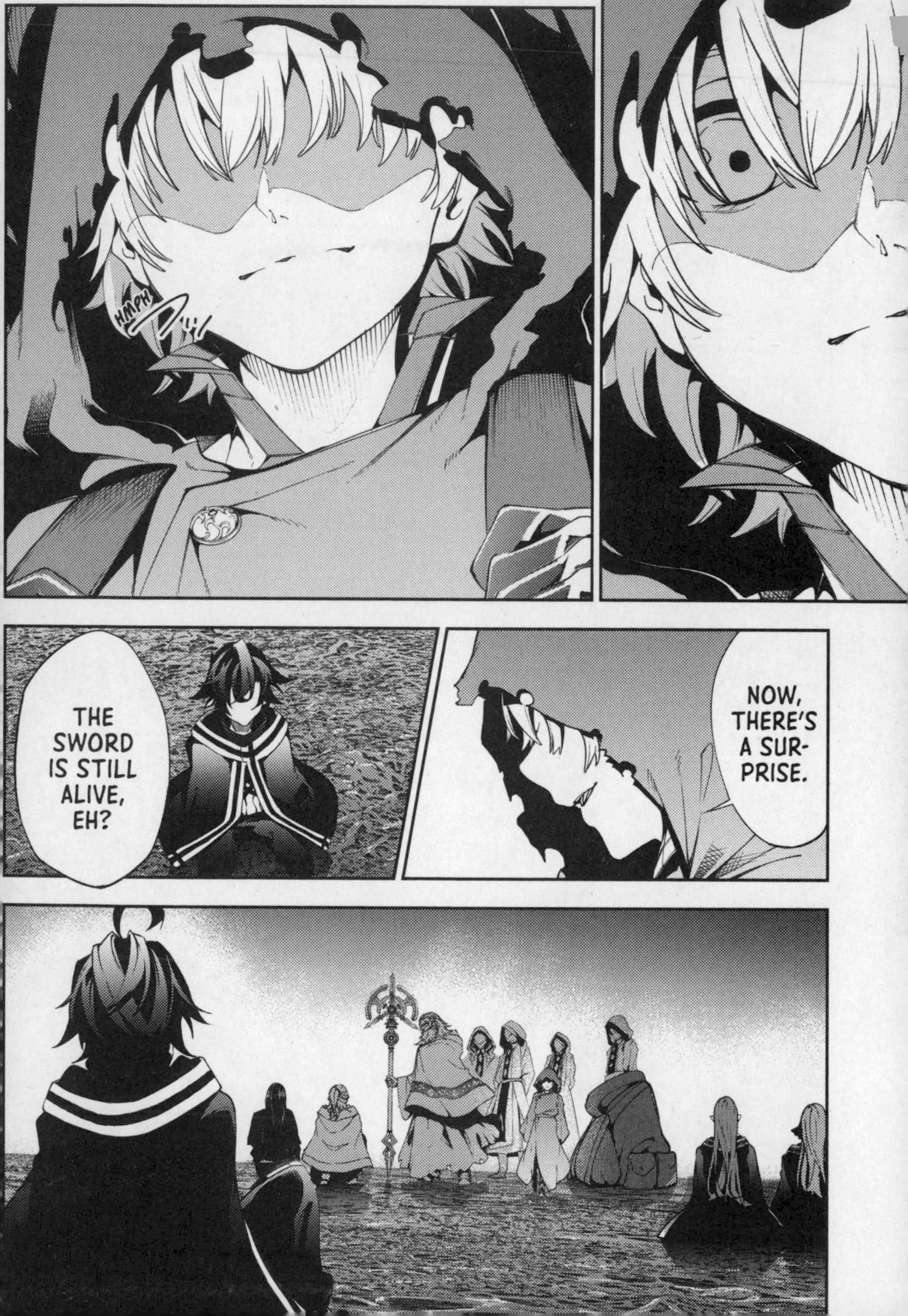
HMPH
NOW, THERE'S A SUR-PRISE.
THE SWORD IS STILL ALIVE, EH?

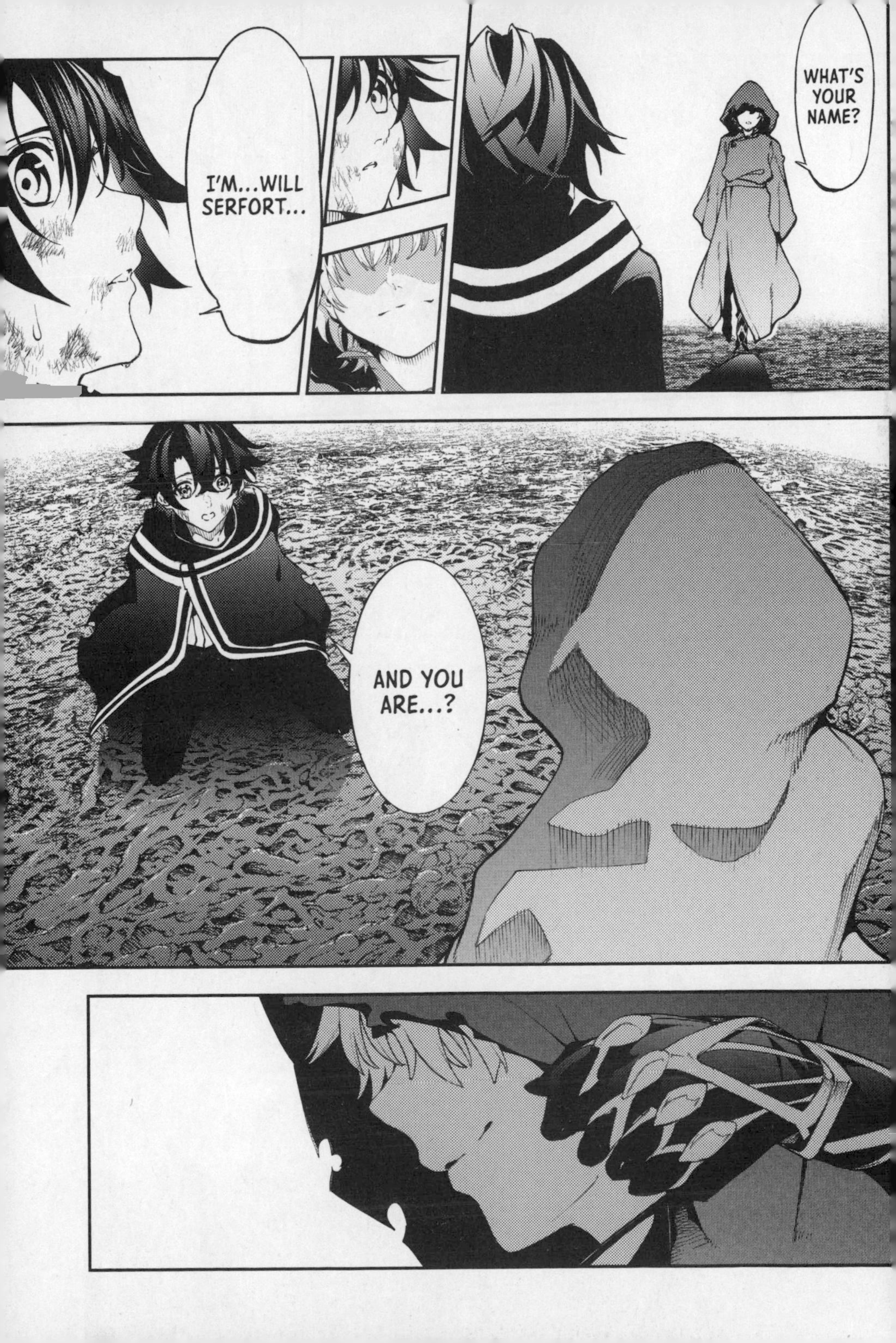
WHAT'S YOUR NAME?
I'M...WILL SERFORT...
AND YOU ARE...?

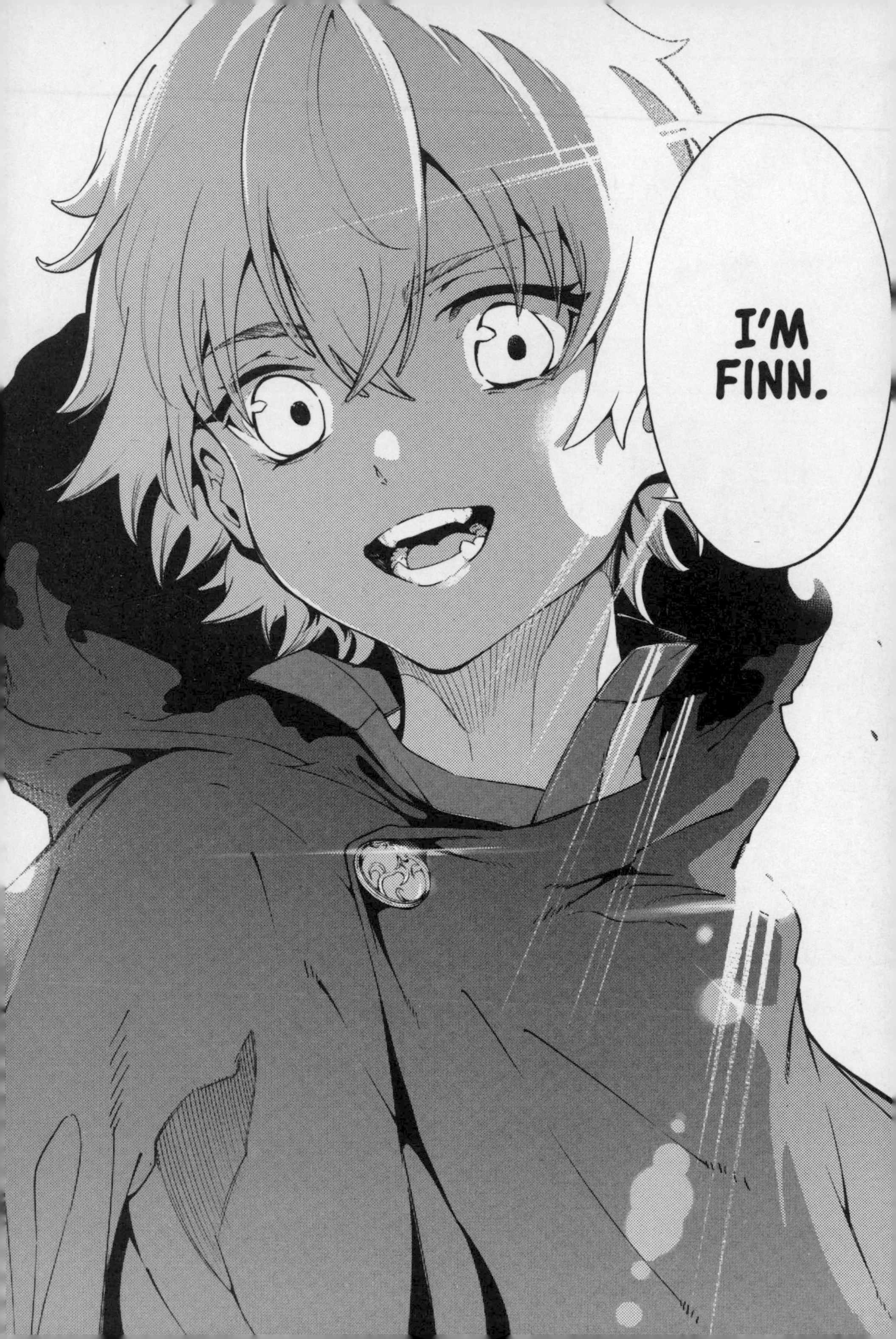
I'M FINN.

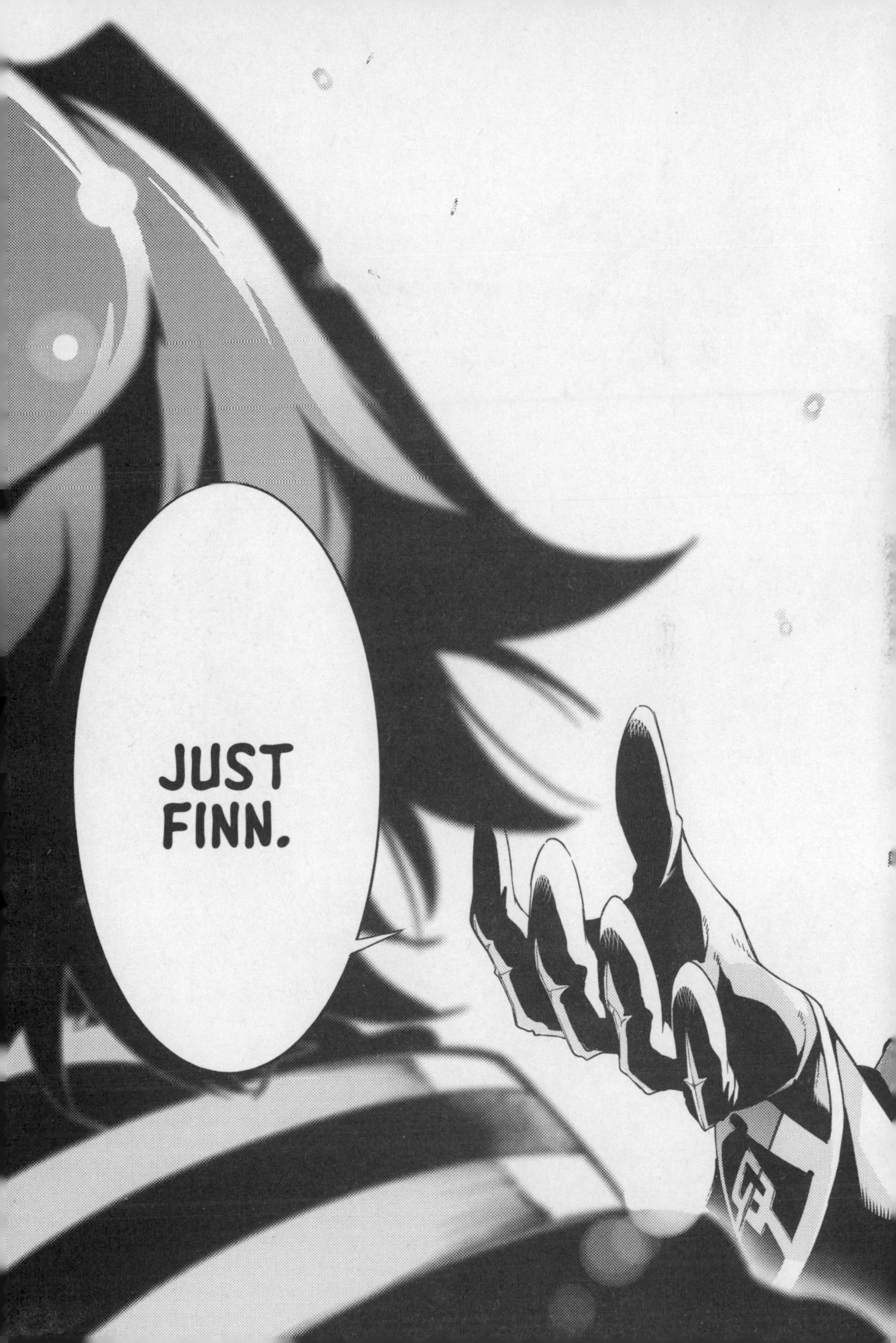
JUST FINN.

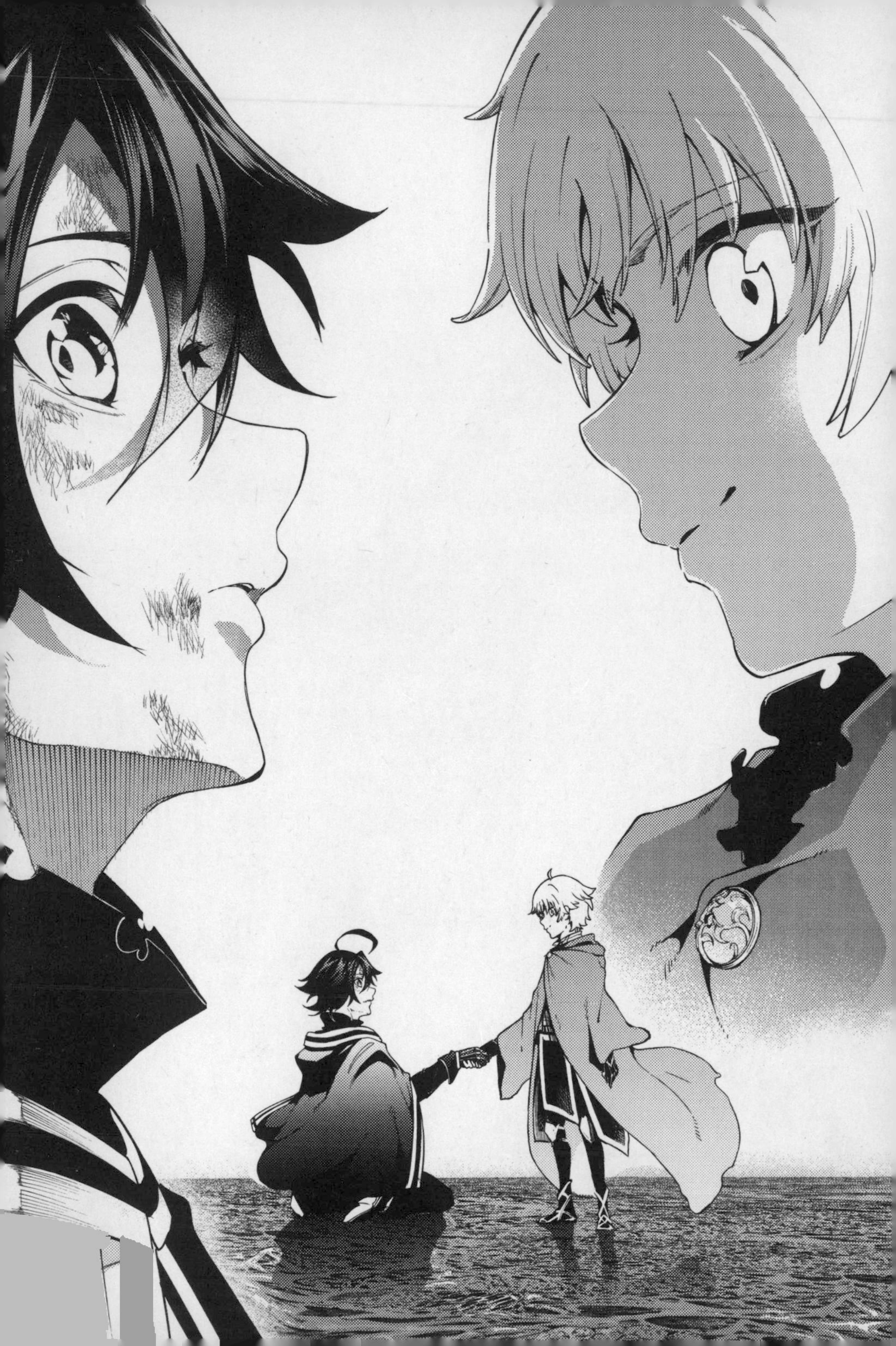

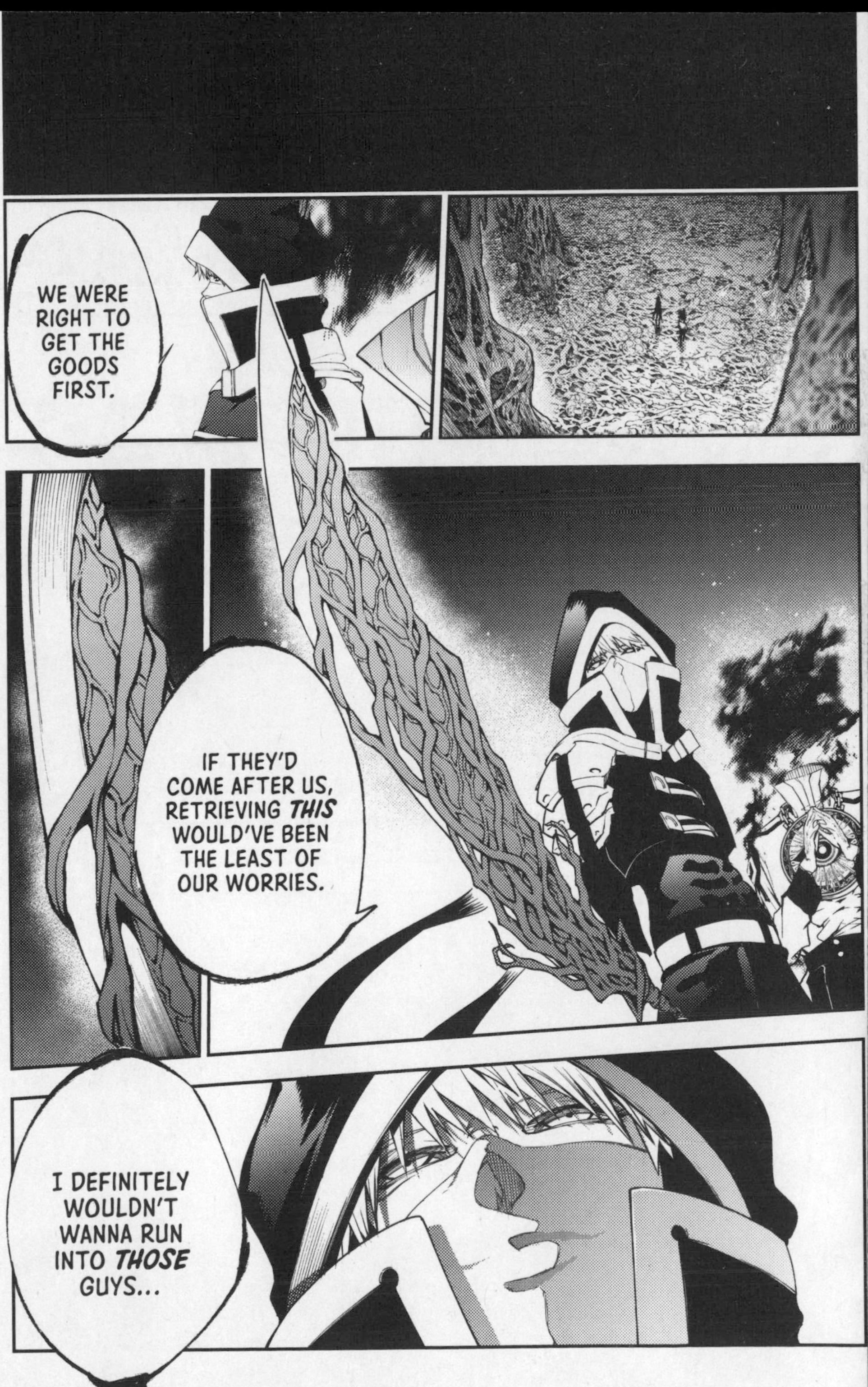
WE WERE RIGHT TO GET THE GOODS FIRST.
IF THEY'D COME AFTER US, RETRIEVING *THIS* WOULD'VE BEEN THE LEAST OF OUR WORRIES.
I DEFINITELY WOULDN'T WANNA RUN INTO *THOSE* GUYS...

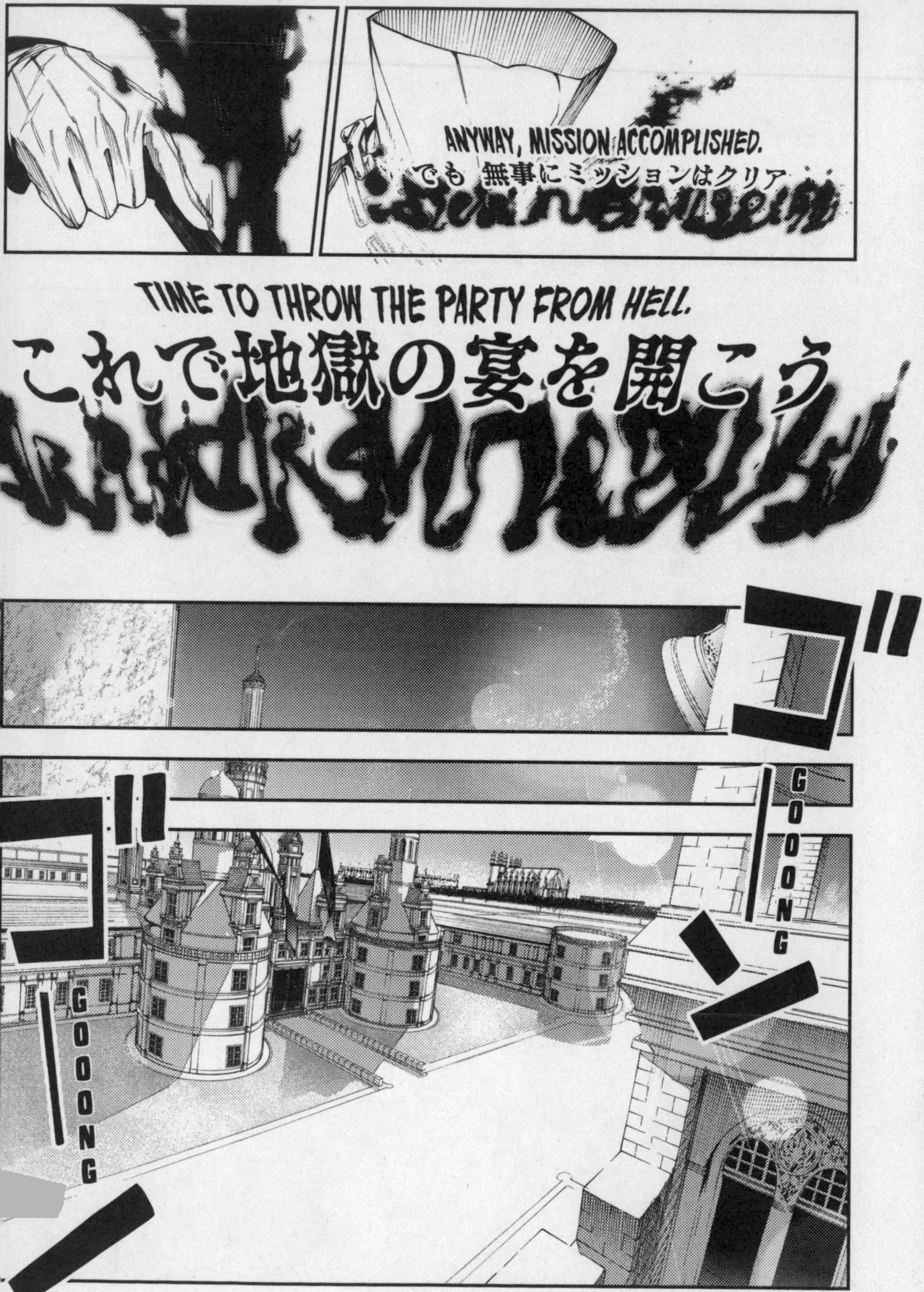
ANYWAY, MISSION ACCOMPLISHED.
でも 無事にミッションはクリア
TIME TO THROW THE PARTY FROM HELL.
これで地獄の宴を開こう
ゴ
ン
GOOONG
ゴ
ン
GOOONG

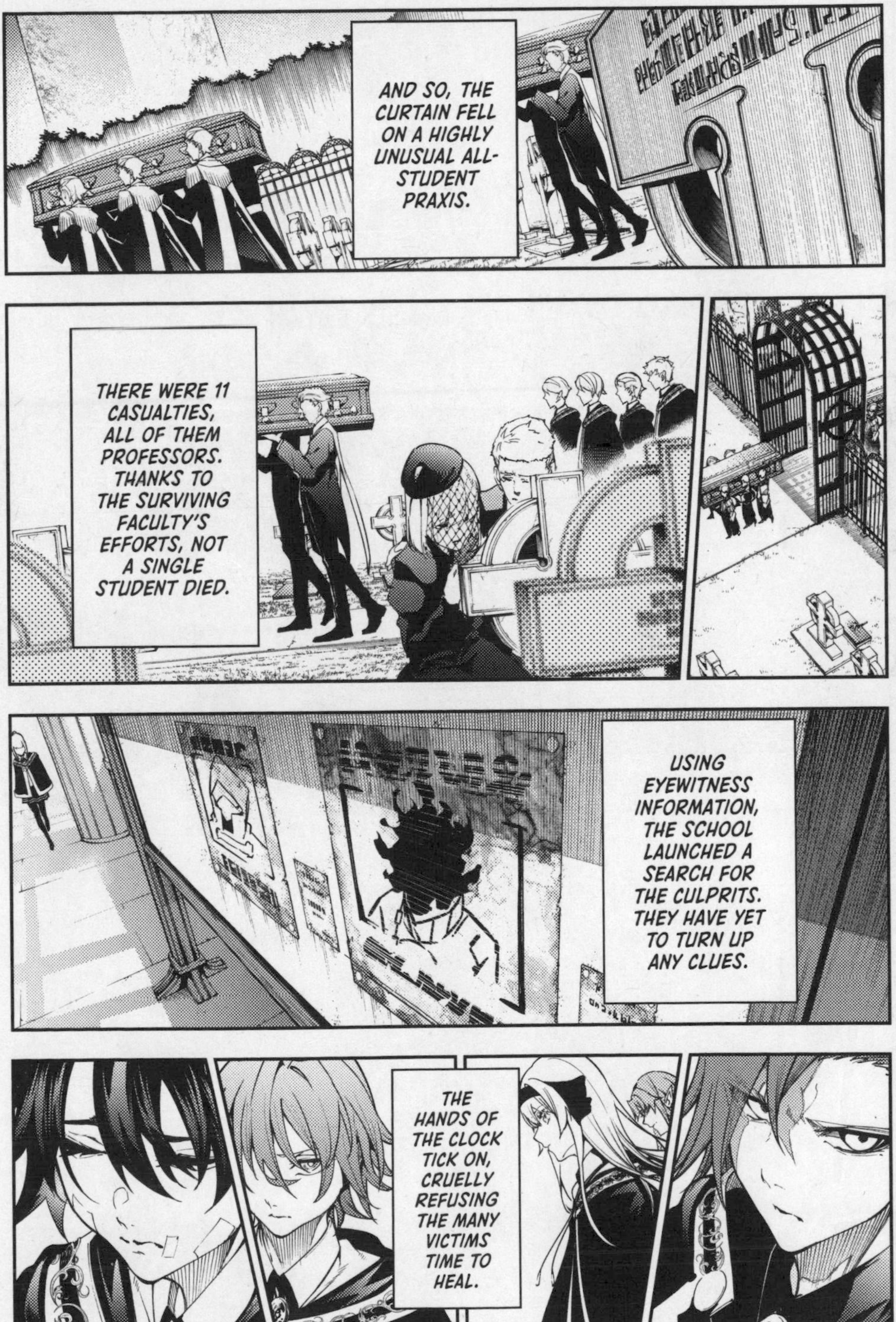
AND SO, THE CURTAIN FELL ON A HIGHLY UNUSUAL ALL-STUDENT PRAXIS.
THERE WERE 11 CASUALTIES, ALL OF THEM PROFESSORS. THANKS TO THE SURVIVING FACULTY'S EFFORTS, NOT A SINGLE STUDENT DIED.
USING EYEWITNESS INFORMATION, THE SCHOOL LAUNCHED A SEARCH FOR THE CULPRITS. THEY HAVE YET TO TURN UP ANY CLUES.
THE HANDS OF THE CLOCK TICK ON, CRUELLY REFUSING THE MANY VICTIMS TIME TO HEAL.

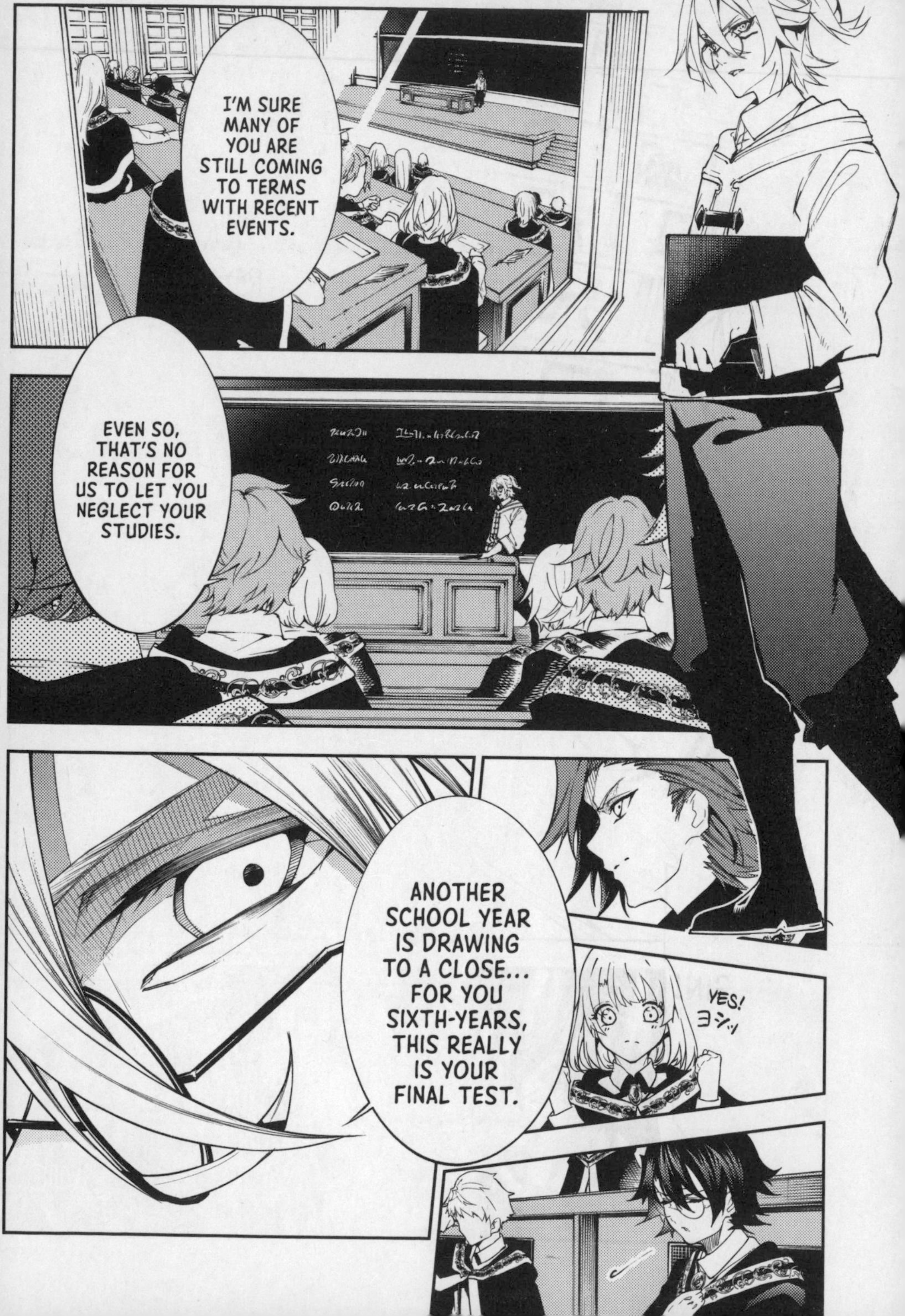
I'M SURE MANY OF YOU ARE STILL COMING TO TERMS WITH RECENT EVENTS.
EVEN SO, THAT'S NO REASON FOR US TO LET YOU NEGLECT YOUR STUDIES.
ANOTHER SCHOOL YEAR IS DRAWING TO A CLOSE... FOR YOU SIXTH-YEARS, THIS REALLY IS YOUR FINAL TEST.
YES!
ヨシッ

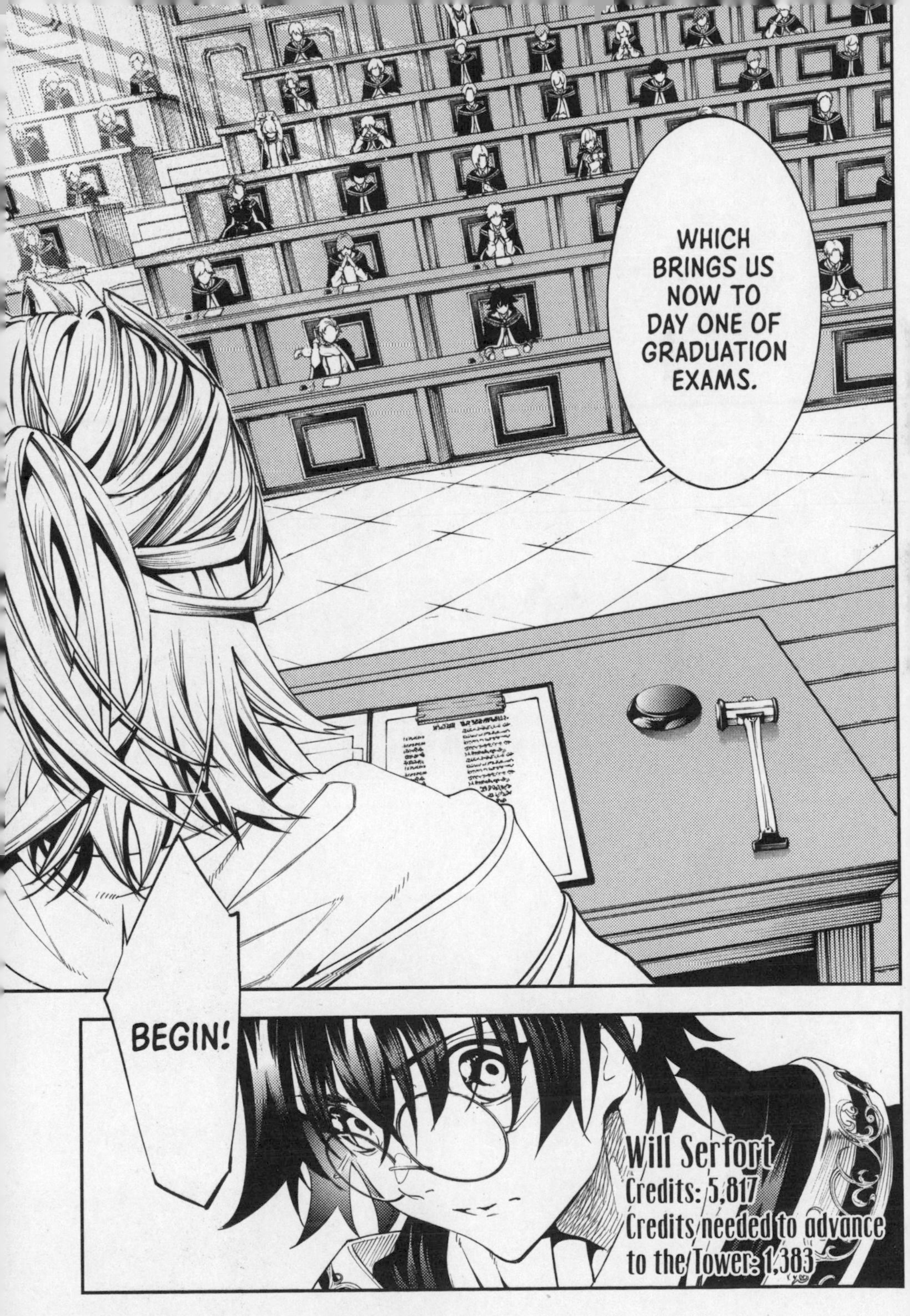
WHICH BRINGS US NOW TO DAY ONE OF GRADUATION EXAMS.
BEGIN!
Will Serfort
Credits: 5,817
Credits needed to advance to the Tower: 1,383

Wistoria
Wand and Sword

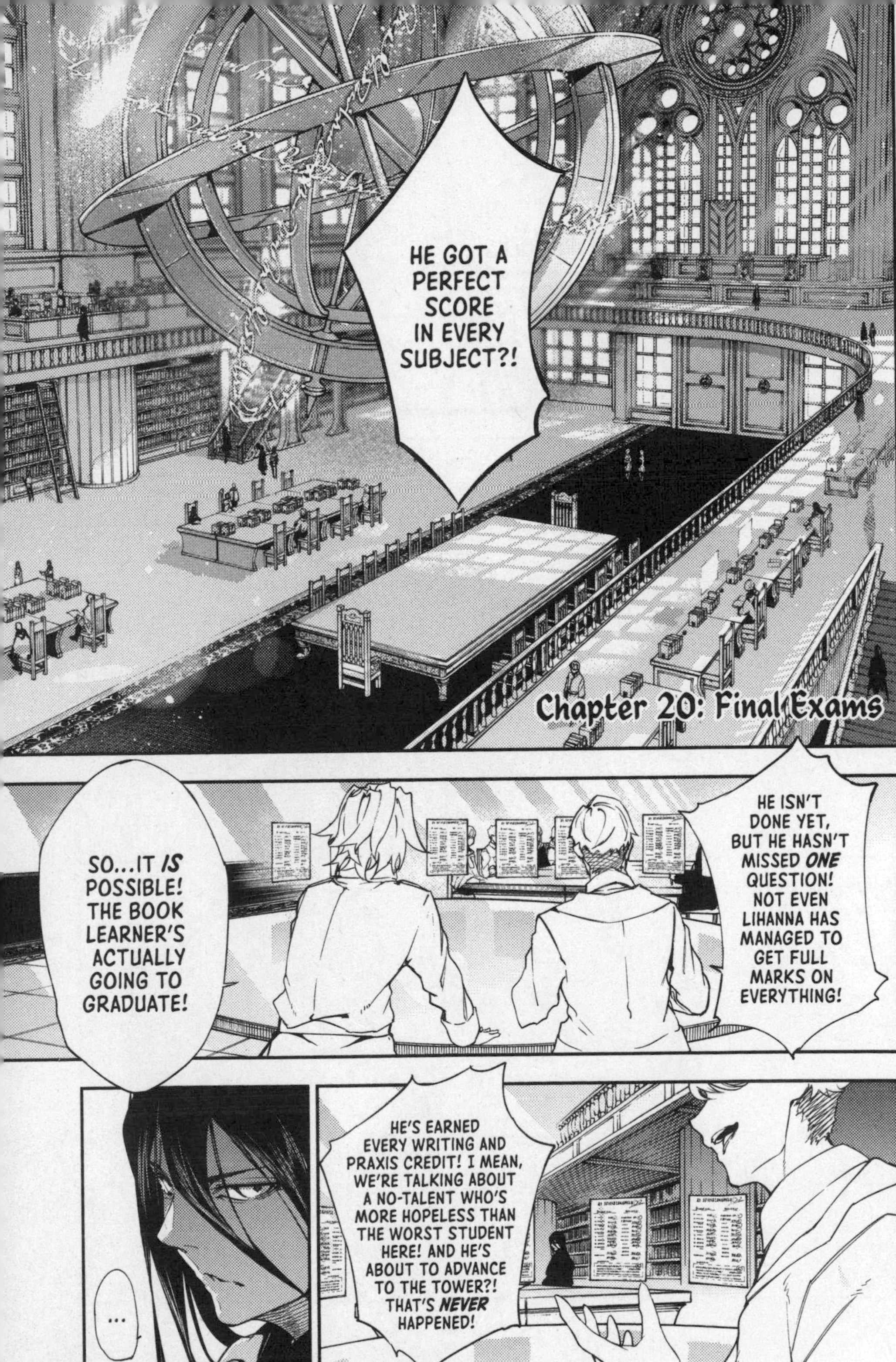
HE GOT A PERFECT SCORE IN EVERY SUBJECT?!
Chapter 20: Final Exams
HE ISN'T DONE YET, BUT HE HASN'T MISSED *ONE* QUESTION! NOT EVEN LIHANNA HAS MANAGED TO GET FULL MARKS ON EVERYTHING!
SO...IT *IS* POSSIBLE! THE BOOK LEARNER'S ACTUALLY GOING TO GRADUATE!
HE'S EARNED EVERY WRITING AND PRAXIS CREDIT! I MEAN, WE'RE TALKING ABOUT A NO-TALENT WHO'S MORE HOPELESS THAN THE WORST STUDENT HERE! AND HE'S ABOUT TO ADVANCE TO THE TOWER?! THAT'S *NEVER* HAPPENED!
...

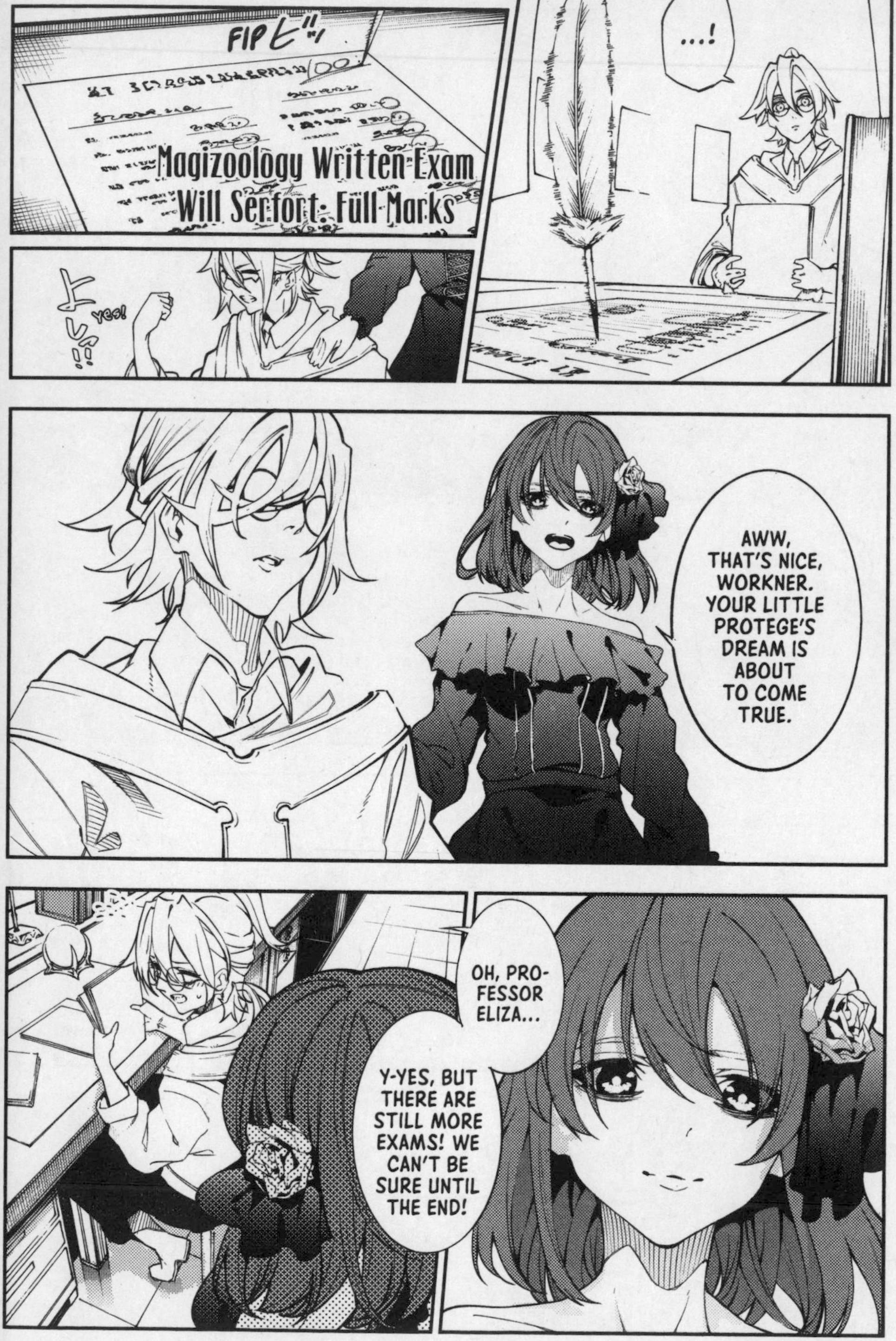
...!
FIP
Magizoology Written Exam
Will Serfort: Full Marks
YES!
AWW, THAT'S NICE, WORKNER. YOUR LITTLE PROTEGE'S DREAM IS ABOUT TO COME TRUE.
OH, PRO-FESSOR ELIZA...
Y-YES, BUT THERE ARE STILL MORE EXAMS! WE CAN'T BE SURE UNTIL THE END!

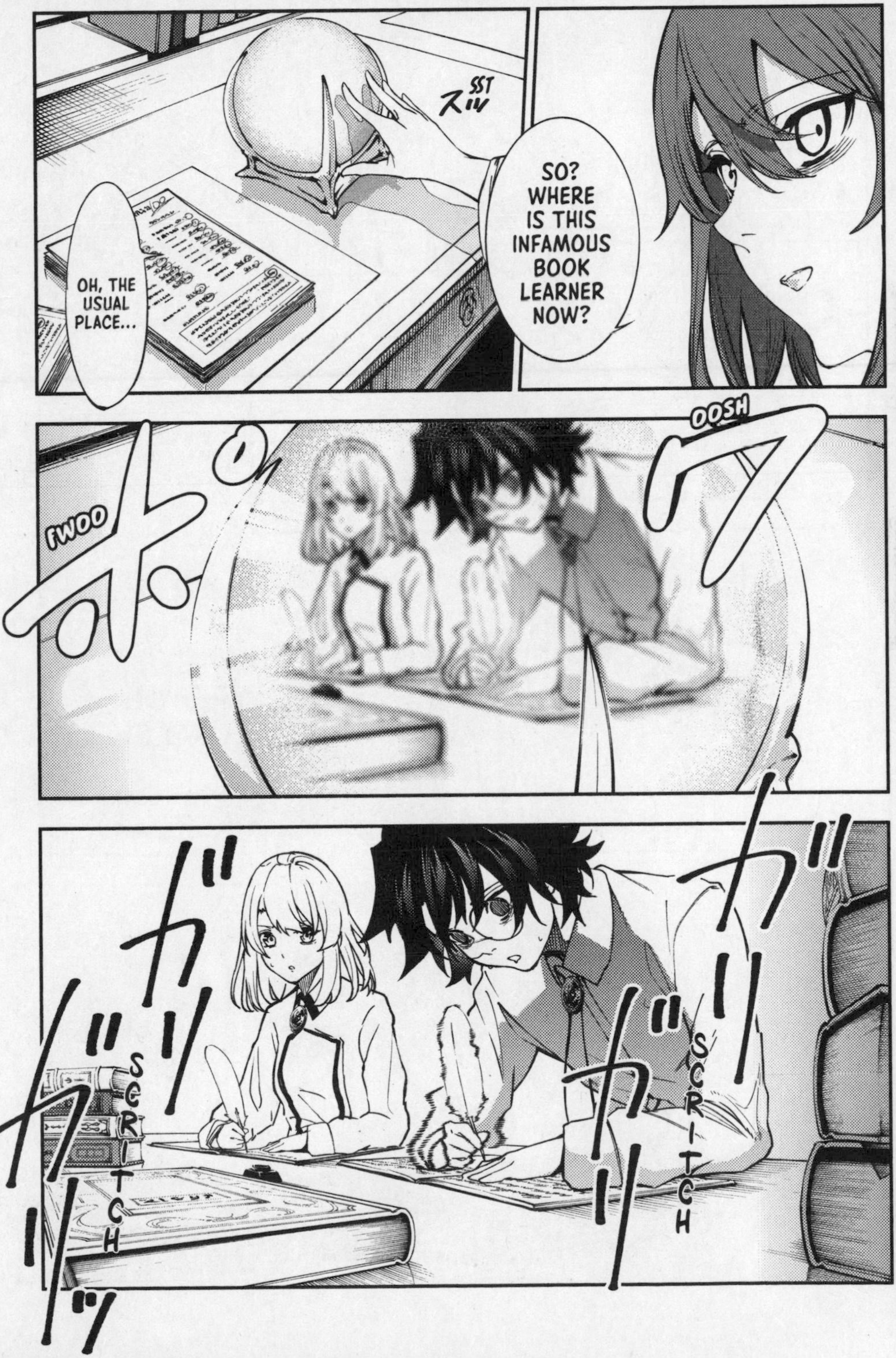
SO? WHERE IS THIS INFAMOUS BOOK LEARNER NOW?
SST
OH, THE USUAL PLACE...
OOSH
FWOO
SCRITCH
SCRITCH

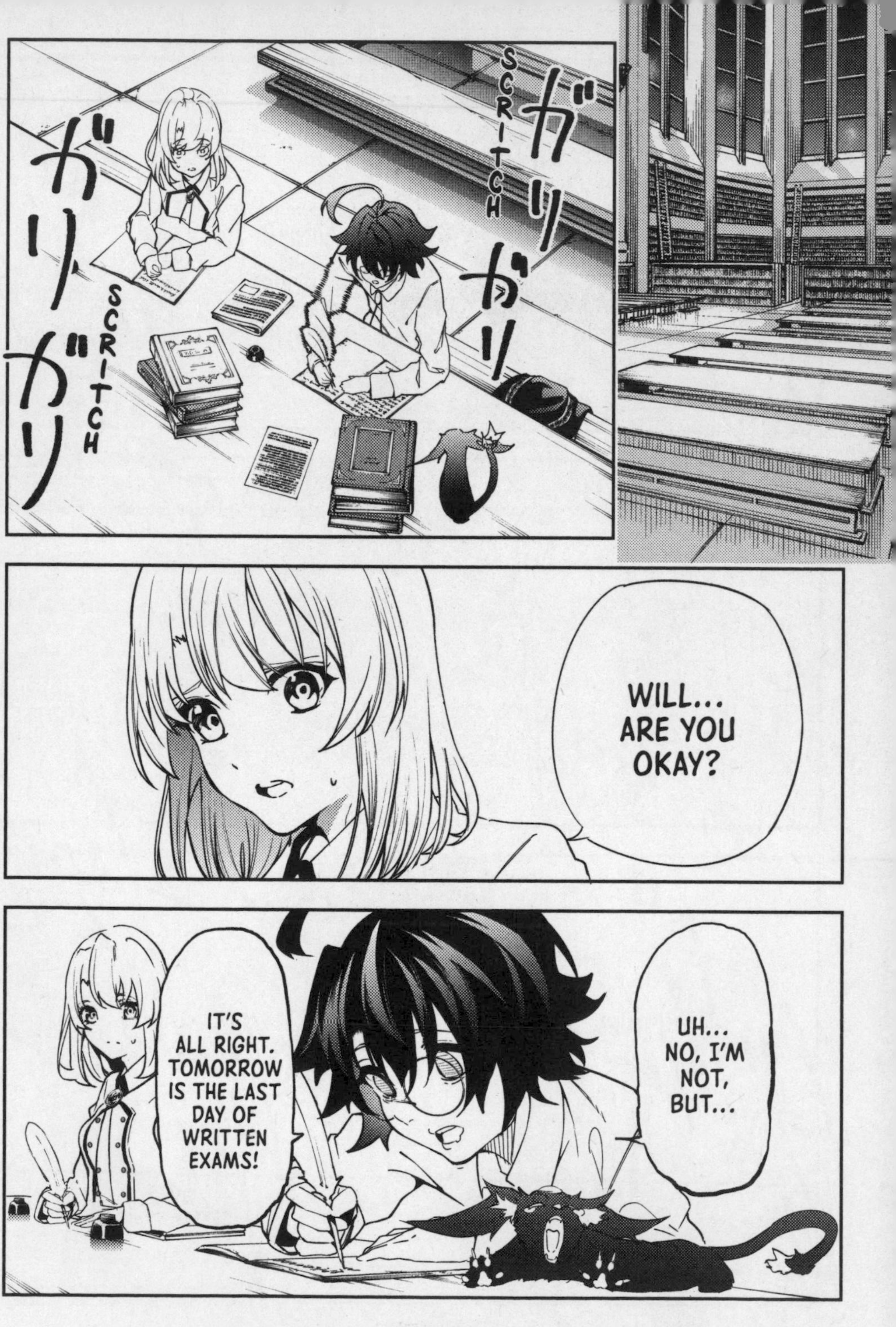
ガリガリ
SCRITCH
がりがり
SCRITCH
WILL... ARE YOU OKAY?
UH... NO, I'M NOT, BUT...
IT'S ALL RIGHT. TOMORROW IS THE LAST DAY OF WRITTEN EXAMS!

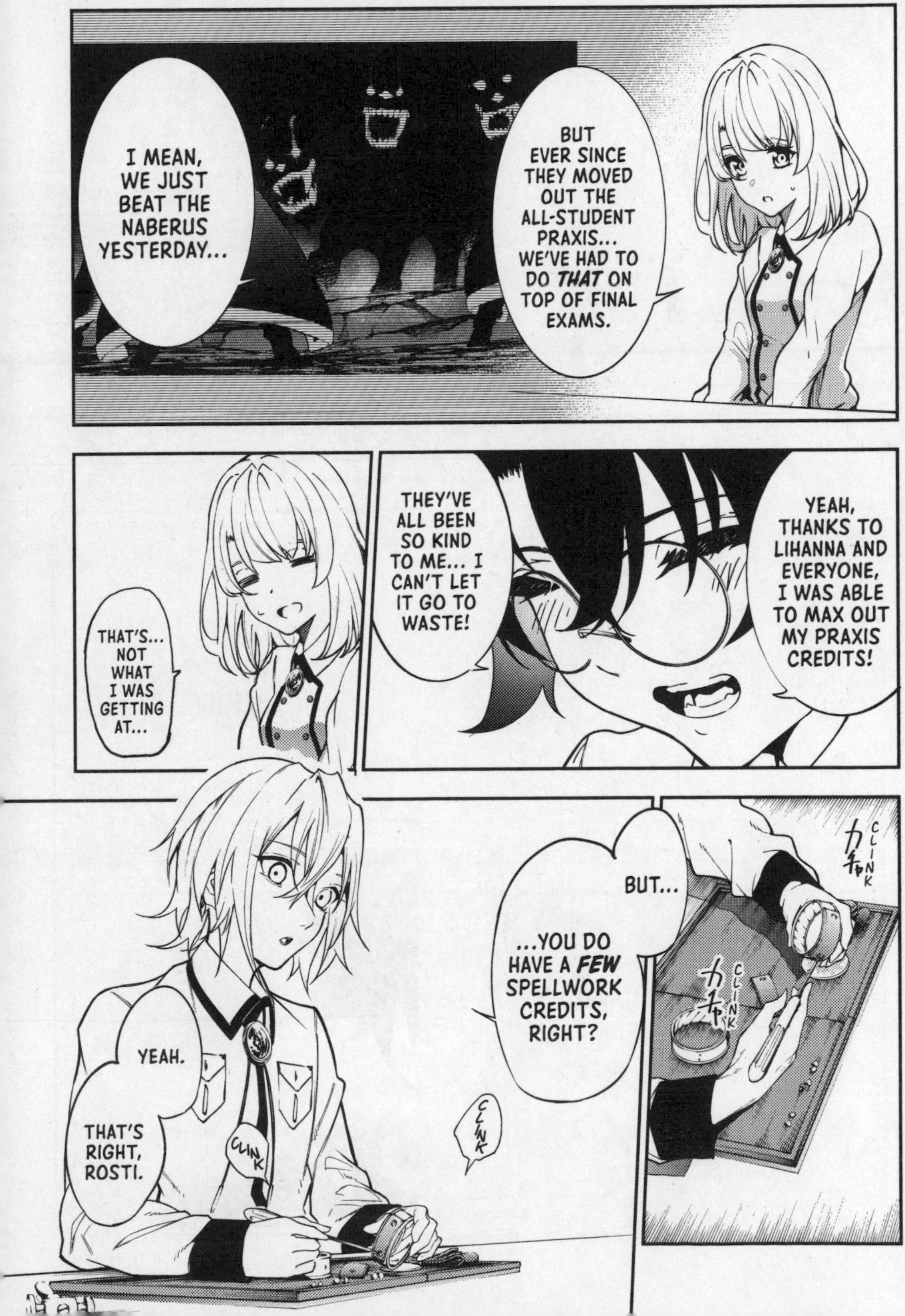
BUT EVER SINCE THEY MOVED OUT THE ALL-STUDENT PRAXIS... WE'VE HAD TO DO *THAT* ON TOP OF FINAL EXAMS.
I MEAN, WE JUST BEAT THE NABERUS YESTERDAY...
YEAH, THANKS TO LIHANNA AND EVERYONE, I WAS ABLE TO MAX OUT MY PRAXIS CREDITS!
THEY'VE ALL BEEN SO KIND TO ME... I CAN'T LET IT GO TO WASTE!
THAT'S... NOT WHAT I WAS GETTING AT...
カチャ CLINK
BUT...
カチャ CLINK
...YOU DO HAVE A *FEW* SPELLWORK CREDITS, RIGHT?
CLINK
YEAH.
CLINK
THAT'S RIGHT, ROSTI.

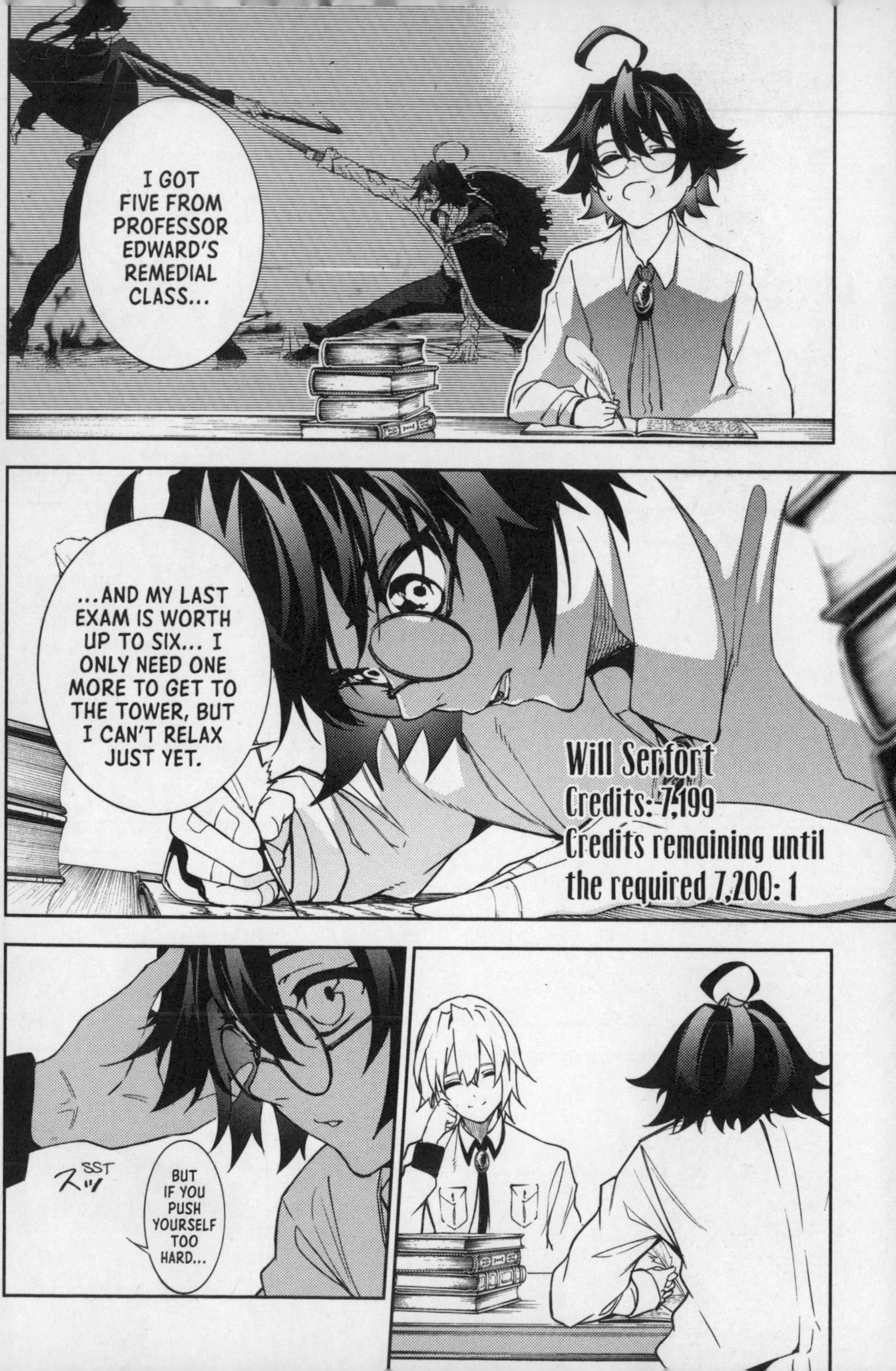
I GOT FIVE FROM PROFESSOR EDWARD'S REMEDIAL CLASS...
...AND MY LAST EXAM IS WORTH UP TO SIX... I ONLY NEED ONE MORE TO GET TO THE TOWER, BUT I CAN'T RELAX JUST YET.
Will Serfort
Credits: 7,199
Credits remaining until the required 7,200: 1
SST
BUT IF YOU PUSH YOURSELF TOO HARD...

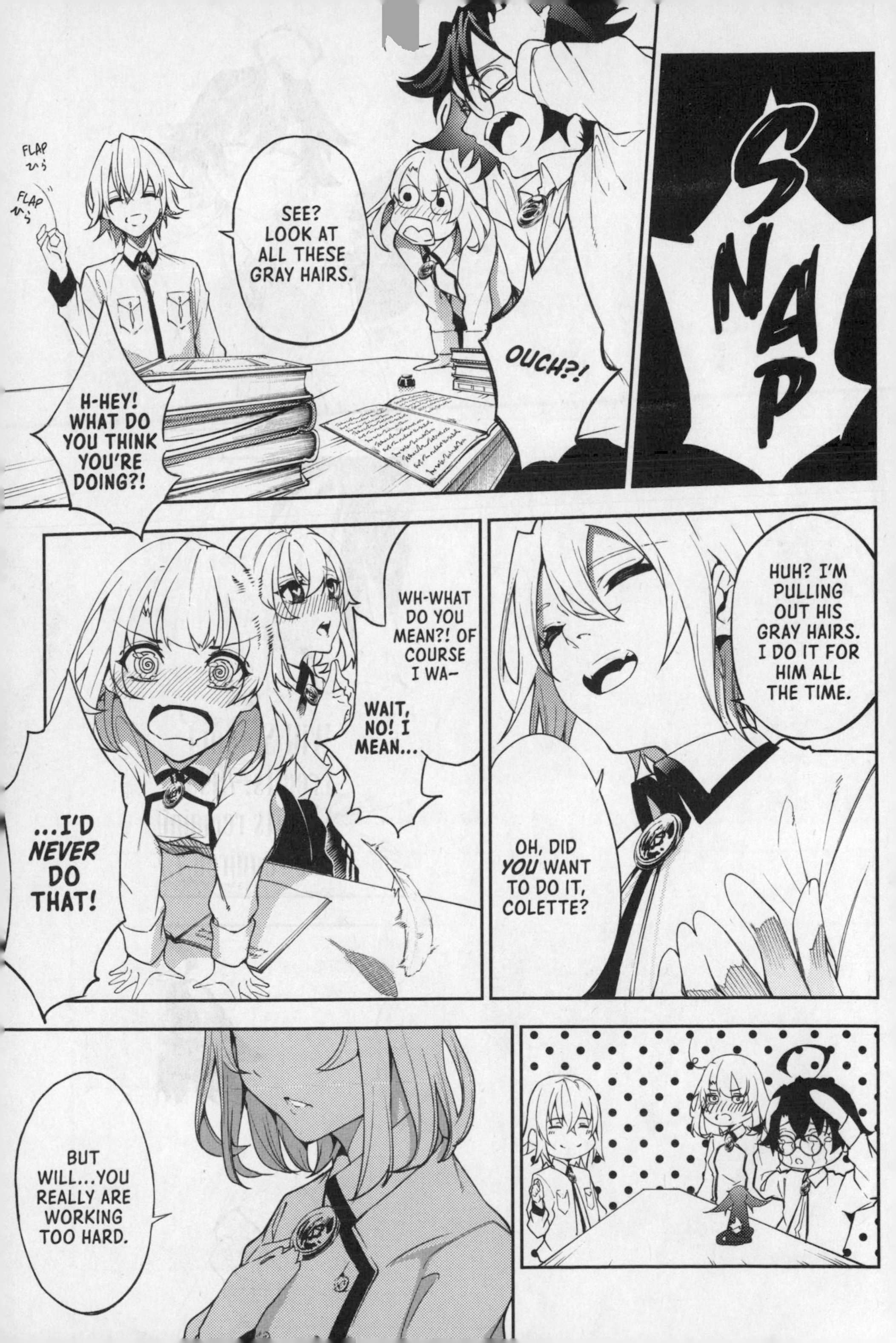
SNAP
OUCH?!
SEE? LOOK AT ALL THESE GRAY HAIRS.
FLAP ひら
FLAP ひら
H-HEY! WHAT DO YOU THINK YOU'RE DOING?!
HUH? I'M PULLING OUT HIS GRAY HAIRS. I DO IT FOR HIM ALL THE TIME.
OH, DID *YOU* WANT TO DO IT, COLETTE?
WH-WHAT DO YOU MEAN?! OF COURSE I WA—
WAIT, NO! I MEAN...
...I'D ***NEVER*** DO THAT!
BUT WILL...YOU REALLY ARE WORKING TOO HARD.

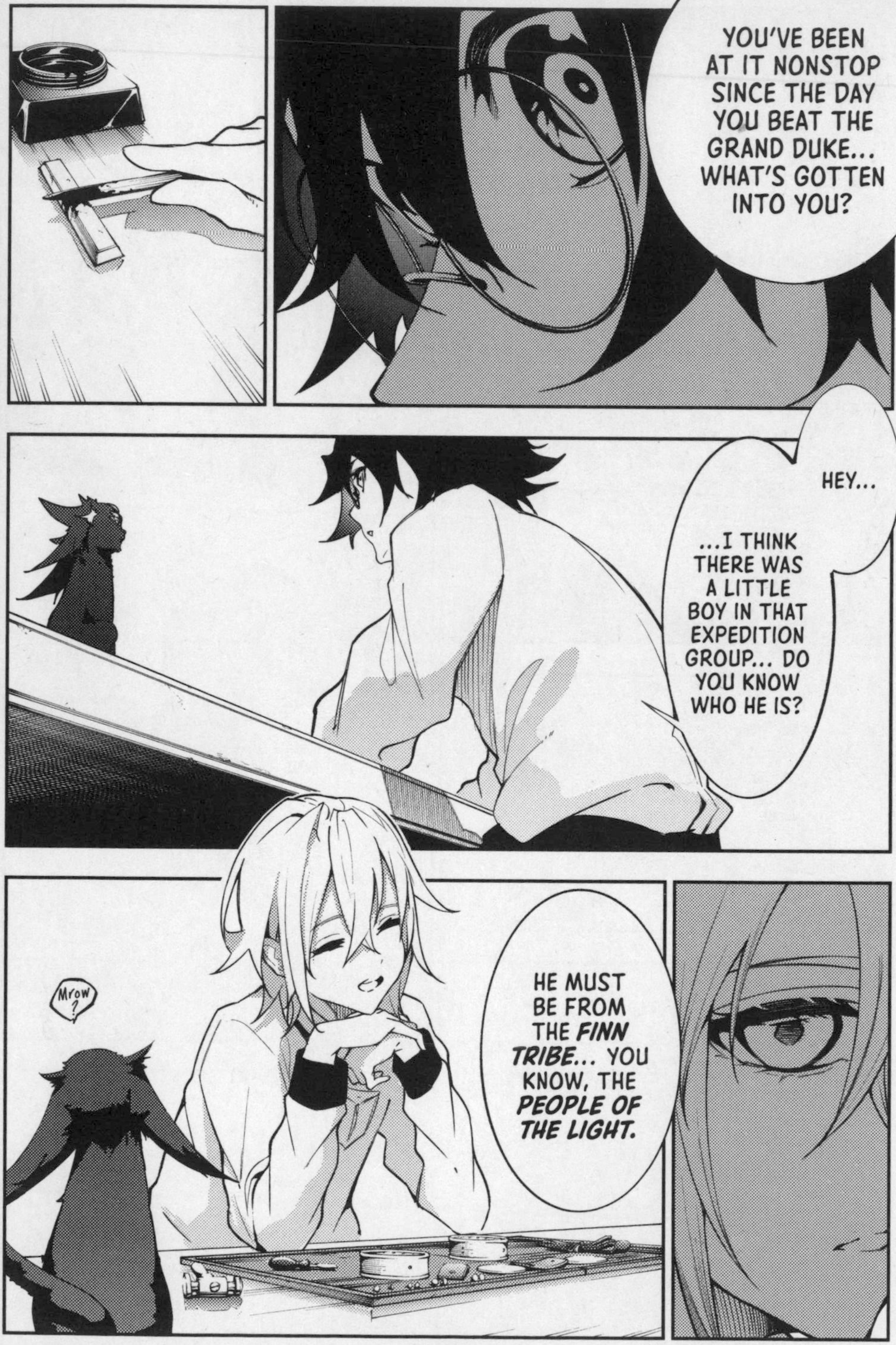
YOU'VE BEEN AT IT NONSTOP SINCE THE DAY YOU BEAT THE GRAND DUKE... WHAT'S GOTTEN INTO YOU?
HEY...
...I THINK THERE WAS A LITTLE BOY IN THAT EXPEDITION GROUP... DO YOU KNOW WHO HE IS?
HE MUST BE FROM THE *FINN TRIBE*... YOU KNOW, THE *PEOPLE OF THE LIGHT.*
Mrow?

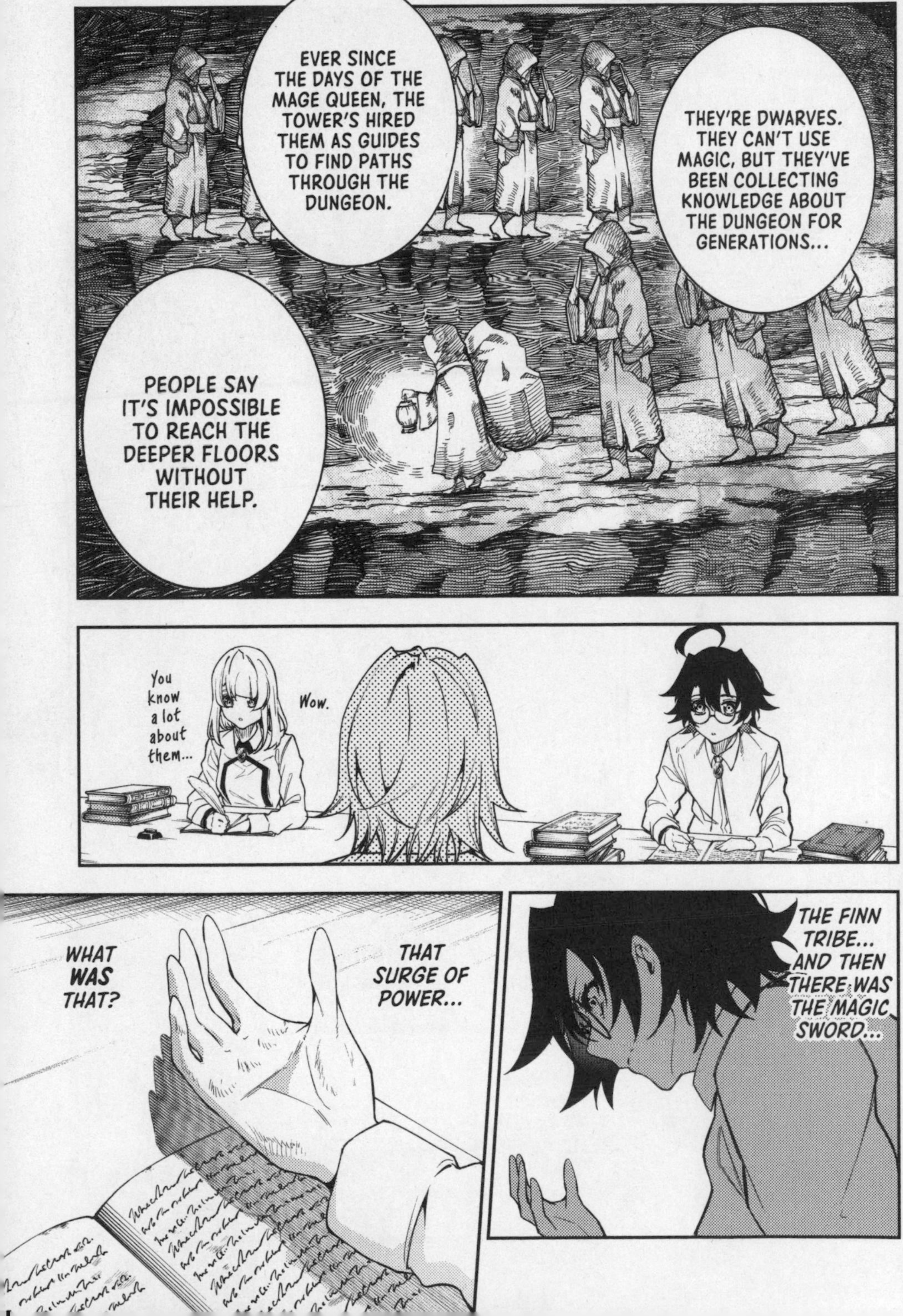
THEY'RE DWARVES. THEY CAN'T USE MAGIC, BUT THEY'VE BEEN COLLECTING KNOWLEDGE ABOUT THE DUNGEON FOR GENERATIONS...
EVER SINCE THE DAYS OF THE MAGE QUEEN, THE TOWER'S HIRED THEM AS GUIDES TO FIND PATHS THROUGH THE DUNGEON.
PEOPLE SAY IT'S IMPOSSIBLE TO REACH THE DEEPER FLOORS WITHOUT THEIR HELP.
Wow.
You know a lot about them...
THE FINN TRIBE... AND THEN THERE WAS THE MAGIC SWORD...
THAT SURGE OF POWER...
WHAT WAS THAT?

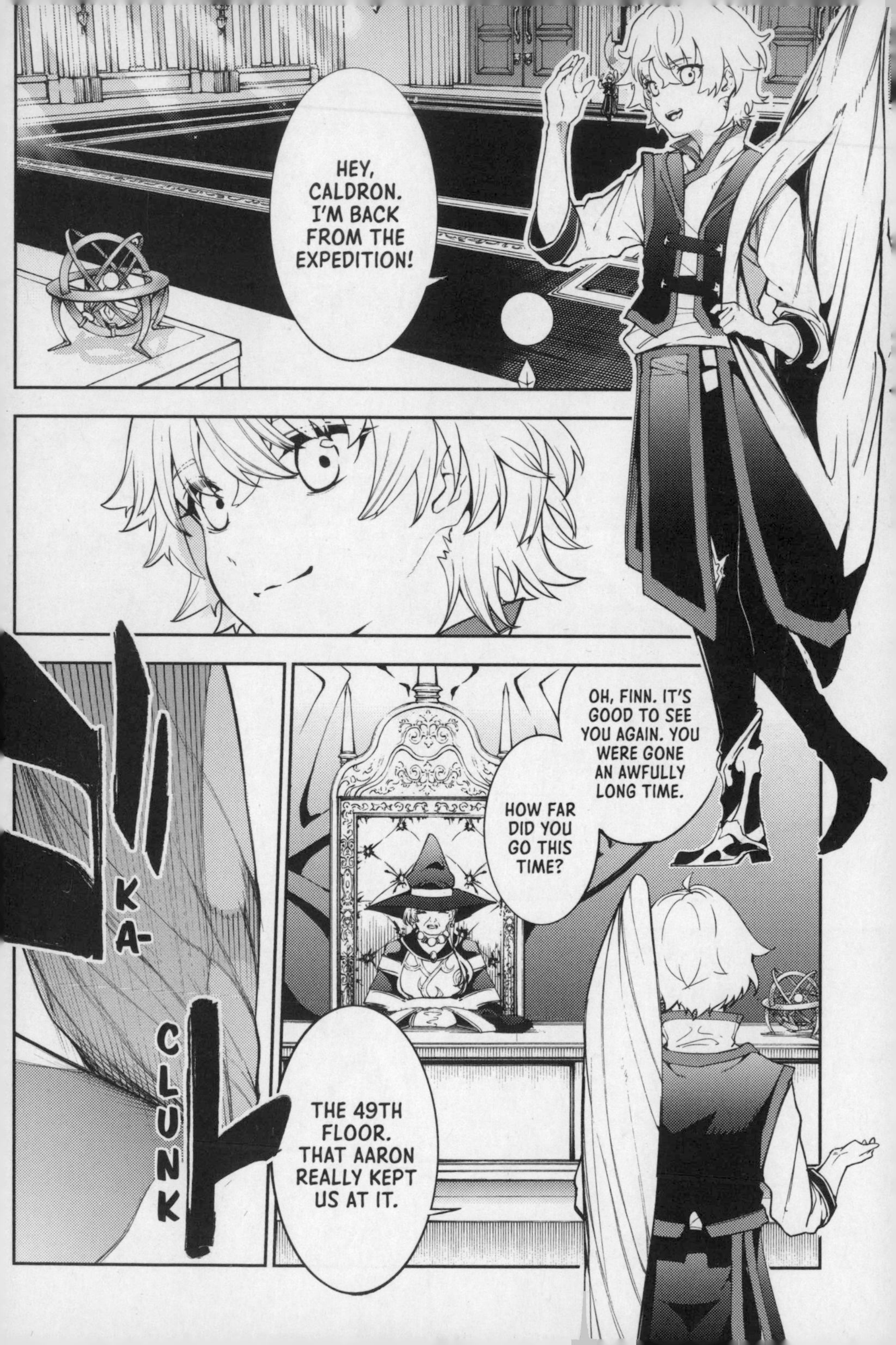
HEY, CALDRON. I'M BACK FROM THE EXPEDITION!
OH, FINN. IT'S GOOD TO SEE YOU AGAIN. YOU WERE GONE AN AWFULLY LONG TIME.
HOW FAR DID YOU GO THIS TIME?
THE 49TH FLOOR. THAT AARON REALLY KEPT US AT IT.
KA-CLUNK

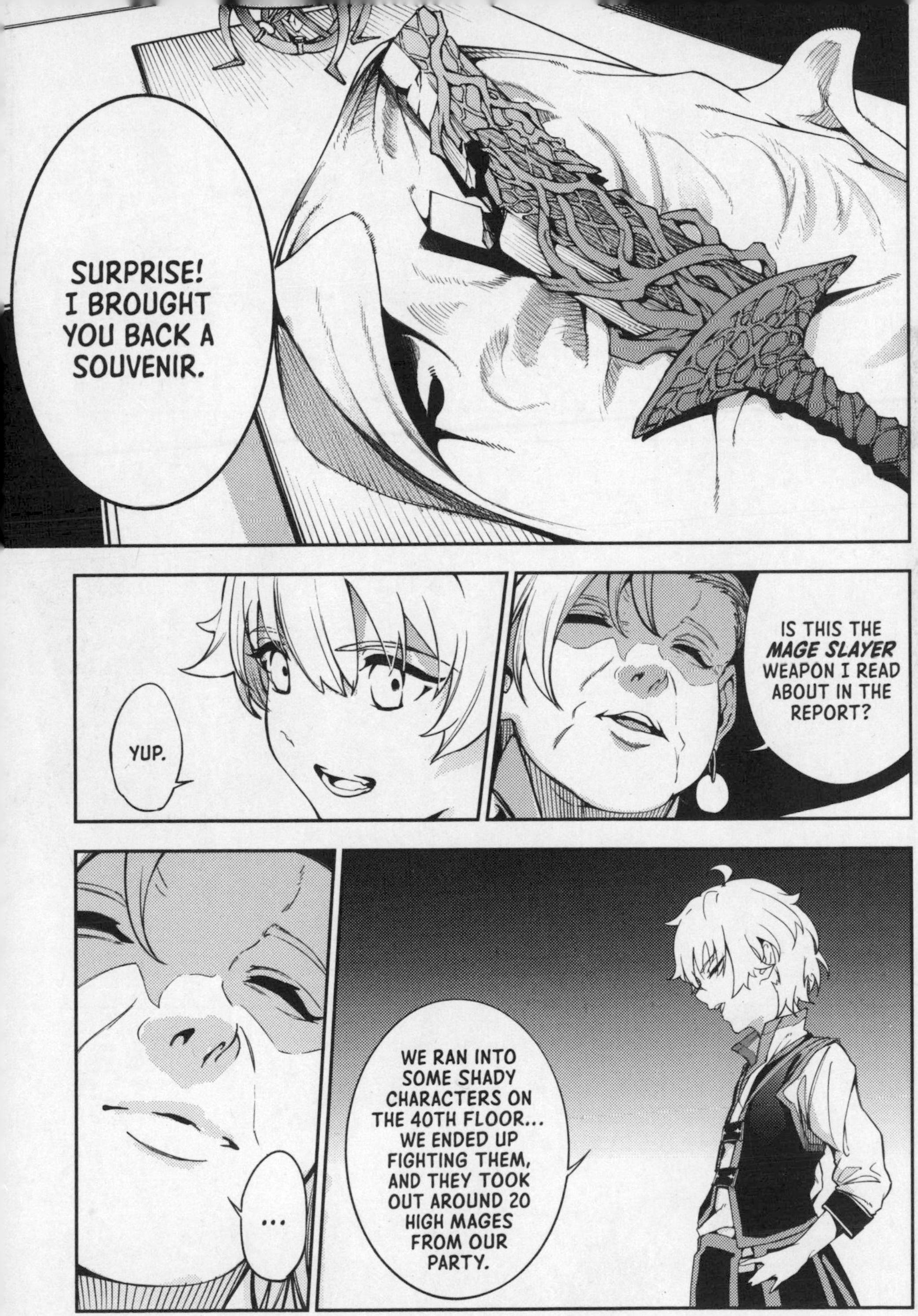
SURPRISE! I BROUGHT YOU BACK A SOUVENIR.
IS THIS THE *MAGE SLAYER* WEAPON I READ ABOUT IN THE REPORT?
YUP.
WE RAN INTO SOME SHADY CHARACTERS ON THE 40TH FLOOR... WE ENDED UP FIGHTING THEM, AND THEY TOOK OUT AROUND 20 HIGH MAGES FROM OUR PARTY.
...

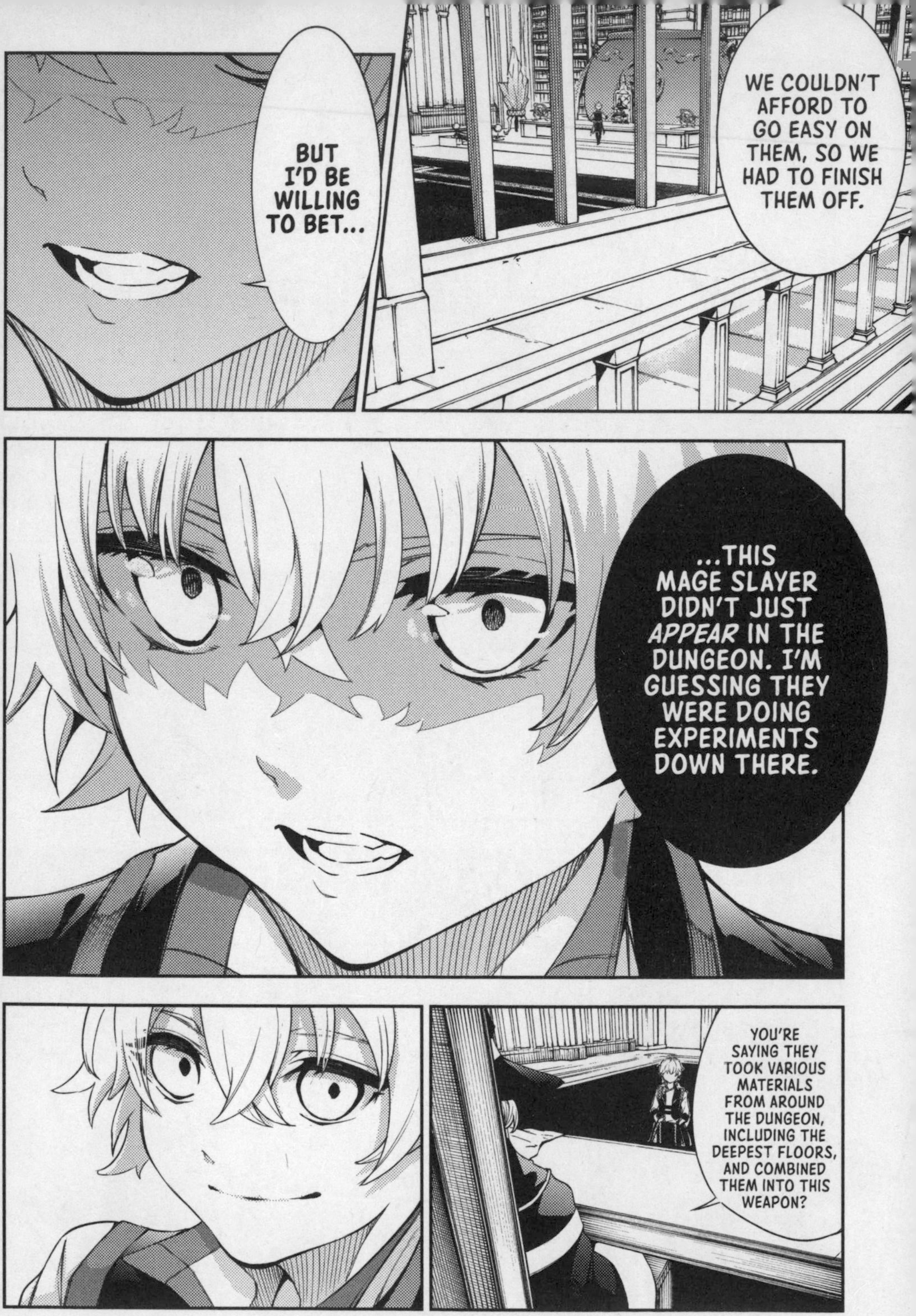
WE COULDN'T AFFORD TO GO EASY ON THEM, SO WE HAD TO FINISH THEM OFF.
BUT I'D BE WILLING TO BET...
...THIS MAGE SLAYER DIDN'T JUST *APPEAR* IN THE DUNGEON. I'M GUESSING THEY WERE DOING EXPERIMENTS DOWN THERE.
YOU'RE SAYING THEY TOOK VARIOUS MATERIALS FROM AROUND THE DUNGEON, INCLUDING THE DEEPEST FLOORS, AND COMBINED THEM INTO THIS WEAPON?

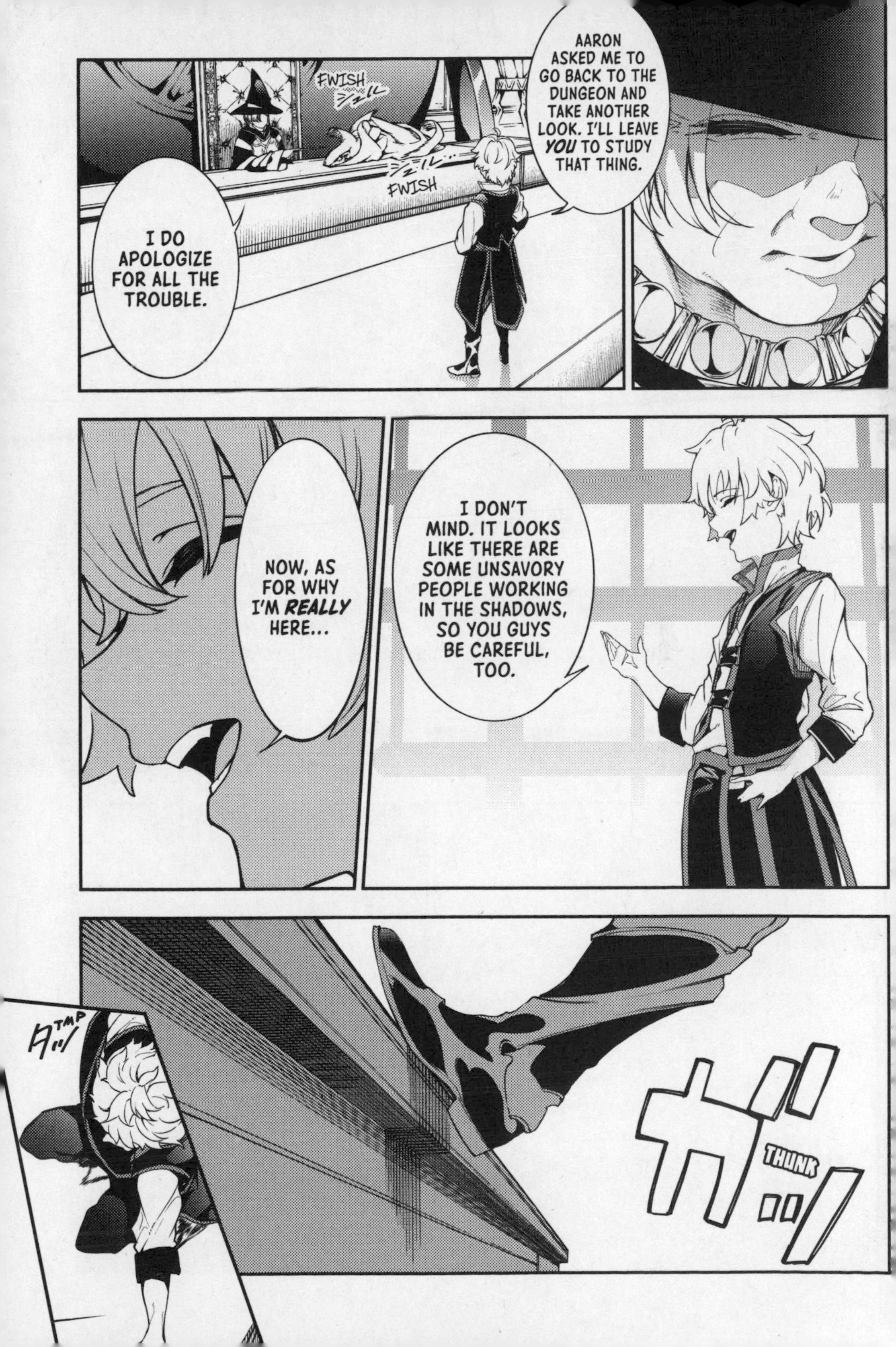
AARON ASKED ME TO GO BACK TO THE DUNGEON AND TAKE ANOTHER LOOK. I'LL LEAVE *YOU* TO STUDY THAT THING.
FWISH
FWISH
I DO APOLOGIZE FOR ALL THE TROUBLE.
I DON'T MIND. IT LOOKS LIKE THERE ARE SOME UNSAVORY PEOPLE WORKING IN THE SHADOWS, SO YOU GUYS BE CAREFUL, TOO.
NOW, AS FOR WHY I'M *REALLY* HERE...
THUNK
TMP

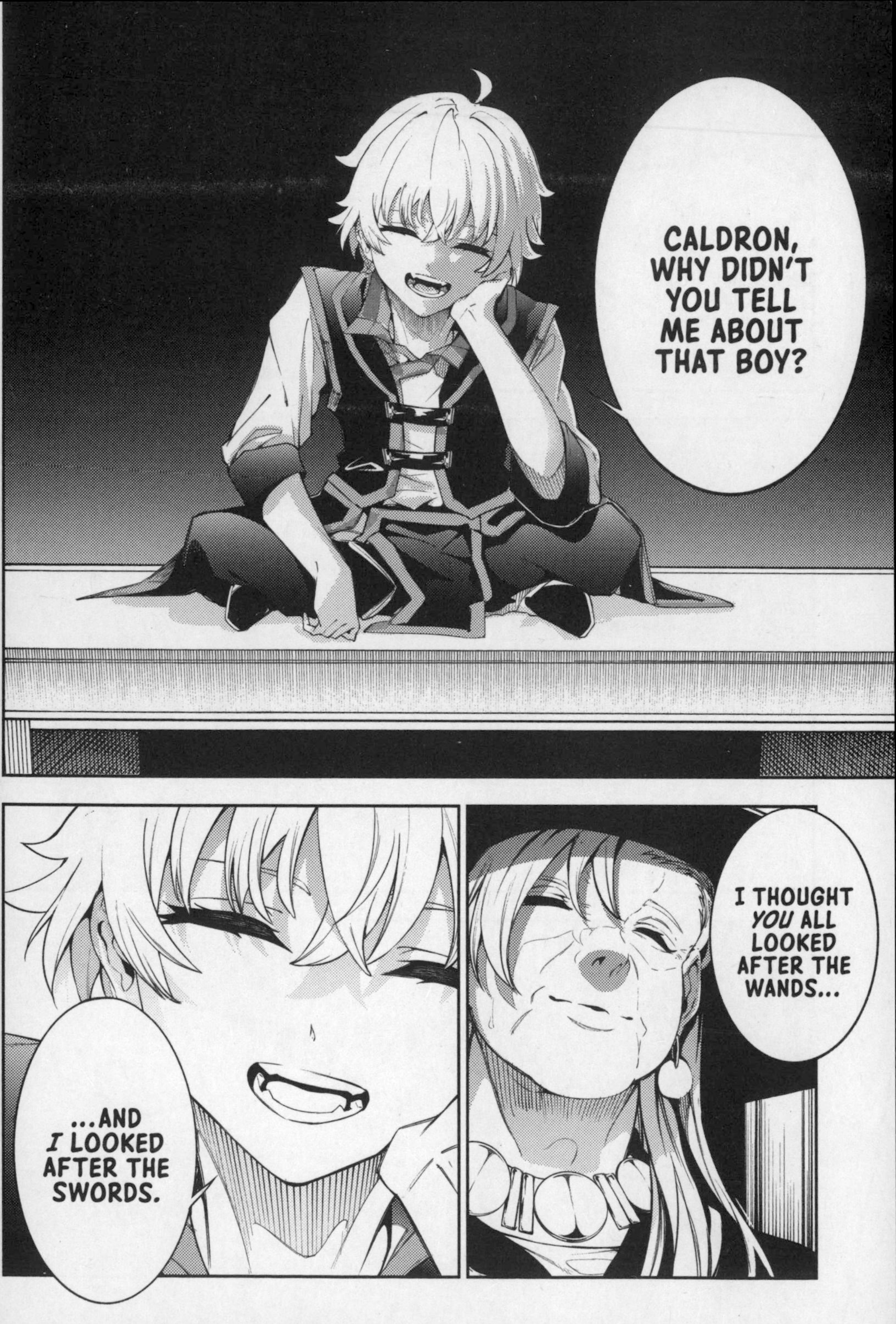
CALDRON, WHY DIDN'T YOU TELL ME ABOUT THAT BOY?
I THOUGHT *YOU* ALL LOOKED AFTER THE WANDS...
...AND *I* LOOKED AFTER THE SWORDS.

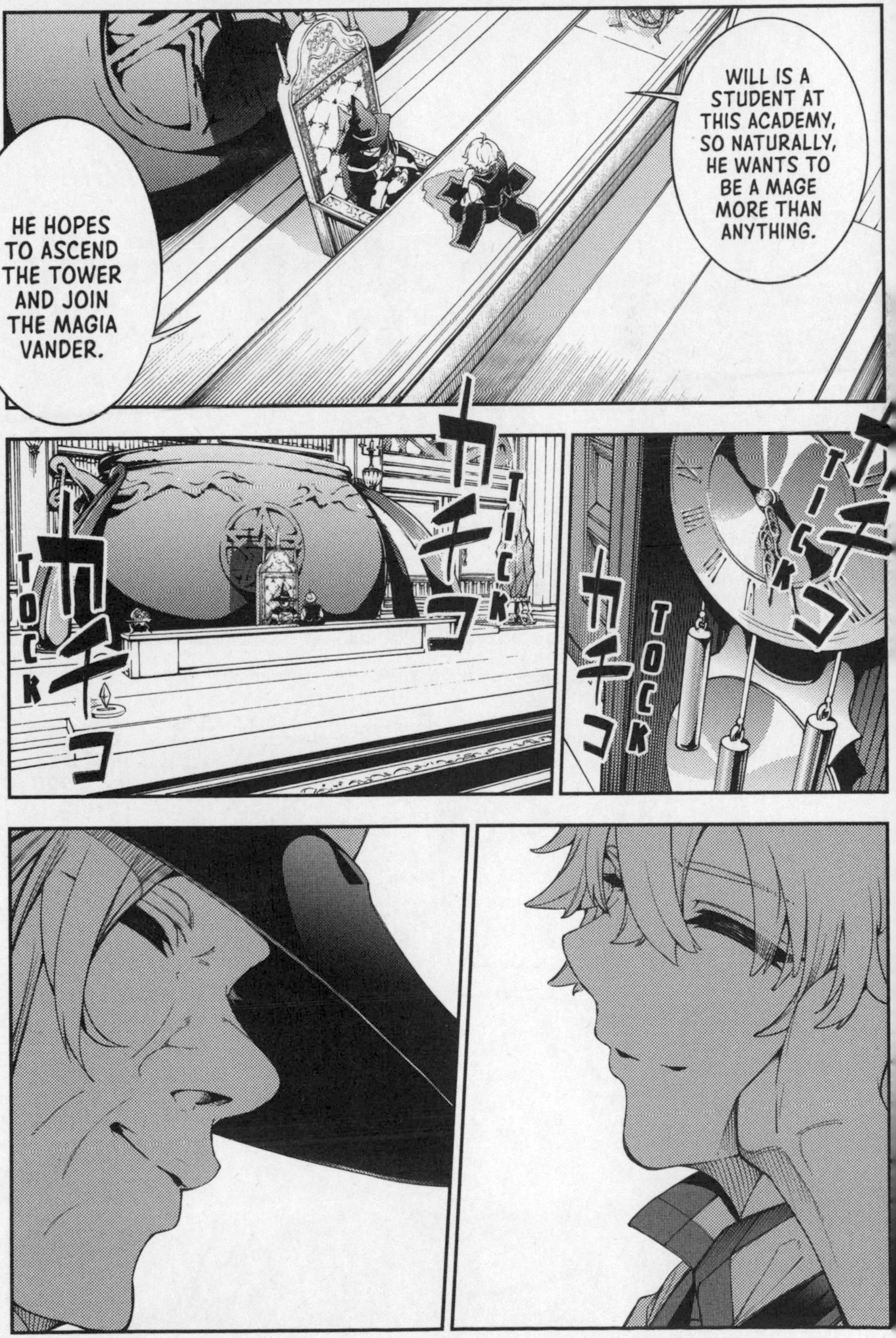
WILL IS A STUDENT AT THIS ACADEMY, SO NATURALLY, HE WANTS TO BE A MAGE MORE THAN ANYTHING.
HE HOPES TO ASCEND THE TOWER AND JOIN THE MAGIA VANDER.
TICK
TOCK
TICK
TOCK

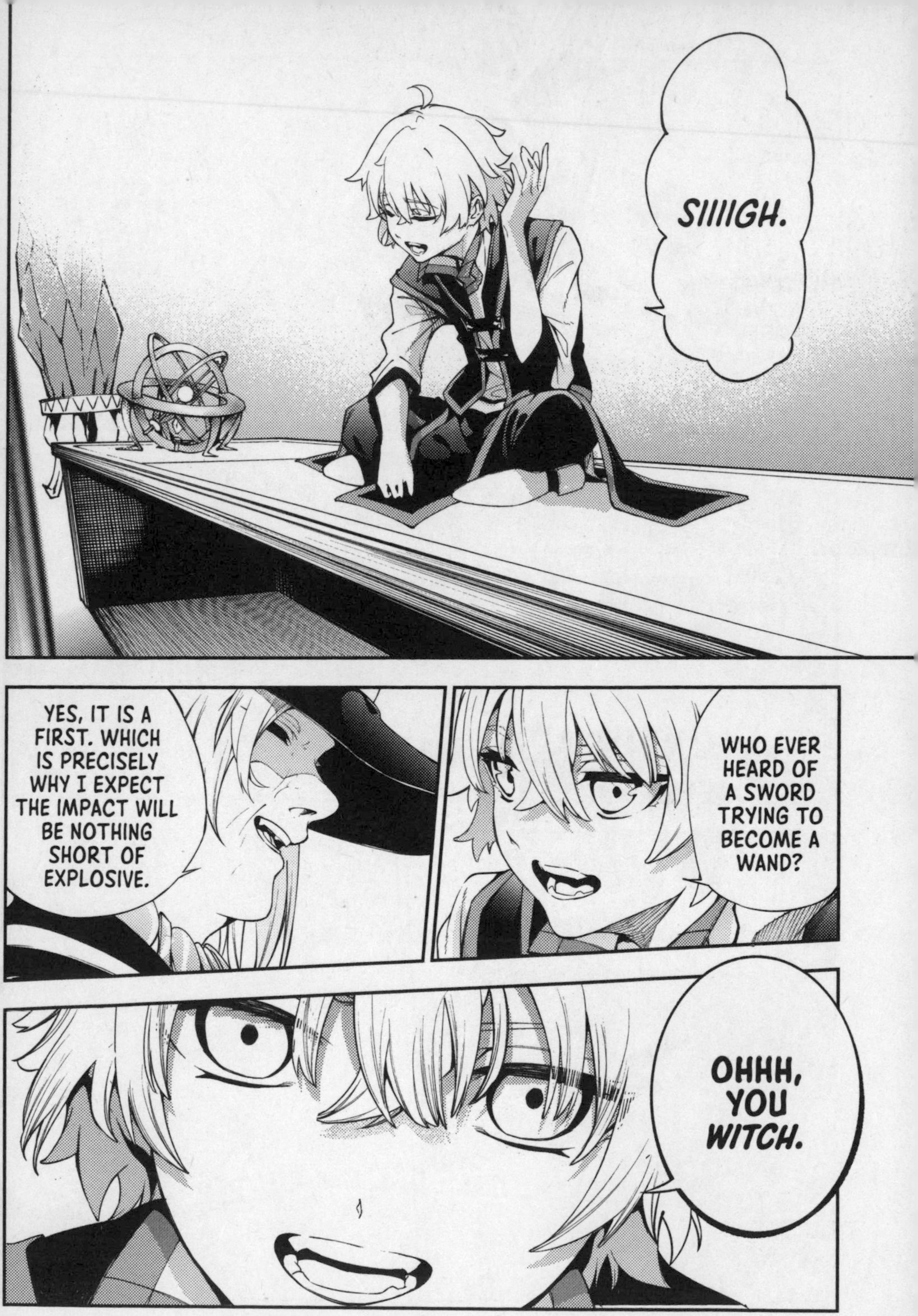
SIIIIGH.
WHO EVER HEARD OF A SWORD TRYING TO BECOME A WAND?
YES, IT IS A FIRST. WHICH IS PRECISELY WHY I EXPECT THE IMPACT WILL BE NOTHING SHORT OF EXPLOSIVE.
OHHH, YOU WITCH.

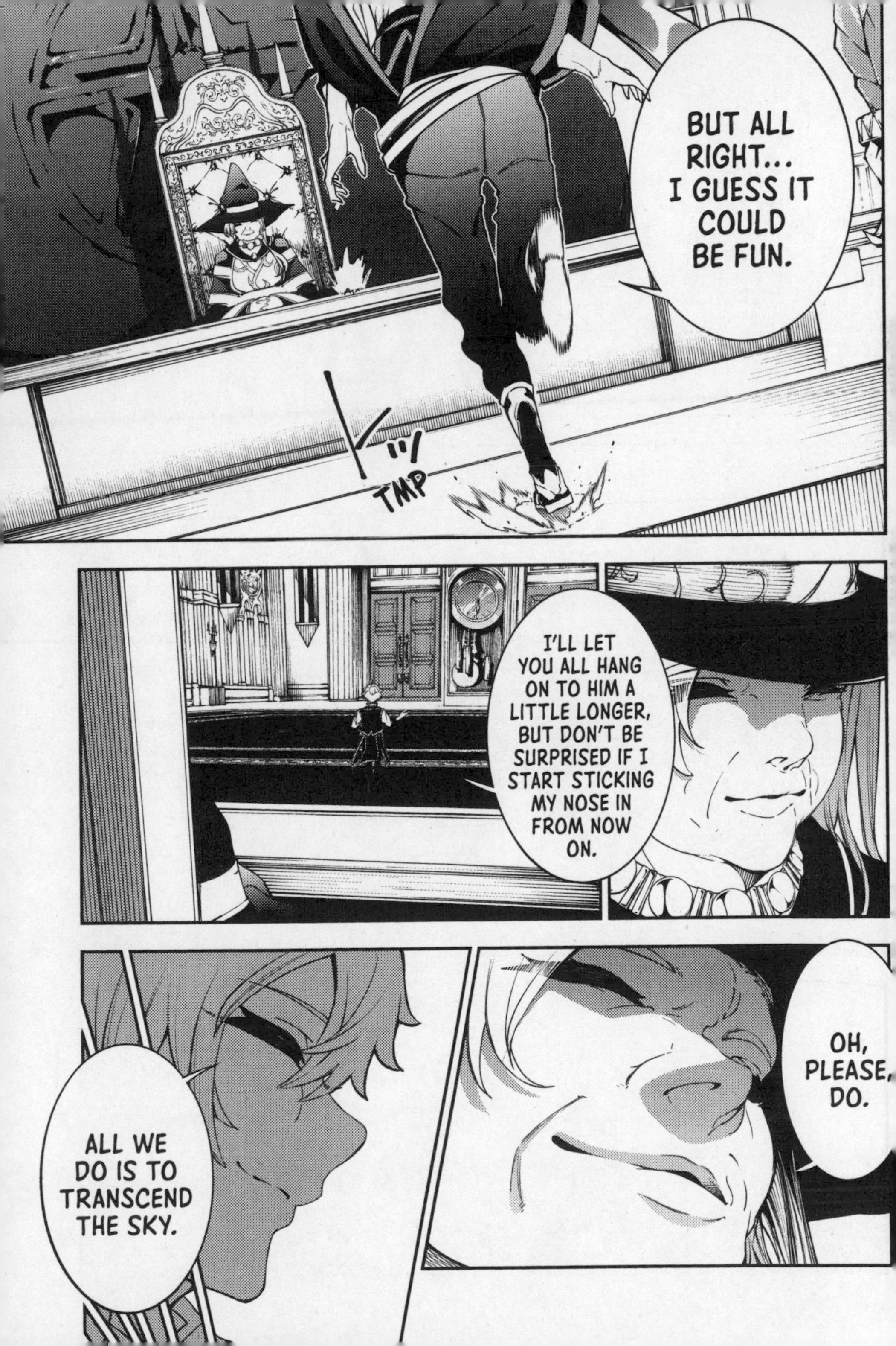
BUT ALL RIGHT... I GUESS IT COULD BE FUN.
TMP
I'LL LET YOU ALL HANG ON TO HIM A LITTLE LONGER, BUT DON'T BE SURPRISED IF I START STICKING MY NOSE IN FROM NOW ON.
OH, PLEASE, DO.
ALL WE DO IS TO TRANSCEND THE SKY.

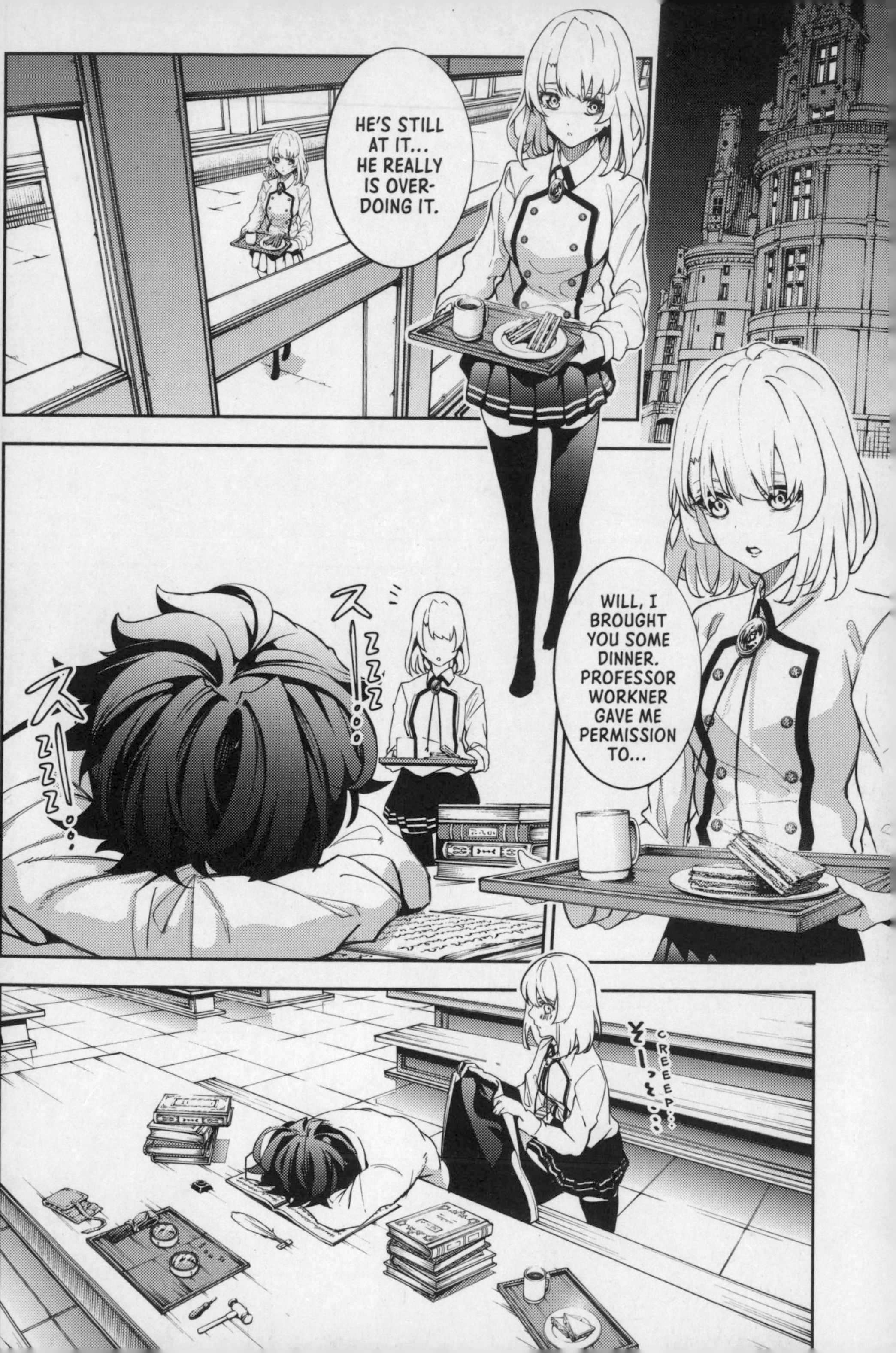
HE'S STILL AT IT... HE REALLY IS OVER-DOING IT.
WILL, I BROUGHT YOU SOME DINNER. PROFESSOR WORKNER GAVE ME PERMISSION TO...
zzz...
zzz...
CREEP...

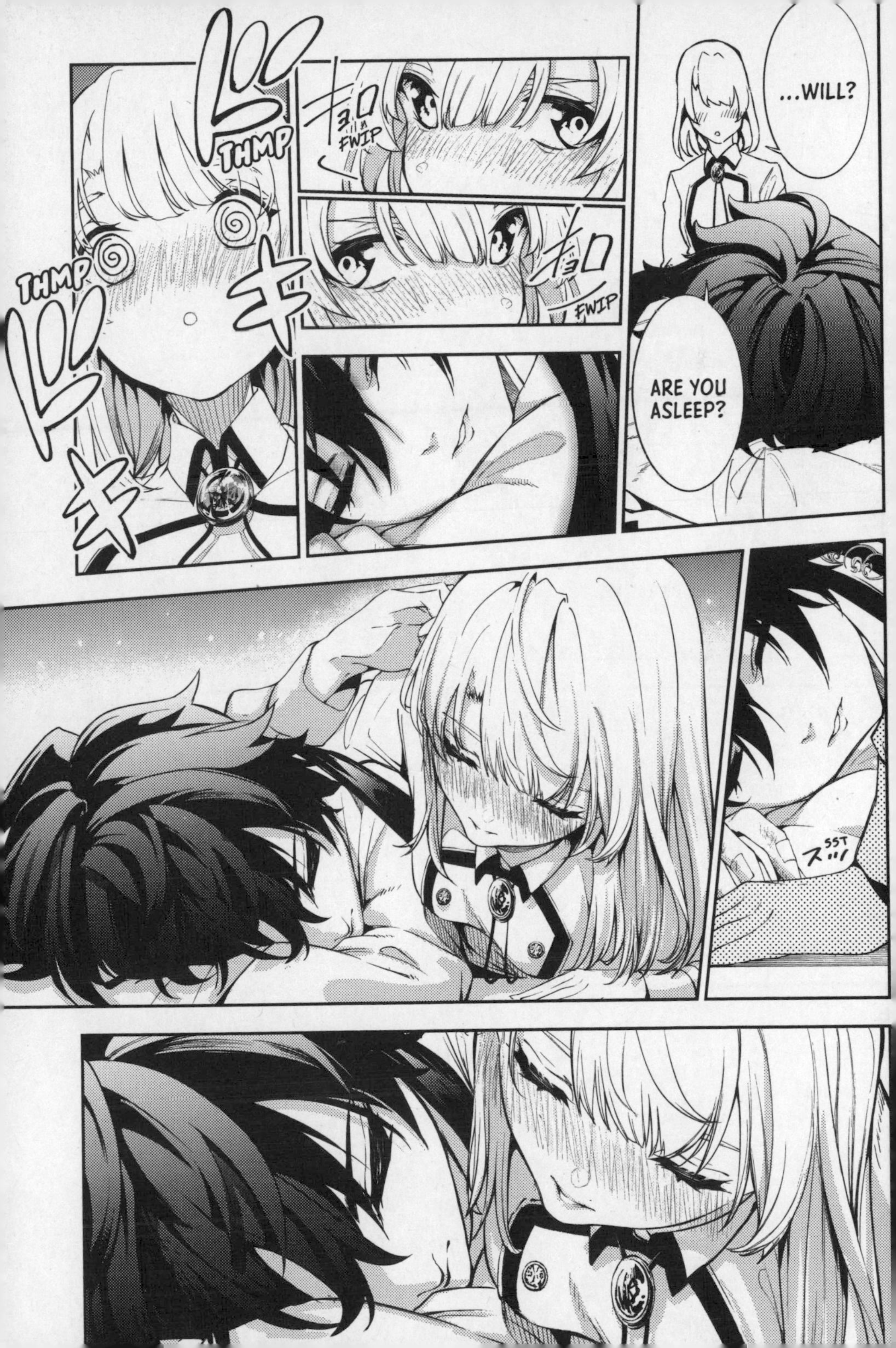
...WILL?
ARE YOU ASLEEP?
FWIP
FWIP
THMP
THMP
SST

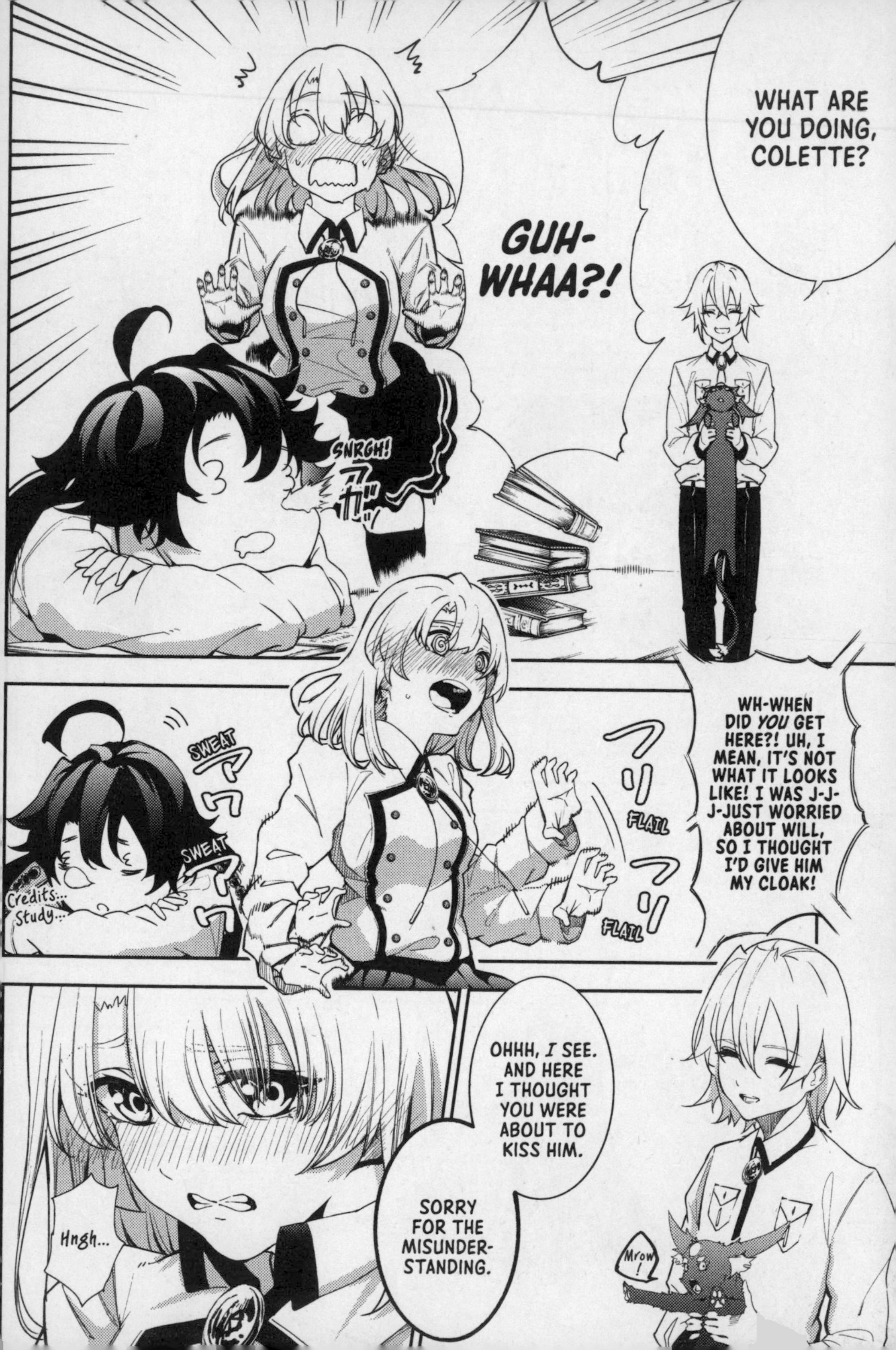
WHAT ARE YOU DOING, COLETTE?
GUH-WHAA?!
SNRGH!
WH-WHEN DID *YOU* GET HERE?! UH, I MEAN, IT'S NOT WHAT IT LOOKS LIKE! I WAS J-J-J-JUST WORRIED ABOUT WILL, SO I THOUGHT I'D GIVE HIM MY CLOAK!
FLAIL
FLAIL
SWEAT
SWEAT
Credits... Study...
OHHH, *I* SEE. AND HERE I THOUGHT YOU WERE ABOUT TO KISS HIM.
SORRY FOR THE MISUNDER-STANDING.
Mrow!
Hngh...

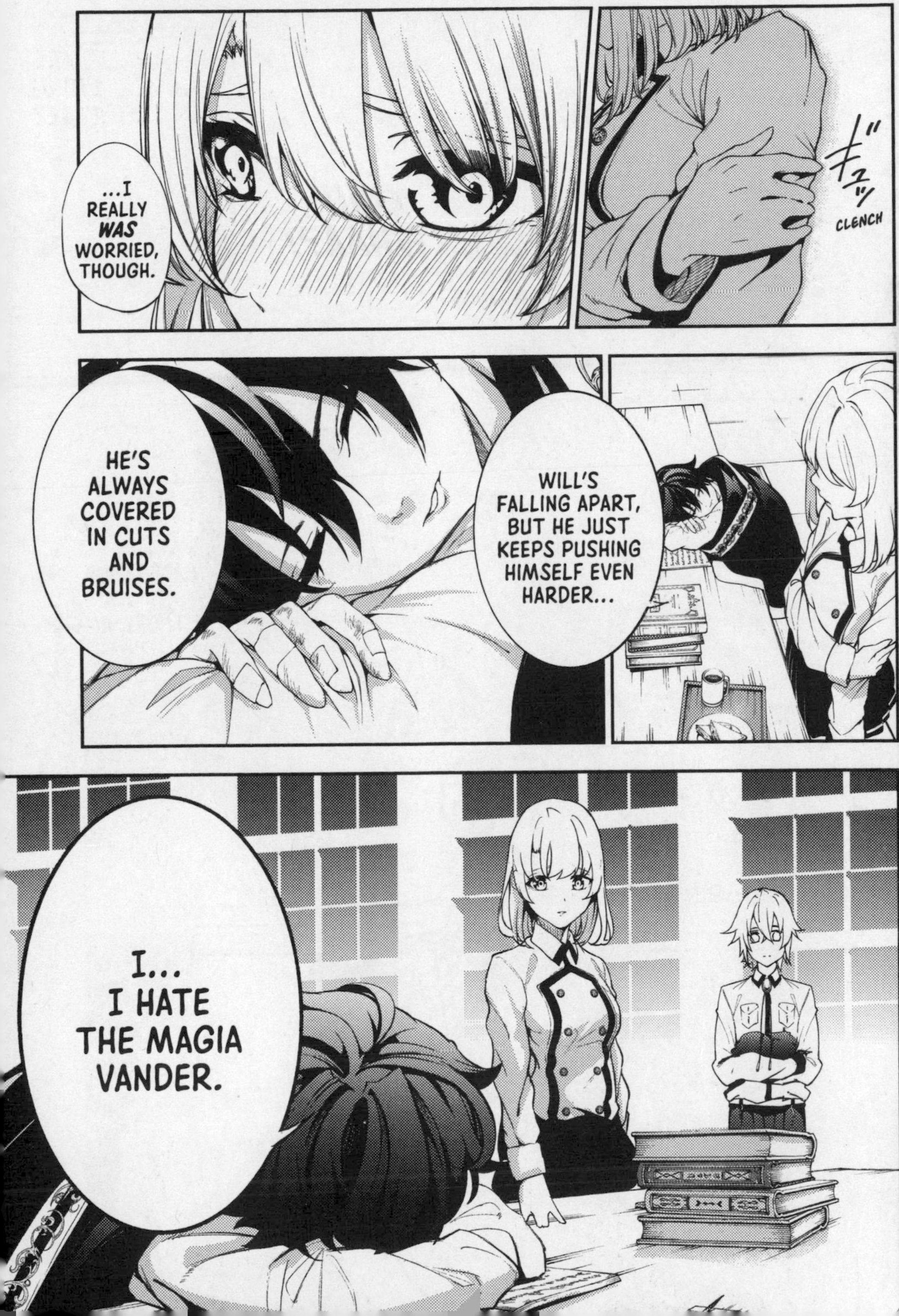
ギュッ
CLENCH
...I REALLY **WAS** WORRIED, THOUGH.
WILL'S FALLING APART, BUT HE JUST KEEPS PUSHING HIMSELF EVEN HARDER...
HE'S ALWAYS COVERED IN CUTS AND BRUISES.
I... I HATE THE MAGIA VANDER.

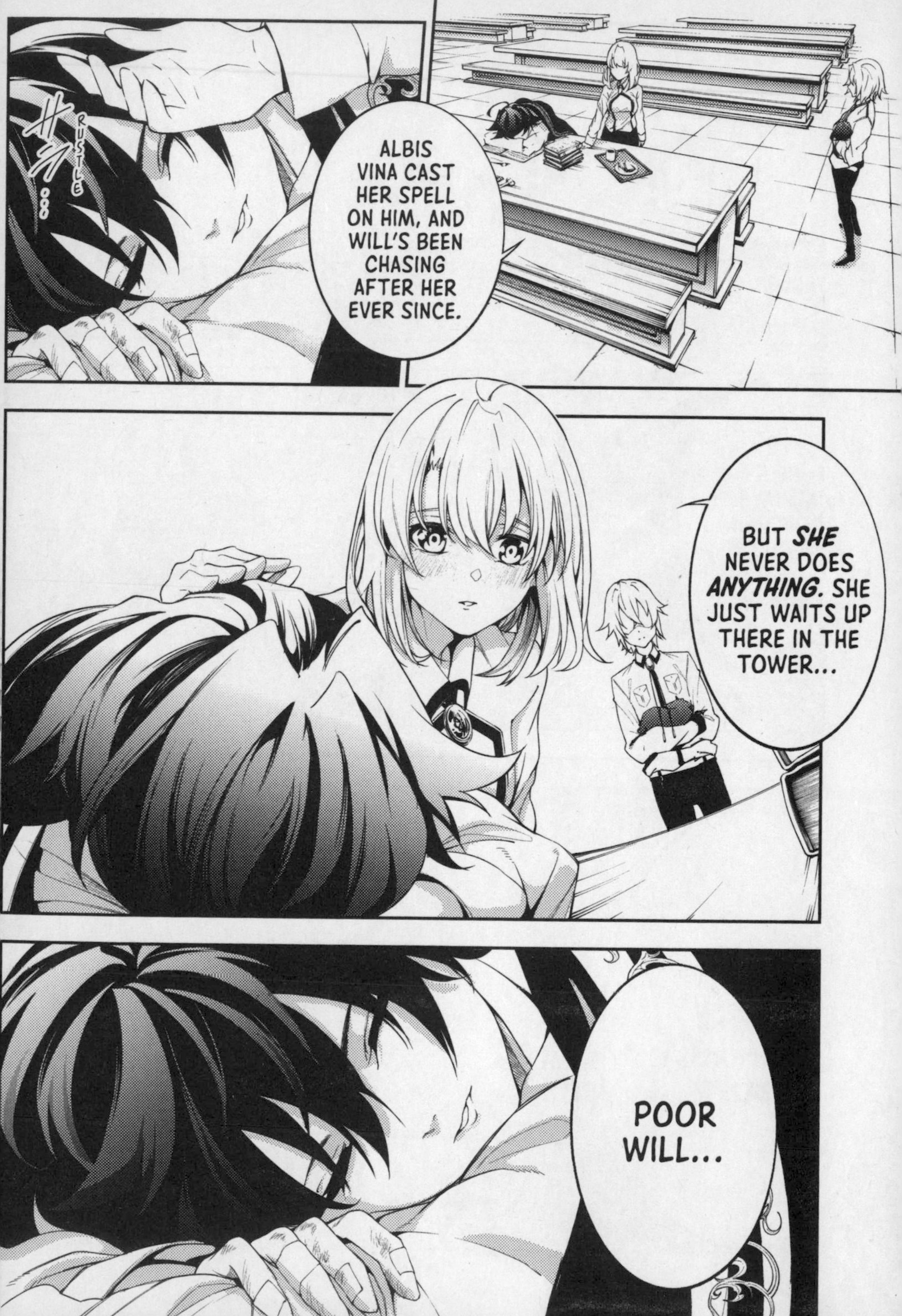
ALBIS VINA CAST HER SPELL ON HIM, AND WILL'S BEEN CHASING AFTER HER EVER SINCE.
RUSTLE
BUT *SHE* NEVER DOES ***ANYTHING.*** SHE JUST WAITS UP THERE IN THE TOWER...
POOR WILL...

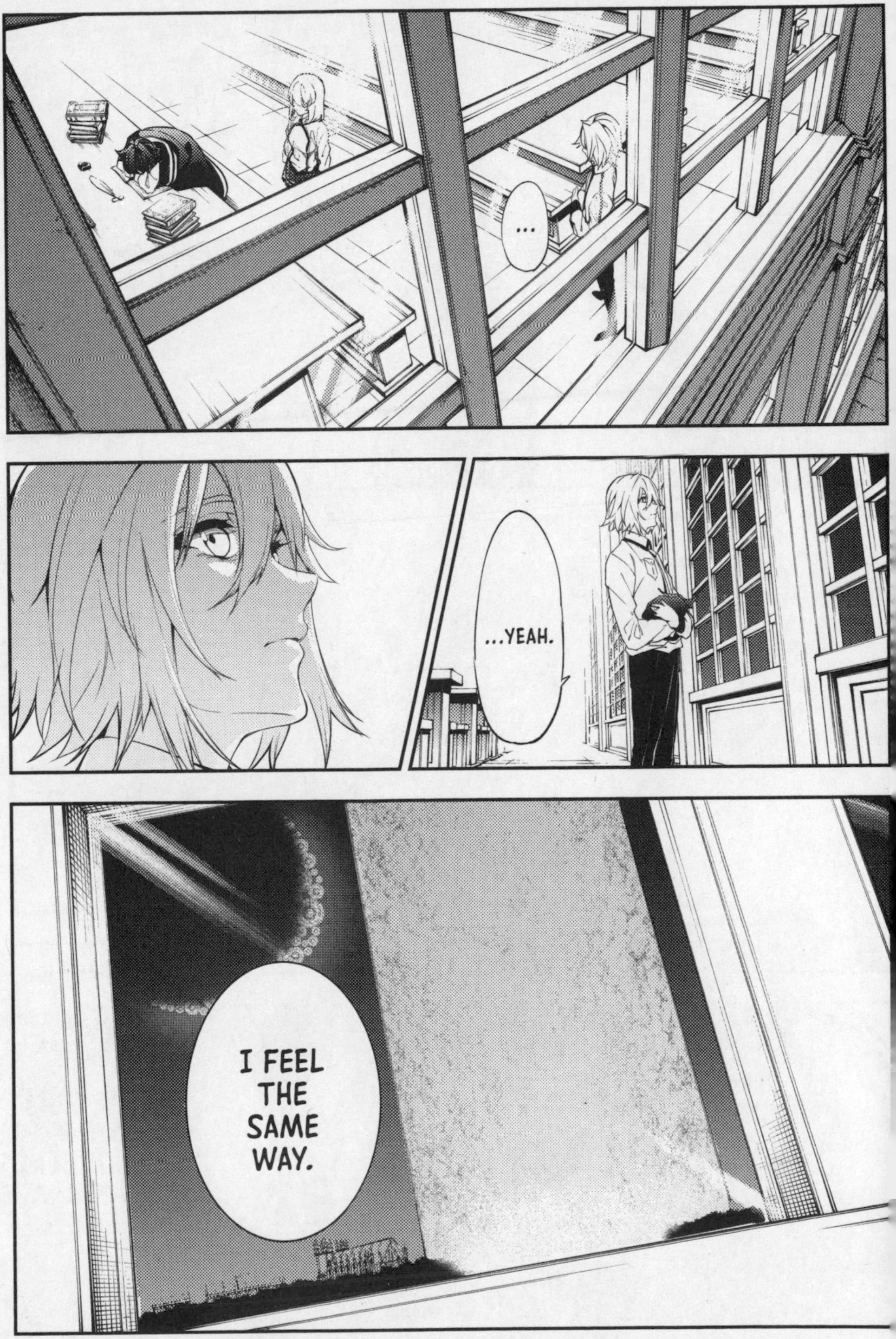
...
...YEAH.
I FEEL THE SAME WAY.

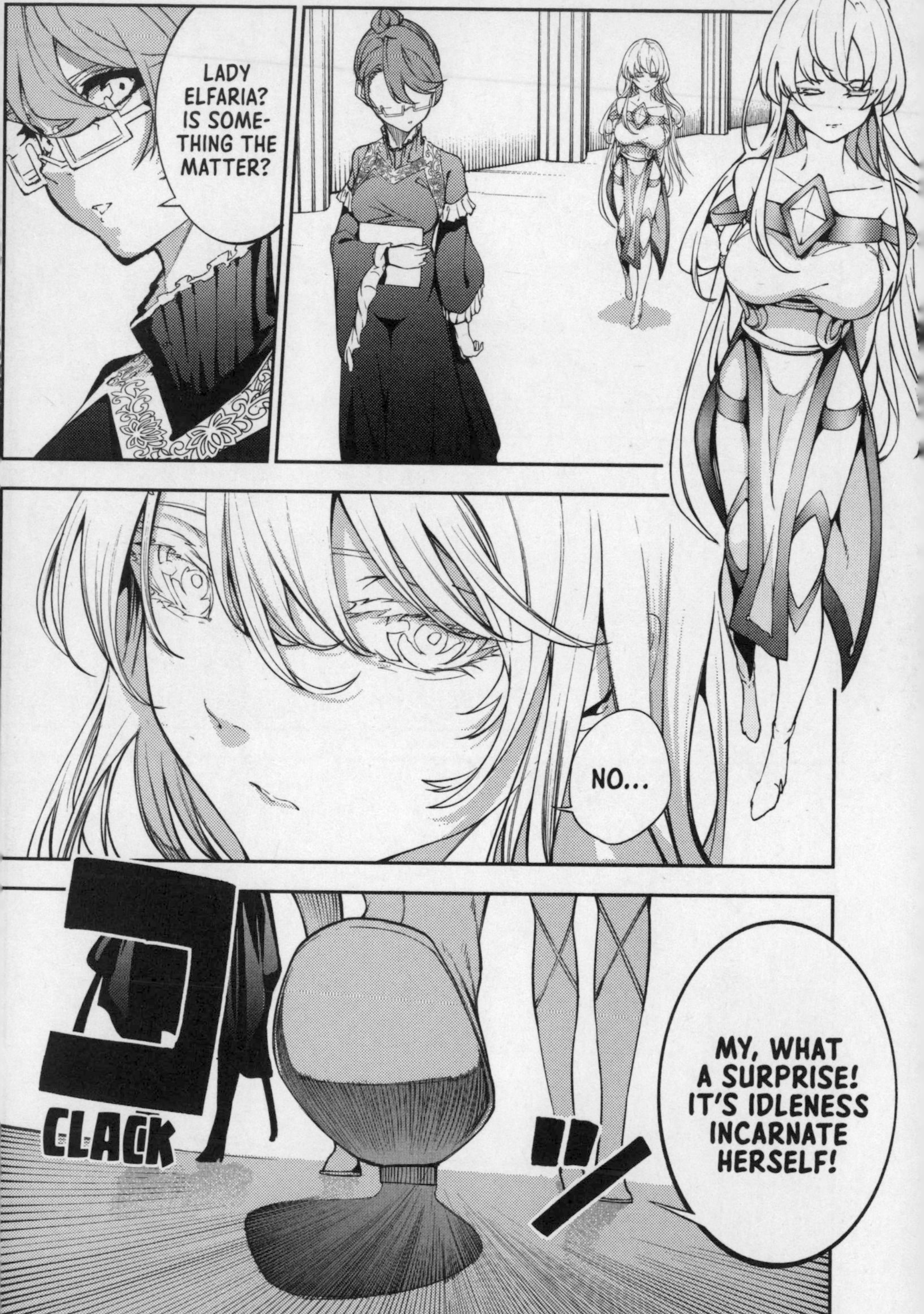
LADY ELFARIA? IS SOMETHING THE MATTER?
NO...
MY, WHAT A SURPRISE! IT'S IDLENESS INCARNATE HERSELF!
!!
CLACK

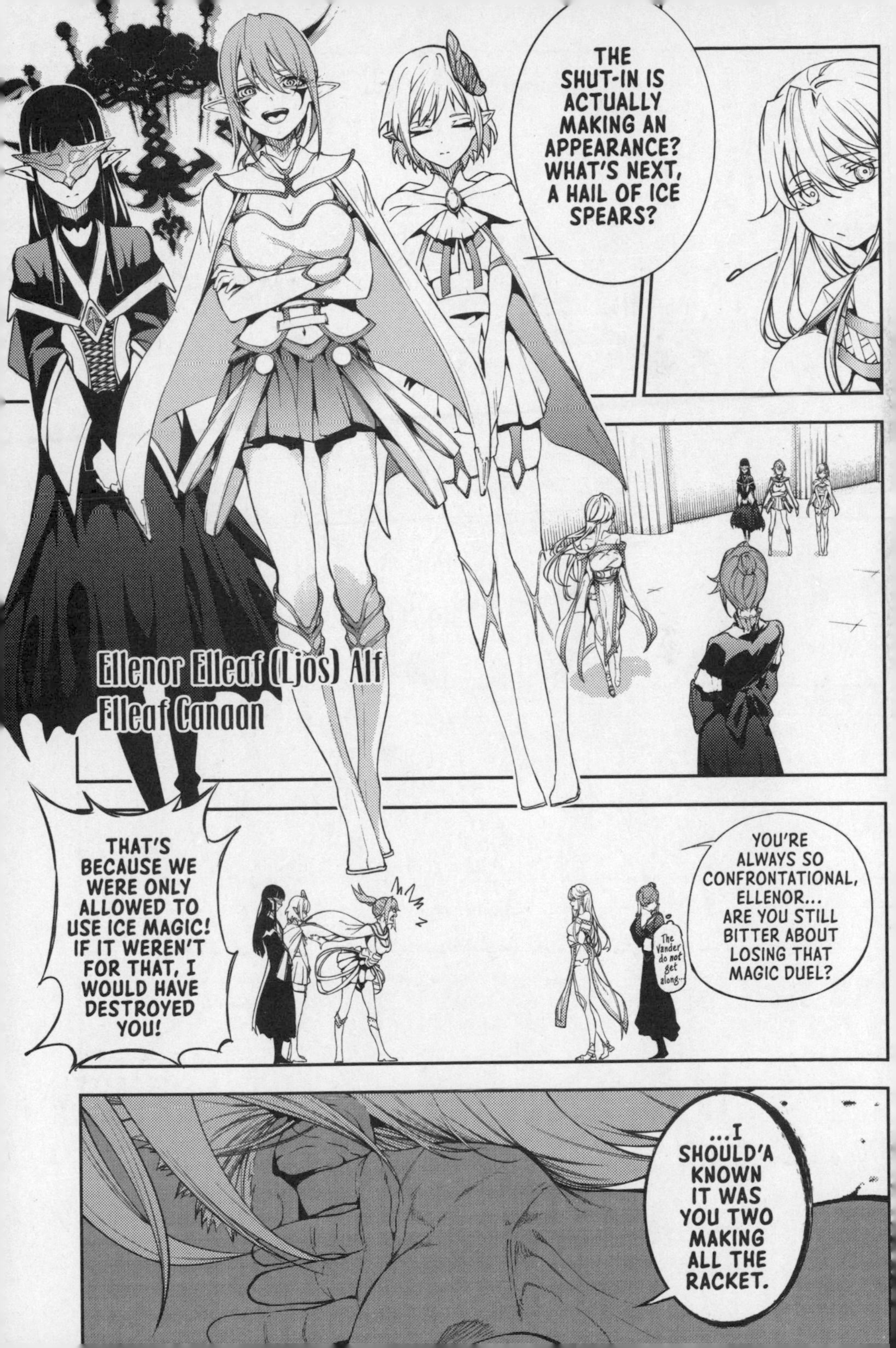
THE SHUT-IN IS ACTUALLY MAKING AN APPEARANCE? WHAT'S NEXT, A HAIL OF ICE SPEARS?
Ellenor Elleaf (Ljos) Alf
Elleaf Canaan
YOU'RE ALWAYS SO CONFRONTATIONAL, ELLENOR... ARE YOU STILL BITTER ABOUT LOSING THAT MAGIC DUEL?
The Vander do not get along...
THAT'S BECAUSE WE WERE ONLY ALLOWED TO USE ICE MAGIC! IF IT WEREN'T FOR THAT, I WOULD HAVE DESTROYED YOU!
...I SHOULD'A KNOWN IT WAS YOU TWO MAKING ALL THE RACKET.

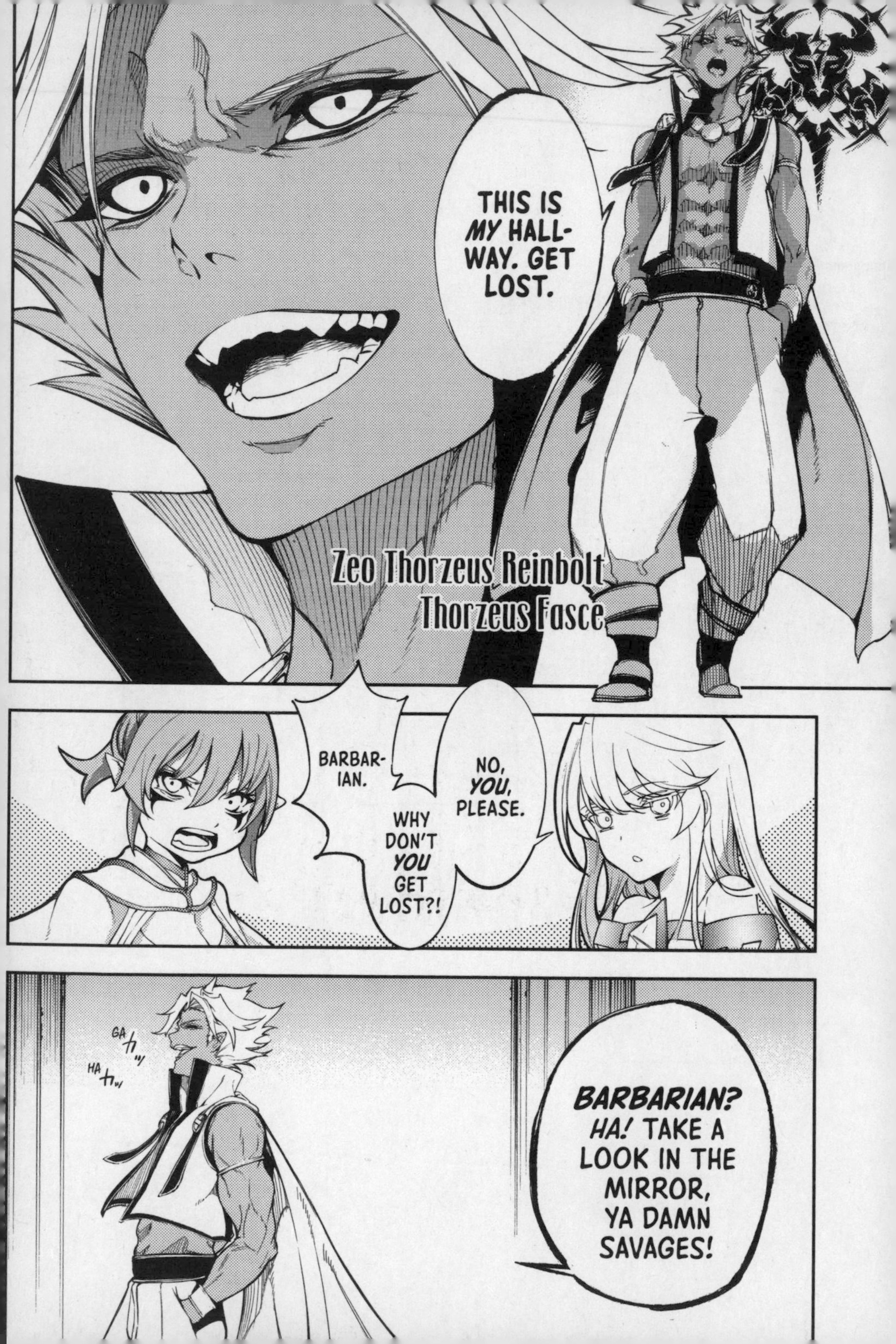
THIS IS MY HALLWAY. GET LOST.
Zeo Thorzeus Reinbolt Thorzeus Fasce
NO, YOU, PLEASE.
BARBARIAN.
WHY DON'T YOU GET LOST?!
GA
HA
BARBARIAN? HA! TAKE A LOOK IN THE MIRROR, YA DAMN SAVAGES!

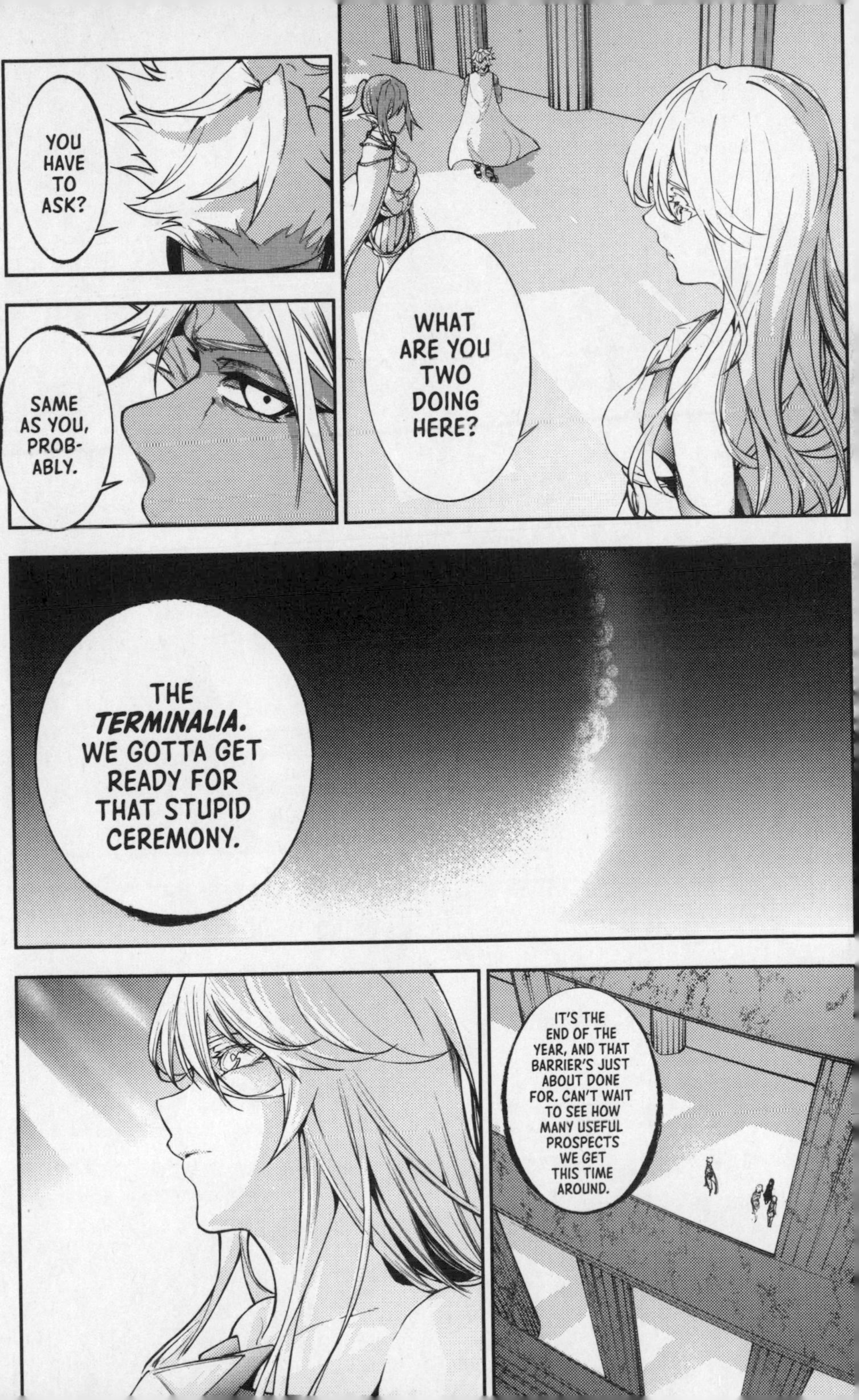
WHAT ARE YOU TWO DOING HERE?
YOU HAVE TO ASK?
SAME AS YOU, PROB-ABLY.
THE *TERMINALIA.* WE GOTTA GET READY FOR THAT STUPID CEREMONY.
IT'S THE END OF THE YEAR, AND THAT BARRIER'S JUST ABOUT DONE FOR. CAN'T WAIT TO SEE HOW MANY USEFUL PROSPECTS WE GET THIS TIME AROUND.

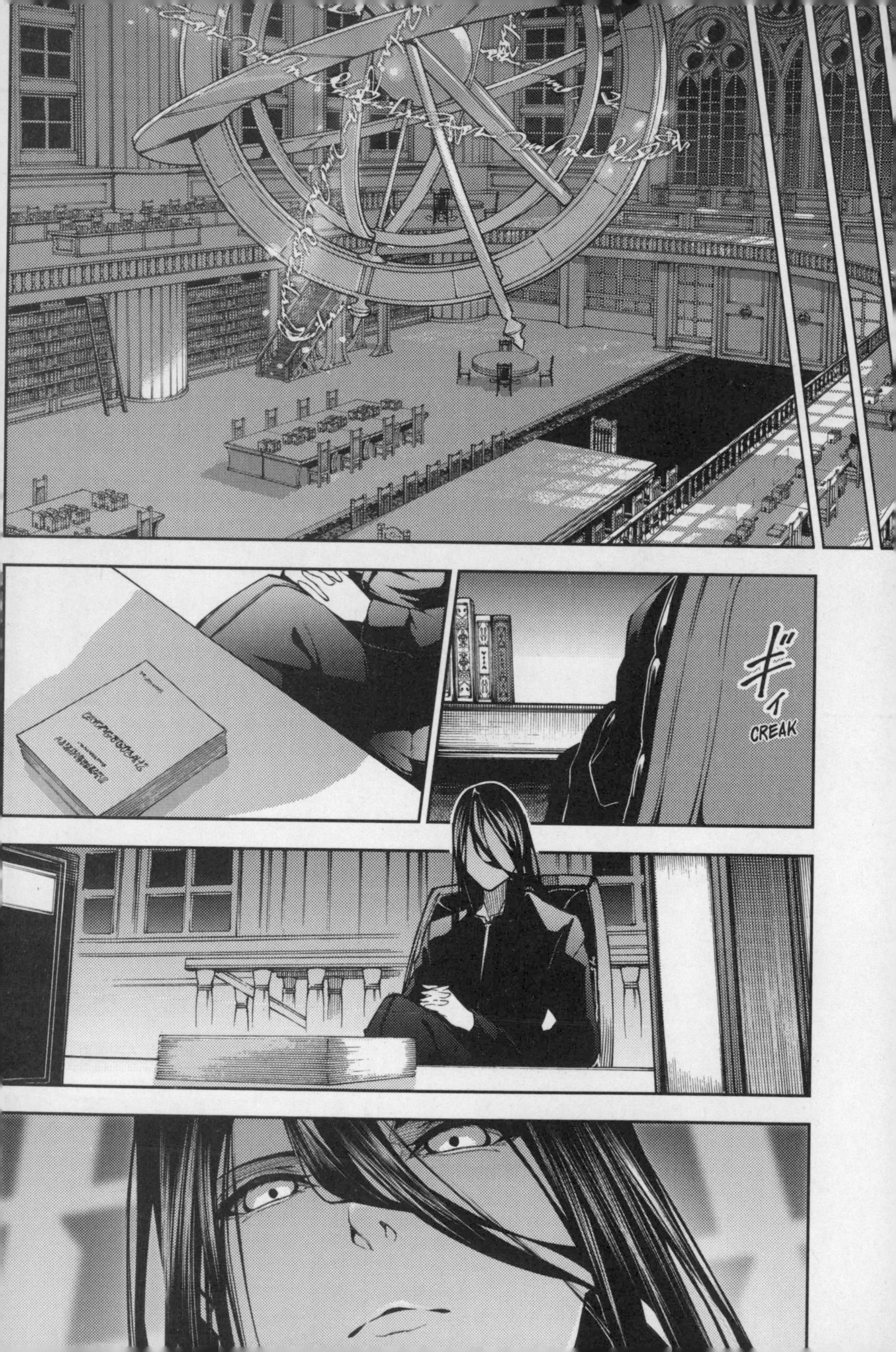
ギィ
CREAK

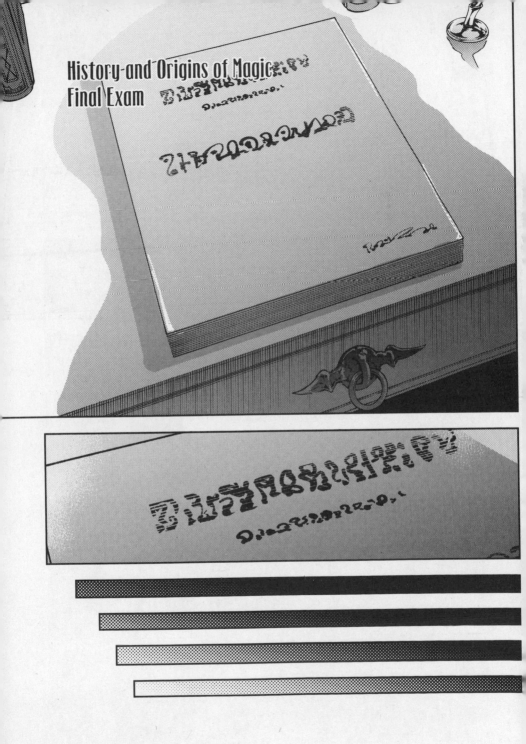

History and Origins of Magic:
Final Exam

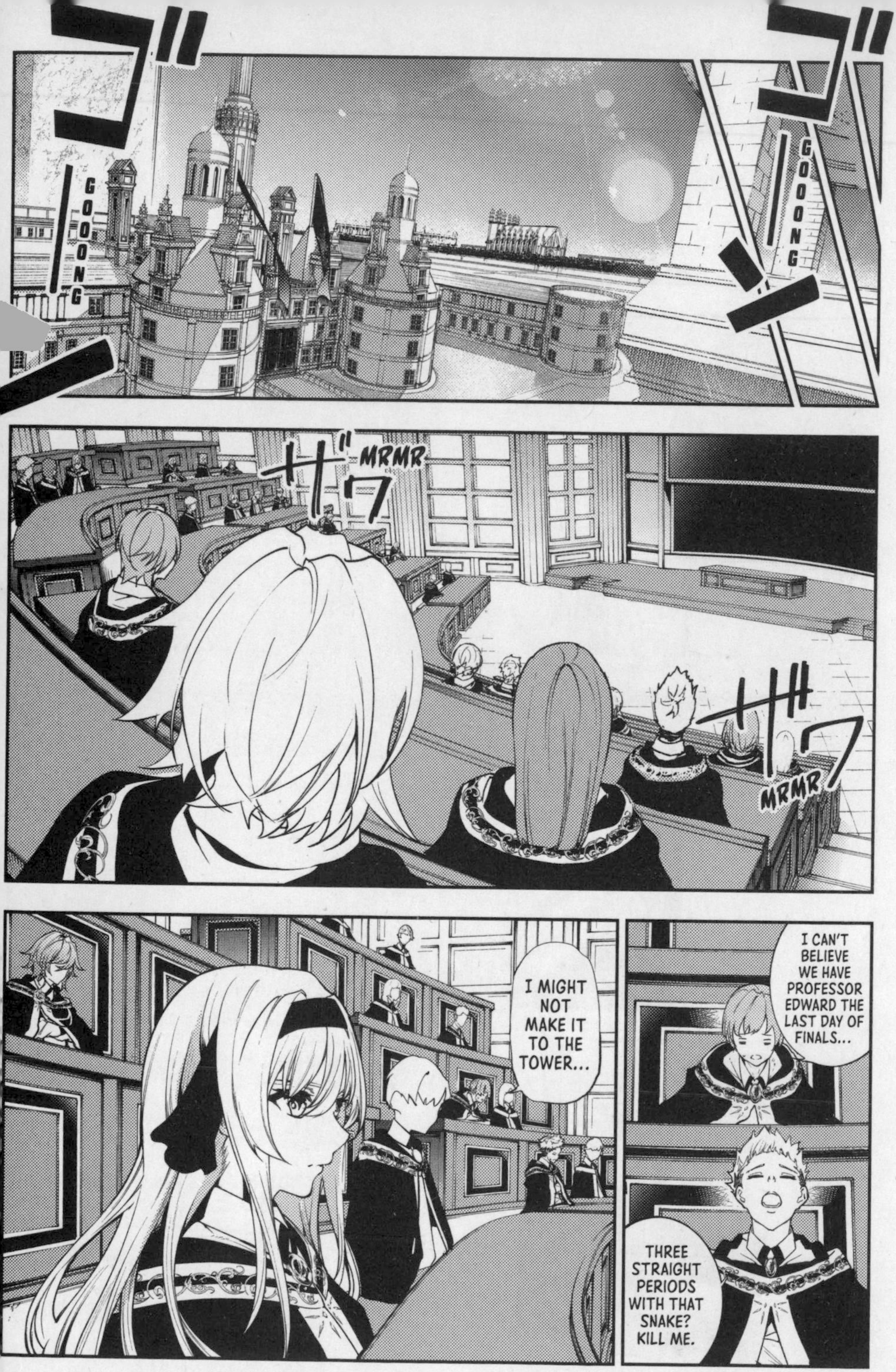
GOOONG
GOOONG
MRMR
MRMR
I CAN'T BELIEVE WE HAVE PROFESSOR EDWARD THE LAST DAY OF FINALS...
THREE STRAIGHT PERIODS WITH THAT SNAKE? KILL ME.
I MIGHT NOT MAKE IT TO THE TOWER...

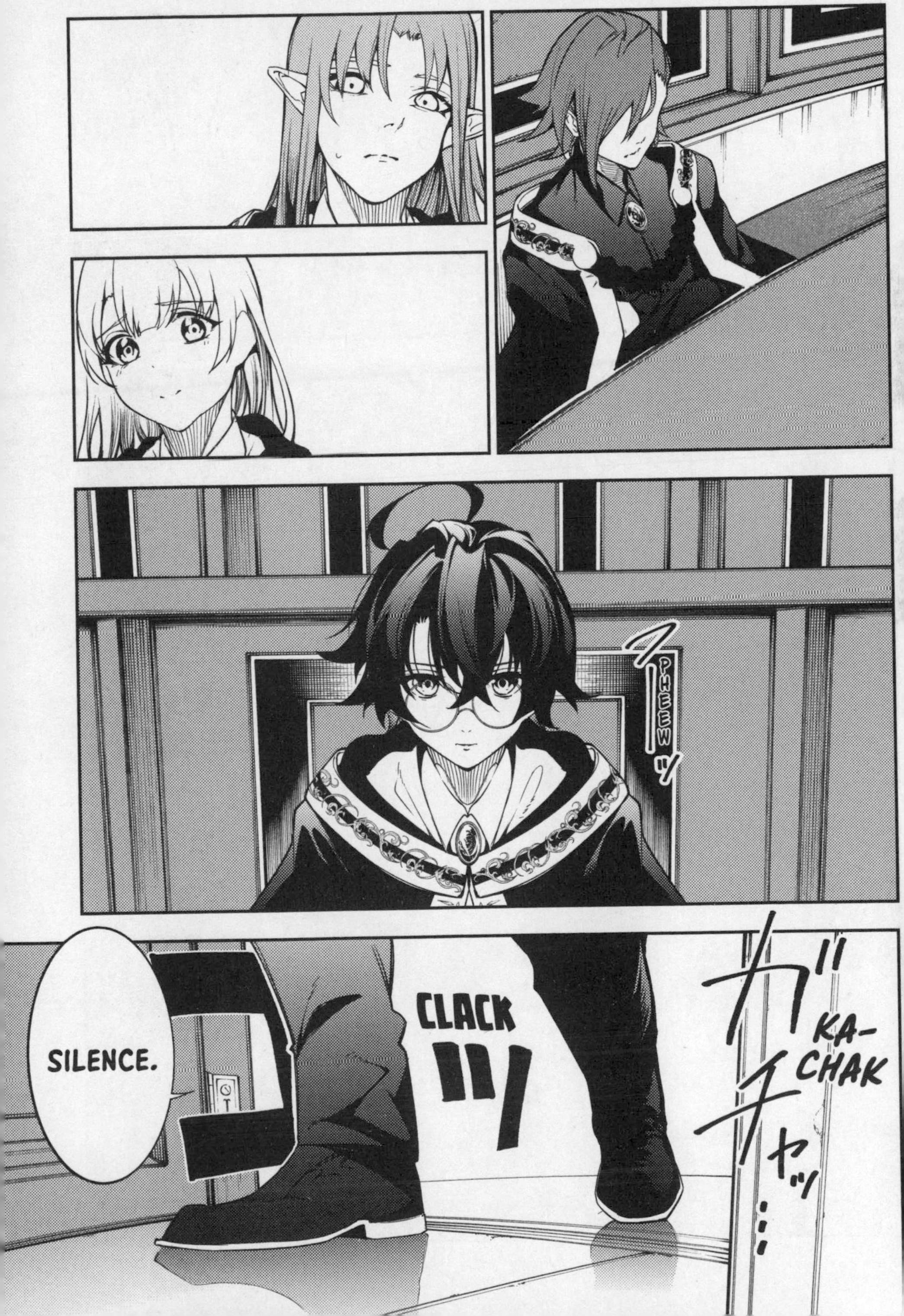
PHEEEW
ガチャッ…
KA-CHAK
CLACK
SILENCE.

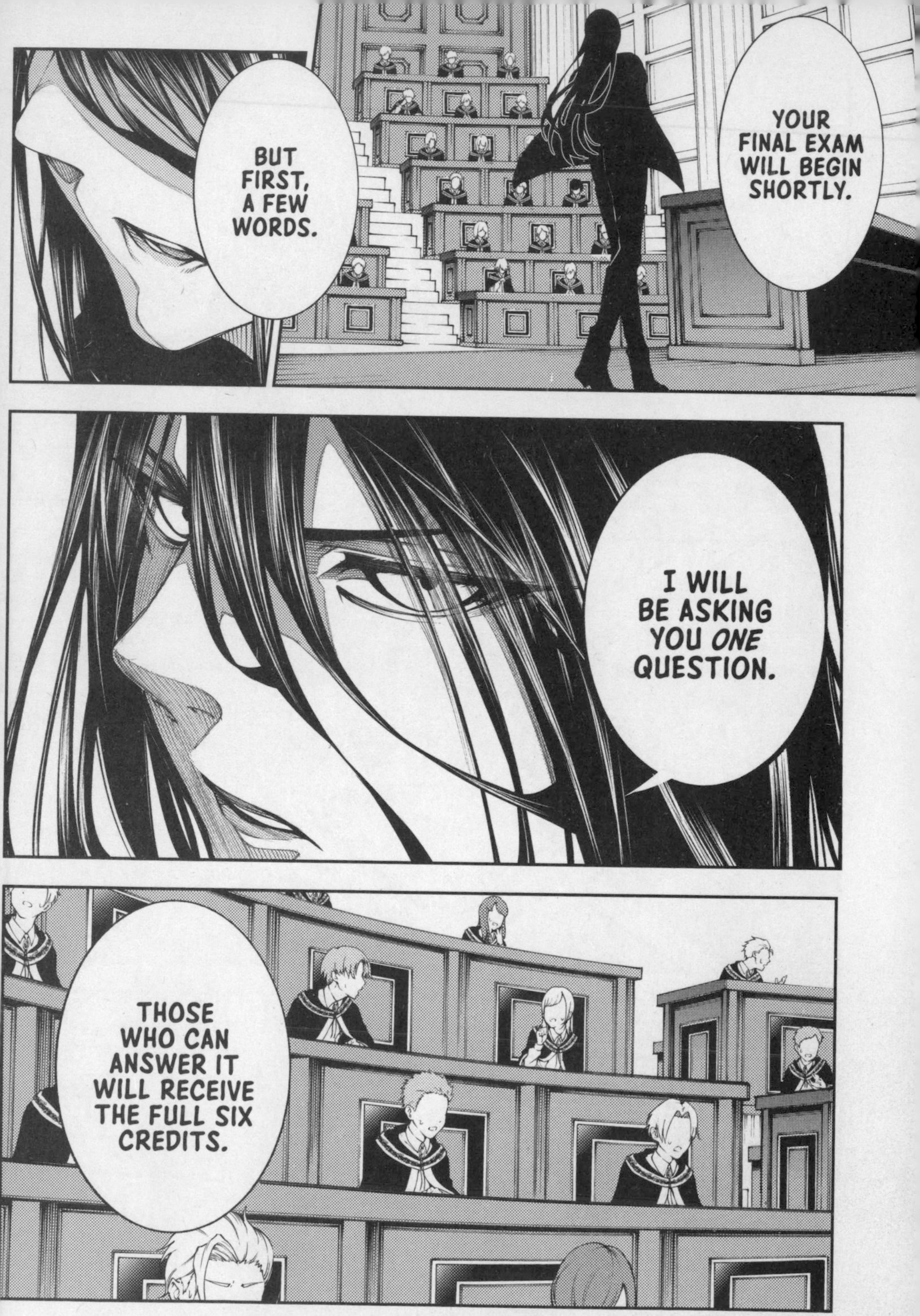
YOUR FINAL EXAM WILL BEGIN SHORTLY.
BUT FIRST, A FEW WORDS.
I WILL BE ASKING YOU *ONE* QUESTION.
THOSE WHO CAN ANSWER IT WILL RECEIVE THE FULL SIX CREDITS.

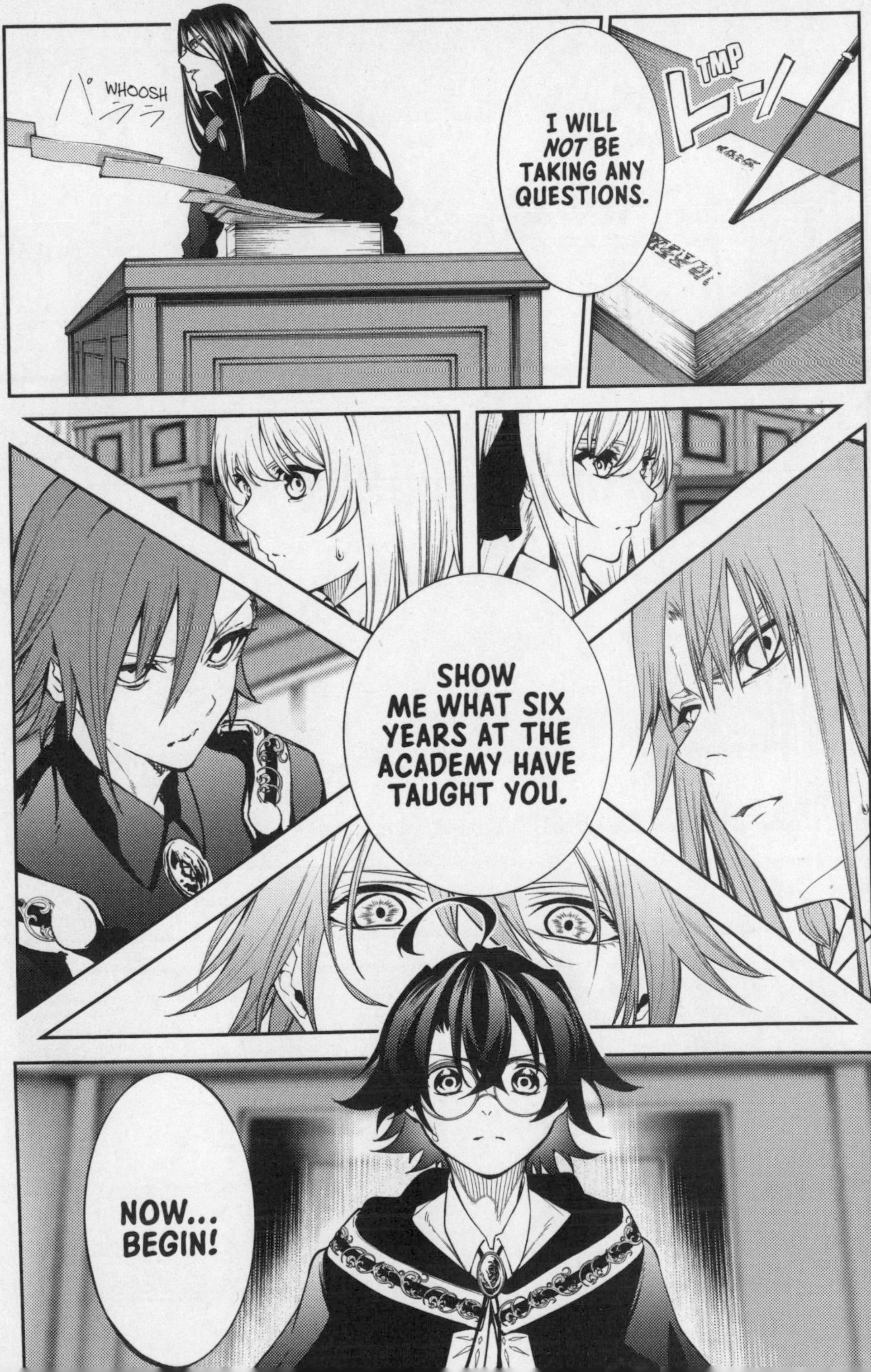
TMP
I WILL *NOT* BE TAKING ANY QUESTIONS.
WHOOSH
SHOW ME WHAT SIX YEARS AT THE ACADEMY HAVE TAUGHT YOU.
NOW... BEGIN!

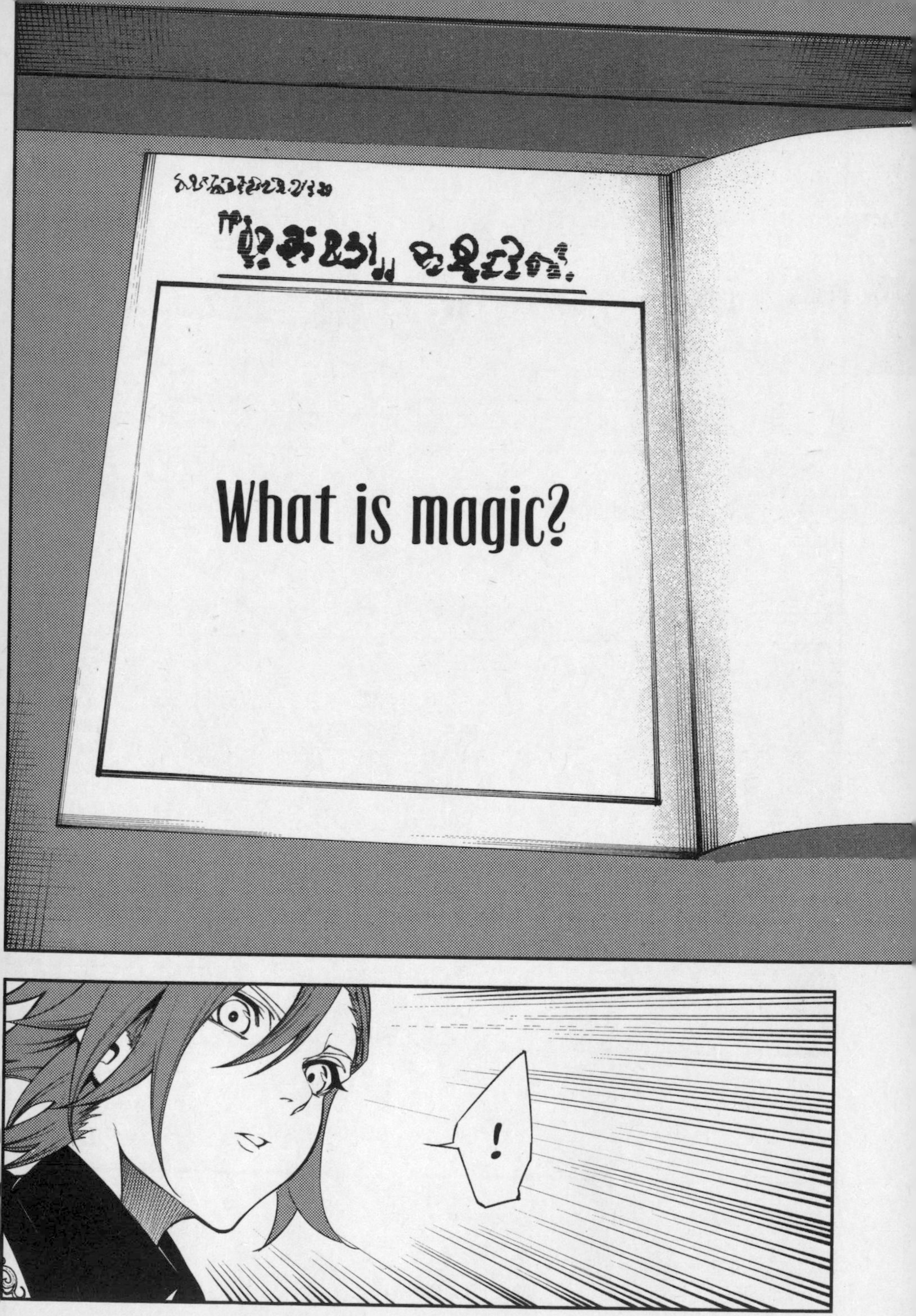
What is magic?
!

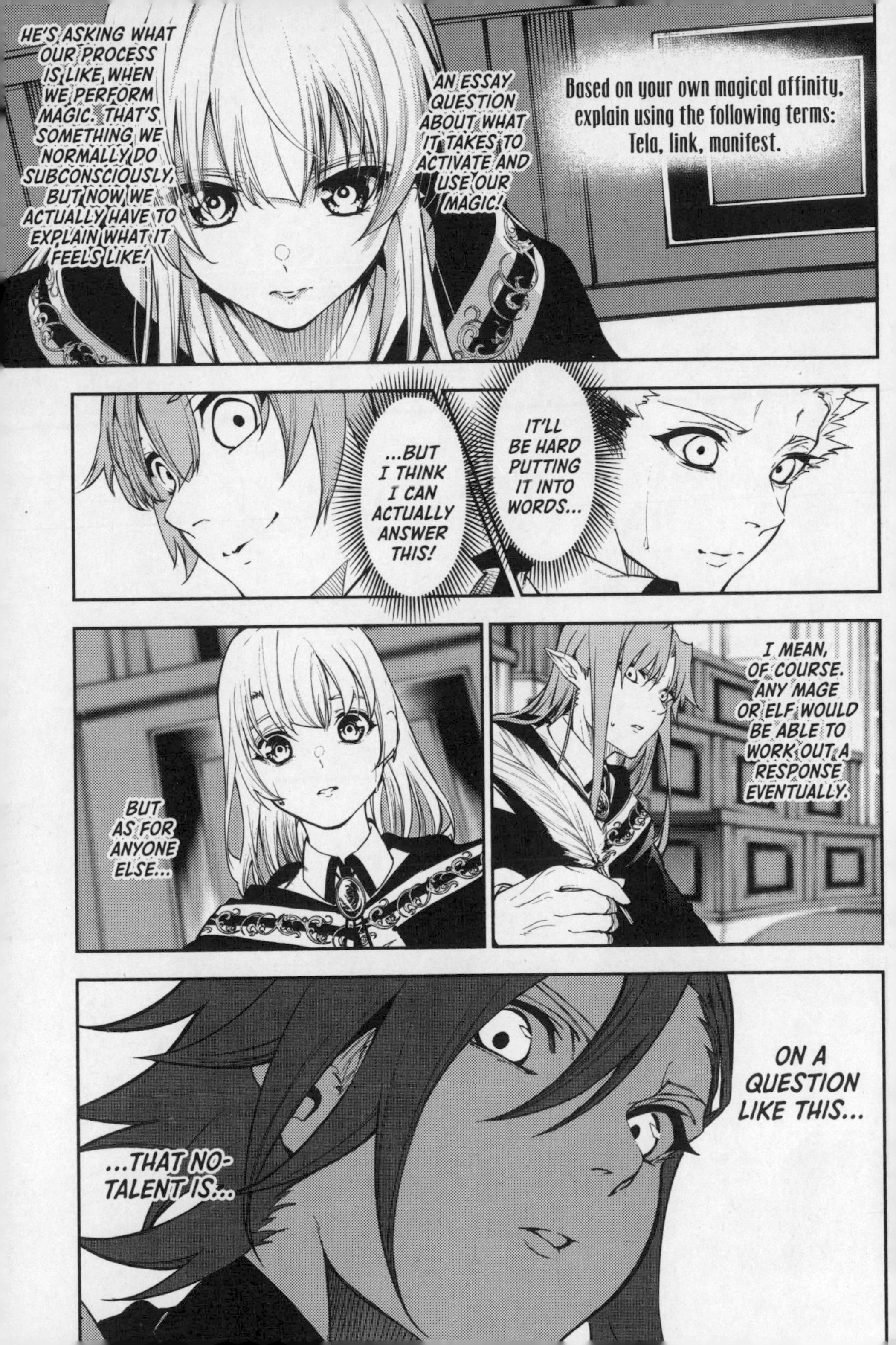
Based on your own magical affinity, explain using the following terms: Tela, link, manifest.
AN ESSAY QUESTION ABOUT WHAT IT TAKES TO ACTIVATE AND USE OUR MAGIC!
HE'S ASKING WHAT OUR PROCESS IS LIKE WHEN WE PERFORM MAGIC. THAT'S SOMETHING WE NORMALLY DO SUBCONSCIOUSLY, BUT NOW WE ACTUALLY HAVE TO EXPLAIN WHAT IT FEELS LIKE!
IT'LL BE HARD PUTTING IT INTO WORDS...
...BUT I THINK I CAN ACTUALLY ANSWER THIS!
I MEAN, OF COURSE. ANY MAGE OR ELF WOULD BE ABLE TO WORK OUT A RESPONSE EVENTUALLY.
BUT AS FOR ANYONE ELSE...
ON A QUESTION LIKE THIS...
...THAT NO-TALENT IS...

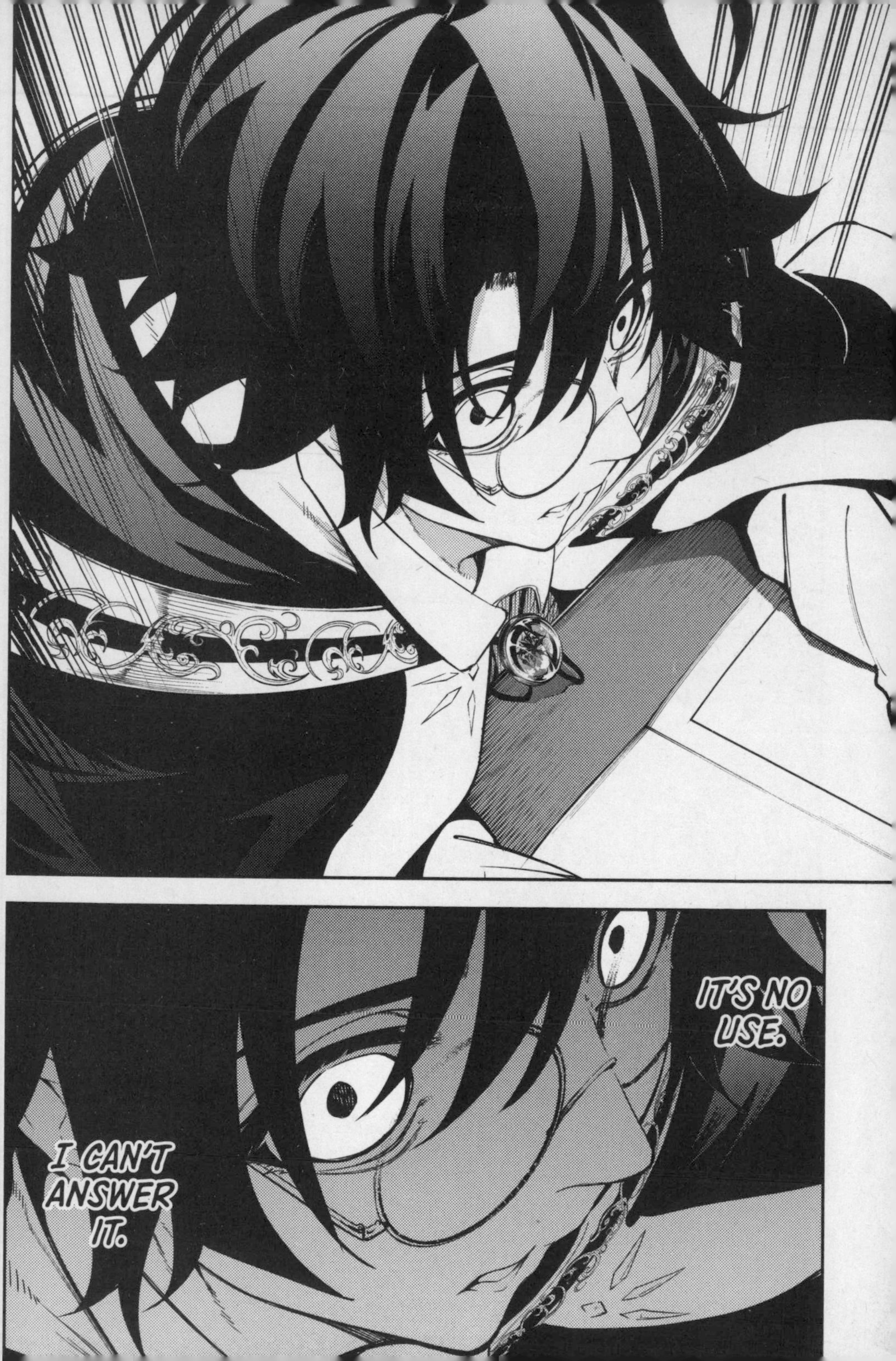
IT'S NO USE.
I CAN'T ANSWER IT.

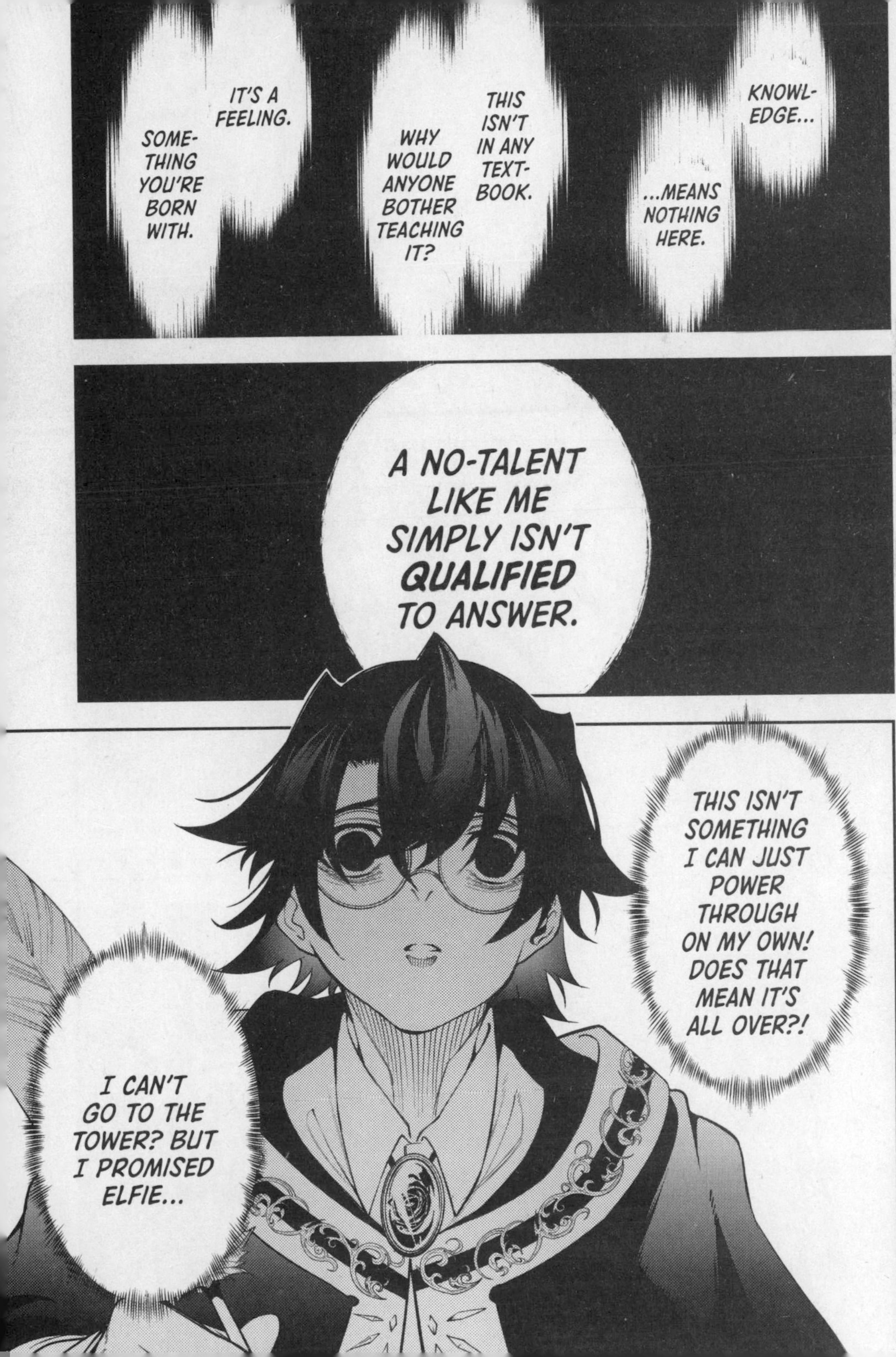
KNOWL-EDGE...
...MEANS NOTHING HERE.
THIS ISN'T IN ANY TEXT-BOOK.
WHY WOULD ANYONE BOTHER TEACHING IT?
IT'S A FEELING.
SOME-THING YOU'RE BORN WITH.
A NO-TALENT LIKE ME SIMPLY ISN'T **QUALIFIED** TO ANSWER.
THIS ISN'T SOMETHING I CAN JUST POWER THROUGH ON MY OWN! DOES THAT MEAN IT'S ALL OVER?!
I CAN'T GO TO THE TOWER? BUT I PROMISED ELFIE...

DON'T GIVE UP!

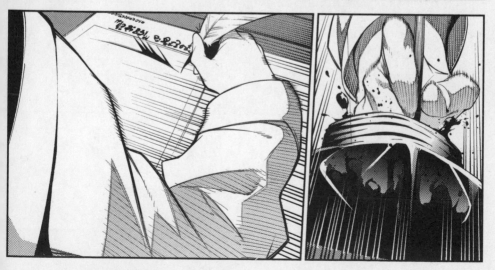

TO ME, MAGIC IS...AN ASPIRATION!

A MIRACLE THAT WILL ALWAYS BE OUT OF REACH!

SOMETHING BEAUTIFUL, YET CRUEL!

MAGIC IS WHAT'S WAITING FOR YOU AFTER ALL YOUR HARD WORK!

I BELIEVE THAT AS LONG AS YOU NEVER GIVE UP, YOU CAN EVEN SURPASS MAGIC, AND I...

I AM A SWORD, NOT A WAND.

TO ME, MAGIC IS...

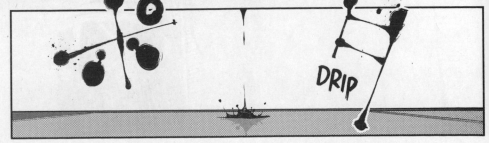

DRIP

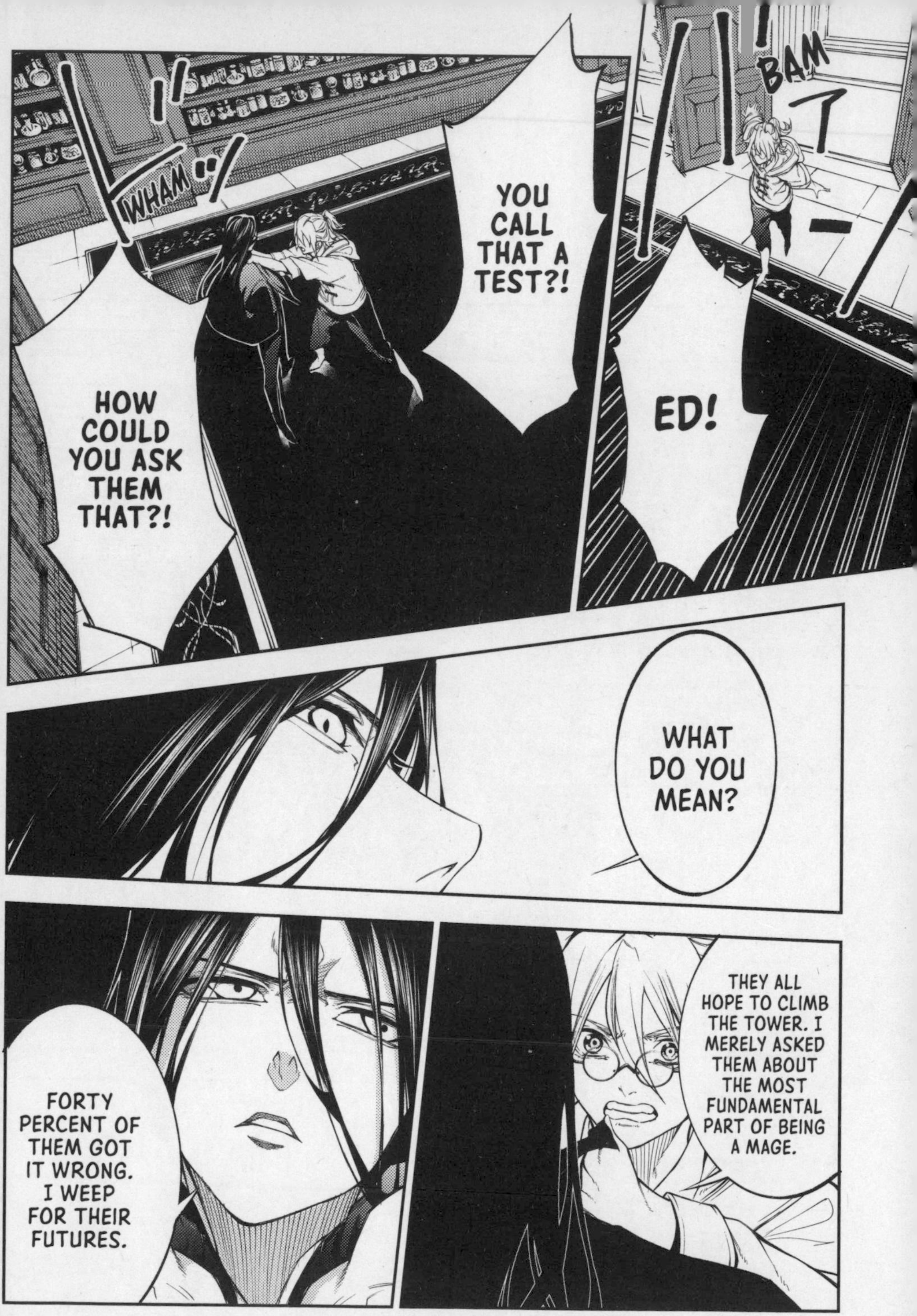
BAM
ED!
YOU CALL THAT A TEST?!
WHAM
HOW COULD YOU ASK THEM THAT?!
WHAT DO YOU MEAN?
THEY ALL HOPE TO CLIMB THE TOWER. I MERELY ASKED THEM ABOUT THE MOST FUNDAMENTAL PART OF BEING A MAGE.
FORTY PERCENT OF THEM GOT IT WRONG. I WEEP FOR THEIR FUTURES.

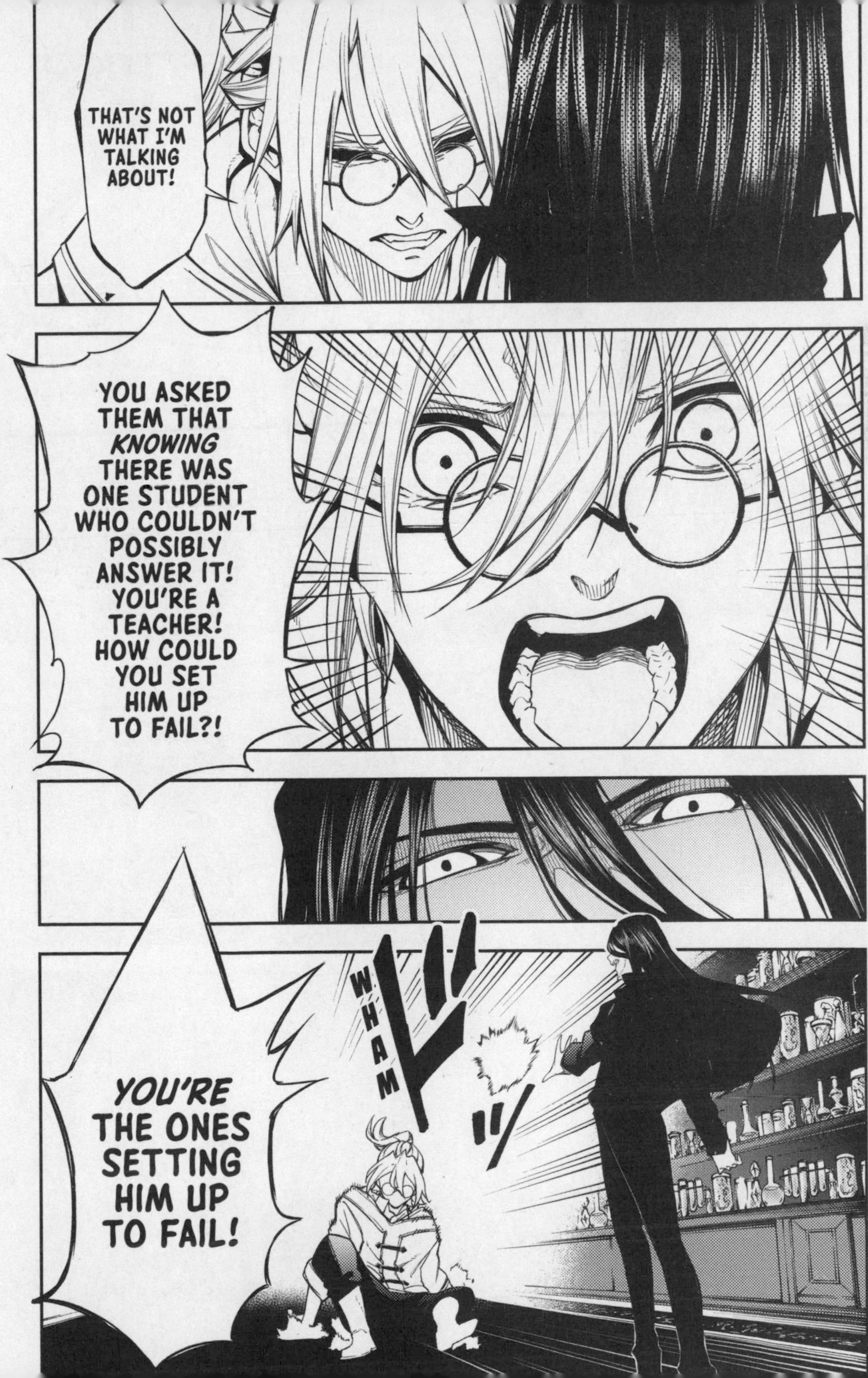
THAT'S NOT WHAT I'M TALKING ABOUT!
YOU ASKED THEM THAT *KNOWING* THERE WAS ONE STUDENT WHO COULDN'T POSSIBLY ANSWER IT! YOU'RE A TEACHER! HOW COULD YOU SET HIM UP TO FAIL?!
WHAM
YOU'RE THE ONES SETTING HIM UP TO FAIL!

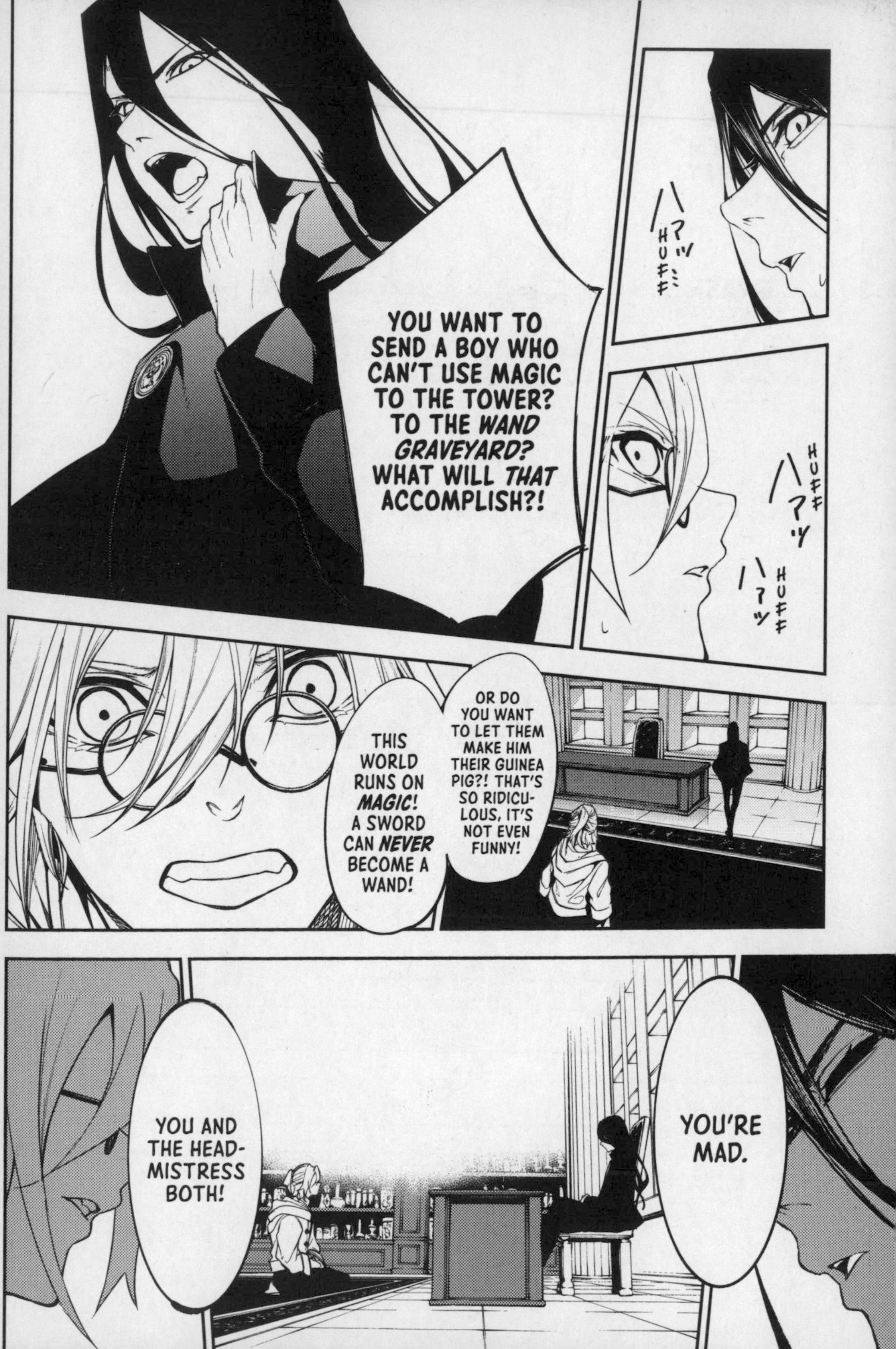

ハァッ
HUFF
ハァッ
HUFF
ハァッ
HUFF
YOU WANT TO SEND A BOY WHO CAN'T USE MAGIC TO THE TOWER? TO THE WAND GRAVEYARD? WHAT WILL THAT ACCOMPLISH?!
OR DO YOU WANT TO LET THEM MAKE HIM THEIR GUINEA PIG?! THAT'S SO RIDICULOUS, IT'S NOT EVEN FUNNY!
THIS WORLD RUNS ON MAGIC! A SWORD CAN NEVER BECOME A WAND!
YOU'RE MAD.
YOU AND THE HEADMISTRESS BOTH!

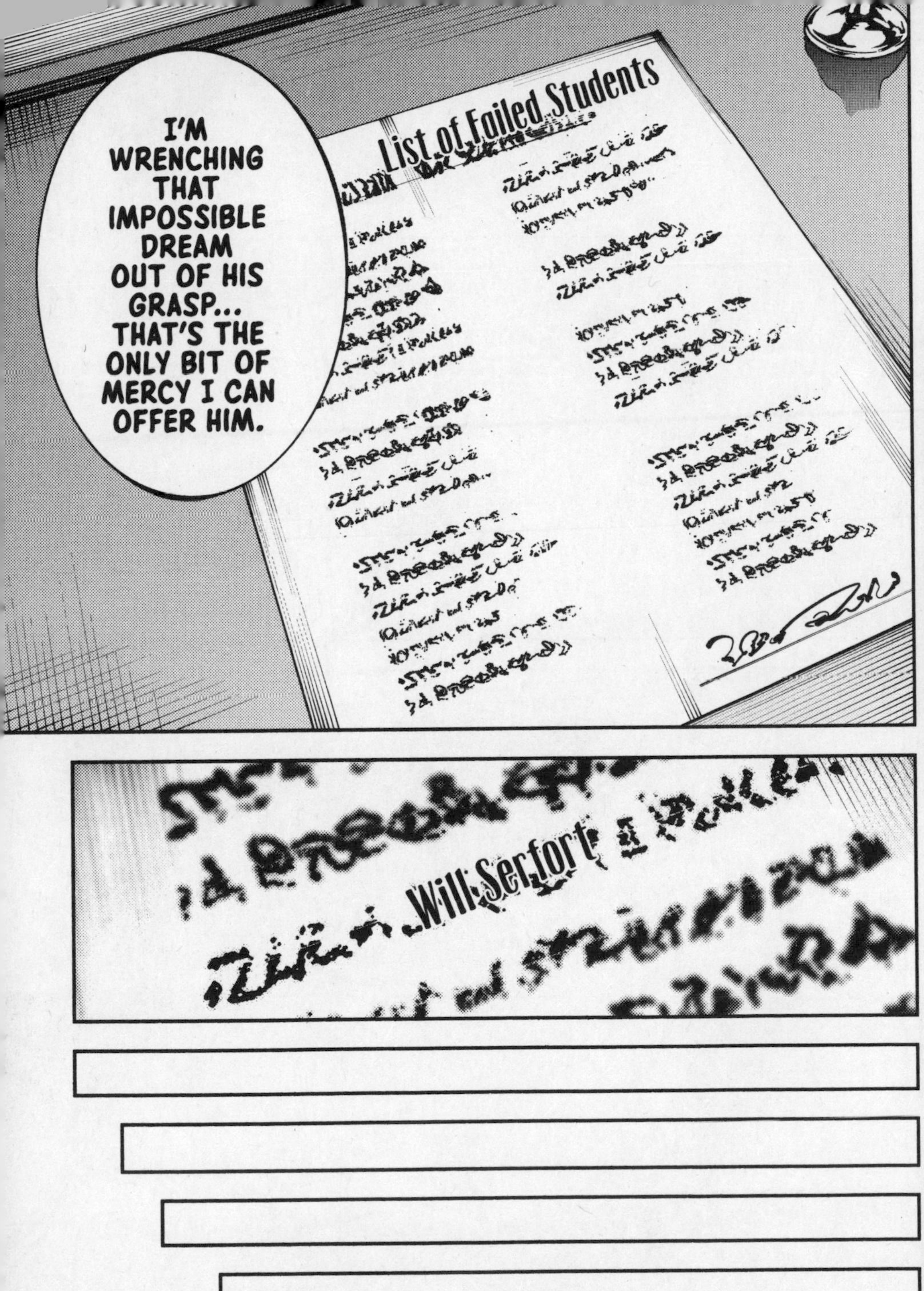
I'M WRENCHING THAT IMPOSSIBLE DREAM OUT OF HIS GRASP... THAT'S THE ONLY BIT OF MERCY I CAN OFFER HIM.
List of Failed Students
Will Serfort

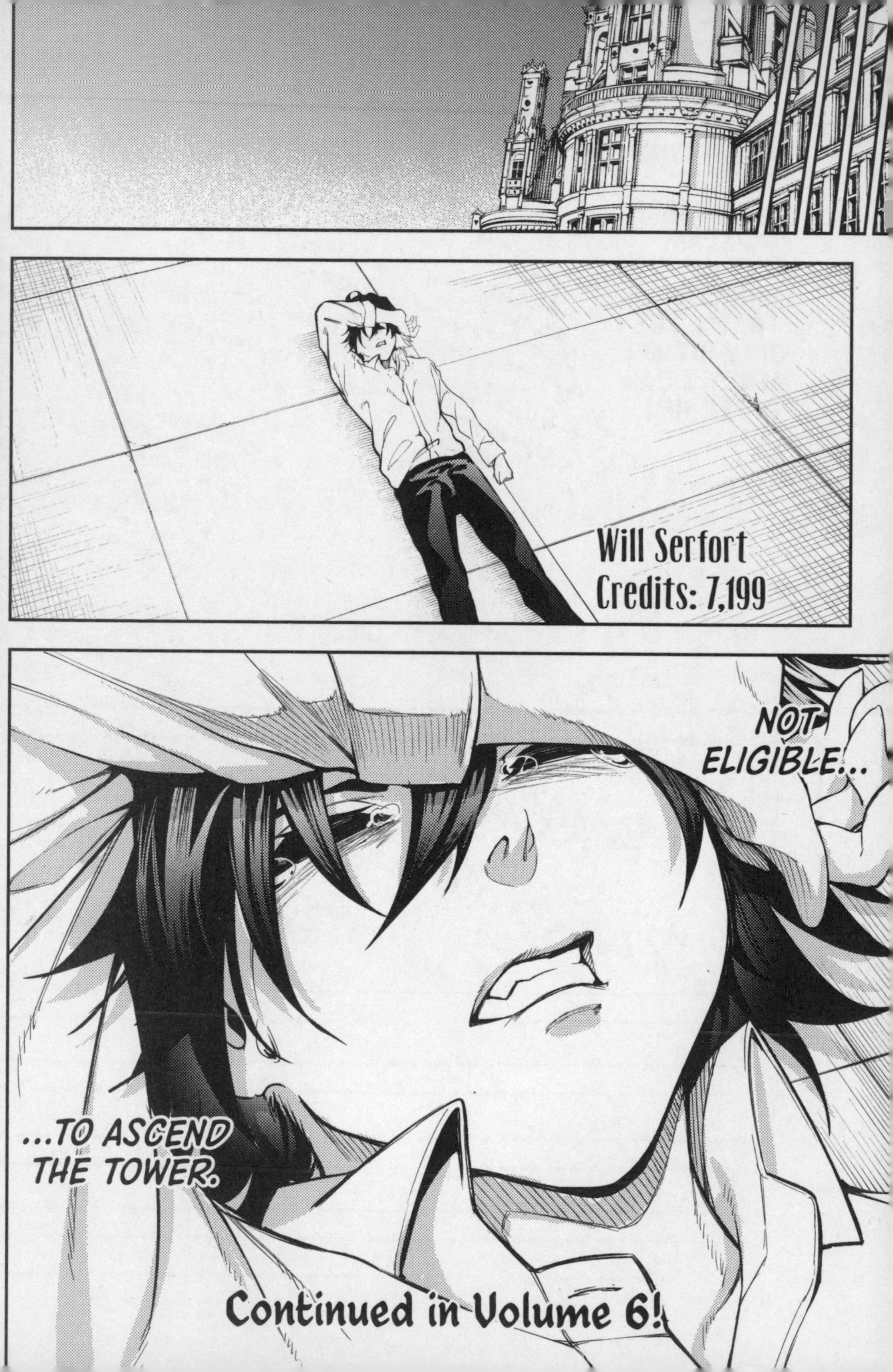
Will Serfort
Credits: 7,199
NOT ELIGIBLE...
...TO ASCEND THE TOWER.
Continued in Volume 6!

Wistoria
Wand and Sword

The Life and Habits of the Icemaiden

Bonus Manga

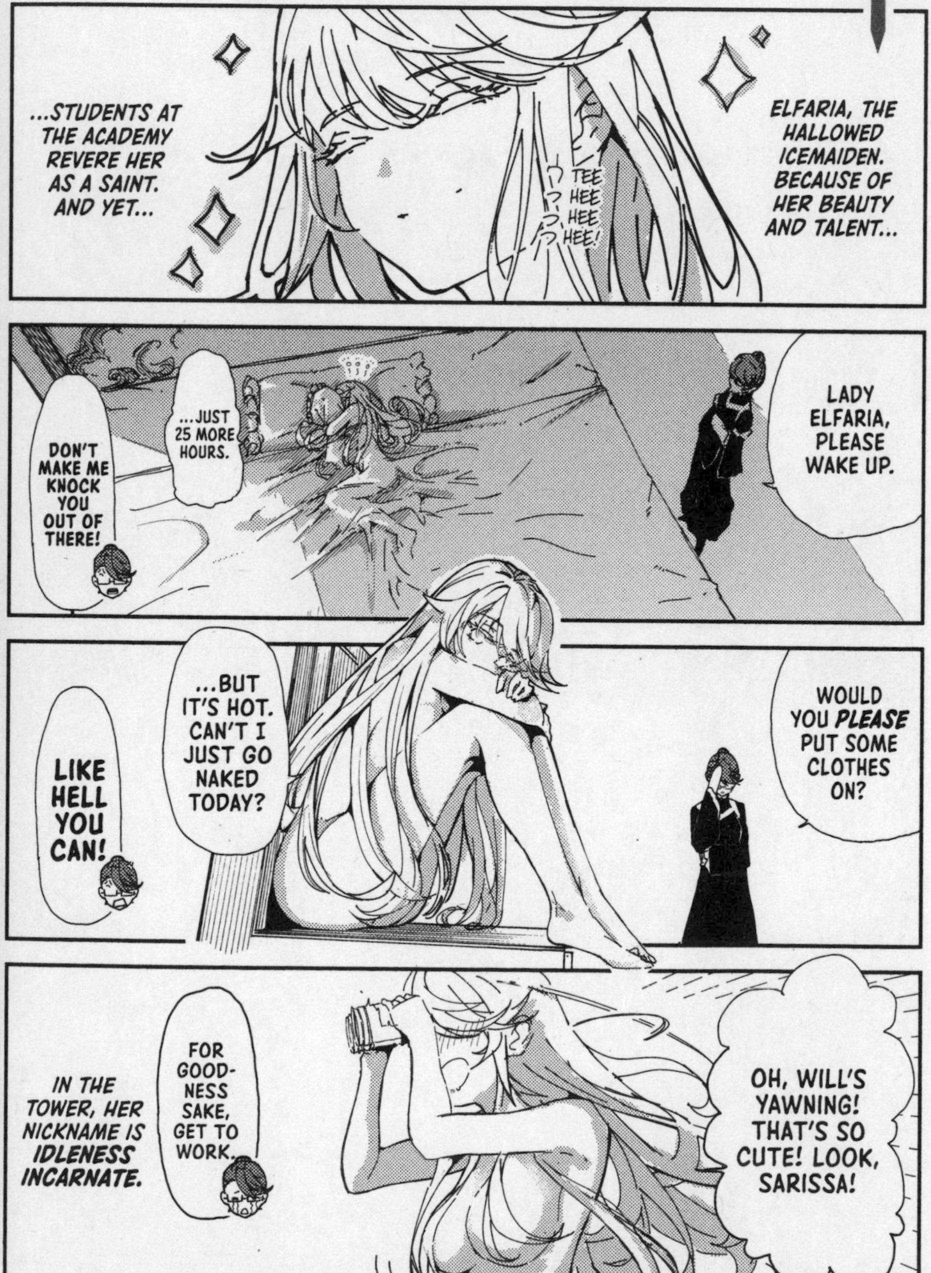
ELFARIA, THE HALLOWED ICEMAIDEN. BECAUSE OF HER BEAUTY AND TALENT...
TEE HEE HEE HEE!
...STUDENTS AT THE ACADEMY REVERE HER AS A SAINT. AND YET...
LADY ELFARIA, PLEASE WAKE UP.
...JUST 25 MORE HOURS.
DON'T MAKE ME KNOCK YOU OUT OF THERE!
WOULD YOU PLEASE PUT SOME CLOTHES ON?
...BUT IT'S HOT. CAN'T I JUST GO NAKED TODAY?
LIKE HELL YOU CAN!
OH, WILL'S YAWNING! THAT'S SO CUTE! LOOK, SARISSA!
FOR GOODNESS SAKE, GET TO WORK.
IN THE TOWER, HER NICKNAME IS IDLENESS INCARNATE.

That Was Ten Years Ago!

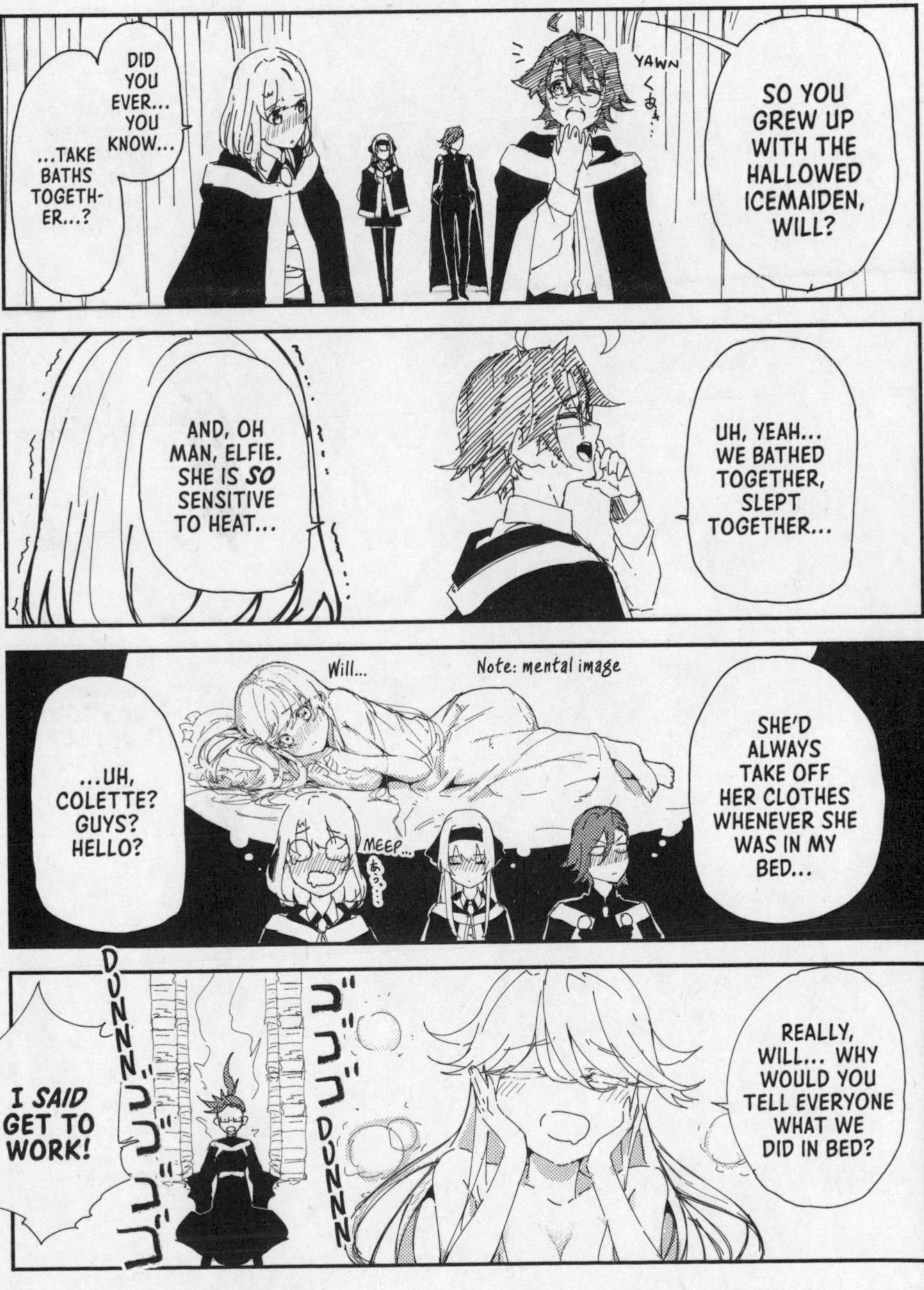

SO YOU GREW UP WITH THE HALLOWED ICEMAIDEN, WILL?
YAWN
DID YOU EVER... YOU KNOW...
...TAKE BATHS TOGETH-ER...?
UH, YEAH... WE BATHED TOGETHER, SLEPT TOGETHER...
AND, OH MAN, ELFIE. SHE IS *SO* SENSITIVE TO HEAT...
SHE'D ALWAYS TAKE OFF HER CLOTHES WHENEVER SHE WAS IN MY BED...
Note: mental image
Will...
MEEP...
...UH, COLETTE? GUYS? HELLO?
REALLY, WILL... WHY WOULD YOU TELL EVERYONE WHAT WE DID IN BED?
DUNNN
DUNNN
I *SAID* GET TO WORK!

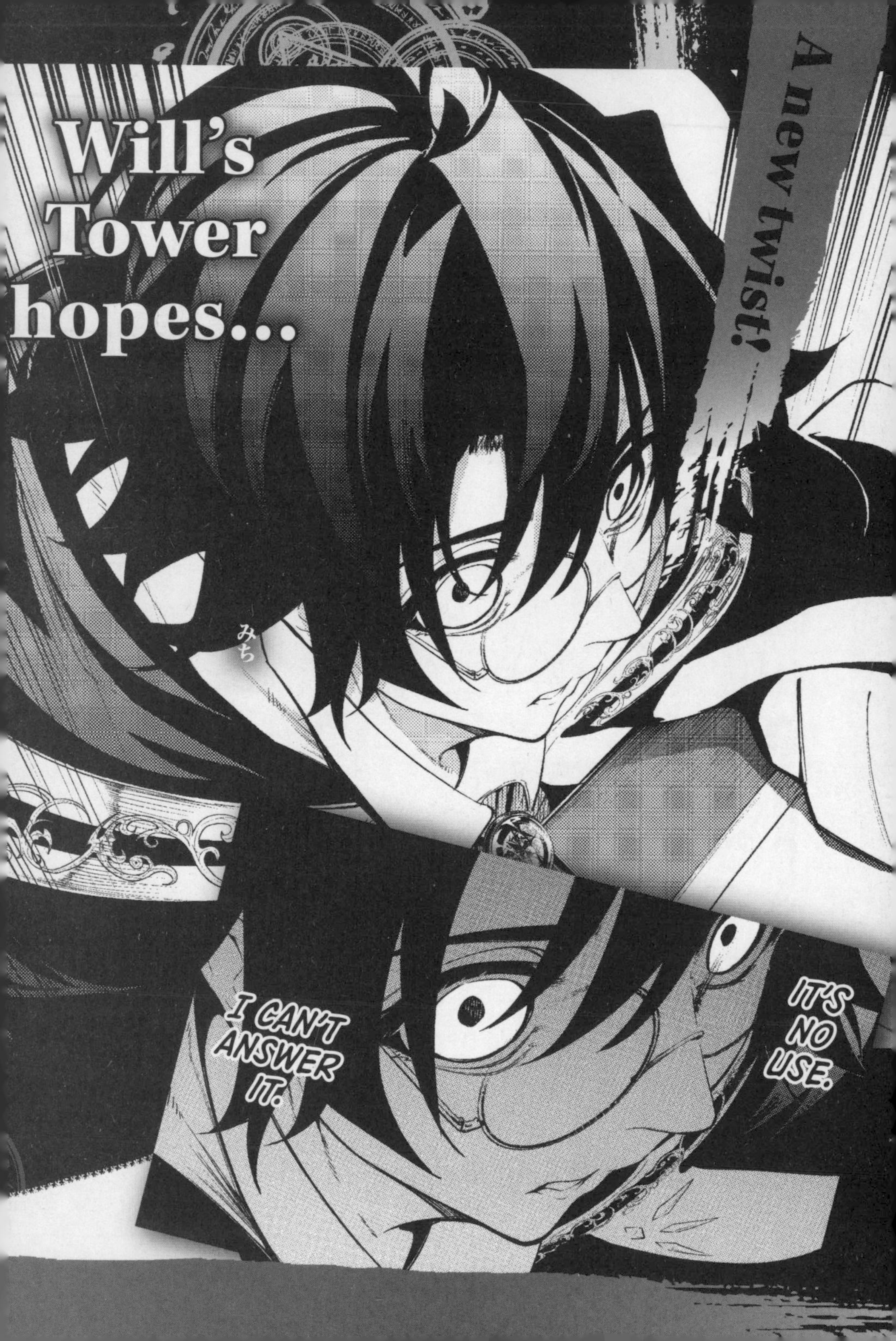
A new twist!
Will's Tower hopes...
みち
IT'S NO USE.
I CAN'T ANSWER IT.

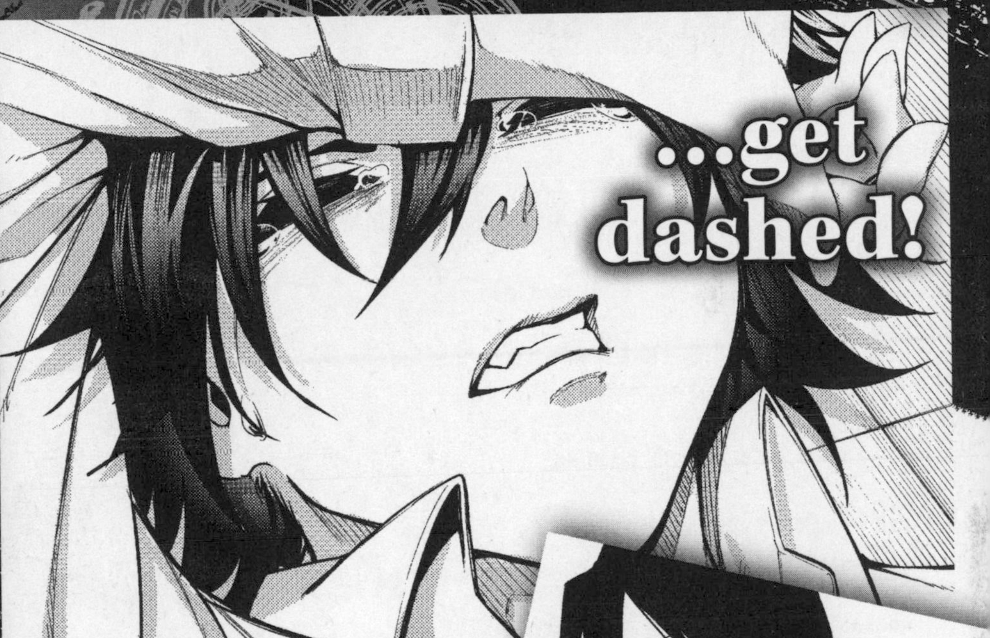
...get dashed!

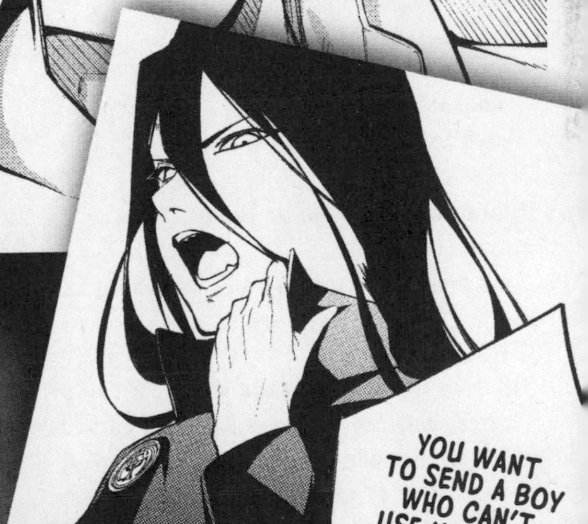
YOU WANT TO SEND A BOY WHO CAN'T USE MAGIC TO THE TOWER? TO THE WAND *GRAVEYARD*? WHAT WILL *THAT* ACCOMPLISH?!

After failing Professor Edward's exam, Will becomes ineligible to ascend the Tower. Will falls into despair, even as the rest of the students prepare to usher in a new school year at the Terminalia. Just then...

Wistoria Wand and Sword 6

EDWARD SERFENCE

Race: Lyzance
Age: 26
Height: 5'9"

Birthday: 22nd of Roemoon
          (August 22nd, in our world)

Likes: Coffee so black that it may as
well be concentrated darkness

Dislikes: Clairie's "killer" cooking

First (magical spell) love: Dark
Deathzone~Arnade Varnatia

Lowest dungeon floor
reached: 33rd

Equipment: Darkviper Wand

Skills: All darkness magic, including the
        highest-level spells

An ascendant who made it to the top of the
Tower, earning the qualification to become
a Magia Vander, before being defeated
by another candidate. He now works as a
professor at Regarden Magical Academy, where
he teaches Dark Magic and History and Origins
of Magic. Ten years ago, he was one of a group
of problem children who enlisted to fight in the
Great War despite still being students.

WORKNER NORGRAM

Race: Lyzance
Age: 26
Height: 5'10"

Birthday: 25th of Ellsmoon
(December 25th, in our world)

Likes: · Magizoology fieldwork
· Food so spicy it brings tears
to your eyes
· Vanilla ice-cream to soothe
his tongue

Dislikes: Cooking battles between Clairie
and Eliza

First (dragon) love: Demon Dragon Fafnir

Lowest dungeon floor reached: 31st

Equipment: · Ashwind Wand
· Crystal for monitoring Will

Skills: · All wind magic
· Dragon's Pulse

Professor of Magizoology. As one of the few
people who understands Will, he always worries
when Will pushes himself too hard. Though he
tends to show his love for his students by being
strict with them, this has made him an object of
terror at the academy. He has earned various
nicknames, including "Remedial Teacher from
Hell," "Four-Eyed Fiend," "Magical Creature
Nut," and "Immortal Workner," and is feared
by friend and foe alike.

Young characters and steampunk setting, like *Howl's Moving Castle* and *Battle Angel Alita*

A boy with a talent for machines and a mysterious girl whose wings he's fixed will take you beyond the clouds! In the tradition of the high-flying, resonant adventure stories of Studio Ghibli comes a gorgeous tale about the longing of young hearts for adventure and friendship!

A SMART, NEW ROMANTIC COMEDY FOR FANS OF *SHORTCAKE CAKE* AND *TERRACE HOUSE!*

A romance manga starring high school girl Meeko, who learns to live on her own in a boarding house whose living room is home to the odd (but handsome) Matsunaga-san. She begins to adjust to her new life away from her parents, but Meeko soon learns that no matter how far away from home she is, she's still a young girl at heart — especially when she finds herself falling for Matsunaga-san.

PERFECT WORLD 1

Rie Aruga

> A TOUCHING NEW SERIES ABOUT LOVE AND COPING WITH DISABILITY

An office party reunites Tsugumi with her high school crush Itsuki. He's realized his dream of becoming an architect, but along the way, he experienced a spinal injury that put him in a wheelchair. Now Tsugumi's rekindled feelings will butt up against prejudices she never considered — and Itsuki will have to decide if he's ready to let someone into his heart...

"Depicts with great delicacy and courage the difficulties some with disabilities experience getting involved in romantic relationships... Rie Aruga refuses to romanticize, pushing her heroine to face the reality of disability. She invites her readers to the same tasks of empathy, knowledge and recognition."
—Slate.fr

"An important entry [in manga romance]... The emotional core of both plot and characters indicates thoughtfulness... [Aruga's] research is readily apparent in the text and artwork, making this feel like a real story."
—Anime News Network

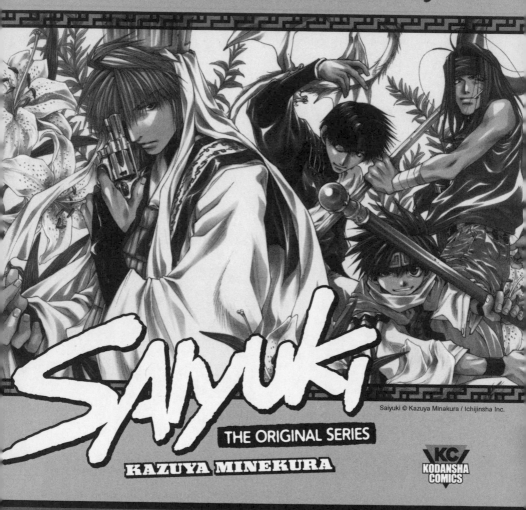

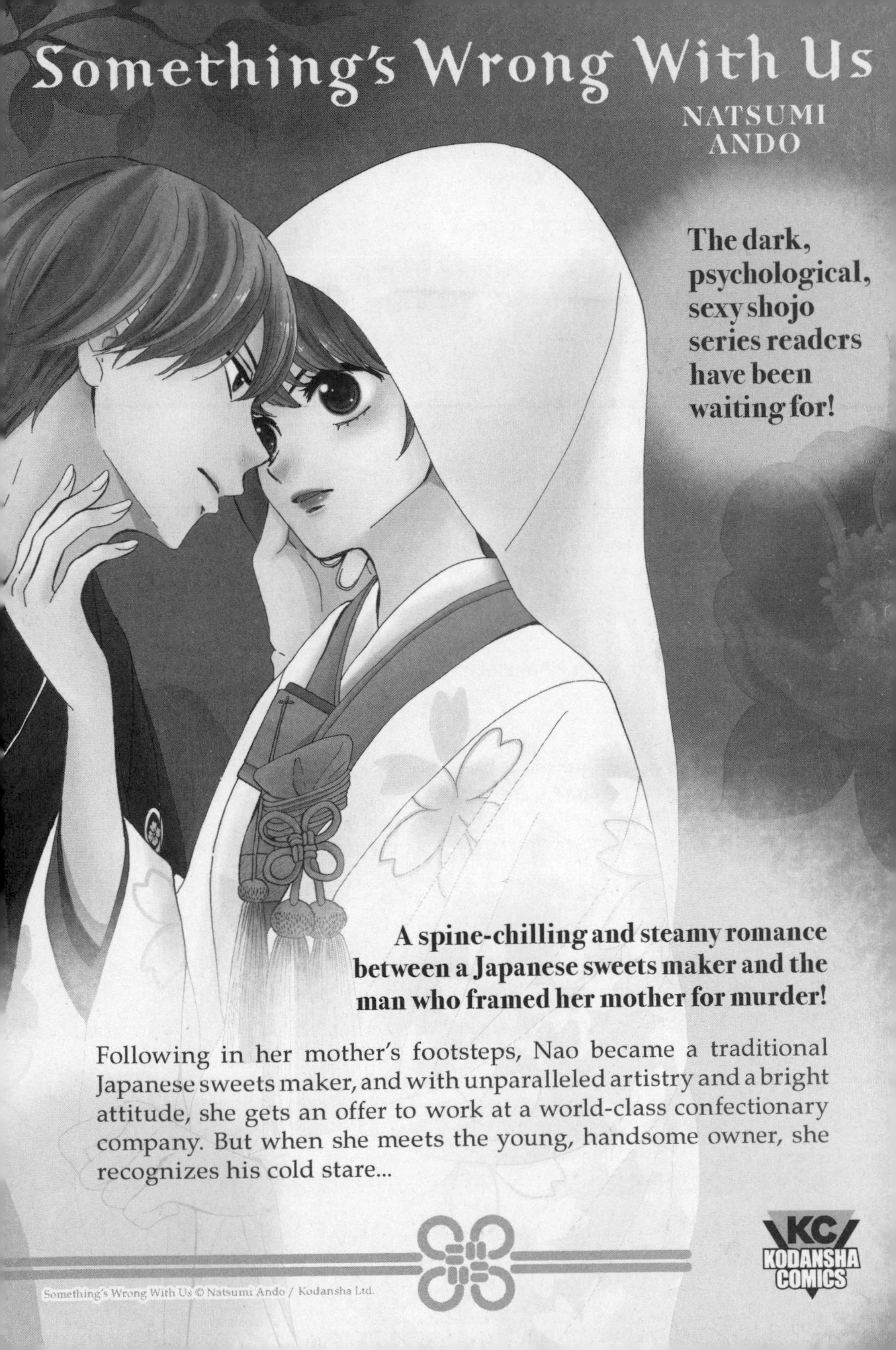
Something's Wrong With Us
NATSUMI ANDO
The dark, psychological, sexy shojo series readers have been waiting for!
A spine-chilling and steamy romance between a Japanese sweets maker and the man who framed her mother for murder!
Following in her mother's footsteps, Nao became a traditional Japanese sweets maker, and with unparalleled artistry and a bright attitude, she gets an offer to work at a world-class confectionary company. But when she meets the young, handsome owner, she recognizes his cold stare...
KC KODANSHA COMICS
Something's Wrong With Us © Natsumi Ando / Kodansha Ltd.

A Kodansha Trade Paperback Original

Published in the United States by
Kodansha USA Publishing, LLC, New York.

Publication rights for this English edition arranged through
Kodansha Ltd., Tokyo.

First published in Japan in 2022 by Kodansha Ltd., Tokyo
as *Tsue to tsurugi no wistoria,* volume 5.

ISBN 978-1-64651-744-2

Printed in the United States of America.

1st Printing

Translation: Alethea and Athena Nibley
Lettering: AndWorld Design
Editing: Andres Oliver
Kodansha USA Publishing edition cover design by Abigail Blackman

Publisher: Kiichiro Sugawara

Director of Publishing Services: Ben Applegate
Director of Publishing Operations: Dave Barrett
Publishing Services Managing Editors: Alanna Ruse, Madison Salters,
with Grace Chen
Production Manager: Emi Lotto

KODANSHA.US

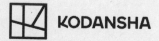